80,000 GOVERNMENTS:
the politics of subnational america

George E. Berkley BOSTON STATE COLLEGE

Douglas M. Fox THE WILLIAM PATERSON
COLLEGE OF NEW JERSEY

allyn and bacon, inc., boston, london, sydney, toronto

Copyright © 1978 by Allyn and Bacon, Inc., 470
Atlantic Avenue, Boston, Massachusetts 02210. All
rights reserved. Printed in the United States of
America. No part of the material protected by this
copyright notice may be reproduced or utilized in
any form or by any means, electronic or
mechanical, including photocopying, recording, or
by any information storage and retrieval system,
without written permission from the copyright
owner.

Library of Congress Cataloging in Publication Data

Berkley, George E.
    80,000 governments.

    Includes bibliographical references and index.
    1. State governments.   2. Local government—
United States.   I. Fox, Douglas M., joint author.
II. Title.
JK2408.B468   350'.000973   77- 26640
ISBN 0-205-06007-2

Interior drawings on pages: ii, xii, 34,
130, 208, 252, 306, and 352 by
Michael Crawford.

80,000 GOVERNMENTS

For ANITA BERLIAWSKY WEINSTEIN, a delightful mother.

For LYELL, MIKE, SALLY, AND BRENDAN.

CONTENTS

PREFACE

Like most instructors who have written in their field, we have done so because we feel the existing texts have not proven satisfactory. It is not that we believe the current textbooks are poorly written or incomplete; rather, they fail, in our opinion, to give the student a sufficiently useful picture of just how the state and local government system works. The very completeness of many of these works, we feel, actually militates against this end. Too often, we have found, students finish a course in this subject feeling stuffed with a great many facts and figures that they look forward to disgorging in an examination and then promptly forgetting. All too often a clear grasp of the overall system and its most basic elements becomes lost.

In an effort to remedy this situation we designed our book to be short. In so doing we, of course, had to leave out a great deal of interesting data, or only touch upon it summarily. Undoubtedly, some instructors will find omissions that they will consider serious. However, the brevity of this book will allow them leeway to use other materials that can bring out those points they feel should be stressed. Since no two instructors have the same preferences and priorities, this should actually work to their benefit.

We have centered our text on one very simple and basic theme, namely that the state and local system consists of nearly 80,000 governments, most of which display a great deal of independence and individuality. We have sought to develop the implications of this fragmentation with an emphasis on the problems that it presents.

Despite its brevity, this book contains some material that existing works in the field omit. One is an appendix on job possibilities in state and local governments which is designed to meet the increasingly vocational orientation of today's students. The other is a chapter on subnational systems in other countries which, we hope, will provide the student with a broader basis for examining and evaluating our own way of doing things.

We wish to thank the several anonymous reviewers who helped us improve drafts of the manuscript for this book. We also appreciate the assistance of Allyn and Bacon editors Robert Patterson and Alan Levitt. Unfortunately, we cannot blame any of these people, should there be shortcomings in the manuscript; these must lie on our shoulders alone.

Douglas Fox wishes to extend a special thank you to Cynthia Mol, who did an extraordinary job of translating his hieroglyphics into a perfectly typed manuscript. George Berkley wishes to acknowledge a similar debt of gratitude to Charlotte Peed.

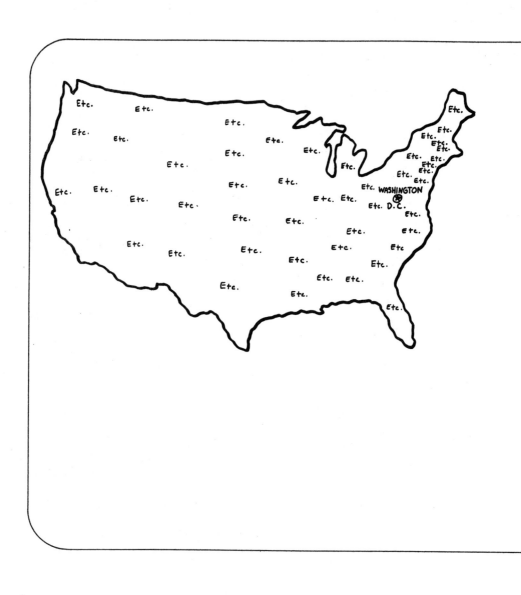

PART ONE

INTRODUCTION

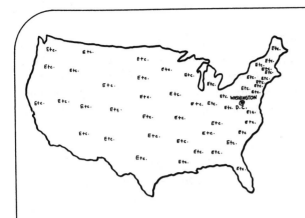

OUR FLOURISHING FRAGMENTATION

CHAPTER ONE

We call ourselves the United States and we take as our motto *E pluribus unum,* or, "in many, one." Such a name and such a motto reveal much about our country and the political system that governs it. We are a nation of bits and pieces and our search and struggle through the years has focused largely on preserving this piecemeal character while establishing national unity. This has proved no easy task, and today, two centuries after our effort to weld a nation out of many disparate parts, these parts still retain a vigor and vitality unparalleled in any other Western land.

The numbers alone to some degree tell the story. The 1972 census of governments showed that in addition to our national government we have 50 state governments, 3,044 counties, 18,516 municipalities, 16,991 townships, 15,780 school districts and 23,886 special districts. We will be examing these many governmental units at closer range in subsequent chapters. Suffice it for the moment to point out that this vast number of governmental entities highlights the fragmented nature of our political system and the fragmented political culture that underlies it.

Be that as it may, where our system is at any one time may be less important than where it is going. What do the trend lines say about the evolving nature of the political system? Are the many American subnational governments losing or retaining their powers? Are they growing or shrinking in number?

Many facts and figures indicate increasing centralization. For example, earlier in this century we had nearly twice as many governments as we have today. Even as late as 1962 we still had over 91,000, or 13,000 more than the 1972 census disclosed. Furthermore, the national government seems to be playing an ever-increasing role in our everyday life. Whether acting through court decisions, congressional legislation, or administrative discretion, Washington seems more and more to be paying the piper and calling the tune.

However, offsetting these centralizing factors and forces, at least to some degree, are other trends. In 1950 the federal government raised and spent 44 billion dollars. By 1972, the figure had grown to 223 billion dollars. Such an increase of 500 percent in a little over two decades seems formidable indeed. But state and local government revenues in this period went from 23 billion to 158 billion, an increase of nearly 700 percent. Thus, while the state and local portion of the revenue pie amounted to 31 percent in 1950, it had reached 41 percent by 1972. All of this means that subnational U.S. government was consuming nearly 15 percent of the country's gross national product by the mid-1970s. To put it another way, the average U.S. citizen was working nearly two months a year to support his state and local governmental system.[1]

But these figures do not tell all of the financial story. In addition to spending their own money, the subnational governments also spend money raised by the national government. Through its vast grant-in-aid and revenue-sharing programs Washington gives substantial sums to these lesser governments for numerous activities that it sponsors or at least sanctions. These programs experienced phenomenal growth beginning in the 1950s, with the result that the federal government was disbursing some 55 billion dollars for them by fiscal 1976. This means that 55 billion was pouring into the coffers of state and local governments to be added to the growing expenditures they were

---

1. U.S. Department of Commerce, *Statistical Abstract of the United States,* 96th ed. (Washington, D.C.: U.S. Government Printing Office, 1975), p. 243.

making with their own funds. Today, state and local governments expend well over half of all government revenues in the United States.

When we turn to employment figures, the trend line becomes even sharper. From 1963 to 1973, the federal government increased the number of its employees by a little over 10 percent, going from a civilian employment payroll of 2.5 million to 2.8 million. However, during this same period, the payrolls of state and local governments swelled from 7.2 million to 11.4 million, an increase of 60 percent. In other words, government employment at the non-national level rose *nearly six times faster* than at the federal level. Though most of these governments were forced to retrench somewhat during the 1974–1975 recession, they still employ approximately four out of every five government workers. [2]

The upshot of all this is that despite the many centralizing trends of recent years, the United States remains a highly decentralized nation. Its 78,267 non-national governments still loom large in the overall political picture, and everyone wishing to know about and understand the American political system must most certainly know and understand them as well.

POLITICAL DECENTRALIZATION: HOW IT ALL BEGAN

The United States began as a collection of scattered and separate settlements, each having little relationship to the others. Their common language and their common tie with Great Britain provided some degree of unity, to be sure, and a slight amount of commerce and trade between them also helped. But generally, each was content to go its own way. These settlements evolved into the colonies that were to become our present-day states but there the evolution by and large halted. Massachusetts showed little concern for the welfare of Virginia and vice versa. To all intents and purposes, the mother country was governing thirteen separate nations.

The growing discontent with Britain's policies made the colonies some-what more cognizant of, and concerned with, each other, and eventually they joined forces to cast off the yoke of British rule. But such unity as they achieved during the War for Independence did not come easily. For example, one reason why the Continental Congress chose George Washington to head the colonial armies in Massachusetts was that Washington was a Virginian. It was felt that this choice would demonstrate to Virginia that this was Virginia's war, too.

2. *Boston Globe,* 10 December 1974.

The Articles of Confederation

After the war had ended, representatives of the colonies once again met in Philadelphia to draw a design for the future. What they put together was less the outline of a nation than a pact between independent principalities. This pact, the Articles of Confederation, established a congress of state representatives to meet in Philadelphia on a more or less continuous basis to take any action that it might deem appropriate to the common welfare.

The Articles required the approval of three-quarters of the states before the Continental Congress could legally act. More importantly, the Articles gave the Congress no real power or resources to actually take action once it had decided to do so. Being a confederation much like the United Nations today, it could only act through its member states. And if any state refused to go along, then the Continental Congress could do little to make it change its mind.

As a result of such a state of affairs, probably not more than one-tenth of all the money the Congress requested from the states was ever paid and even this was in currency of dubious and wildly fluctuating value. When the new government asked for a modest 5 percent tax on imports to carry out the nation's business, the states said no. When it decreased its request the states again said no. As one writer puts it, "The Articles provided for little more than a debating society, in which the debate became increasingly unrelated to the pressing needs of American society."[3]

For obvious reasons, the best men from the colonies soon began to balk at serving as delegates to the Philadelphia talking shop and some states chose not to send any delegates at all. Moreover, of those who did attend, many found more interesting diversions in the somewhat rowdy Pennsylvania city than attending the sessions of Congress.

Meanwhile, the new nation was paying a heavy price for its lack of unity. Division and discord seemed to be the order of the day. Connecticut and Pennsylvania almost came to open warfare over their respective claims to far-off Wyoming, while New York State asserted a claim to Vermont that evoked bitter opposition not just from Vermonters but from the citizens of other states as well.

Communications and transportation were a mess. Washington and some fellow Virginians wanted to improve navigation on the Potomac, but most of the several states through which the river ran turned a deaf ear to the Virginians' plea. Jefferson complained bitterly that it took him five days to go from Baltimore to Philadelphia, a journey that today requires only an hour. It seemed nearly impossible for the states to agree on anything.

3. Richard H. Leach, *American Federalism* (New York: W. W. Norton, 1970), p. 3.

Financial Worries

The major source of controversy was money. New York began taxing New Jersey farm products so heavily as to virtually eliminate them from the New York market. New Jersey responded by slapping a heavy tax on a lighthouse that the New Yorkers had built on Sandy Hook. Connecticut, meanwhile, imposed a heavier tax on goods "imported" from Massachusetts than on those coming from Great Britain. Rhode Island, however, sought to benefit by serving as a low-taxing financial middleman between the larger states, a role similar to that which Switzerland has played in Europe.

Each state could print its own money and many of them proceeded to do so with glee and abandon. As more and more currency poured into the society, its value became steadily less and less. Lenders became less willing to lend while debtors became less eager to redeem. Speculation mounted as money depreciated, and finally when in 1784 the inflationary bubble burst, the country found itself in the grips of its first depression.

The growing financial crises produced great unrest within the separate states themselves. Sections of North Carolina and Pennsylvania threatened revolt against their own state governments while in New England actual uprising occurred in Massachusetts and New Hampshire. Some states began looking overseas for alliances and Washington feared that Kentucky might actually become affiliated with Spain.

Confronted with a degree of chaos and confusion that threatened the disintegration of their new republic, the states dispatched delegates to Philadelphia to see if they could fashion a better arrangement. The delegates spent the long hot summer of 1787 meeting behind closed doors, and when they emerged they had created not only a new nation but a whole new form of government as well.

The Birth of Federalism

The key element in the new constitution was something they called *federalism*. In a confederation such as had up to then existed in the country, the constituent elements (the states) alone possessed sovereign or inherent and intrinsic power. The central government possessed no sovereign or inherent power at all, but had to make do with such power as the sovereign states would give it. (As we have seen, this was not much.) Under a unitary setup, on the other hand, only the central government can lay claim to sovereign power. A unitary state may and usually does have subunits but these subunits only enjoy as much power as the central government chooses to give them. And any power such subunits may

7

be given can be taken away at any time. Great Britain and France are unitary states.

A federal state differs from both a confederation and unitary state by providing for *divided sovereignty*. This means that it allows for a sovereign central government and for sovereign subunits, each possessing powers with which the other is not supposed to tamper. The idea sounds rather simple today but in 1787 it seemed almost revolutionary.

In terms of foreign relations, the powers assigned the federal government by the new constitution were nearly all-inclusive. To it alone fell the right to regulate foreign commerce, sign treaties, or wage wars against foreign powers. Any treaties it signed would become the law of the land and would take precedence over any state laws. The new national government was also given authority to establish an army and navy and to call forth the state militias (now called the National Guard) to "execute the Law of the Union, supress Insurrections and repel invasions."

In domestic matters the powers of the federal government were much more limited. It was given the right to regulate the currency and all trade between the states, two prerogatives which it was to make ample use of during the next two centuries. It was also authorized to tax and spend "to promote the general welfare." Other clauses in the Constitution enabled it to borrow money, set up a postal system, establish a court system, issue copyrights and patents, grant citizenship, and see to it that states honored all contracts and upheld each other's laws.

The Constitution explicitly gave the federal government the right, and even the duty, "To make all Laws which shall be necessary and proper for carrying into execution the foregoing powers, and all other powers vested by this constitution in the Government of the United States." This mandate was backed up by a subsequent clause that decreed that the constitution and all the laws made by the Federal Government under its provisions "shall be the supreme Law of the Land; and the Judges in every state shall be bound thereby, any Thing in the constitution or Laws of any state to the contrary notwithstanding."

Such a conferral of power, though seemingly quite sweeping, nevertheless left most of the country's internal affairs in the hands of the states. Furthermore, three-quarters of the states would have to give their consent before the power relationship could be changed through a constitutional amendment.

It is believed that many of the convention delegates, including some of its leading lights such as Alexander Hamilton and James Madison, really wanted the central government to possess all the sovereign power. In other words, they wanted a unitary state. They created and adopted federalism only as an expedient, possibly temporary, in order to placate their fellow delegates and the people they represented, most of whom feared a strong national government. As it is, they had a hard time selling even federalism to the nation and Madison, Hamilton, and John Jay felt it necessary to write a series of newspaper articles (*The Federalist*) carefully pointing out the limitations of the new sovereign government and the great powers still left in the hands of the states. It took a good deal of persuasion of this nature before the requisite majority of the states agreed to accept the new government.[4]

The Evolution of Federalism

Today, we sometimes praise our system of divided sovereignty, which gives us a sovereign national government and fifty sovereign states, as something almost divine in nature. We should keep in mind that its origins were quite different. It was concocted by and large by men who didn't really believe in such a system but who felt it a necessary expedient. "As the constitutional father well understood," Morton Grodzins, one of the foremost students of federalism has written, "the federal structure is a means, not an end."[5]

The federalist compromise hammered out at the Philadelphia convention and enshrined in the country's new constitution gave us a government that could and did impose some measure of national unity. When whiskey makers in Western Pennsylvania refused to pay the federal government's new excise tax, President George Washington personally led a detachment of militia men to stamp out their rebellion. When South Carolina refused to obey the nation's tariff laws, President Jackson used both coercion and conciliation to persuade the state to back down. When rebellious Rhode Islanders set up a rival government in their own state, President Tyler crushed it by merely threatening to use federal force. And when the South started to secede from the Union, Abraham Lincoln did use force to preserve the constitutional compact.

Fortunately the federal government has usually managed to handle most disputes between itself and the states, as well as disputes between the states themselves, in a more conciliatory fashion. When Ohio and Michigan militiamen clashed in 1835 over the side of the state line on which the city of Toledo fell (a clash that luckily caused only the death of one mule and a finger wound to an

---

4. Ibid., p. 9. Some scholars apparently believe that federalism was intended to be a temporary scheme, lasting only until such time as the former colonies cohered into a unitary state. Other scholars would not go so far but most agree that federalism was born out of expediency and compromise. In his introduction to the 1937 Modern Library edition of *The Federalist,* Professor Edward Mead Earle remarked that "there is no doubt that many members of the Federal convention were nationalists at heart. . . ."

5. Morton Grodzins, "The Federal System," in *Goals For Americans* (New York: The American Assembly, Columbia University Press, 1960).

Ohio soldier) President Jackson stepped in. He awarded Toledo to Ohio but mollified Michigan by giving it the Upper Penninsula. [6] And, to take a more recent example, there is the "Lobster War" that broke out between Maine and New Hampshire in 1973. New Hampshire lobstermen cut the traps of Maine lobstermen, claiming that these out-of-staters were fishing illegally in New Hampshire waters. Maine conservation officers reacted by arresting two New Hampshire lobstermen for allegedly committing the same offense in Maine waters. In this case, as in many such altercations, one of the parties eventually turned to the Supreme Court for assistance. [7]

At this juncture we could do well to take cognizance of the forceful role the Supreme Court has often played in riding herd on the forces of fragmentation that still beset the system. With such a strong nationalist as John Marshall as its first chief justice, it soon established itself as the final arbiter of all disputes involving the new constitution. It ordered Georgia to honor its contracts with the Cherokee Indians and stopped Maryland from taxing the federal government's property. "The national government . . . is the government of all," wrote Marshall in one of his most famous decisions. "Its powers are delegated by all; it represents all, and acts for all . . . the nation, on those subjects which it can act, must necessarily bind its component parts." [8]

But be that as it may, the early federal government, aside from preserving the union and enforcing minimal requirements of the Constitution, left most domestic matters to the states and their local governments. Jefferson, for example, seemed to regard the federal government as, for the most part, merely a department of foreign affairs (though he actively pursued interests in this area). In 1854, President Franklin Pierce, in carrying out this "hands-off" policy, refused to grant the states land on which they could erect insane asylums.

Foreign observers were often struck by the prominent, even dominant, role that state and local governments played in running the country's affairs. Alexis de Tocqueville, the French statesman, who visited our shores in the 1820s, noted that "the governments of the states in reality direct society in America." [9] And an English peer, Lord James Bryce, who toured the country toward the end of the century, remarked on how rarely the average American

6. *The New York Times* of June 5, 1973 carried a story saying that a group of Toledo residents, including the city's mayor, had formed the Select Committee to Arrange a New Deal to Avoid Litigations (SCANDAL) to demand some $11 billion in reparations from the state of Michigan. The figure is based on the alleged damage that Michigan troops inflicted on Toledo cabbage crops in the 1835 fracas, with interest compounded to the present day. The group said it would use the money to build a wall along the Michigan-Ohio border to prevent Ohioans from purchasing cheaper liquor and lottery tickets from Michigan.

7. An account of the "Lobster War" can be found in the *Boston Globe,* 1 July 1973.

8. *McCulloch v. Maryland* (1819).

9. Alexis de Tocqueville, *Democracy in America* (New York: Alfred A. Knopf, 1945), p. 86.

10

came into contact with his national government. "The police that guard his house, the local boards which look after the poor, control highways, impose water rates, manage schools—all these derive their legal powers from his state alone."[10]

The Great Depression of the 1930s, and the New Deal programs that the Roosevelt administration launched in the hope of ending it, created a change in this state of affairs. With the states nearly paralyzed, the federal government was forced to intervene in domestic affairs on an unprecedented scale. Soon federally raised or created funds and federally employed men and women were engaged in a variety of activities heretofore left in the hands of the states and localities. Federal controls also began extending into many new areas of American life. In the meantime, the Supreme Court, which, as we have seen, has often defended and extended federal power, began doing so again, establishing federal standards in civil rights, civil liberties, and a host of other matters.

Nevertheless, state and local government was scarcely quashed by the lengthening shadow of Washington. During the New Deal era, for example, Congress managed to put substantial control over administrative programs into state and local hands. This trend has to some extent persisted to the present day. Then, state and local government spending and employment, as we have seen, has shot up at a much faster rate than that of the federal government since the early 1960s. In addition, local patriotism has far from died out. In May 1945, for example, Fort Worth, Texas was displaying signs saying "Buy Bonds and Help Texas Win the War,"[11] and in 1975, Alabama was still flying its state flag over its statehouse with the U.S. flag relegated to a shorter flagpole on the capitol grounds.[12]

It should also be noted that the states, despite increased Supreme Court rulings in such matters as civil rights and civil liberties, still retain a fair degree of discretion. A state can determine whether or not it wants to run a welfare program or even operate a school system. It can allow its residents to marry at fourteen or prevent them from marrying until forty. Indeed, most of the civil and criminal laws that govern our behavior are still state laws. As Robert E. Merriam, chairman of the federal government's Advisory Committee on Intergovernmental Relations, reminds us, "The states retain the essential power to do anything short of abrogation of constitutional rights or conflict with federally pre-empted legislative areas that they would like to within their own borders."[13]

10. James Bryce, *The American Commonwealth,* 3rd ed. (New York: Macmillan, 1909), p. 313.

11. John Gunther, *Inside U. S. A.* (New York: Harper & Brothers, 1947), p. 815.

12. Alabama finally changed the positions of the U.S. and state flags in the fall of 1976.

13. Robert E. Merriam, "American Federalism: A Paradox of Promise and Performance," in Advisory Commission on Intergovernmental Relations, *Toward a More Effective Partnership* (Washington, D.C.: U.S. Government Printing Office, 1975).

11

But if the state has succeeded in retaining a good deal of legal power as well as political clout, what about cities, towns, counties and all the other instrumentalities of the subnational system? How are they faring?

Here we come to an important point that the student should bear continually in mind while probing into the subject. *Local government has no sovereignty.* Its institutions and policies exist only at the will and whim of the states. Therefore, any state can abolish or create, modify or merge any local government operating within its borders. Consequently, when we speak of the power of states we are speaking, to some degree, of the power of localities as well, for local government, in many respects, is merely an extension of the state government.

To sum up, then, our federal nation has undergone great changes in the cause of its two-hundred-year existence. However, it still remains a highly decentralized system, one that has no parallel in the modern world. Such decentralization provides us with numerous benefits but also saddles us with numerous problems. It is to these aspects that we will now turn.

GRASS ROOTS DEMOCRACY: DELIGHTS AND DILEMMAS

CHAPTER TWO

Federalism by its very nature implies a certain degree of decentralization. The sharing of sovereignty between a nation's central government and its subunits leads of necessity to a devolution of power and a dispersion of functions away from the center and toward what we call the "grass roots." This is the avowed aim of federalist government.

However, the federal framework established in our constitution fails to account for the extensive degree of political decentralization that has always characterized our political system. After all, federalism *per se* stops at the statehouse. While the states possess sovereign powers, their local governments, as we have seen, can make no such claim. However, as matters stand, local governments in practice share a great deal of the power of their sovereign states.

They possess more prerogatives and carry on more functions than the local governments of any other Western country. Political decentralization in the United States does not stop at the statehouse but extends to the smallest subdivisions of our political system.

What this means is that the United States as a nation has long been committed to the concept of what is called "grass roots democracy." This belief in breaking government down to the smallest size possible has permeated our creed and culture since its earliest days. It was responsible for the creation of a national government that would share sovereign power with the states. And it was and is responsible for the fact that the states themselves have always felt constrained to turn over many of their powers and functions to local governments.

THE DELIGHTS

Why have we always adhered so to the concepts and concerns of grass roots democracy? Why do we like to keep government small? What benefits does such a system bestow?

Former Vice-President Nelson A. Rockefeller sees four main advantages in what he calls the federal idea, an idea that signifies not only powerful and activist states but vigorous local government as well.[1] First, such a system "fosters diversity within unity." It allows the people of Wyoming, the people of Louisiana, and the people of Massachusetts the maximum opportunity to solve their own problems and meet their needs in their own way. Second, the federal idea "permits and encourages creativity, imagination, and innovation in meeting the needs of the people." Third, the system "gives scope to many energies, many beliefs, many initiatives and enlists them for the welfare of the people. It encourages diversity of thought, of culture, and of beliefs. It gives unparalleled opportunity for the development of private institutions—social, political and economic." Fourth, and finally, "the federal idea is characterized by a balance which prevents excesses and invites the full, free play of innovation and initiative."[2]

Flexibility

Expanding on Rockefeller's ideas, we see that grass roots democracy fosters flexibility. It offers an attractive alternative to having all policies made by, and

1. See: Nelson A. Rockefeller, *The Future of Federalism* (Cambridge, Mass.: Harvard University Press, 1963).
2. Ibid., Chapter 1.

14

executed from, one central source. It gives each locality more opportunity to do things in its own way.

Individuality

The admirers of grass roots democracy feel that by fostering flexibility, it produces government that can best meet the needs of the people. Each area has its own special problems and potentialities—what better way to respond to them than with a governmental apparatus designed solely for the area concerned. The further we can go in this direction, i.e., giving each locality its own government, the more responsive and responsible the political and governmental system becomes.

Hand in hand with these claimed advantages goes the one of enabling the citizen to play a greater role in government and making him feel more effective by doing so. It is hard to hear one man's voice among tens of millions of other voices. In a smaller arena a single voice stands a better chance. The fewer people a government has to serve, the more attention it can give to those it does serve and the more opportunity it can give them to make a meaningful impact on its activities.

Participation

This brings us to another factor favoring political decentralization. In providing more opportunities for citizens to play a role in government, it helps fulfill one of the basic prescriptions of democracy, namely participation. A person obviously would seem to have a greater chance to perform government service if there were many small governments than if there were one large one. Well over a half-million Americans hold elective office while countless others serve as appointees on various boards and commissions. No other nation quite duplicates this degree of citizen involvement. Presumably, it has invigorated and enriched our democratic way of life.

Political Experience. An attendant advantage to this phenomenon is the practice and training it gives to those few who go on to higher political office. In Great Britain, for example, the opportunities to hold a significant local office before running for Parliament are not nearly so great. (This will be discussed more fully in Chapter 27.) Consequently, a newly elected member of the British Parliament must usually start out with comparatively little experience in making important government decisions and in coping with the pressures that such decisions frequently generate. In this country, a newly elected congressman may well have

15

served in critical posts at the state and/or local level and so will have received the training that his British counterpart lacks. Each level of our political system serves, to some degree, as a farm team, preparing its more able members to move into the major leagues.

Party Politics

This training function becomes still more critical when a party is out of power at the national level for a long period of time. For example, from 1860 to 1912 only one Democratic candidate, Grover Cleveland, succeeded in winning the presidency. Furthermore, the Republicans controlled Congress for most of those years. The Democratic Party might well have atrophied and died had not it managed to maintain control and governance of several states and major cities. As a result it maintained its viability and the Democrats were ready to take office when the Democratic governor of New Jersey, Woodrow Wilson, won election to the presidency in 1912.

The Republicans, it should be noted, experienced a similar but not so lengthy exile in this century. From 1932 to 1952 the Democrats controlled the White House and for all but two years of that period they dominated Congress as well. However, the Republicans managed to win important offices at state and local levels. They thus prepared themselves to resume power at the national level in the 1950s.

The opportunities that our system offers for the parties lead us to another and perhaps deeper reason for its widespread acceptance. Decentralization can serve as a defense against despotism. When power is dispersed, when it is scattered through fifty state governments and reallocated by them through tens of thousands of local governments, it becomes difficult indeed for any one individual or group to gain absolute control. The majority party in control of the national government must continue to reckon with numerous other governments, many of them controlled by the minority party. Grass roots democracy thus thwarts monolithic absolutism.

However, there is also a more positive side to this aspect of our decentralized system. In preventing one political group from taking full charge, we give other groups a chance to grow. New parties have frequently originated in one or two states and, once established there, have on occasion spread throughout the country. In other words, our federalist system provides political movements that have a sectional base with a chance to get started and prove themselves.

Many of the movements that spring up in this fashion are somwhat extremist or eccentric and perhaps it is just as well that they rarely go on to become viable nationwide parties. But they do provide a valuable means of

16

expression for dissatisfied citizens and often call to the attention of our major parties important developments in our society. When such a movement begins to gain ground, one or both of the major parties usually make some effort to accommodate the concerns that created it.

This brings us to a final feature of our system that its backers often cite in its defense. Our states and localities act to some degree as laboratories, testing out new ideas and new programs. Often one state will approach a problem in one way, a second state in another, and another state in a third way. Their individual results may provide the rest of the nation with some valuable clues as to what to do. Or a state or local government may strike out in a new field and its success or failure will offer valuable lessons to others.

Examples of such experimentation and pioneering abound. In 1965 Massachusetts passed the nation's first truth-in-lending bill. It required vendors to tell their customers just what rate of interest they would have to pay for buying things on time. Since credit charges came to about 18 percent in most retail sales and since those were days of comparatively low interest rates generally, Massachusetts merchants feared their customers would revolt if the bill became law. However, no such revolt occurred. The customers continued to buy on credit pretty much as before. The following year Congress passed similar legislation for the entire nation.

There are numerous other examples of states taking the lead over the federal government in enacting law and instituting programs. Minnesota began monitoring radiation in the atmosphere before Washington conceded that such monitoring was useful. Wyoming instituted land use regulations with regard to open cut mining in 1969. The following year, Vermont set up a plan of district environmental commissions, coupled with an imaginative scheme of tax relief. Oregon pioneered with anti-litter laws while Hawaii has forged ahead with still more dramatic efforts at scenic preservations.

As is evident, these experimental efforts at the state level have proven useful not only to other states but also to the national government. When the Arab oil embargo of 1973 brought our energy crisis into the news, some of the states began reducing their speed limits in order to conserve gasoline. The federal government subsequently made a lower speed limit national policy. Furthermore, while Washington hesitated to take such a drastic step as gas rationing, Oregon originated the idea of every-other-day rationing, an idea that many other states quickly adopted.

Finally, we should note that federalism and grass roots democracy in general has managed to win not only the acceptance but also the approval of the American people. Polls have frequently indicated that the country's citizens do feel closer to, and do show preference for, their state and local governments over

17

their national government. For example, a poll taken in the late 1960s showed that only 18 percent of those sampled felt the federal government spends money more wisely than the states.[3]

The concept of political decentralization has also succeeded in enlisting the support of leading political thinkers on all sides of the system. The distinguished liberal Supreme Court Justice Louis D. Brandeis noted in 1920 that, "The Great America for which we long is unobtainable unless that individuality of communities becomes far more highly developed and becomes a common American phenomenon. . . .The growth of the future—at least of the immediate future—must be in quality and spiritual values. And that can come only through the concentrated, intensified striving of smaller groups. The field for special effort shall now be the state, the city, the village. . . ."[4]

A good half a century before Brandeis penned these words, an equally distinguished conservative writer, the British statesman Lord Acton, gave the concept of decentralization an even warmer embrace. "A great democracy must either sacrifice self-government to unity or preserve it by federalism," he wrote. "The coexistence of several nations under the same state is a test, as well as the best security, of its freedom." And, he added, ". . . it is also one of the chief instruments of freedom. . . ."[5]

THE DILEMMAS

From the foregoing it would seem that political decentralization offers citizens an unmixed blessing. Unfortunately, that is far from being the case. Despite its numerous advantages and assets, our federalist ideal, and the grass roots democracy it has spawned and nourished, carries a high price tag.

Perhaps no one better summarized the problems better than the British socialist Harold Laski. After spending some time in the United States during the 1930s, Laski wrote an article in which he capsuled in a few brief sentences the disadvantages and dilemmas of the federal concept:

> It is insufficiently positive in character; it does not provide for sufficient rapidity of action; it inhibits the emergence of necessary standards of uniformity; it relies upon compacts and compromises which take insufficient account of the urgent category of time; it leaves the backward areas a restraint, at once parasitic and

3. See: *Nation* (17 November 1969), p. 18.

4. Quoted in *New Republic* (5 July 1969), p. 20.

5. See Acton's essay "The History of Freedom in Antiquity," reprinted in Gertrude Himmelfarb, ed., *Essays on Freedom and Power* (Boston: Beacon Press, 1949). Acton also says of federalism, "By multiplying centers of government and discussion, it promotes the diffusion of political knowledge and the maintenance of healthy and independent opinion."

18

poisonous, on those who seek to move forward, not least, its psychological results are depressing to a democracy that needs the drama of positive achievement to retain its faith.[6]

Laski's central point is that divided government tends to become inactive government. A fragmented political system experiences great difficulty in responding to the needs and desires of its citizens. Because it is piecemeal in nature, it tends to respond to problems in a piecemeal fashion. And such response as it does make can often come about only after prolonged deliberation and negotiation, for too many power centers must consent and cooperate before the system can act at all.

This point has been underscored by other writers. Herbert Croly, an American social scientist who wrote at the turn of this century, also expressed dismay at the workings of our decentralized system. No government can be efficient, he claimed, unless its powers equal its responsibilities. But, said Croly, such is not the case in our own land. It is often possible for even just one of its many parts to stymie action by the whole. Consequently, the majority becomes easily thwarted.[7] And even such a backer of federalism as ACIR (Advisory Commission on Intergovernmental Relations) chairman Robert P. Merriam admits that "the capacity to plan well for the future, and then act in accordance with plans, is one of our weakest points."[8]

Examples abound to illustrate the point these writers are making, and we will come across many of them in the pages and chapters which follow. At this juncture, let us spotlight just one of them, the Potomac River Basin Compact.

Not long after World War II discussion arose in the Potomac River area about the need for instituting some water resource management plan for the important waterway. Nothing was done about it until the spring of 1965, however, when, fearful that the federal government would take steps on its own if they continued delaying, the District of Columbia and the four states that enclose the river began deliberations in earnest. It was not until late 1970 that they succeeded in drawing up a mutually agreeable plan for the waterway, and then the plan had to go before the respective legislatures of the four states for approval. It managed to win the endorsements of the legislative bodies of Maryland and Pennsylvania without too much trouble, but in Virginia and West Virginia it ran into difficulties. By the mid-1970s, a full ten years after serious

6. Harold M. Laski, "The Obsolescence of Federalism," in *New Republic* (3 May 1939).

7. This point is developed in Croly's landmark work, *The Promise of American Life,* first published in 1909 and reprinted by Capricorn Books (New York: 1964). See in particular Chapters 11 and 12.

8. See: Robert Merriam, "American Federalism: A Paradox of Promise and Performance" in Advisory Commission on Intergovernmental Relations, *Toward a More Effective Partnership* (Washington, D.C.: U.S. Government Printing Office 1975).

planning had begun, and nearly a quarter century after the possibilities of such a project had surfaced, the first concrete step had yet to be taken to put a water resource management plan into action.[9]

Associated with the difficulties and delays that grass roots democracy fosters are the pronounced tendencies toward confusion and competition among its many constituent elements. When New York City dumps its garbage out to sea, some of the waste material washes back on New Jersey's beaches. Meanwhile, residents of New York City's Staten Island section complain bitterly that dust and soot from heavily industrialized Paterson, New Jersey are polluting their suburban environment. Urban states enact stringent controls on the purchase of guns only to encourage a flourishing trade in the import of firearms from more permissive rural states. And when the Supreme Court allows communities to set obscenity standards for themselves, it sets off widespread confusion not only in the pornography market but also among legitimate book and magazine dealers and even law enforcement agents.[10]

Sometimes the disorder that results from divided government leads to consequences that seem more humorous than harmful. A former district attorney in Upper Michigan relates how he campaigned enthusiastically for one day in a logging village. At about midnight when he was buying drinks freely for customers in a local tavern he glanced up at a map on the wall and found that the town was situated a full twelve miles outside his election district.[11] Elsewhere in the Midwest, the late journalist John Gunther wrote of drinking in a tavern in Kansas City, Missouri one Saturday night when he was suddenly asked to shift from one end of the bar to the other. It seems that all drinking had to stop at midnight in Missouri in those days, but since the other end of the bar was located across the Kansas line where light (3.2 percent) beer was still purchaseable, a customer could simply move his seat and go on drinking.[12]

Then there was the case of the Arizona governor who invented "Osborne time." Governor Sidney P. Osborne yielded to none in his devotion to President Franklin Roosevelt. However, he was even more fanatical in his detestation of daylight saving time. When Roosevelt put the nation under daylight saving time during World War II, Osborne refused to go along. He reversed the federal edict on his own authority and kept his state on solar time. Needless to say, this move created considerable confusion for airlines and railroads with carriers passing

9. This information was supplied by Dr. James A. Medeiros, former Associate Professor of Political Science, Northeastern University.

10. For an interesting and informative review of the unintended consequences of the Supreme Court's decision, see a dispatch by Jon Nordheimer headlined "Smut, Variously Defined, Is Booming Nationwide," in *New York Times,* 19 May 1974.

11. Robert Traver, *Small Town D. A.* (New York: E. P. Dutton, 1958), p. 17.

12. John Gunther, *Inside U. S. A.* (New York: Harper & Brothers, 1947), p. 352.

through his state. Arizona continued to run on "Osborne time" throughout the War.[13]

States not only possess the potential for disturbing and even, on occasion, destroying federal policy in domestic matters, but can even jolt the federal government's foreign policy as well. In the spring of 1960, California was preparing to execute its most famous convict, Caryl Chessman. Sentenced to death many years before for sex crimes, the brilliant death row inmate had kept the executioners at bay with one strategem after another. In the meantime he had written several books that had brought him and his case international fame. Now, time had finally run out and his execution date had been set.

Chessman's case, however, had acquired such renown that his scheduled execution touched off demonstrations around the world. Even the Vatican newspaper asked that his life be spared. President Eisenhower, meanwhile, was preparing to leave on a trip to South America, where pro-Chessman sentiment was running particularly high. The State Department asked California Governor Edmund Brown (father of current California governor Edmund Brown, Jr.) if he could stop the execution. Brown, who was personally opposed to capital punishment, managed to secure a brief reprieve until the President's trip was over.[14]

Other efforts at securing state and local support of U.S. foreign policy efforts have met with less success. At different times, several states and localities have discriminated against citizens of various ethnic groups, damaging U.S. relations with the countries from which these groups come. When Mayor Mirioni of Detroit snubbed the visiting deputy premier of the Soviet Union in 1959, and when both Mayor Lindsay of New York City and Governor Rockefeller of New York State declined to greet King Faisel of Saudi Arabia in 1966, U.S. foreign policy efforts suffered a setback.

It should be kept in mind that the confusion and competition that tend to permeate a system based on grass roots democracy are not confined to relations among the states or between states and the national government. The same problems tend to flourish at the local level as well. In 1969, a series of student riots shook Isla Vista, the university section of Santa Barbara, California. A subsequent study showed that more than thirty jurisdictions have some authority over the community. The resulting tangle of government services and directives was thought to have contributed to the widespread student unrest.

This lack of coordination and cooperation that our decentralized political

13. Ibid., p. 899.

14. A brief discussion of the Chessman case and its political consequences will be found in: Bunzel and Lee, *The California Democratic Delegation of 1960,* Inter-University Case Program #67 (Indianapolis: Bobbs-Merrill).

system produces not only makes action difficult but also makes the pinpointing of responsibility for any action even harder. Since usually no one unit of government has untrammeled authority for the carrying out of a project or program, it becomes inconvenient and often impossible to give credit or, as is most frequently the case, assess blame. A system of divided powers lends itself to buck-passing. Thus, not only is it burdensome for government to act decisively in our country but also in many cases it becomes easy for it to refrain from doing so, for even those who are monitoring its activities most closely will often find it perplexing to know who is at fault. Since in a democracy the government should, above all, be able to be held responsible by its citizens, this particular feature of decentralization tends to undercut democracy itself.

Political decentralization also imposes such a great financial cost that it frequently is looked upon as a luxury. "With our thousands upon thousands of governmental-units," says Merriam, "there is gross duplication of administrative machinery." And he adds, "Foreigners sometimes observe that only America with its bountiful resources could afford a governmental system like ours." [15]

The cost of maintaining our complex governmental setup has been documented in many ways. For example, in a study done in 1966 the Committee on Economic Development found that the refusal of local governments to join together for joint purchasing was adding some $82 million a year to their purchasing costs. (The figure would be nearly double that today.) The CED also cited a 1960 study in Illinois that found that abolishing all the state's townships and consolidating the state's 102 counties into 24 would cut the costs of local government by as much as 40 percent. [16]

Grass roots democracy probably bears responsibility for the fact that our government actually employs a higher percentage of the work force than do the governments of many semi-socialist countries. For example, in Sweden approximately 17 percent of the nation's work force are classified as government employees. In this country the figure is slightly over 18 percent. Yet in Sweden nearly every doctor, nurse, hospital worker, school teacher, and professor is an employee of the government as are significant numbers of actors, opera singers, and the like. In other words, government in Sweden, which is a unitary state, manages to perform far more functions while employing relatively fewer people than does government in the United States.

There are other financial costs of our decentralized system that do not show up in the actual expenditures of government operations. Every so often a building located near a town or city line burns down simply because the fire

15. Merriam, "American Federalism."
16. *Modernizing Local Government* (New York: Committee for Economic Development, 1966).

station closest to it was located across the line in another community. This adds to everyone's insurance costs. And when a business located in a community such as Fridley, Minnesota has to make out tax returns to eleven different jurisdictions it must of necessity include such a bookkeeping burden in the cost of its products. Such problems individually may seem minor but overall they add up.

Finally, there are the costs imposed because most American governments are simply too small to cope with their challenges and demands in the most intelligent and practical manner. The CED, in the study previously mentioned, found that "very few local units are large enough in population, area, and taxable resources—to apply modern methods in solving current and future problems." [17]

Critics of grass roots democracy also repudiate some of the specific advantages that its defenders claim for it. The argument that the subunits serve as pioneers in trying out and testing new techniques and ideas draws the disdain of these critics. "The states . . . have not proved themselves laboratories of experiment, seeking knowledge and experience to be shared cooperatively," writes one author. "Rather, their efforts have too often been aimed at closing each other in, or, at least, at a kind of economic one-upmanship. Identity of long-run interests has played second fiddle to short-term politics. Even where issues have had strong state implications, states seem willing to pass the most troublesome ones (and therefore the most exciting ones) to the federal level, avoiding the necessity of energetic involvement with them. . . ." [18] Another author echoes these sentiments: "The growth of a leviathan in Washington, it can safely be asserted, is due in large part to the defaults of the states in exercising power in areas where they had a legitimate claim and every reason to act." [19] Such critics denigrate the examples of state and local enterprise cited in the previous section, maintaining that when it comes to the big issues, it falls almost invariably to the national government to take the lead.

The vaunted advantage that political decentralization ostensibly confers by providing government that is closer to, and more responsive to, the people also has come under attack. If it really does this, say critics, then why is it that people seem to show less interest in local and state affairs than they do in national events. Such evidence as exists often bears these critics out. Alan K. Campbell, a leading authority on subnational government in the United States, concedes that "on the average, participation in elections in smaller units is less

17. Ibid.
18. John P. Wheeler, Jr., "A Great Partnership," National Civic Review (April 1969).
19. Richard H. Leach, American Federalism (New York: W. W. Norton, 1970), p. 42.

23

than in larger units." Furthermore, he notes, "that ideal of American Democracy, the New England town meeting, has also been found by recent scholars to have been elitist controlled with relatively little citizen participation." [20]

Since it does seem to be the case that people tend to vote more actively in national elections than in state elections, and often more frequently in state elections than in local ones, we might do well to pause for a moment to consider why this occurs. What lies behind this steady falloff in citizen interest and involvement as government gets closer to home?

The Royal Commission, which Great Britain set up in 1966 to examine local government in that country, may have hit upon part of the answer. The Commission concluded, among other things, that any public function must be fairly large in order to be interesting. Small government can usually spend only limited amounts of money, tackle only small-scale problems, and attract as leaders only people of limited stature. Its activities lack the drama and color of events that go on in the larger arenas of political action. Tied in with this is the fact that it frequently fails to secure sufficient news media coverage, especially by the metropolitan press and television. Thus, its ability to ignite the interest of the average voter suffers.

Another factor resulting in citizen apathy is the immense complexity of the system that our grass roots democracy has created. In order to participate effectively the citizen must keep tabs on the activities of his nation, his state, his country, his municipality, his school district, and any special districts and other institutions that may play a role. And since, as we saw earlier, the activities and responsibilities of these governments frequently overlap, the task of intelligently monitoring them can become almost impossible. A Canadian writer, in commenting on the somewhat more limited decentralized system in his own county, speculated, "Federalism, in the sense that it divides powers between the provinces [states] and the central government, cannot be comprehended by vast segments of the electorate." [21]

A third factor influencing this rather puzzling lackadaisical attitude towards grass roots government is the accelerating mobility of our society. At least forty million Americans change their residence every year. In many cities and towns more than 35 percent of the population turns over annually. We have, as one commentator puts it, become a "nation of strangers." To the extent that this is so, it impairs the workings of grass roots democracy, for in order to participate meaningfully in local and state government people must possess the knowledge and incentive to do so. A people on the move, shifting from one locality to another

20. Alan K. Campbell, "Functions in Flux," in Advisory Commission on Intergovernmental Relations, *Toward a More Effective Partnership.*

21. John Porter, *The Vertical Mosaic* (Toronto: University of Toronto Press, 1965), p. 48.

24

and even from one state to another, often fail to develop any intimate involvement with their own subnational governments. However, since no matter where in the country they move they remain American citizens, their interest in national affairs will usually continue.

To the extent that political decentralization may stifle rather than stimulate certain forms of political participation, it runs counter to, rather than reinforces, democratic values. Still another democratic value that may suffer or at least sustain some damage under such a system is equality. For any number of reasons, one state is often richer than another state, and even within any given state, one locality may be richer than other. To the degree that each state or locality is self-contained, the citizens of those that are richer benefit; the residents of the other lose. In 1969, the nation's oil companies paid Alaska nearly a billion dollars for rights to pump that state's vast oil reserves. The sum was six times Alaska's current budget. In the meantime, many other states not blessed with a resource such as oil were desperately trying to meet their minimal budget needs.

Basing their views on these and other considerations, critics of grass roots democracy deride the claim by its supporters that it is intrinsically more democratic. These critics point out that a high level of democracy has managed to coexist nicely with a high degree of political centralization in Great Britain and some other northern European countries. At the same time, many South American dictatorships have managed to live comfortably with at least some degree of federalism in their lands. [22]

Going still further, it can even be argued that federalism and other forms of political decentralization have shown no special ability to preserve democratic systems from the threat of dictatorship. The fragile democracy that Germany was struggling to maintain before the advent of Adolph Hitler was a federal system, and this actually may have contributed to that democracy's demise. For one thing, while the Nazi Party was outlawed in much of democratic Germany for a time, it was permitted in the state of Bavaria. This gave the Nazis a sectional base upon which to build. Then, when they did become a nationwide movement, they found that the individual governments of the states or municipalities were each too weak to curb their frequently unruly and unlawful tactics. There were thirty-three police forces in Germany at that time and the Nazi Party soon became stronger than any one of them.

An interesting contrast is provided by France, with a more centralized government that narrowly managed to avert joint Fascist and Communist takeover. The Fascist and Communist groups all summoned their supporters to assemble outside the French Parliament on the night of February 24, 1934.

22. This point is brought out by William H. Riker in his provocative and underappreciated book *Federalism* (Boston: Little, Brown and Co., 1960).

Once assembled, the groups proceeded to storm the Parliament building. The beleaguered French government had decided not to call in the Army to help for fear that the Army might side with the Fascists. Fortunately, the central government did control the country's entire police system, so it had been able to summon police reinforcements from throughout the nation. The beefed-up police barricades held the demonstrators at bay until dawn, when the attackers finally dispersed. The leaders of the extremist parties were never able to mobilize such a mob again. French democracy was saved, thanks in large part to a centralized police force. [23]

It is part of our good fortune that such menacing events have rarely occurred in this country. But detractors of decentralization point to the discrimination against blacks, Indians, Mexican Americans, and, at one time, Oriental Americans in various states and communities as examples of how sectional policies can strike at democratic values. Furthermore, many a city and county boss and, on at least one occasion, a state governor have functioned as virtual dictators within their bailiwicks. As Grant McConnell puts it, "Decentralization to local or functional small units does not make for democracy; indeed, in the sense that democratic values center about liberty and equality, it creates conditions quite hostile to democracy." [24]

GRASS ROOTS DEMOCRACY: LIBERAL OR CONSERVATIVE?

As the student has now had a chance to see, there is no agreement on whether our highly decentralized system deserves hosannas of praise or howls of protest. Undoubtedly, there is a good deal of merit in the claims of both its defenders and its detractors. Both sides provide ample food for thought, with the truth probably lying, as it usually does, somewhere between the two extreme positions. Substantially more agreement exists on the question of whether grass roots democracy serves liberal or conservative democracy best. Most observers place it on the conservative side of the spectrum.

The reasons behind this judgment are not difficult to discern, and, in fact, have already been suggested in the previous discussion. Let us examine them more closely.

Grass roots democracy tends to curb vigorous government action. The division of political power among so many different instrumentalities keeps any one of them from acting with vigor and force. As a result, while decentralization

23. For an account of this event see: William L. Shirer, *The Collapse of the Third Republic* (New York: Pocket Books, 1971), pp. 190–199.

24. Grant McConnell, *Private Power and American Democracy* (New York: Alfred A. Knopf, 1966), Chapter 4.

leads to a proliferation of government payrolls, it also leads to lessened overall governmental action, at least in many instances. The fact that so many different governmental units exist to check each other helps to put a brake on government action generally. As one writer has noted, "Federalism builds into our political system veto politics: a certain conservative bias which tends to expand geometrically as access points on all governmental levels increase and new constituencies are created." [25]

The governmental competition that political fragmentation creates constitutes a second cause for the system's conservatism. Although competition should and sometimes does spur grass roots governments into taking new initiatives, it more often acts to tie their hands. A few hypothetical examples illustrate how this works.

Let us assume that there are two comparable and adjoining states, A and B. State A decides to increase substantially its welfare benefits. Soon certain trends start to reveal themselves. While welfare clients in state B will certainly not all at once pack up their bags and head for more generous state A, nevertheless, state A finds that its welfare rolls are now starting to rise somewhat more rapidly than those of state B. The more generous allowances probably have at least some slight impact in encouraging some impoverished people to settle in state A rather than in state B. (The new welfare policy may also encourage a few more of the state's own citizens to apply for aid.)

State A has already had to increase its taxes somewhat to pay for its new welfare program. Now it finds that because of the increase in its number of clients it must raise its taxes still more. However, as the tax burdens of state A tend to grow increasingly heavier than those of State B, it discovers that the resources to pay those burdens are growing slimmer. What is happening? Simply this: as the comparative tax burden between the two states becomes more unfavorable for state A, some of the resources that help pay that tax burden my have started to drift to state B.

Again, we must not expect to see any sudden or sharp changes. But, for example, if an industrial concern in state A is planning to build a new plant, it may now find state B a more attractive site to locate the facility than state A. Or if a retired person of means is planning to take up residence in the region that the two states comprise, he may now find state B to be a more idyllic locale.

As a result of these trends, state A may find itself trapped into a vicious cycle. It must raise its taxes to pay for its new welfare programs. But in so doing it is tending to increase the number of people that the programs serve—and this may force it to increase taxes still more. At the same time, it finds its tax base

25. Donald E. Haider, *When Governments Come to Washington* (New York: Free Press, 1974), p. 307.

27

shrinking or at least failing to rise at its former rate. This puts increased pressure to tax the remaining taxable resources still more and this, in turn, tends to diminish them more, as increasing numbers of businesses and high-income people find state A less and less appealing.

Let us take another somewhat simpler example of how the competition that characterizes a decentralized political system can curtail governmental action. Let us assume now that both state C and state D have numerous wood pulp mills that are polluting the rivers and fouling the air (pulp mills often give off a horrendous stench) in both states. State C decides to crack down. It passes a series of antipollution laws that require its pulp producers to purchase new and expensive equipment and to adopt new and expensive procedures.

The results in this case are not hard to predict. Pulp mills cannot, of course, easily pack up and move to another state. But to the extent that the pulp mills of state C are forced to shoulder new expenses, they become less able to compete with mills located in lackadaisical state D. Thus, many of state C's mills will find it increasingly difficult to raise investment capital for expansion and some may well find themselves forced to lay off workers. A few may even be forced out of business.

These two hypothetical examples should provide some insight into how our piecemeal political system acts as a brake on governmental action. We will see numerous (and far from hypothetical) examples of these same forces at work throughout the text. These tendencies are by no means limited to the states alone. The same competitive restraints often operate among localities. Under grass roots democracy, so it has been said, the slowest ship tends to determine the speed of the fleet.

There is a third way in which decentralization seems to shift the system slightly to the right. It is an observable, if not easily explainable, fact that people tend to become more conservative as the government they are dealing with moves closer to them. The same person who may support a liberal president may prefer a less liberal governor and a still less liberal mayor.

A large constituency, such as the nation itself, has a much easier time invoking within us what might be called the larger feelings and responses, or, if you like, higher and more altruistic commitments. Our country can inspire and instill within us a love of its symbols and a devotion to its ideals. It can move us to forget or forego our more selfish sentiments and focus our attentions on the loftier levels of patriotism. When President John F. Kennedy said, in his first inaugural address, "Ask not what your country can do for you; ask what you can do for your country," he received a remarkably enthusiastic response. Yet if, say, a district city councillor were to say the same thing to his constituents—

namely, do not ask what the city can do for you but what you can do for it —in all likelihood he would not remain a city councillor much longer. The small constituency induces us to think of our personal, everyday concerns. Most people want their city councillors to have the potholes in their streets repaired, not to try to appeal to their nobler natures.

Many social scientists have drawn attention to this rather peculiar feature of grass roots democracy. Edward Banfield has pointed out that, strange as it may seem, presidents have on occasion feared to propose tax cuts because of hostile responses from taxpayers. Michael Regan has noted that, "It is demonstrably harder to obtain approval for public welfare expenditures in many states and cities than in Congress."[26] Says another social scientist, Grant McConnell, "Material values are much more characteristic of narrow than of broad constituencies; 'altruistic,' 'sentimental,' or 'public' interests are more readily given expression and support in large constituencies."[27]

An interesting illustration of this tendency can be found in the policies and programs of declared Socialists when they have been elected to office. Several American cities in the past have on occasion voted in Socialist mayors. Generally, these mayors have refrained from taking the dramatic steps their credos would seem to demand. Bridgeport, Connecticut, for example, reelected for many years a Socialist mayor who earned local popularity and a certain amount of national fame by refusing to spend the taxpayers' money to clear away snow. The good Lord put it there, and the good Lord can take it away, he was accustomed to say.

To sum up, then, decentralization works to make American democracy somewhat more conservative than it might otherwise be. It does this by creating a network of checks and counterchecks that tend to impede and impair governmental action; by substituting competition for cooperation, which tends to make most of our various governments hesitate before adopting costly programs; and by making us all take more provincial and more personal positions toward many government issues. No wonder, then, that right-wing politicians and entrenched economic interests have long served as champions of grass roots democracy. As President Theodore Roosevelt once remarked, "It is a comical fact that the most zealous upholders of state's rights are big businessmen."[28]

Two additional points merit attention before bringing our examination of this particular aspect of grass roots democracy to a close. For one thing, to say

26. Michael Reagan, "Uncle Sam Is Really Needed," in *New York Times Magazine*, 13 September 1964.

27. McConnell, *Private Power and American Democracy*, p. 117.

28. Quoted in Leach, *American Federalism*, p. 38.

29

that decentralization injects a somewhat more conservative flavor into our political system than might otherwise be the case is not to say that this is necessarily bad. Conservatives often point out that constraints on government action preserve individual freedom and permit greater economic growth. The fact that big business can usually protect its interests more easily at state and local levels has enabled it to spearhead the country's great economic expansion, they say; and if people tend to become less idealistic and more selfish when it comes to government that is closer to them, then, say conservatives, this may also be to the good. After all, idealism, they maintain, has often led the way to greater tyranny and human suffering than has the intelligent pursuit of self-interest. Adolph Hitler, conservatives like to point out, created a vigorous, centralized government backed by a good deal of idealistic fervor.

The second point to be considered is that like so many other features of modern life, our decentralized government is also undergoing change and modification. During the 1960s, the radical left, using such terms as "community control" or "community power," joined, in effect, their opposites on the right in attacking government centralization. At the same time, many of those who might be deemed moderate conservatives began to express second thoughts about grass roots democracy. For example, the Committee on Economic Development, an organization consisting largely of business leaders, published several salient reports calling for increased centralization in government. One of its studies actually suggested that 80 percent of all the local governments in the United States be phased out of existence. In a time of crisis and change, the subnational system finds itself with strange enemies, and even stranger allies.

THE CONTEMPORARY CHALLENGE

This country and this people, John Jay once noted, "seem to have been made for each other, and it appears as if it was the design of Providence that an inheritance so proper and convenient for a band of brethren, united to each other by the strongest ties, should never be split into a number of unsocial, jealous, and alien sovereignties." [29] Jay's comment was not just a hopeful observation. He was pleading the case for the new constitution and exhorting his fellow citizens to ratify it. The Constitution was designed to alleviate the dissensions and divisions that had wracked the country during its first few years of independence. It was designed to end a system of "unsocial, jealous, and alien sovereignties."

29. This statement appears in Number 2 of *The Federalist Papers*. (There are many editions of this work.)

To a great extent, the Constitution has succeeded in doing just that. The union thus created has preserved itself, although it has on occasion needed to use force to do so. Yet the question of whether or not it functions in anywhere near the optimal manner has continued to instigate disputes and ignite controversies through its two centuries of existence. Early in this century Herbert Croly claimed that democracy should be "a living movement in the direction of human brotherhood."[30] Federalism, he said, tends to forestall rather than foster such growth for it substitutes competition for cooperation and animosity for amity and thereby keeps people apart more than it brings them together.

Most other writers have felt differently. Writing at roughly the same time as Croly, James Bryce pointed out that local self-government, as we know it in this country, "creates among the citizens a sense of common interest in the common affairs, and of their individual as well as their common duty to take care that those affairs are efficiently and honestly administered."[31] A half-century later, Daniel Elazar, an authority on federalism, echoed these sentiments. Federal democracy, claims Elazar, has served the nation well, providing it with an energetic government able to respond to greater changes than any government has ever had to face before.[32]

The crises of the 1960s and 1970s, however, have prompted a good deal of reappraisal not only by the pundits but also by the people themselves. For example, in 1965, a Harris poll showed 43 percent of the population expressing confidence in local government. A similar poll in 1975 found that the figure had dropped to 14 percent. This was only 1 percent more than the figure of those expressing confidence in the national government, the smallest gap ever recorded between the respective popularity of the two types of government since polling became a regular feature of our political process. Clearly something was amiss.

The Advisory Commission on Intergovernmental Relations has given voice to some of these concerns, noting, at the same time, that they are nevertheless not all that new. In a 1974 report entitled *American Federalism: Into the Third Century,* the commission stated:

> For nearly 200 years now, Americans have tried to reconcile the twin goals of diversity and unity through a federal system of government, with a sharing of power between a national government on the one hand and state and local government on the other. . . . Today, as at other times, the question is raised,

30. Croly, *Promise of American Life,* p. 271.

31. James Bryce, *The American Commonwealth,* 3rd ed. (New York: Macmillan, 1909), p. 426.

32. This point comes through in almost all of Elazar's writings on federalism. For a full exposition of his views see: *American Federalism: The View from the States* (New York: Thomas Crowell, 1966).

among statesmen, scholars, and citizens, as to whether such a system of shared and divided powers is equal to the complex and critical nature of domestic government in the United States. [33]

An attempt to deal with this question and to discover or at least discuss, some possible answers will occupy our attention in the chapters that follow.

33. Advisory Commission on Intergovernmental Relations, *American Federalism: Into the Third Century* (Washington, D.C.: U.S. Government Printing Office, 1974).

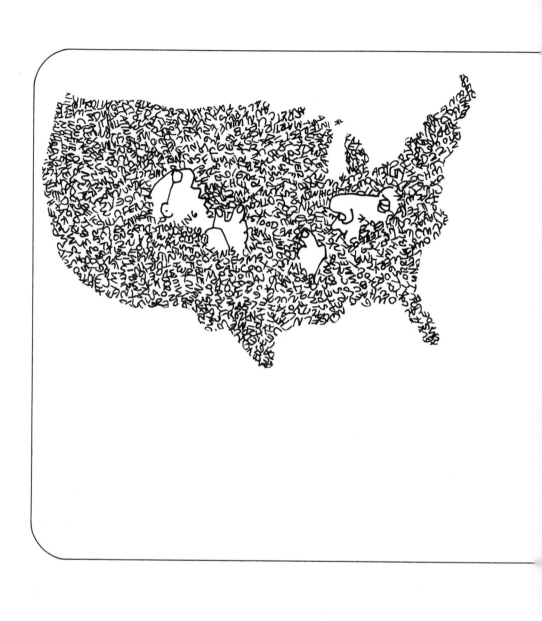

PART TWO

STATE GOVERNMENT

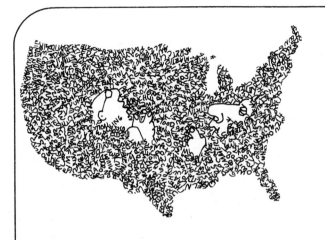

STATE CONSTITUTIONS

CHAPTER THREE

State government does not loom large in the public consciousness. The average American finds national and local affairs much more interesting and involving. A survey conducted in one Michigan city, for example, disclosed that while most of the respondents found national issues to be highly significant, only 2 percent felt state problems to be of much interest and importance. The news media seem for the most part to take a similar view. A consistent reader of the *New York Times* will be struck by how little coverage that comprehensive newspaper gives to events in Albany compared to goings on in New York City and Washington, and even London and Paris. And a noted network TV commentator, David Brinkley, casually remarked some years ago that the states might just as well go out of existence since there wasn't much left for them to do any longer.

The facts and figures, however, belie such attitudes. In Chapter 1 we called attention to the fact that since 1960 governmental expenditures and employment have grown at a faster rate at state and local levels than at the national level. Zeroing in for a closer look, we find that state government has grown the fastest of all. While local government revenues and expenditures went from twelve to seventy-four billion dollars in the years 1950 to 1974, state government revenues and expenditures shot up from eleven to eighty-four billion. Thus, the states started the period spending one billion less than their local governments and ended the era spending ten billion more. In terms of employment, local government payrolls increased almost two-and-one-half times (from 3,228,000 to 7,872,000) but state payrolls rose nearly three times (from 1,057,000 to 2,937,000). As political scientist Martha Derthick points out, ". . . the state governments are not atrophying. They have plenty to do, and more all the time."[1]

Writing about the states as a group, however, is not all that easy, for substantial differences exist between them. The largest (Alaska) is 483 times as large as the smallest (Rhode Island). Many (Alaska, New York, California, Massachusetts) are comparatively well-off, while others (Mississippi, Louisiana, Alabama, etc.) are comparatively poor. Some states are quite literate (in Massachusetts some 63 percent of the population reads daily newspapers); others are much less so (in Louisiana only 34 percent of the population are daily newspaper readers).

More important for our purposes are the differences between states in terms of their political cultures. In the politics of a state like Minnesota, corruption is minimal, personality conflicts are subdued, and much attention is focused on issues. In a state like Louisiana, the political climate is somewhat different, for stealth and skullduggery have frequently characterized its political doing. Finally, to make matters more complicated, some states are almost torn in half by conflicting political cultures. Edmund Brown, Sr., admits that toward the end of his last term as governor of California, he gave serious thought to trying to divide the state in two, making California's liberal north into one state and its conservative south into another. In his memoirs, he says he would have pushed for such a division if he had not had to institute a major water project, which required joint action on both sections of the state.[2]

All of this makes generalizing about state governments frequently inconvenient and sometimes impossible. Nevertheless, the states do display certain

1. Martha Derthick and Gary Bombardier, *Between State and Nation: Regional Organizations of the United States* (Washington, D. C.: Brookings Institution, 1974), p. 22.

2. Edmund G. Brown, *Reagan and Reality: The Two Californias* (New York: Praeger Publishers, 1970).

characteristics and customs that distinguish at least most of them, though in varying degrees to be sure. Consequently, we can examine them as a group provided we keep in mind that what may be true for most states is not necessarily true for all of them, and that even in the states for which it is true, substantial differences do exist.

As a sovereign power in its own right, every American state is legally entitled to have a constitution, and, as it so happens, each of the fifty states has one. Such constitutions are not really necessary for the workings of a federal system and in other federal countries such as Canada, West Germany, and Switzerland, the sovereign subunits are able to get along without them. That all our states have seen fit to promulgate such documents of fundamental law provides yet another indication of our greater commitment to political decentralization. Some of our state constitutions actually predate the U.S. Constitution, with the Massachusetts Constitution being the oldest such document in effect in the world today.

What are these state constitutions like? At first glance they seem remarkably like the U.S. Constitution. They all provide for a separation of powers with a separately elected chief executive and a separately elected legislature that in all but one state (Nebraska) consists, as does Congress, of an upper house and a lower house. As a matter of fact, the upper chamber is everywhere referred to as the senate while the lower chamber is sometimes called the house. (Many states, however, call their lower chamber the assembly.) Each state constitution also establishes an independent judiciary and sets forth a bill of rights that in most cases incorporates such procedural safeguards as writ of habeas corpus, trial by jury, protection against double jeopardy, and the like.

The similarity between state constitutions and the U.S. Constitution means that these state charters are also similar to each other. Indeed many states have borrowed whole sections of their constitutions from other states. The New Hampshire Constitution, for instance, is almost a carbon copy of that of Massachusetts. This tendency to adhere to a general pattern has distressed some of federalism's backers, who view it as a failure to take advantage of the opportunities a federal system provides for experimentation and innovation. As Lord Bryce noted, "So far from abusing their power of making themselves unlike one another, the states have tended to be too uniform, and have made fewer experiments in institutions than one could wish."

As we subject these state constitutions to a closer look, we do, however, find one significant feature that differentiates them from the national constitution. State constitutions are longer, usually much longer. While the constitution that governs the United States contains about 7,000 words and can be read in less than an hour, many state constitutions go on to almost interminable lengths.

39

Louisiana once held the prize in this regard. Its constitution once ran to over 235,000 words, making it rival the Old Testament in length. It was finally shortened in 1974 to 35,000 words—still five times longer than the U.S. Constitution. Meanwhile, Alabama retains a constitution of over 100,000 words, California operates under a constitution of more than 32,000 words and the Texas Constitution comes to well over 60,000 words. Even the shortest state constitutions, those of Vermont, Connecticut, and Rhode Island, amount to nearly 8,000 words each.

Why should states, even relatively small ones, need such elongated constitutions when our national government, embracing so many activities and powers, manages to govern with a much shorter one? What makes the typical state constitution such a long-winded document?

One reason is simply poor draftsmanship. Those who have authored such documents have frequently fallen prey to verbosity, rambling on and on to say something that could be said in very few words. Parts of some state constitutions read more like exhortations to virtue than stipulations of law. The Massachusetts Constitution, for example, says, "It shall be the duty of Legislatures and Magistrates . . . to countenance and inculcate the principles of humanity and general benevolence, public and private charity, industry and frugality, honesty and punctuality in their dealings, sincerity, good humor, and all social affections, and generous sentiments among the people."

Even when it comes to setting standards, state constitutions frequently substitute sermons for specifications. Thus, the Maryland Constitution demands that judges should be "most distinguished for wisdom and sound legal character," while the Texas constitution requires the University of Texas to be an institution "of the first class." Indeed, this sermonizing note tends to run through many state constitutions, adding a good deal of superficial and superfluous wordage.

Preachiness and prosiness, however, are far from being the sole sources of verbosity in the state constitutions. A more important reason for the great length of these documents is their preoccupation with detail. California's constitution specifies what powers the legislature may exercise in setting the time limit of wrestling matches, while Georgia's Constitution offers a $250,000 reward to the first person to strike oil in that state. Utah's fundamental law requires all the state school systems to teach the metric system; Oklahoma's requires all state schools to teach domestic economy. South Carolina's constitution devotes considerable space to spelling out what constitutes a "durable hard surface" for the streets of Greenville.

Before Louisiana's constitution was modified it was something of a paragon of prolixity. For example, the document contained provisions concerning the New Orleans Zoo, and it also devoted five whole pages to various details concerning the operation of the sewer system in East Baton Rouge Parish.

This mania for minutiae that state constitutions seem to exhibit is prompted by various factors. For one thing, since early days we have tended to view government with fear and distrust. Because of this, many of the early constitution writers inserted numerous provisions limiting and checking the powers and prerogatives of their various organs of government. Succeeding experience only aided and abetted this trend. The financial panic of 1837, for example, caused many states to place a constitutional limit on the amount of money their legislatures could borrow on the credit of the state. Later in the nineteenth century the corrupt and irresponsible behavior of many state legislatures and of state government produced a whole wave of constitutional amendments designed to further curb and constrain their powers. The people became fearful of leaving even the smallest matters to the discretion of their elected officials.

Another factor fostering extensive and detailed provisions in state constitutions is the limited scope of judicial determination at the state level. When it comes to interpreting our national constitution, the U.S. Supreme Court has rarely shown itself hesitant to fill in the gaps as to what it does and doesn't mean and to apply its more general provisions to a wide variety of specific cases. State supreme courts have rarely shown the same aggressiveness and assurance. The state courts have tended to take a more limited view of their role as interpreters and have thereby left more room for constitution writers and amenders to spell out further specifics.

By far the most important reason for cramming these constitutions with detail is the prevalance and potency of state interest groups. Many of the provisions and particulars that clutter up state constitutions reflect an interest group at work. The constitutions of Arizona, Arkansas, Florida, Kansas, Mississippi, Nebraska, and South Dakota all contain "right-to-work" provisions which reflect the work of business interests by outlawing the union shop. The constitutions of Hawaii, Missouri, New Jersey, and New York guarantee workers the rights to bargain collectively and to join trade unions, which reflect the activity of organized labor.

It should be kept in mind that not all interest groups are economically oriented. There are all kinds of interest groups representing all kinds of points of view and motivated by all kinds of reasons. A veterans' group may seek to have patriotic celebrations in the schools, a religious group may fight to outlaw beano, a conservation group may seek to protect the public forests from encroachment. The Massachusetts Constitution, for example, contains a lengthy provision extolling the glories of Harvard College and conferring certain privileges on that institution. This provision results from the efforts of a one-man interest group,

41

John Adams. As the author of the state's constitution and a loyal Harvard alumnus, Adams saw to it that the interests of his alma mater were duly provided for and protected.

THE CONSEQUENCES OF COMPREHENSIVENESS

It is not difficult to decipher just what prompts interest groups to seek to inscribe protective clauses into state constitutions. As the state's fundamental body of law, the constitution commands a respect and, in some cases, a reverence that an ordinary law passed by a legislature and signed by a governor does not elicit. More importantly, a law can be easily repealed; a constitutional provision cannot. Constitutions are not as easy to change as ordinary laws. Therefore an interest group gains greater protection by making its concerns a matter of constitutional provision rather than of normal legislation.

The vast detail in state constitutions has had many effects on state governments, which, in the view of most political observers, are almost all bad. A constitution by its very nature, wrote the first chief justice of the U.S. Supreme Court, "requires that only its great outlines should be marked, its important objects designated." Otherwise, John Marshall went on to observe, it "would partake of the prolixity of a legal code and could scarcely be embraced by the human mind." Furthermore, a constitution is intended "to endure for ages to come, and, consequently, to be adapted to the various crises of human affairs . . . . It would have been an unwise attempt to provide by immutable rules, for exigencies which, if foreseen at all, must have been seen dimly, and which can best be provided for as they occur." [3]

The U.S. Constitution meets Marshall's criteria but most state constitutions obviously do not. As a result, they have made state governments heir to all the evils against which Marshall warned. Governors, legislators, and other state officials find themselves straightjacketed by their confining, circumscribing clauses and consequently cannot easily adapt state policies and programs to meet changing needs. Sometimes even the smallest measures run afoul of constitutional restrictions. For example, a provision in New York State's constitution, which decrees that the state's public forests shall be kept "forever wild," produced constitutional crises on two occasions when the state attempted to construct some ski trails in its woodlands.

One significant way in which these constitutions protect special interests is through a device called *earmarked funds*. An interest group will often seek to have a particular form of revenue designated for a certain type of expenditure

3. *McCulloch v. Maryland* (1819).

42

and for that expenditure alone. The most famous—some would say notorious—example of this is the earmarking of gasoline taxes for highway construction and maintenance. Highway interests in virtually every state have at one time or another succeeded in having such revenues so earmarked and in many states this protection has been written into the state constitution.

It is not always possible or even necessary for a special interest or, as in the case of highways, a group of special interests to have all the revenues from a certain tax allocated for its purpose alone. Sometimes an interest group wants only a portion of the tax allotted to its concerns, while other interests may succeed in having the remaining portions of the tax assigned to their specific areas of activity. The result is that up to two-thirds of all government revenue in some states is earmarked. The governor of Georgia in 1967, to take just one example, had discretion over only two million dollars of the state's income. The rest was already spoken for.

In view of all this, it is no wonder that state constitutions have evoked little enthusiasm from political scientists or, for that matter, state political leaders. Former North Carolina governor Terry Sanford has few kind words to say for such documents. State constitutions serve, he says, as "the drag anchors of state progress and permanent cloaks for the protection of special interests and points of view." [4]

MODERNIZING CONSTITUTIONS

Anchors can be lifted and constitutions can be changed. Indeed, if they were not amendable they would never have become so suffused with detail. Georgia's present constitution was adopted in 1945. By 1975, it had been amended nearly 700 times. Louisiana has had as many as eighty constitutional amendments on a single election ballot. Finally, in 1970 the state's increasingly exasperated voters, confronted with fifty-three proposed amendments on the ballot, voted down all of them. This revolt prompted the state's political leaders to set a brand new constitution before the citizens in 1974.

The amendment process varies from state to state. Tennessee's is considered the most difficult. A constitutional change in that state must be approved twice by a majority of all members of the state legislature, the second time by a two-thirds vote. Then the amendment goes before the voters, who must approve it by a majority as great as the majority of those voting for governor. This last roadblock is more serious than is apparent at first glance, for many voters don't bother to vote on constitutional amendments at all. Consequently, while a

4. Terry Sanford, *Storm over the States* (New York: McGraw-Hill, 1967), p. 84.

majority of those voting on the proposed amendment may favor it, the amendment may still lose, for the number of yes votes it garners can easily fall short of the number of votes received by the winning candidate for governor.

Other states have made the process somewhat looser, but most of them follow the same general pattern. Usually the proposed change must be first approved by the legislature and then ratified by the voters. However, as almost everywhere else in the subnational political system, exceptions are fairly numerous. Eighteen states allow their citizens to initiate constitutional changes without the prior approval of the legislature. On the other hand, one state, Delaware, does not even require citizen approval. Passage by two successive legislatures is enough to insert any number of amendments into the Delaware Constitution.

An alternative to legislative enactment of constitutional change is the constitutional convention. Such a convention may be called by the state legislature or, in a few states, may be called into being through a referendum initiated by a citizen petition drive. (A specified number of citizens sign a petition to put the proposal for a constitutional convention on the ballot.) Constitutional conventions may be limited or general. A limited convention is one convened for scrutinizing only certain specific portions of the constitution. A general convention is given the right to propose any number of changes anywhere in the constitution. A few states require that the question of whether to call a constitutional convention be automatically put before the voters every ten years or so.

Although constitutional conventions often reflect a desire to take constitutional change out of the hands of the state's political leaders, they rarely succeed in doing so. Delegates to such conventions are often elected from legislative districts on partisan slates. As a result, legislators and other politicians often end up serving as delegates. However, citizens other than professional politicians usually manage to provide some input and occasionally succeed in seizing the leadership. The Michigan constitutional convention of 1961–1962 elected George Romney, then president of American Motors, as its vice-chairman. Romney's well-regarded leadership of some of the proceedings prompted the Republican Party to choose him as its candidate for governor in the next election. (He was elected and went on to become a candidate for President and then the Secretary for Housing and Urban Development in President Nixon's cabinet before resigning from public life.)[5]

One problem particularly annoying to constitutional reformers is that when it comes to the substantial structural changes in government that modernization mandates, the people themselves frequently say no. During the

5. For an insightful picture of the problems and politics of constitutional conventions see Albert L. Sturm's account of the Michigan experience, "Making A Constitution," *National Civic Review* (January 1964).

1960s voters in Rhode Island, New York, Kentucky, North Dakota, Pennsylvania, Maryland, North Dakota, Utah, and Idaho all rejected efforts to bring their constitutions up to date. In 1970, Oregon voters turned down, by a 3–2 vote, a proposed new constitution that represented some ten years of careful preparation.

However, Hawaii, Connecticut, Massachusetts, New Jersey, and Tennessee all approved fairly sweeping changes in their constitutions and California, Pennsylvania, and Wisconsin voters accepted somewhat lesser revisions. Furthermore, the pace of constitutional change picked up in the 1970s as certain critical governmental problems became increasingly apparent and increasingly appalling. As a matter of fact, during the 1972–1973 legislative year, all but three states took some action to alter their constitutions. The current of change that has been sweeping through modern society seems finally to have penetrated the none-too-hallowed but all-too-impregnable sanctuary of state constitutionalism as well.

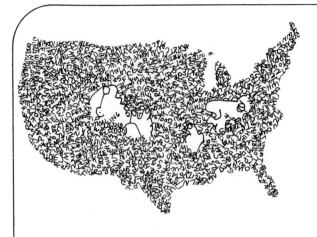

POLITICAL PARTIES

CHAPTER FOUR

Most Americans feel that their country is essentially governed by two political parties, the Democrats and the Republicans. Most American political scientists, however, disagree. In their view, the United States is governed by a wide variety of parties that tend to shift and spread themselves all over the democratic political spectrum. According to these political scientists, the political decentralization that characterizes our political system characterizes our party system as well.

Leaving aside such parties as the American Independence Party, which George Wallace created in 1968 to advance his presidential candidacy, or such parties as the Conservative and Liberal Parties of New York, which are limited to that state alone, one can put the number of American political parties at 102.

This includes the 50 state Democratic Parties, the 50 state Republican Parties, and the national Democratic and Republican Parties. Dividing the parties in this way does seem to make more sense than classifying them into only two, Democrats and Republicans. The states, as was stressed in earlier chapters, are essentially sovereign and the independence they show in so many matters appears in the party system as well.

When we look more closely at the two national parties, we see that essentially they exist to nominate candidates for the presidency and vice-presidency. For this purpose they assemble for a week every four years, but even then the delegates vote on a state-by-state basis. True, each national party maintains a full-time party headquarters and each sets up a national committee consisting of varying numbers of representatives from each state. But the respective national committees and the national party apparatus possess relatively little power. They can set the guidelines for the national convention, give election materials and assistance to the state parties, and issue pronouncements on national party policy. Beyond that, they can do little.

When we drop our gaze to the state level we may find a stronger party mechanism at work—but the emphasis is on the word *may*. The state parties are themselves split into county, city, ward, precinct, and other units, many of which may hold substantial degrees of power. In Illinois, the chairman of the Cook County Democratic Committee, who has often served as the mayor of Chicago at the same time, usually plays a greater role in determining the policies and programs of Illinois's Democratic Party than does the Illinois state committee itself.

In terms of actual machinery, the lowest level of party organization is the precinct. Above that comes the ward. Then there may be city and county committees as well as other groupings. An example of the latter would be the party committees formed in each congressional district in some states. On top, at least theoretically, of this vast panorama of party organization are the state committees. For the party holding the governorship, there is an additional level of command, for the governor serves as the leader of his own state party.

The locus of power varies from state to state and may vary within any state from time to time. A strong governor may consolidate a good deal of power at the very top. More rarely, a state committee may exert considerable weight in party affairs. County party organizations play an especially important role in many states. This is particularly true in the South, where county "courthouse gangs" often headed by the county sheriff wield considerable leverage in state party affairs. In Massachusetts, on the other hand, county and even city committees scarcely exist. (Yet, to point up the variations still more, in New York, which is also a northeastern urban state, county party organizations are quite important.)

Other factors frequently complicate this already rather muddled situation. In addition to the official structural demarcations, geographic, religious, economic, ethnic, and other divisions also tend to keep state parties from becoming unified entities. In the Democratic Party of Louisiana, for example, the Protestant and Anglo-Saxon northern party units are usually at odds and sometimes at war with party organizations in the French and Catholic south. Political figures also may divide party organizations. In any one state, one political leader may be able to claim the loyalty of some groups, another will be able to command the adherence of others, while a third leader will hold sway over still others.

As a result, no state party truly duplicates the party bearing the same label in another state. Furthermore, within any state, the balance sheet of power may change from one election to the next as issues come and go and as political leaders rise and fall. And even at any one time, party influence is never completely concentrated at any level or within any pair of hands. The nature of our political system and the party system it has given rise to usually prevents such centralization from taking place.

ONE-PARTY STATES AND TWO-PARTY STATES

The diversity that state parties so often exhibit is sometimes furthered by another factor that tends to complicate and curb party development. In many states one party greatly overshadows the other in size and support. Indeed in some states this imbalance has reached the point that these are, to all intents and purposes, one-party states.

The South in particular has suffered from this political malady. There the Democrats dominated nearly every elective office in several states through the course of many decades. The firm enlistment of these states in the ranks of the Democrats earned for them the title of the "solid South." The causes for this peculiar phenomenon were many but most crucial seems to have been the desire to perpetuate segregation. Competition between the two parties, it was feared, would eventually lead one of them to bid for the black vote and this would bring down the whole rickety structure of segregation. Thus, the Republican Party remained a slim and shadowy affair whose prime function was to obtain and dispense federal patronage whenever the Republicans were in power in Washington. In state after state, the Democrats ran the entire show.

Although the rigidity with which the southern states clung to the Democratic Party was never fully duplicated elsewhere, some states did show an adherence to the Republican Party that almost rivaled it. In Maine and Vermont, for example, it was nearly as difficult for a Democrat to win state office as it was for a Republican to do so in Georgia and Alabama. A few midwestern states, such as Kansas, were only slightly less zealous upholders of the Republican banner.

This situation has changed substantially in recent years. In the South, there are at least a few Republicans in every state legislature, while in the North, Democrats have at times managed to become the party in power in Maine and Vermont. This has led some observers to conclude that the era of one-party states is over. Each state now has a viable if somewhat vitiated two-party system.

Technically speaking, such a view is undoubtedly correct. However, the Republican Party in the South, though very much alive, has scarcely become a potent force. In many southern states the Republicans have yet to win an important statewide office or to elect even a significant number of candidates to the legislature. In the meantime, some northern states have become more imbalanced than they were a generation ago. For example, in 1955 Massachusetts Republicans controlled the governorship and the state senate, and Democrats controlled the house and formed a sizeable minority in the senate. During the early 1960s the Democrats captured both houses of the legislature and have held them ever since, with Republican representation shrinking after each election. They also established a seemingly unbreakable grip on all the statewide offices except the governorship, and in 1974 they took over the governorship as well. Thus, today Massachusetts has become almost a one-party state.

Finally, even many of those states that can boast of a robust two-party system contain cities, counties, or other areas where no critical party opposition exists. Many of the country's larger cities are today so predominantly Democratic that the Republican Party has essentially ceased to exist as a political force in their municipal governments. Meanwhile, some rural areas remain almost as strongly dominated by Republican politics.

Political scientists have generally disparaged one-party politics. Since such politics still remains a feature in some sectors of state and local government, it behooves us to understand why they do so.

As was noted in Chapter 1, democracy requires accountability, and without a vigorous opposition party such accountability becomes hard to achieve. A spirited and sizeable opposition party will only too quickly take the governing party to task for its miscalculations and misdeeds and will usually try to offer alternatives to its policies. The clashes between the two parties tend to focus the voter's attention on the issues and to inform and educate him as to what is happening and what is at stake. The more evenly the two parties are matched, the better these functions are performed.

In a system of two competing parties, each of the parties usually tends to become more unified and better disciplined. This will simplify the citizen's task of checking on them, for he will only have to watch two distinct groups rather than try to keep tabs on a varied assortment of individuals. Personalities will count for less and issues will count for more. Corruption should diminish since it would seem much more difficult to bribe an entire and quite visible party organization, especially one that is being continually eyed by its rival party, than to pay off many independent individuals.

In states and localities where the opposition party is too weak, the dominant party tends to become less disciplined and less unified. Lacking a competing party sufficiently strong to keep it on its toes, the party in power usually starts to break down into factions. This, too, provides opposition and alternatives within the governing process, but many see the checks and balances that result from factions as far less satisfying than those that result from party competition.

A faction, it should be noted, lacks the coordination and coherence of a party. Its members may frequently switch sides on various issues. Indeed, factions may organize over one issue and then dissolve. A new issue then creates new factions. Even the leaders of factions change as issues change. A further and perhaps more important result is that a faction is much less visible than a party. Factions are not institutionalized. They do not educate the electorate and controversies between factions do not involve the electorate. Voters almost never identify with factions the way they do with parties.

V. O. Key, Jr., a political scientist who pioneered in the study of state government, felt that the absence of competing parties in the southern states tended to make governments in these states much less responsible and responsive to the wishes of the people. Instead it made it easier for special interests, especially moneyed interests, to work their will, for they found it easier to control factions than parties. [1] Later political scientists sought to test out Key's thesis and found some, but only some, evidence to support it. Strong party competition, their studies indicate, may play some role in, for example, the desire of state governments to operate liberal welfare programs, but social and economic factors seem to constitute much more important components in state policymaking.

However, although Key's thesis about party competition has only been partially verified, most students of state government still feel that these governments function best when two parties of near equal strength exist to compete for the prizes of power. As professor and former state senator Duane Lockard has

1. V. O. Key, Jr., *Southern Politics in State and Nation* (New York: Alfred A. Knopf, 1949), pp. 308–310.

put it, "Where there is competition there is a possibility for improvement, for the simple reason that the ins are opposed by the outs and each tries to turn to its advantage any indiscretion of the other. The visibility of the major parties and the pressures of election uncertainty are disciplinary rods and may induce a certain caution."[2]

In summary, then, we find that the evolution of one-party states into two-party states is a desired development in state politics. However, this evolution still has a long way to go in many states and its benefits will never, in and of themselves, resolve all the many problems that plague state government.

WHO CAN VOTE AND WHO CANNOT

Democratic government rests on popular consent. Citizens must have a voice, ultimately a determining one, in deciding its programs and policies. This voice usually takes the form of a vote. Therefore, a democratic system must seek to enable and encourage the maximum number of its people to express their wishes through the ballot.

No democracy, however, has ever extended the franchise to everyone. Elementary school children are commonly excluded. So are those suffering from extreme forms of mental illness. Prisoners lack the right to vote in most, though not all, democratic countries. More controversial restrictions have centered on financial status, race, and sex. There are also such problems as deciding the age people must attain or the length of time they must reside in a locality before they can gain access to the ballot box.

The Constitution left the issue of voting qualifications largely in the hands of the states. Most of them responded by granting suffrage to all white males who had reached the age of twenty-one, who possessed a certain minimal amount of property, and who had resided in their states for at least a year and in their community for at least six months. Such limitations strike us as being highly exclusionary if not actually elitst today, but in those days they seemed quite liberal. If they did not make the new nation into a full-fledged democracy, they certainly made it more democratic than any contemporary country. The course of history since then has been one of gradually extending the voting privilege to wider and wider sectors of the population.

The first barriers to the ballot to fall were property qualifications. They were not very severe to begin with and usually kept only a minority of citizens from the polls. As the democratic spirit spread through the country, they soon

2. Duane Lockard, *The Politics of State and Local Government* (New York: Macmillan, 1963). See also his *New England State Politics* (Princeton, N.J.: Princeton University Press, 1959), in which he tested Key's thesis with somewhat mixed results.

began to crumble. By the time Andrew Jackson took office they had pretty well vanished.

Removing restrictions because of sex, however, took almost a century longer. Agitation for giving women the right to vote did not gain much support among men or, for that matter, among women until late in the nineteenth century. But once the movement for women's suffrage did spring up it succeeded rapidly in moving forward, and following World War I women joined the electorate.

Opening up the electorate to blacks proved to be a still more drawn-out and difficult process. While the black freemen of the North soon gained voting rights, their much more numerous enslaved brothers of the South enjoyed no rights at all. The Civil War, and the constitutional amendments it gave birth to, were supposed to give the South's black citizens the full rights of citizenship. For a while they seemed to do just that and black political leaders not only sat in state legislatures but also went to Washington to take seats in the House of Representatives and the U.S. Senate. But soon a reaction set in. White segregationists seized power in the southern states and devised numerous and often noxious ways of depriving black citizens of the right to vote.

A chief means used to exclude black voters was the device of the white primary. For many decades nominating elections or primaries were deemed to be private affairs and therefore invulnerable to constitutional regulation. By maintaining themselves as one-party states and by making the Democratic primary the real election, southern states easily managed to keep most blacks from participating in the electoral process.

The U.S. Supreme Court began taking an increasingly jaundiced view of exclusionary methods and from the turn of the twentieth century on the court placed increasing restrictions on their use. It finally outlawed white primaries completely in 1944.[3] However, the South was not without other means of keeping its electorate nearly all white. Southern states had long used other practices such as poll taxes, literacy tests, and, at a local level, outright physical intimidation to keep black citizens from showing up at the polls on election day.

These exclusionary techniques came under attack not only by the Supreme Court but also by the nation's political leaders. In 1956 a Democratic Congress passed, and a Republican president signed, the first civil rights bill since Reconstruction. When John F. Kennedy took office some four years later, he assigned voting rights top priority in his civil rights program. His successor, Lyndon Johnson, signed the Voting Rights Act of 1965 into law, and his successor, Richard Nixon, signed the Voting Rights Act of 1970. Meanwhile the

3. In *Smith v. Albright.*

53

Twenty-fourth Amendment outlawing the payment of poll taxes as a requirement for voting in national elections was ratified in 1964. The following year the
Supreme Court outlawed poll taxes as a requirement for participating in state
and local elections. [4]

This brief summary fails to do full justice to a long and laborious movement in American history, a chapter filled with episodes of horror as well as
incidents of heroism. But the goal of widespread suffrage has for the most part
been achieved. As the United States entered its third century, almost as many
blacks as whites were enrolled on southern voting lists, and the small discrepancy which remained could easily be explained by differences in income and
educational levels. The presence of blacks as leaders of several southern counties and municipalities including the region's foremost city, Atlanta, suggests that
this particular civil rights battle has been won.

Another curb on electoral participation has also become less effective in
recent years. In 1968, residency requirements prevented an estimated five
million otherwise eligible citizens from voting. The Voting Rights Act of 1970
forbade any state from imposing a residency requirement of more than thirty days
on voting in national elections. It also required the states to make special
provisions for absentee voting and for registering new residents. Two years later,
the Supreme Court declared Tennessee's one-year residency rule to be unconstitutional for even state and local elections. This invalidated any one-year
residency rules in effect in other states. States can now prescribe a residency
period of no more than sixty days as necessary for a person to cast ballots for
local and state candidates.

The age limit of twenty-one remained a stable fixture in our electoral
architecture until 1944. At that time, Ellis Arnal, then governor of Georgia,
criticized the practice of drafting youths to fight while not allowing them to vote.
As a result of Arnal's leadership, Georgia soon became the only state that
allowed eighteen-year-olds the right to vote. (Ironically, this progressive move
did little or nothing to help the state's blacks, most of whom, whether eighteen or
eighty, continued to go unregistered.) In later years Kentucky, Hawaii, and
Alaska also reduced their voting age but there the movement stopped. No other
states took similar action until Congress, in the 1970 voting rights acts, attempted
to legislate a lowering of the age to eighteen. The Supreme Court in a 5-to-4
decision said the legislation was constitutional as applied to voting in national
elections but not as concerned state and local ones. Setting the age limits for the
latter type of elections, said the Court, was a state matter. However, the

4. *Harper v. Virginia State Board of Elections.*

following year the necessary three-quarters of the states ratified a constitutional amendment giving eighteen-year-olds the right to vote in all elections.

Although the extension of the franchise to the eighteen-to twenty-one-year group passed almost effortlessly, it aroused great fear in some small town residents whose communities contained large colleges and universities. They feared that hordes of radical students would troop to the polls in the next election and take over their communities. However, these fears proved largely groundless. Most students preferred to maintain their voting residency in their home towns. And in those municipalities where student voting power did become a potent force, such as Madison, Wisconsin, no drastic upheavals occurred.

A final factor that sometimes determines the size and shape of the electorate is simple fraud. So many of Chicago's precincts voted so overwhelmingly for John F. Kennedy in 1960 that many Republicans strongly suspected outright chicanery. They reportedly feared to ask for an official recount, however, lest evidence turn up showing that their own party cohorts had tampered with the ballots in rural areas. When John D. Rockefeller IV became state secretary of West Virginia in 1969, he sponsored public hearings on voting irregularities. The hearings disclosed that thirty-three of West Virginia's fifty-five counties had more registered voters than they had adult residents. One man testified under oath that his brother had voted regularly since dying in a 1964 automobile accident.[5] In Mississippi in 1971, the Delta Ministry of the National Council of Churches charged widespread cheating at the polls.

Corruption of the voting process has a long history in this country but fortunately this particular phenomenon of our subnational political system seems to be dying out. Voting machines make vote fraud more difficult—though by no means impossible. Statewide computerized voter registration, pioneered by South Carolina in the late 1960s, does still more to eliminate such practices. And the increasing surveillance by the news media, backed by the increasing sophistication of the citizens, appears to be adding the finishing blows. Fraud-free election results are now the rule in most states and localities and soon may be the rule in all of them.

THE PRIMACY OF PRIMARIES

When American voters march to the polls at election time to perform their civic duties, they customarily find lists of candidates already drawn up and waiting for

5. Richard Reeves, "One Rockefeller Who May Make It," New York Times Magazine, 4 October 1970.

their choices. How are these lists prepared? Who decides what candidates shall be each party's nominees for the various offices at stake?

At one time party leaders chose these candidates through a variety of conclaves called caucuses or conventions. The rank-and-file voter was not without influence in the process, for those making the decisions usually kept in mind whom the average citizen would prefer to vote for come election day. In other words, they wanted to pick candidates who would win. Furthermore, if the voter wished to take the time and trouble, there were often opportunities to participate in choosing the party leaders who would make the decisions. However, most voters nevertheless had little direct say in the nominating process. For the most part they had to wait until the final election when they could cast their ballots for the nominees of one party or another.

The system struck many as being far from satisfactory. This was especially true in the South where, as we have already seen, one-party dominance had become the rule after the Civil War. A one-party political system obviously deprives the voter of any meaningful choice in the final election. If his vote is to count for something in a one-party state, then it must be cast during the nominating process, for the nominees selected in this type of state are almost automatically elected.

This state of affairs prompted Georgia in 1876 to establish an election for choosing party nominees. An Atlanta newspaper at the time explained the rationale behind this new type of election.

> If parties were evenly divided perhaps the old caucus plan would do. Then there would be two good tickets for local offices in the field. The knot of worthies who, under that plan would gather in a room just large enough to hold them, would be on their good behavior. They would remember their constituents, and would confine their logrolling within prudent bounds. But when as in our local politics, they have nothing to fear from the opposition, there is little guarantee that the delegate system would give the voters a square chance . . . we prefer the easier, simpler plan of direct voting. [6]

The primary election as a device for allowing the voters to determine directly who shall be the party nominees soon spread throughout the South, and its growth did not stop there. Many non-southern states were also vicitims of one-party systems that gave the voter no real choice in final elections. Furthermore, many if not most of them suffered from extensive corruption, at least partially as a result. Soon these states too began turning to the primary as a solution. Such nominating elections were seen as a sure method of destroying

6. Quoted by Alan Snider in *Just Beginnings* (New York: McKenzie Press, 1958), p. 118.

political machines and ending boss-ruled conventions. By 1915 most of our states had made some provision for party primaries. [7]

The advent of party primaries did not spell the immediate demise of party conventions. Many states continued to hold these party conclaves for the purpose of selecting at least potential nominees. But it now became possible to challenge the convention-picked designees in a subsequent primary and such challenges began to occur with increasing frequency. Gradually, party conventions shrank in importance and in most states eventually disappeared. In 1967, New York, after fifty years of intermittent debate, finally scrapped its noisy convention system altogether. [8] Massachusetts did so in 1974. By the bicentennial year, primaries had become the country's major method of nominating party candidates.

Primaries essentially fall into two categories—open and closed. The closed primary is by far the most popular and is used in forty-one states. In most states using the closed primary only those voters already registered in a political party can vote and they can vote only for candidates in their own party. However, the closed primary is usually more open than it first may appear. For one thing, independents in at least some states can vote in either party's primary. If they do so, they will then have "R" or "D" placed after their names on the voting lists, but they can always go to the local election office later and have the party designation erased if they wish to resume their independent status. Even those who have registered in one party can vote instead in the other party's primary if they take the step of going to the election office ahead of time and changing their party affiliation. As with the independents, they can always change back to their former status afterward.

The open primary makes such crossing-over much easier. In seven states, each voter simply picks the ballot sheet of the party primary he wishes to vote in regardless of his own party status. Thus, a registered Republican who wishes to vote in the Democratic primary instead of his own party primary simply does so. The remaining two states, Washington and Alaska, have what might be called a wide-open primary. In these two states each voter has the right to choose candidates in any political party. [9] Thus a Republican, after designating which

7. For what is probably the best account of the rise of the primary system see: V. O. Key, Jr., *American State Politics* (New York: Alfred A. Knopf, 1956), especially Chapters 4, 5, and 6. See also his *Politics, Parties, and Pressure Groups,* Chapter 14.

8. A dispatch headlined "Many Democrats Assail State Nominating System" in the April 3, 1970 *New York Times* provides a revealing picture of the charges often leveled against state conventions.

9. In the "wide-open" or "blanket" primary as it is most often called, the voter cannot, however, choose a nominee from more than one party for the same office. What he can do is go back and forth between the two parties, designating his choice, say, for senator from one party, his choice for governor from another, etc. Of course, he may simply vote for nominees in his own party if he wishes.

candidates he would like to see carry the banner of his own party in the final election, can then go ahead and list his choices for Democratic party nominees as well. Democratic voters can similarly help select the Republican party's nominees.

The question now arises as to whether or not primaries do indeed fullfill their major purposes. Reformers turned to them with enthusiasm, hoping that they would democratize and clean up the political processes. The two major goals of primaries could perhaps be described as participation and purity. It was thought that primaries would help take away power from political machines, increase the involvement of the citizenry, educate and inform the voters through the additional campaigning which they necessitate, and allow more potential candidates more opportunities to win offices. Have they succeeded in accomplishing such ends?

To some degree they obviously have. One can point to many instances where the rank-and-file voters have nullified the workings of party bosses and where able candidates have managed to win nominations despite the opposition of such bosses. The primary and its secret ballot available to all registered voters who wish to associate themselves with a political party has often become a mighty force for civic improvement.

Nevertheless, despite the obvious opportunities they present for bettering the ballot process, and despite their growing popularity, primaries have generally failed to fulfill the expectations they have so often aroused. In the view of some, they create more problems than they solve.

New York State's experiences provide a good example of some of the problems that primaries may present. As earlier noted, the Empire State abandoned its convention system in 1967. Some three years later *The New York Times* reviewed the results. It did not find them favorable. Though all registered voters could now participate in the nominating process, no more than 20 to 30 percent of the Democrats were bothering to do so. Such low turnouts as well as multiple candidates for nominations meant that as few as 5 percent of the state's Democrats could select their party's nominee for the U.S. Senate that year.

The situation with the Republicans was still worse. The strong leadership—some would say domination—exercised by then governor Nelson Rockefeller had resulted in a hand-picked slate of his candidates. There were no contests of any significance in the Republican primary that year. Said the *Times*, "Something is missing in the primary system." [10]

The difficulties confronting New York reflect some of the dilemmas of the primary system generally. Primaries have usually failed to arouse the citizen

10. *New York Times*, 21 June 1970, "News of the Week in Review."

58

interest and involvement for which reformers had hoped. This fact, combined with the fact that any number of candidates may enter their names, means that it is possible for only a tiny minority to decide the party nominees. A voting bloc of 5 to 15 percent of the party's registered voters (and, of course, representing an even smaller percentage of the entire electorate) may thus decide who will be nominated and who will not.

Such factors as these make primaries vulnerable to manipulation. For example, two candidates representing different sectors of the party electorate may vie for a particular post. Each may then try to induce other candidates from the opponent's group to also enter the race. In this way each hopes to split the opponent's vote. Thus, if an Irish-American and an Italian-American are the principal candidates, the Irish-American may seek to persuade other Italian-American candidates to join the race while the Italian-American may encourage other Irish-American hopefuls to do the same. As a result, the party voter finds a bewildering number of names on the ballot and the winner may be nominated by a relative handful of voters.

However, candiates frequently find deliberate manipulation of this kind unnecessary, for important primary contests, unless firmly controlled by a strong party leadership (as happened with the Republican Party in New York under Rockefeller), have usually been able to attract a good number of entrants on their own. Sometimes otherwise obscure citizens possessing the names of famous people try their luck. Candidates named Daniel Boone, Brigham Young, and Mae West have run in Oklahoma's primaries. In 1952, a bookkeeper for a razor blade company entered the Massachusetts primary as a candidate for state treasurer. His name was John F. Kennedy. That year, a more famous John F. Kennedy was running for the U.S. Senate. Thanks to voter confusion, bookkeeper Kennedy not only was nominated in the primary but also went on to win the final election. (As a matter of fact, he did not turn out to be a bad treasurer. He allowed the deputy treasurers, who were career employees, to run things while he confined himself largely to receiving visitors in his spacious and ornate office. Massachusetts voters, struck by his apparent honesty and modesty, if not by his enterprise and vigor, twice reelected him to the position. However, his attempt to move up to governor in 1960 failed and he retired to write a book on his favorite hobby, a card game named whist.)

As might be expected, the problem of too many candidates has been especially severe in the South where party nomination is so often tantamount to election. The 1971 Louisiana primary featured twenty candidates for governor, seventeen of them running on the Democratic ballot.[11] Most southern states

11. *New York Times,* 6 November 1971.

have resorted to a run-off primary in an attempt to provide voters with a meaningful choice. In a run-off primary the two top vote getters for each office in the original primary get to battle it out for nomination. However, as the Louisiana episode just cited illustrates, this has not deterred many from running in the initial primary. It may even have encouraged more people to run, for what frequently happens is that a person with no chance of placing first or second in the initial primary, but hopeful of obtaining a respectable number of votes, will enter his name. After the initial primary is over, he will then bargain with the two top vote getters, hoping to make a deal with one of them for his support in the run-off primary.

Primaries add to the cost of campaigning. It is not unusual for a candidate to spend more money in winning the nomination than in winning the final election. At the same time, it is usually more difficult for candidates to raise money for primary fights. This gives a decided advantage to wealthy contenders or to those willing to make deals with, or elicit funds from, questionable sources. Furthermore the additional costs imposed by primary campaigns are physical as well as financial. Candidates frequently end up in November so exhausted from both campaigns that if they do win, they cannot devote as much energy and effort to their transitional tasks as they would like. They usally have only about two months to prepare themselves for their new posts.

Finally, primaries further weaken the party system. Since the primary is a game in which almost any number can play, and since it often provides little assurance as to who will win—the luck of having one's name first on the ballot has spelled the difference between victory and defeat in many cases—it becomes increasingly difficult to hold the parties to account. To the extent that primaries do damage the party leadership and open up the process, they make it possible for candidates who do not concur with basic party policy to become party standard-bearers. The lines of demarcation between the parties become even more blurred, factions form around various candidates, and party discipline and party accountability tend to dissipate.

None of this is meant to suggest that primaries are an unmitigated evil. They have frequently led to the unseating of bosses and the democratizing of the electoral process. But, as with so many reforms, reality has fallen short of expectation.

REFERENDA

Like primary elections, referenda seek to give the average voter more opportunity to participate directly in the political process. Actually, referenda go farther than primaries, for they afford the voter a chance not just to help nominate candidates but also to help legislate. As we saw earlier, all states but Delaware require all constitutional changes to be placed before the voters for ratification. In addition, some state legislatures are required by constitutional provision or by previously enacted legislation to allow the electorate to have the final say on many matters. Even when such a step is not necessary, state legislatures sometimes voluntarily place some issues on the ballot to allow the voters to say yes or no. Finally, citizens themselves sometimes initiate referenda by gathering sufficient signatures and meeting such other requirements as their state may have prescribed for putting a citizen-inspired proposal on the ballot.

Even more so than primaries, referenda reflect our abiding desire for direct democracy. They also are subject to many of the advantages and disadvantages which primaries offer. On the asset side of the balance sheet, referenda do permit more grass roots participation, stimulate voter interest in state affairs, and make political representatives more responsible and more responsive to citizen concerns. Frequently they serve as a valuable check on governmental misbehavior. When Massachusetts legislators gave themselves a substantial pay raise in the closing hours of their 1960 session, the state's citizens responded angrily. A citizen's group managed to put a proposal on the ballot for the next election calling for repeal of the pay raise. It was overwhelmingly approved by the voters.

But referenda also suffer from some of the liabilities of primaries. Again let us take an example from New York State to illustrate some of the problems they so frequently present. On November 4, 1969, voters in the Empire State were asked to approve four constitutional amendments. They appeared on the ballot as follows:

AMENDMENTS

AMENDMENT NUMBER ONE—LOANS FOR HOSPITALS AND RELATED FACILITIES

1 Shall the proposed amendment to Article seventeen of the Constitution inserting a new Section seven therein, to provide for the loan of the money or credit of the State, a municipality or a public corporation acting as an instrumentality of the State or municipality to certain corporations or associations for the purpose of providing hospital or other facilities for the prevention, diagnosis or treatment of human disease, pain, injury, disability, deformity or physical condition and for facilities incidental or appurtenant thereto as may be prescribed by law, be approved?

61

AMENDMENT NUMBER TWO—JOB DEVELOPMENT AUTHORITY

2

Shall the proposed amendment to Article ten, Section seven (renumbered eight) of the Constitution, increasing from $50,000,000 to $150,000,000 the maximum aggregate principal amount for which the Legislature may make the State liable as guarantor at any one time for bonds issued (exclusively of bonds issued to refund outstanding bonds) issued by a public corporation (Job Development Authority) created for the purpose of making loans to non-profit corporations to fiinance the construction of new industrial or manufacturing plants in this State or the acquisition, rehabilitation or improvement of former industrial or manufacturing plants in this State to improve employment opportunities in any area of the state, and providing that bond anticipation notes and any renewals thereof issued by any such public corporation shall mature within seven years after the respective dates of such notes rather than five years after such dates, be approved?

AMENDMENT NUMBER THREE—CONSERVATION, THE STATE NATURE AND HISTORICAL PRESERVE

3

Shall the proposed amendment renumbering Section four of Article fourteen to be Section five and inserting therein a new Section four declaring the policy of the State to conserve and protect its natural resources and scenic beauty and to encourage the development and improvement of its agricultural lands, providing that the Legislature in implementing such policy shall include adequate provision for the abatement of air and water pollution and of excessive and unnecessary noise, the protection of agricultural lands, wetlands and shorelines and the development and regulation of water resources, and providing for the establishment of the State Nature and Historical Preserve outside of the forest preserve counties and regulating the disposition of the lands thereof, be approved?

AMENDMENT NUMBER FOUR—APPORTIONMENT

4

Shall the proposed amendment to Article three of the Constitution, inserting a new Section five-a therein, to provide that, for the purpose of apportioning Senate and Assembly districts pursuant to the provisions of Article three which precede the new section, the term "inhabitants, excluding aliens" shall mean the whole number of persons, be approved?

As these suggested amendments illustrate, referenda proposals frequently involve complicated issues that require a good deal of study and background. Few voters can give such issues the attention intelligent decision-making would seem to mandate. And the more proposals there are on the ballot, the more difficulty the typical voter is likely to have. The result is that many voters tend to vote randomly or not at all on these proposals.

The confusion and complexity that referenda create make them, like primaries, frequently subject to manipulation. In California, a state partial to referenda, several public relations firms have become specialists in promoting referenda proposals. They employ people to gather the signatures to put the issue on the ballot and then they conduct an active promotional campaign to win voter approval. Many special interests have used their services to get legislation beneficial to them enacted. Voters in many cases may have approved the referenda largely on the basis of billboards and radio jingles put out by the PR firm. With many referenda to vote on—there were twenty-two on the ballot in the California election of 1972—a voter would need to make almost a full-time study in order to vote intelligently on them all.

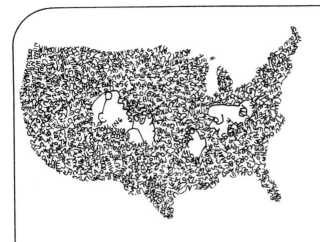

WHOSE INTEREST?

CHAPTER FIVE

Anyone who wishes to understand American politics must learn a good deal about interest groups. They elect and defeat many political leaders, write many of our laws and block the passage of others, aid administrators in carrying out some programs and deter them from carrying out others. Interest groups undergird and, at the same time, overshadow much of our governmental system.

The pervasiveness and often predominance of interest group activity in the American polity springs from a variety of sources. We are, for one thing, a large and heterogeneous nation. In terms of agriculture we have cotton farmers, sheep ranchers, wheat growers, chicken raisers, cattle ranchers, etc. In terms of industry, we make all kinds of goods from basic industrial commodities such as steel and aluminum to finished products such as computers, automobiles, textiles, and so forth. We mine coal and iron, catch fish, drill for oil, teach school, and record racing bets.

When it comes to noneconomic activities, we are perhaps even more diversified. Some of are white, some of us are black, and some of us are neither. Some of us who are white are Anglo-Saxon, others are Polish, others are Italian, and others come from numerous different lands. Some of us are Protestant, some are Catholic, some are Jewish, others adhere to still other religions, while some profess no religious ties at all. Even when it comes to leisure-time activities, differences abound. Some of us like to hunt and fish, others prefer to go to museums and concerts, while still others enjoy working for charitable institutions.

All of these differentiations designate at least potential interest groups. Because so many such differentiations do exist, interest groups abound.

Our size and diversity, however, do not adequately explain the role interest groups play in our politics. Other factors have also fostered their growth and influence. One of these may be our weak political parties. Some have claimed that an absence of party discipline and party accountability provides a fertile field for interest groups. Certainly the looseness of our political system generally, with the many points of access it provides, and the many openings it offers for those who wish to influence its activities, stimulates for interest group activity.

If interest groups seem to thrive in our political system, they flourish especially in our statehouses. Their representatives testify at hearings, buttonhole legislators in corridors, and knock on the doors of administrative agencies. We have already seen them at work in drafting state constitutions and we shall run into them again and again as we continue to examine the workings of the subnational system. At this point, however, we would do well to focus some attention on interest groups generally in order to establish a framework for subsequent study.

THE NATURE OF INTEREST GROUPS

Interest groups come in all shapes and sizes, exhibiting all kinds of contours and colorations, motivated by all manner of reasons and rationalizations. Some are large and some are small. Some are tightly knit and highly structured; others are rather loose and amorphous. Some are permanent while others are *ad hoc*, formed to deal with one particular issue and ready to dissolve once it is resolved. Some are broad-range while others are concerned with only one narrowly defined issue. Some seem selfish while others seem self-sacrificing. All, however, are prompted by the pursuit of power in the sense that they seek to work their will and influence the behavior of others.

66

Most of us, when we think of interest groups, tend to think first of business groups. Research suggests that we may be right in doing so. One researcher asked legislators in all fifty states to name the interest group each considered to be influential. When he compiled his list of some 3,000 groups, he found that 43 percent of them fell into the business category. Manufacturing, utilities, transportation, liquor, oil interests and financial institutions were among those most frequently cited. Other studies show that the majority of all registered lobbyists are business representatives. Even in a rural state such as South Dakota two-thirds of all the registered lobbyists represent business interests.[1]

Such research tends to lend credence to the popular view that business usually gets its way in the statehouses of the nation. Popular historians, meanwhile, have pointed out how in some states just one interest and sometimes just one company seems to hold the state in a firm grip. The power of Anaconda Copper in Montana and the influence of Kennicott Copper in Arizona are but two examples of this phenomenon.

However, the view that business runs the show at the statehouse is somewhat oversimplified. Although business representatives may clutter statehouse corridors, they usually do not act in unison. Most business influence is expended in internal warfare; i.e., business groups spend more time, money, and energy fighting each other than anyone else. Representatives of drugstores, for example, may seek to get a bill passed forbidding any store without a registered pharmacist on the premises from selling certain kinds of nonprescription medicines. Representatives of the new cut-rate cosmetic and health goods store industry then leap to ward off this attack on their interests and the battle is joined.

This kind of internecine rivalry duplicates itself throughout the state political spectrum. At one time the railroads and the truckers waged bitter, protracted warfare until finally the ever-shrinking railroads began to give up. Even within a particular industry, skirmishes often arise. Small banks may seek to limit the right of the big banks to expand into their territories, prompting the big banks to strike back.

When one or two industries or just one or two business firms are the major part of the state's economy they still may encounter difficulty in dominating the state's political system. During the days Anaconda seemed to run Montana, some politicians were able to make their way without surrendering themselves to Anaconda's control. Indeed, a few found that denouncing Anaconda regularly seemed to help their careers.

1. John C. Wahlke, "Organization and Procedure," in Alexander Heard, ed., *State Legislatures in American Politics* (Englewood Cliffs, N.J.: Prentice-Hall, 1966), p. 145.

If any one state today is in the grip of a particular business, that state would seem to be Delaware. This state is so small and its main employer, Dupont Chemical, so large that it seems that the former should be a puppet of the latter. However, three political scientists who studied this situation did not find this to be the case. Although the state government wanted the company to prosper so that it could provide more employment, tax revenue, and other benefits for Delaware, it did not always march to Dupont's drumbeat. Dupont, meanwhile, because it was so large and so visible often hesitated to make its full weight felt. The elephant may fear to dance among the chickens lest it become the target for too much rancor and, eventually, repression. As the study found, "A business can be too big to be politically effective along some lines. Nowadays many really big corporations are not eager to dance among the chickens; the consequences are or may be too unpleasant." [2]

Finally, we should keep in mind that numerous as they are, and well-organized as they can be, business interests are yet only a minority among all state interest groups. Church groups, labor groups, veterans groups, ethnic groups, and hosts of others all make their presence known. Their power varies from group to group, from issue to issue, and from one time to another. Veterans groups were once a most potent force in state government but their influence has dwindled in recent years. Ethnic groups can marshall a good deal of support when it comes to naming a particular square after one of their illustrious members or, better yet, having his birthday declared a state holiday. The rest of the time they may be relatively quiescent. Religious groups may take part in numerous matters relating to their basic beliefs but usually find themselves much more effective in some matters than others.

As interest groups strive to secure acceptance of their points of view they may, often unwittingly, enter into rather curious coalitions. In many states, church groups and gambling interests have often fought alongside each others in opposing legalized gambling. In Mississippi, Protestant fundamentalists and the bootleggers' lobby succeeded for many years in defeating efforts to repeal the state's prohibition law. (A sheriff's raid on a free-flowing party at a Jackson country club in 1966 finally persuaded the legislature to legalize drinking. Among the many prominent people at the party was the state's governor.)

Two kinds of interest groups have become considerably more important in terms of influence and impact in recent years. Labor groups, particularly government employee unions, have experienced great growth since 1962, when President Kennedy signed an order allowing federal government workers to form unions and bargain collectively. His action stirred many state governments

2. Raymond A. Bauer et al., *American Business and Public Policy* (Cambridge, Mass.: MIT Press, 1963), Chapter 16.

to do the same, thereby unleashing a wave of governmental unionism at the state and local level. These unions are more affected by what state government does and does not do than by national government and they have lost little time in involving themselves in state politics. As Neal R. Peirce notes, the unions can deliver not only manpower but also money. The labor movement contributed 1.7 million dollars to state campaigns in California alone in 1974, making it the largest single contributor in the state. "In state after state, legislators who buck the unions are pinpointed for defeat—and often retire voluntarily," writes Peirce. [3]

Of all governmental unions, the most powerful appear to be teachers' groups. One study of four states—California, New Jersey, Ohio, and Tennessee—found that legialators in three of these states (California, New Jersey, and Tennessee) named the state teachers' association as the state's single most powerful interest group. In the fourth state, Ohio, the teachers' group was ranked second. (The Ohio Farm Bureau was placed first.) [4] Teaching is the country's largest industry in that more people teach than do anything else. This fact, plus the generally favorable image that education enjoys, has enabled the country's teachers to become a formidable force in the arena of state government.

The other interest groups that have emerged as an increasingly influential factor in the formulation of state policy are what are called public interest groups. These organizations profess, often with legitimacy, to have no personal interest whatsoever in the programs and policies they advocate. They support the cause of good government generally as they perceive it. They include such organizations as the state units of the League of Women Voters and Common Cause. In addition, other groups devoted to a narrower range of issues also consider themselves to be serving the common good. These include consumer, conservation, and civil rights groups.

Defining just what is a public interest group often presents obstacles. Church groups, for example, almost inevitably believe they are acting in the public interest. Even business groups like to claim that securing government action favorable to their concerns benefits the citizenry as a whole. On the other hand, some people consider consumer groups to be responsible for driving up prices and reducing employment opportunities by advocating policies that allegedly increase business costs and reduce business investment. Moreover, conservationists are often accused of being elitists who wish to preserve woodlands and wildlife for their own private pleasures since they are the ones who

3. Neal R. Peirce, "Showdown with Public Employee Unions," *Boston Globe,* 9 August 1975.

4. John C. Wahlke et al., *The Legislative System* (New York: John Wiley & Sons, 1962), pp. 318–319.

make most use of them. However, it is generally recognized that such groups do differ somewhat from the common run of interest groups and thus may claim a different classification.

Although public interest groups have been around in some form for quite awhile, they did not come to the fore until the mid-1960s. The 1970s saw them start to take a leading role in many states, and, as we will have occasion to see, they seem destined to play an ever-expanding role in the future of American federalism.

HOW INTEREST GROUPS WORK

The term "interest group lobbyist" conjures up in the minds of many the image of a sinister and shadowy figure skulking through the statehouse halls bearing a little black satchel stuffed with crisp bills to be slipped surreptitiously to corrupt officials. Such practices have indeed gone on in many statehouses in the past and probably still go on in some of them. However, although interest group activity continues to be regarded as cruder and more free-wheeling and less visible at the state government level than it is in Washington, it usually does not assume the dimensions that cynics so often imagine.

Interest groups work in a variety of ways. They testify before legislative and administrative hearings, distribute printed material containing their views to public officials, and solicit meetings with the more important of these officials. They often try to publicize their cause in the news media and may seek to reach the average voter in other ways as well. Most interest groups, feel that their cause is just and that if they can only get the "facts" out, the electorate will eventually support them. And even if their publicity efforts fail to create a groundswell of public opinion in their behalf, such efforts should, they hope, alert officialdom that they constitute a force with which to be reckoned.

What about their more suspicious and subterranean activities? The statehouse scandals that surface from time to time indicate that such doings still go on. However, outright payoffs do seem to have diminished in frequency and extent. Instead, legal or quasi-legal techniques often come into play. Thus, lobbyists for a particular interest may purchase tickets to a campaign fund-raising dinner for a candidate and the candidate may pocket some of the funds raised for his personal use. It is interesting to note that even incumbents from safe districts who need little in the way of campaign financing frequently hold such fund-raising functions. (Of course, the candidate must declare all funds that he uses for his personal needs on his income tax form or he will be liable to federal prosecution. Such prosecutions have taken place.)

70

Many questionable interactions between officials and interest groups are more subtle. For example, an electric utility may install new power lines or a phone company may improve the phone service in the districts of key legislators. Racetracks may provide legislators and top administrators with season tickets. Sports teams may send their star players to address little league affairs or to give exhibition performances in response to requests from important state officials. Local governments, which are also interest groups competing for state favors, may speed up a tax abatement for a relative or friend of an important member of the state's governing apparatus.

The roles of interest groups in state government thus involve a complex network of actions and interactions. Relatively few of these actions may involve outright illegality. Many more may occur in a sort of gray area between what is legal and what is illegal. Still, the majority of interest group activities probably do not involve illegality or even grave moral impropriety. Indeed, some may even have a salubrious effect on the workings of state government.

THE USES OF INTEREST GROUPS

Too often, we tend to view interest groups as pernicious parasites eating away at the fabric of our political system. While their actions and activities sometimes do give cause for concern or even for alarm, the fact that they are so active and abundant may indicate that they also fill a need. Our political system does require a certain amount of interest group activity in order to operate at all effectively.

Interest groups perform an educational and informational function. They educate and inform the public but, more importantly perhaps, they educate and inform the public's officials. They may point up weaknesses in proposed legislation or in existing programs. They frequently provide important facts and figures that legislators and administrators need in order to discharge their tasks properly. A bill may contain a "sleeper" clause that could cause a whole slew of problems. The interest group that opposes the bill will call attention to this fact. An administrative program may be failing to accomplish its purposes or may be creating injurious side effects. Again, an interest group will bring this to light. Similarly, if a problem exists that requires new legislation or new administrative action, an interest group will usually spotlight it as well as propose solutions.

It can be said that the vastness and complexity of American society, coupled with the weakness of the political system which governs it, make interest group activity necessary. In this way minority interests can gain an opportunity to participate in the political process. Otherwise, they easily find themselves passed over and trampled on. Furthermore, political representation in our system is based on geography. Politicians are elected from, and remain beholden to, specific geographic areas. An industry or a profession, a religious creed or a political belief, an ethnic group or a hobby group can too easily go unrecognized within the framework provided by *areal* politics. Interest groups, however, can rectify this by offering opportunities for *functional* representation. Many of the issues that fall within the province of politics do not concern areas as such and the lively play of interest group politics acknowledges and attests to this fact.

Finally, while interest groups do seem to plague state government in a variety of ways (and we shall have ample occasion to see them in an unfavorable light in the chapters that follow), things are changing all the time. Certain trends indicate that their more alarming abuses are gradually diminishing.

Research has turned up a rather interesting phenomenon in regard to interest groups. *The fewer interest groups there are, the more powerful they are.* Conversely, as the number of interest groups rises, the weaker their influence on government becomes.[5] What seems to occur is that numerous interest groups tend to cancel out the influences of each other. They still perform their role of providing information and nonareal representation; indeed they perform it better because they now must compete with so many other interest groups. But when so many competing interest groups are in the arena, they tend to keep each other from becoming too powerful. Faced with diverse and competing interest groups, the public official finds it easier to adopt those policies that he believes conform most to the public good.

Maine offers an example of just how this works. At one time the state seemed to be essentially run by three large companies, the Central Maine Power Company, the Great Northern Paper Company, and the Bangor and Aroostock Railroad. There were at the time few other active interest groups in the state. Today, Maine has labor unions, fishermen's unions, organized conservation groups, and a host of alert organizations anxious to influence government action. The result is that no interest today really controls the state the way the "Big 3" used to do. (Another factor is the emergence of a fairly strong two-party system. The Big 3 found it much easier going when one party, the Republicans, pre-dominated and no effective opposition existed to call it to account.)

What has occurred in Maine has happened in many former single-interest states. More and more interest groups have arisen in states that previously contained very few. As a result, interest group control over state government has noticeably declined. The interest groups are more conspicuous now than ever

5. Harmon Zeigler presents and develops this point in "Interest Groups in the States," in Herbert Jacob and Kenneth Vines, eds., *Politics in the American States* (Boston: Little, Brown and Co., 1965).

before yet their very visibility has curbed their influence. And each usually finds that it must make a better case for its cause in order to gain the ear of officialdom and the support or at least acceptance of the public.

Another favorable development in interest group politics is the rather sudden and startling surge of the public interest group. Such groups may have axes of their own to grind, albeit ideological ones, and they may not always be correct in the facts they present or the proposals they promote. But they do provide an antidote to many of the more crassly self-seeking groups that have too often haunted statehouses in the past. They have begun to affect state politics considerably and may affect it much more in the future. This trend we shall have ample occasion to witness as we continue our explorations in state and local government.

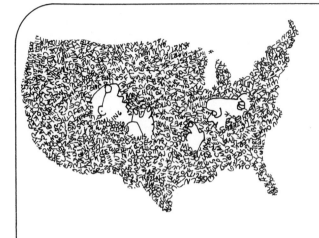

LEGISLATURES

CHAPTER SIX

The colonial legislatures served, in many respects, as the launching pads of our country's liberty. Being the popular assemblies of the increasingly unruly colonies, they vigorously and vociferously challenged royal ruthlessness and championed the forces of freedom. To be sure, not all legislators nor, for that matter, all legislatures were eager to shake off the coils of colonial rule. Some counseled caution; others even fought to maintain the existing relationship to the mother country. Nevertheless, as the colonists' main political instruments for asserting their demands, they gradually became the incubators of insurgency and independence. It can be said that the seeds of American democracy were sown in the country's state legislatures.

State legislatures today do not bulk so large on the political horizon. The growth of the federal government has greatly overshadowed their activities. Other changes within the states themselves have worked to weaken their once primary position. Yet the 7,600 members of our state legislatures still play, in many respects, the determining role in the operations of our state governments. As one observer has noted, "Anyone writing of the state as an instrument of government must write of the legislature. To indict the state is to indict the legislature."[1]

THE PROBLEM OF STATE LEGISLATURES

In the early part of the nineteenth century two worthy citizens of Brownhelm, Ohio, Judge Henry Brown and the Reverend Caleb Pitkin, journeyed to the state capital at Columbus. Their goal was to secure a charter for a new university. The legislators quickly agreed to grant the charter but just as quickly fell to wrangling bitterly amongst themselves as to where to locate the university. As the fight over the site continued, Judge Brown advised the Reverend Pitkin to return home. Said the jurist to the clergyman, "Dealing with legislatures is work for a sinner, not a minister."[2]

This anecdote encapsules the problems that have continually beleaguered and bedeviled our state legislatures and those who have attempted to deal with them. These problems can be succinctly summarized: Throughout our history, the state legislatures have displayed a remarkable bias toward behaving in an irresponsible manner.

This somewhat perverse predilection toward irresponsible behavior assumes many dimensions. For one thing, at least some of our state legislatures have countenanced and even coddled a good deal of corruption. In 1964 an Illinois legislator wrote an article for a national magazine in which he estimated that about one-third of his colleagues accepted payoffs.[3] A few years later, another Illinois legislator, state senator and later U.S. Senator Adlai Stevenson III, filed a bill to give the state's governor the power to investigate corruption within the legislature. (Needless to add, Stevenson's fellow lawmakers promptly killed the bill.)

Of course the Illinois legislature of the 1960s may not have been typical, but there are indications that it was far from unique. Scandals have erupted in

---

1. Frank Trippett, *The States: United They Fell* (Cleveland: World Publishing Co., 1967), pp. 2–3.

2. Related by James L. Heaphey in "Public Administration and Legislature," *Public Administration Review* (September/October 1976).

3. Paul Simon, "The Illinois Legislature: A Study in Corruption," *Harper's Magazine* (September 1964).

most state legislatures from time to time. Even California's legislature, which one survey judged to be the best in the country, has failed to escape the taint of wrongdoing.

Corruption can take many forms. The method that most frequently comes to mind is a payoff to a legislator to vote for or against a particular piece of legislation. Another, and less obvious—though at the same time more aggressive—means for a morally lax legislator to pad his salary is for him to file what is called a "fetcher bill." Such a bill is expressly designed to produce such anxiety and alarm in an interest group that the group will pay off the lawmaker to kill his own legislative offspring. The irony is that the legislator often earns plaudits for filing the bill in the first place. Thus, measures to curb the activity of racetracks or to reduce the interest rates that small loan companies may charge may gain for the legislator the image of champion of the people. Yet, he may at the same time be using these bills to squeeze some money out of the affected interests.

Many payoffs to receptive legislators take legal or quasi-legal forms. Those wishing to secure a lawmaker's support on a particular issue may, for example, simply purchase tickets to a fund-raising dinner for his campaign. Afterwards the legislator may pocket some of the funds for his own use. If he reports the funds on his income tax, then he may avoid breaking any law. However, gift giving from lobbyist to legislator may take many forms. A New Hampshire racetrack, for example, for many years ran a free bar opposite the state house for thirsty legislators.

Interest groups do not seek and secure legislative support solely through the use of inducements. Threats may work equally well. This is especially true for broader-based, noncommercial groups. In this case, it is usually their ability to deliver votes for or against a legislator that causes him to support their interests. Veterans groups, sportsmen's associations, trade unions, etc., may resort to a variety of strategies to cajole or coerce a state legislator to vote as they wish. It is not an unusual sight during a roll-call vote to see an interest group representative sitting in the statehouse gallery taking down the names of legislators who vote "wrong." Many a state legislator has looked up to the gallery, gulped, and then proceeded to vote not as his conscience or his constituency would have wanted but as his needs for political survival seem to dictate. (In a few states, lobbyists in the gallery have been seen giving signals to key legislators on the floor.)

Not all lobbyists act so brazenly, of course. And we should also keep in mind that their efforts, as noted in the preceding chapter, can prove helpful as well as harmful to the processes of government. Nevertheless, the feeling abounds, and a fair amount of data exists to support it, that lobbyists all too often play too strong a role in the operations of state legislatures. New York State, for example, is considered to have one of the nation's better legislative bodies. However, *The New York Times* has noted that a few lobbyists, representing powerful labor unions or business organizations, "are so well integrated into the legislative process that they are regarded as more influential than many Assemblymen or Senators."[4]

But interest group pressures and payoffs, important as they often have been, do not bear the sole responsibility for the numerous failings of our state legislatures. Frequently, state legislatures display shortcomings when they are reacting only too faithfully to majority sentiments. Their members often respond too rapidly and too rigorously to sensitive and emotional issues that have momentarily fanned public ardor.

When a wave of demonstrations and riots swept U.S. campuses during the Viet Nam War, many state lawmakers rushed to pass punitive legislation against the protesters. Even in a comparatively liberal state such as New York, the legislature sped through a bill requiring any college or university receiving state funds to suspend any student who had received a ten-day jail sentence for campus disorder. In California, a legislative committee set up a panel of law school professors to study the marijuana problem. When the panel recommended in 1969 that only the sellers and not the buyers of marijuana be punished—the same legal situation that already existed for prostitution—the committee lost no time in firing the entire panel and burying its suggestions.

Other issues also frequently spur state legislators into headlong action. Let a teacher of a sex education course make an inadvertent remark that gets printed in a newspaper and a legion of lawmakers will file bills abolishing or modifying sex education in the schools. Let a particularly grim murder take place and bills restoring capital punishment or tightening up existing capital punishment statutes will pour into legislative hoppers. Delaware abolished capital punishment in 1958. Three years later, when a black man beat and stabbed to death a white woman, a bill restoring capital punishment sailed through the state's senate in two days.

Racial issues have particularly inflamed southern legislators to hostile and hasty action. When a young black named Julian Bond won election to the Georgia legislature in 1966, the lawmakers voted 184 to 12 to bar him from taking his seat. They supposedly based their action on the fact that Bond had endorsed a strong statement opposing the Viet Nam War. Bond had to go to the Supreme Court to obtain his right to represent his constituents. In 1959 the Arkansas legislature voted to bar any member of the National Association for the Advancement of Colored People from state employment on grounds that the civil

4. *New York Times*, 1 February 1970.

rights organization was communist controlled. Only 6 of the 135 members of the legislature dared to oppose the measure.

Professor Malcom E. Jewell, who is perhaps the country's foremost student of state legislatures, has observed that, "Most legislators recognize that their constituents pay little attention to most of the issues that come up for consideration in the legislature. The issues that lead to intensive pressure within a district are likely to be emotional or moral, such as the regulation of liquor or the liberalization of abortion laws." [5]

In the all-too-frequent stampede to respond to emotionally or morally inflammatory issues, state legislatures have sometimes passed or threatened to pass legislation that could actually defeat the ends they have in mind. In 1807 the Kentucky legislature, fired up over Great Britain's actions against U.S. vessels on the high seas, readied a bill to forbid Kentucky's courts from making citations of British law in deciding cases. Such a bill would not have caused one iota of damage to Britain but would have nearly paralyzed court operations in Kentucky since U.S. law was then based almost wholly on British law. Fortunately the astute American statesman Henry Clay, who was then serving in the Kentucky legislature, managed to point out to his colleagues the follies of their ways. [6]

As this incident suggests, some of the rash and ridiculous actions taken by state legislatures have stemmed from sheer ignorance or ineptness. Examples of this are by no means scarce. The Indiana legislature once passed a twenty-four-million-dollar highway program for the Indianapolis area and then somehow succeeded in losing it. The measure simply disappeared after passage and so the governor could not sign it into law before the legislature adjourned. No new bill on the program could be passed for two years. [7] Poor draftsmanship has been responsible for many legislative boners. Ohio once passed a bill requiring that the state coat of arms be engraved on state officials while Kansas once enacted legislation requiring that trains meeting each other on a single track should each proceed to a siding. Then, under the terms of the bill, neither train should move until the other had passed! [8]

On occasion a disgruntled lawmaker will take advantage of the shortcomings of the system to make a point while at the same time having some fun. Thus, some wag once attached a rider to a bill in the Alaskan state legislature

5. Malcom E. Jewell, *The State Legislature: Politics and Practice* (New York: Random House, 1965), p. 7.

6. Glyndon G. VanDeusen, *The Life of Henry Clay* (Boston: Little, Brown and Co., 1937), p. 49.

7. United Press International dispatch dated March 14, 1961, quoted in Duane Lockard, *The Politics of State and Local Government* (New York: Macmillan, 1969), p. 289.

8. See: Russell W. Maddox and Robert E. Fuquay, *State and Local Government*, 3rd ed. (New York: D. Van Nostrand Company, 1975), p. 145.

abolishing all salaries for state legislators. His unattentive colleagues passed the bill, rider and all. The culprit claimed afterward, with some justification, that his experiment proved that "some members did not know what they were voting for."[9] Some ten years later, a Texan legislator went him one better. He introduced a resolution, which his colleagues duly passed, honoring one Albert DeSalvo for his efforts at population control. The person so honored by the Texan lawmakers had been convicted some time before of being the Boston Strangler.

LEGISLATIVE IRRESPONSIBILITY: REASONS AND RATIONALES

The picture we have drawn of legislative incapacity is perforce a generalized one and is therefore subject to numerous qualifications. Many state legislatures have performed quite well over the years and even the poorest of them have, at least on occasion, risen to the challenges that confront them. Furthermore, most legislators are neither corrupt nor inept. Yet, from the days of Thomas Jefferson, our state legislatures have on the whole been found wanting. In the minds of many who have studied them, and in the minds of many more who have served in them, they have generally failed to measure up to more than minimal standards of responsibility.

Why is this so? Why have these bodies that the U.S. Supreme Court once called "the fountainhead of representative government in this country" set such a poor example of democracy at work?

The reasons are many. To begin with, state legislatures suffer from the same problem that plagues all of state government, namely a lack of visibility. As we saw in the preceding chapter, most Americans devote little time and attention to state affairs. State governments simply do not loom large in the public consciousness. This lack of visibility leads to a lack of accountability and this, in turn, provides for, or at least permits, irresponsible behavior.

However, the problem for state legislatures is compounded by the fact that the legislators themselves are quite physically fragmented. Every state except Nebraska has two legislative chambers. The upper chambers, or senates, range in size from 20 members in Alaska and Nevada to 67 in Minnesota, while the lower chambers go from 40 members in Alaska and Nevada to 400 in tiny New Hampshire.[10] It is sometimes said that anyone with a large enough family in New Hampshire can almost be assured of winning a seat.

9. This item appeared, appropriately enough, in the *New York Times*, 1 April 1961.

10. *Book of the States, 1974–1975* (Lexington, Ky.: Council of State Governments, 1974), p. 54.

The fact that there are so many state legislators plus the fact that they are usually grouped into two separate chambers aggravates the problems of visibility. It is much more difficult for the public and its watchdogs such as the press to keep track of many legislators rather than few. Similarly, it is more taxing to follow the activities of two legislative chambers than one.

Further intensifying this visibility problem is the fact that our state legislatures have spawned a great number of legislative committees to assist them in their labors. There are over sixteen hundred standing committees to process the bills and carry out the overseeing operations that constitute the main work of state legislative bodies. This renders the task of studying state legislative activities all the more taxing. As a result, most legislative behavior fails to elicit the scrutiny it needs to insure proper operation.

The lack of visibility also plays a role in another basic reason why state legislatures have through the years received low marks for responsibility. Essentially, it detracts from the potential prestige of those who choose to serve in state legislatures. What people do not watch they usually do not esteem and the fact that they do not watch their state legislatures very closely indicates that they do not hold legislative service in high regard. As a result, many citizens of high caliber who might be motivated to serve in state legislatures direct their energies elsewhere.

Other factors also tend to discourage many distinguished or dedicated citizens from becoming state legislators. State capitals are often located relatively far from a state's major population centers. This means that most of those who become state legislators must travel some distance from home to attend the sessions. In many cases it means living in the state capital for at least some months a year. A public-spirited citizen might well be willing to uproot himself if serving in a state legislature conferred as much prestige and pay as serving in Congress. But, of course, it does not.

The problem of pay often outweighs lack of prestige and geographical inconvenience in discouraging well-qualified people from seeking state legislative office. Salaries for state lawmakers have in many states been so low that one observer once noted that "at least 75 percent of the voters can't possibly afford to serve."[11] Rhode Island lawmakers, for example, receive only one-half the daily pay earned by their own doorkeepers, while New Hampshire's legislators pocket about two hundred dollars a year in salaries. A respected Texas legislator, Richard Cory, quit in 1970, saying he could no longer live on his scant $4,800 yearly wage. Added Cory, "There are only three ways a man can stay in the

11. James Nathan Miller in "Our Horse and Buggy Legislatures," *Reader's Digest* (May 1965).

81

legislature and spend the time the job needs—be rich, have an angel, or be on the make."[12]

The Texan lawmaker's resignation cannot be viewed as a rare event. Faced with such dismaying factors as low pay, little prestige, and the need for long travel or yearly relocation, many state legislators do likewise. As a consequence, the turnover in state legislative bodies is high. Nearly one-third of all state lawmakers are freshmen, serving their first term. Thus, it has been said, the typical state legislator is a bird of passage. Unlike federal legislators, who usually remain in congress until defeat or retirement, the majority of state lawmakers sooner or later drop out—often sooner than later. This means, among other things, that the average state legislature contains a high number of individuals who are inexperienced in the procedural and substantive problems that they must face.

Of course, not all the members of our state legislatures are amateurs. Many do stay on for long periods of time and as they acquire skills in maneuvering and manipulating, they acquire positions of leadership. Who are these leaders? Frequently, they come from small towns and rural areas. At the start of the 1970s, for example, the leaders of the South Carolina house and senate both came from the state's most rural county. In Oregon the Speaker of the House was from a town of less than fifteen hundred people, while the chairman of the chamber's important ways and means committee claimed to be the biggest hog rancher in the state. Even in New York, where four-fifths of the population are city dwellers, the heads of both the senate and the assembly usually come from semirural communities.

The consequences of rural leadership are many. Urban problems often are neglected or treated in a simplistic and hostile fashion. Indeed, the sophistication needed for tackling most of the complex problems that beset the modern state is often lacking. New techniques of governance, such as program budgeting, often receive short shrift. The old dies hard when the "squires," as they are sometimes called, are in the saddle.[13]

Rural elements, especially farmers, have comprised a disproportionate number of the rank-and-file of our state legislatures as well. But increasingly in recent years they have been supplanted by others. The largest single group in most state legislatures today is that of lawyers, closely followed in many states by members of the real estate profession and insurance agents. The reason for the predominance of such groups is not hard to understand. All of them benefit

12. *Texas Observer*, 2 January 1970.

13. For an informative analysis of the power of rural representatives in state legislatures see: A. James Reichley, "The Political Containment of the Cities," in *The States and the Urban Crisis* (Englewood Cliffs, N.J.: Prentice-Hall, 1968).

professionally from whatever publicity, prestige, and power they can derive from their positions. And, unlike ordinary wage earners or corporation executives, they can usually leave their affairs in the hands of associates while participating in the legislative session.

A wide variety of other groups is also represented in statehouse legislative chambers. Farmers, though not as numerous as they once were, still occupy many seats. Labor leaders, teachers, housewives, and others also serve. In 1974, a Nevada woman named Beverly Harrell became the Democratic nominee from her district for the state's lower house. She received nationwide publicity owing to the fact that she was the operator of a brothel in one of the state's two counties where prostitution is legal. (She did not win despite the fact that Nevada's state secretary smilingly posed with her for a campaign picture.)

As has been indicated, the most powerful single occupational group in most state legislatures today is from the legal profession. Their numbers, plus their skills at debate and draftsmanship, frequently give lawyer-lawmakers a decisive hand, especially in issues which affect them. For example, in 1972, bills to provide no-fault auto insurance plans were introduced into thirty-seven state legislatures. The concept had already been tried out in one state, Massachusetts, and had led to a sizeable reduction in car insurance rates. However, it also led to much less business for attorneys. As a result, all but two states voted down the scheme. This occurred even in New York, where it was backed by the state's powerful Governor, Nelson Rockefeller; most of the state's newspapers; various good government groups; the insurance industry; and business and labor generally. It was only when a few Empire State legislators who had opposed the plan were defeated in the fall elections that the other members became concerned enough to enact a modified no-fault system the following year.[14]

Legislative service, it should be kept in mind, is a part-time profession. Therefore, most state lawmakers continue to practice their other vocations while legislating the state's business. This provides a continual potential for conflicts of interest. One way in which this potential reveals itself is in the composition of legislative committees. The lawmakers naturally gravitate to those committees that process legislation and oversee administrative agencies that deal with their own economic interests. As Professor Jewell has noted,

> The Senate banking committee in Alabama, for example, a few years ago had a majority of bankers. The alcoholic beverage control committee in the Maryland House recently consisted mostly of tavern-keepers, beer distributors, and lawyers representing liquor interests. Florida committees dealing with citrus products and

14. *New York Times,* 3 October 1972.

forestry have been made up almost entirely of citrus-growers and representatives of the forestry interests. In a recent session of the Kentucky legislature all members of the House who were veterans were put on the veterans' committee, all insurance agents were on the insurance committee, and most of those on the agricultural committees were farmers.[15]

Adding to and aggravating all these problems are a variety of other problems that tend to weaken or even wreck the ability of state legislatures to discharge their duties diligently. One such problem is the sheer volume of legislation, which has grown almost astronomically in recent years. Many state legislatures process over a thousand bills a year and some handle more than five thousand. Furthermore, the bills themselves have become quite complex in step with the increasing complexity of modern-day life. Yet the average legislator lacks not only the time but also the expert staff assistance that he needs in order to gain sufficient knowledge of many of the bills upon which he must act. It should come as no surprise then to find all sorts of whimsical factors entering into legislative decision making. For example, Earl W. Brydges, a former president of the New York Senate, once pointed out that "many votes are decided by the accident of who sits next to whom." According to Brydges, a legislator often turns to the legislator next to him, asks how his neighbor will vote, and then votes the same way.[16]

A final factor contributing to the capriciousness of legislative behavior is the limited session. Many state institutions restrict the time their legislature can stay in session. Alabama lawmakers are allowed only thirty-six days to transact the state's business. Wyoming gives its lawmakers forty days. Other states have longer time limits but the average is sixty days. This places a heavy burden on the legislature's members, especially during the sessions' final days when the so-called adjournment rush has begun. During this time legislative chambers frequently become scenes of madness and mayhem as floods of bills come pouring forth from committees requiring prompt action before time runs out.

As midnight approaches on the last legal day of the session, legislative leaders frequently resort to stopping or covering the clock in order to gain a few extra hours. And when the weary lawmakers troop out of the state house in the early hours of the morning, many have only the foggiest notions of the decisions they have made and the work they have done. No wonder, than, a New York court once declared, in the course of handing down a decision in 1866, that "No man's life, liberty or property is safe while the legislature is in session."

15. Jewell, *The State Legislature*, p. 99.
16. Earl W. Brydges, "New Frontiers in Legislative Staffing," *State Government* (Autumn 1966).

84

THE RISE OF REFORM

In 1960 Risley Clairborne (Pappy) Triche led the fight in the South Carolina house to block desegregation of the state's public schools. In 1972, Triche led another fight, this one a drive to push through bills that would protect blacks from discrimination in employment. Triche commented on his conversion in these words:

> I know what some of you think. I know what some of the people outside the halls of this House are going to think—"Oh, but listen to that segregationist. Isn't that the guy who offered all the segregation bills in 1960 and fought our public school systems."
>
> The only reply I can make to that, gentlemen, is that yes, that occurred. And at the time in the state of development in the history of our state, we thought we were correct. And now we find that we were wrong.[17]

The conversion and contrition of "Pappy" Triche indicates that something is stirring in the statehouses of the nation. Other signs have also indicated the fact that state legislatures are undergoing something of a transformation. The same year that Triche led the floor fight to pass antidiscrimination bills, the Georgia legislature, the same body that had banned Julian Bond from taking his seat just a few years before, voted overwhelmingly for a bill barring school board members from sitting on the boards of private schools. This legislation was designed to prevent such board members from using public school property to help operate segregated private schools.

The signs of change are by no means confined to civil rights. In a host of ways state legislatures are displaying a new diligence and dedication. For example, in 1973, as the waves of the Watergate scandal began to ripple through the nation, at least half of the country's state legislatures passed what the citizen reform organization Common Cause called "significant laws aimed at money and secrecy" involving state politics. Many states enacted "sunshine laws," which opened up hitherto secret committee and commission proceedings to the public. Many also passed laws tightening up campaign financing practices. Control over lobbyists also figured in many new bills that were enacted into law. Commented Common Cause, "There was enough state progress in 1973 to put Congress to shame."[18] (By 1976 forty-four states had passed some new legislation in this area.)

17. Neal R. Peirce, *The Deep South States of America* (New York: W. W. Norton, 1974), p. 62.
18. Common Cause, *Report from Washington,* (February 1974). See also: "Housecleaning for State Politics," *Christian Science Monitor,* 5 June 1974.

By the mid-1970s even the demeanor of state legislatures was showing signs of improvement. In Alabama, legislators were no longer buying peanuts from barefoot boys passing up the aisles and washing down the snacks with nips from pocket flasks. In Massachusetts, observers no longer saw a bookmaker standing in the hallway outside the lower house chamber, taking bets from legislators and other statehouse employees.

Accompanying these changes in legislative output were some more fundamental changes in structure and procedure. In 1963, only twenty state legislatures met every year. By 1973, over forty state legislatures were holding annual sessions. In 1963 only eighteen houses and twenty-two senates had fewer than twenty-one standing committees. By 1973 some thirty houses and thirty-four senates had fewer than twenty-one such committees. One half of the states had also set up electronic roll calls, while a full two-thirds had established units to evaluate the work of administrative agencies. The state legislatures of the nation seemed to be seriously getting down to business.

Bolstering this trend was a dramatic increase in legislative pay. From 1950 to 1970 the average compensation for state lawmakers jumped over 500 percent. In 1970, it reached an average of $13,256 for a two-year term.[19] By 1972, the average had risen to $14,500 and it has continued to rise since. By 1975, California was paying its legislators more than $40,000 a year. (However, New Hampshire, which had remained at the bottom of the list in terms of remuneration, was still paying its lawmakers $100 a year).

Some more basic developments have served to aid and abet the forces of change. One is the increase in good government organizations and their growing awareness of the importance of state government in general and state legislatures in particular. The League of Women Voters, Common Cause, and other groups have focused, through their state chapters, considerable energy and effort on state legislative problems. More specifically oriented organizations, such as the Council of State Governments and the Citizens Conference on State Legislatures, have also served to spur the turnabout trend. Colleges and universities have also lent a hand with the use of internships and other devices to increase student awareness of, and input into, state legislative bodies. In 1974 the State University of New York at Albany began offering an M.P.A. in legislative administration. The following year Indiana University announced plans to do the same.

A constitutional change and a new constitutional interpretation did a great deal to lay the groundwork for this upsurge in reform. The new interpretation was made in the early 1960s when the U.S. Supreme Court ruled that seats

19. Associated Press dispatch from Kansas City dated August 8, 1970 in the *New York Times*, 9 August 1970.

86

in state legislatures must be apportioned equally on the basis of population.[20] In other words, each member of a legislative chamber must represent roughly the same number of people.

The Supreme Court's one-man, one-vote dictum set the stage for a drastic shake-up in the composition of most state legislatures. Up to then, many states had apportioned their senate seats on a different basis from population. California, for example, had allocated a senate seat to each of the state's counties. This meant that the senator representing populous Los Angeles county represented over twenty times as many people as the senator representing more rural Orange county. After the ruling Los Angeles county had to be given twenty times as many senate seats as Orange county. Each person's vote, said the court, must count as much as every other person's vote.

Although state senates bore the brunt of the Court's decision, lower houses did not remain unaffected. Although most states had originally provided for lower house districts of roughly equal population, many had failed to redraw these districts to keep up with population shifts. The fact that two districts were equal in population at the turn of the century did not necessarily mean that they were both equal a half century later. Tennessee, the defendant in the first of these cases to reach the Supreme Court, had not reapportioned its legislative districts in over sixty years.

The Supreme Court rulings affected, in varying degree, nearly every state. Under pressure from the Court, state after state redrew at least some of its legislative districts. The "squires" were the biggest losers since their rural districts were the ones that had tended to be most overrepresented. Howvever, some central cities also lost seats in the state house since they too had failed to maintain their share of the state's population. The big gainers were the suburbs, which had generally been scoring the greatest population gains. The suburban legislators who began taking their seats in legislative chambers of this time showed a slickness and sophistication that their country or even central city colleagues lacked. Whether conservative or liberal, the suburban lawmaker was usually more amenable to change and more vulnerable to pressure from good government interest groups. At the same time, he was typically less partial and prone to the old-fashioned techniques that smacked so strongly of corruption and connivance.

Some years after the reapportionment decisions—in 1971—the Twenty-sixth Amendment was enacted. This amendment lowered the voting age to eighteen. This change created not only younger voters but also younger legislators. In Vermont, an eighteen-year-old and a nineteen-year-old won elec-

20. There were two important Supreme Court decisions on this matter: *Baker* v. *Carr* (1962) and *Reynolds* v. *Simms* (1964).

87

tion to the state's house of representatives. In Kansas four young Democrats with a combined age of 88 years defeated four incumbents whose combined age was 239. In some states the average legislator's age became younger than the average voter's age.

This new breed of state legislator, younger, better educated, and better paid than his predecessor, was producing a new breed of legislative leader. Massachusetts offers an interesting illustration of this transformation. In the early 1960s, the state's two chambers were led by men who had never gone beyond high school. The Speaker of the House, known as the "Iron Duke," suffered from severe drinking problems. He would occasionally go off on binges, leaving actions in the house stalled awaiting his return to sobriety. When he died of a heart attack in 1965, he was under indictment for corrupt practices. The leader of the senate was involved in a number of businesses, including a liquor store, and was also on the payroll of a construction company though he had no experience or training in construction work. In the early 1970s, the leaders of the state's senate and house were both ex-schoolteachers, one of whom was still in his early thirties. Although each was controversial neither had ever been accused by even his enemies of engaging in tainted or tawdry activities.

These changes, dramatic though they have often been, do not mean that the reform wave has crested. In the view of most observers much still remains to be done. One of the more sweeping steps that still occupies a prominent place on many a reformer's agenda is combining the customary two legislative chambers into one. Nebraska took this step in 1934, replacing its senate and house with one legislative body. However, although the unicameral concept seems to have worked quite well in this midwestern state, no other state has followed suit.[21] Nevertheless, backers of unicameralism, whose ranks include the National Municipal League, many state chapters of the League of Women Voters, numerous political scientists, and a few prominent state legislators, refuse to give up. They point to the greater visibility and accountability that one legislative chamber could offer over two and they also note that in no other federal country in the world do the sovereign subunits have two legislative houses. Furthermore, all of our larger cities now operate with only one legislative body, and these cities are larger in population than many of our states.

The drive for unicameralism, which seemed stalled for many years, has begun showing signs of revival recently. This new interest in one-house legislatures started in 1971 when a former Speaker of the California House, Jess Unruh, wrote an article blasting the evils of bicameralism and urging the adop-

21. For an assessment of Nebraska's experience with unicameralism see: A. C. Breckenridge, *One House for Two* (Washington, D.C.: Public Affairs Press, 1958).

tion of unicameralism instead.[22] In 1972, unicameral amendments appeared on the ballot in North Dakota and Montana. They received substantial but not majority support. In 1975, a California state senator named Arlen Gregorio, with the backing of several state political figures, launched a new drive to establish a one-hundred-member, single-house legislature in that state. League of Women Voters chapters in Florida, Montana, and Maine were also working for a similar step in their respective states.[23]

Other reforms, including better financing arrangements for legislative campaigns, have also begun drawing attention. However, although much progress may remain to be achieved, there is little disputing the fact that a great deal has already been attained. Certainly much is at stake. As one of the new breed of legislative leaders has pointed out, "It is the metamorphosis of state legislatures from the past feudal baronies to the modern policy and decision-making centers which may determine whether or not the spirit of cooperative federalism can be truly realized." [24]

22. Jess Unruh, "One House Legislature," *National Civic Review* (May 1971).

23. *National Civic Review* (October 1975), p. 469.

24. David M. Bartley, "The Legislative Organization from a Speaker's Perspective," *Public Administration Review* (September/October 1975). Bartley at the time was the Massachusetts Speaker of the House.

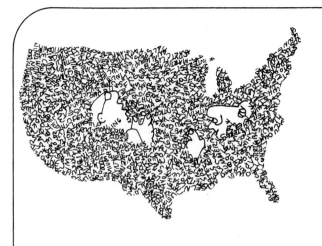

THE GOVERNOR

CHAPTER SEVEN

Many people regard the State governor as simply a president on a smaller scale. Like the president, the governor heads the executive branch as well as his own state party organization. He introduces legislation and represents the state on ceremonial occasions as well as in its relationships with other sovereign entities. He even acts as commander-in-chief of the state militia. Consequently, like our president, the governor wears a variety of hats, so to speak, and plays a diverse role.

The role that comes most frequently to mind when we think of the governor is that of chief executive. Like his larger-scale counterpart in Washington, the governor must see that the laws are faithfully executed. Since this is a rather demanding responsibility, it would seem likely to occupy more of his time and attention than any of the other roles that he must play. In fact, however, it does not. Research indicates that the typical modern-day governor may spend no more than one-fifth of his time on purely administrative matters. At least two of his other roles consume more of his time.

One of these is his role as chief legislator. "More than half of my work as governor," Theodore Roosevelt once said, "was in the direction of getting needed and important legislation."[1] This situation has changed little since his day. If anything, it has intensified. The demands that modern society places upon today's state governments generate more and more increasingly complex pieces of legislation. Only the governor and his administrative agencies possess the knowledge and expertise to formulate most of the policies and draft most of the bills these demands necessitate. And once they are drafted and submitted, the governor must usually work, and work hard, to see that these bills are enacted.

Another role that consumes extensive chunks of the governor's time is that of head of state. In this capacity the governor signs proclamations designating certain days or weeks or months in behalf of worthy causes and organizations; he poses for pictures with numerous people and groups; he addresses dinners, marches in parades, and cuts ribbons at the opening of new installations. But superficial as such responsibilities may seem, they often are very important to the people involved. Thus most governors feel obliged to make ample room for such events in their schedules. New York governor Al Smith once said that his state really needed two governors, one to run the state and the other to attend the ceremonies and rituals.[2]

To discharge the duties of chief executive, chief legislator, party head, and head of state, governors possess certain formal powers and prerogatives. In some states, such as Tennessee and New York, these powers are quite extensive. For example, when New York governor Nelson Rockefeller was having trouble getting the legislature to approve his Urban Development Corporation in 1968, he called certain recalcitrant legislators into his office and simply threatened to cut off their patronage if they didn't go along. In a few hours he had his majority.[3]

1. Quoted in Thomas C. Desmond, "To Help Governors Govern," *New York Times Magazine*, 2 June 1957.

2. Robert C. Wood claims that governors in the three states he studied, New Jersey, Connecticut, and Massachusetts, spend more time in fulfilling their "representative" functions than any of their other functions. See his "The Metropolitan Governor" (PhD. dissertation, Harvard University, 1949).

3. See: A. James Reichley "The Political Containment of the Cities," in *The States and the Urban Crisis* (Englewood Cliffs, N.J.: Prentice-Hall, 1968).

Many southern governors have also wielded considerable power, at least in dealing with their legislatures. The governor of Alabama has often succeeded in dictating which legislators will chair the major committees. The governor of Georgia until the late 1960s had a "hot line" running to the Speaker's rostrum to relay his instructions to the house leadership. Former Louisiana governor Huey Long would frequently storm onto the floor of the state legislature and read the riot act to lawmakers who were not falling in line with his wishes. As late as 1968, the Louisiana Municipal Association could observe that "the powers of the legislative branch are so much under the control and domination of the executive that it no longer deserves to be called a branch. It comes closer to being a twig and a badly bent one at that." [4]

As might be expected, some governors have seriously misused and abused their powers. Huey Long's sins in this respect are notorious, and sometimes they extended into unusual areas. For example, Long on occasion would supersede the coach of the Louisiana State University football team and give directions to the players during a closely contested game. [5]

More recently, Governor George Wallace canceled advertising by the state liquor monopoly in newspapers that showed themselves unfriendly to his administration. [6] He also set up a seven-member secret tribunal called the Sovereignty Commission to carry out special investigations without being required to record its proceedings. Florida Governor Claude Roy Kirk, Jr., raised nearly a half-million dollars through private sources to promote Florida and himself. Until 1972, Mississippi governors operated a "Colonel's fund," which enabled them to appoint wealthy citizens as honorary staff members with the rank of colonel. The appointments were made in return for contributions to the fund, which was used at the governor's discretion.

Some governors have come into conflict with the criminal justice system. Various governors of Oklahoma, West Virginia, and Illinois have gone to jail for violating the law for private gain, and former Vice-President Spiro Agnew's conviction for accepting payoffs covered crimes committed while he was governor of Maryland (such activities had started while he was a county official and extended to his term as Vice-President). [7] In 1977, Agnew's successor as Mary-

4. Quoted in Neal R. Peirce, *The Deep South States of America* (New York: W. W. Norton, 1974), p. 66.

5. For a colorful but accurate account of Long's policies and practices see: T. Harry Williams, *Huey Long* (New York: Alfred A. Knopf, 1969).

6. It is estimated that by 1969 the *Alabama Journal* had lost $400,000 in advertising from the state-run liquor monopoly as a result of its criticism of the governor. (See: *Boston Globe*, 16 November 1969).

7. In regard to West Virginia, former Governor Arch Moore was found innocent of wrongdoing in 1976 following a trial. However, in 1971, former Governor William Wallace Barron was sentenced to twelve years imprisonment and fined $50,000 for bribing a federal jury foreman three years earlier.

land chief executive, Marvin Mandel, was convicted on charges of wrongdoing in office.

However, despite the fact that many governors have exercised remarkable power in their states and some of them have apparently misused it, most political scientists, as well as most governors, have felt that the true problem with state chief executives lies in the opposite direction. Rather than being too powerful, they contend, the typical state governor has not been powerful enough.

For example, if a member of Congress wants to see the president he must nearly always put in a request ahead of time, and unless he is a particularly influential member of Congress, he has no assurance that such a request will be granted. A state legislator usually enjoys musch greater access to his chief executive, as political scientist Alan Wyner has observed: "A standing rule in most governor's offices allows a legislator to see the governor almost any time he wishes. The governor's door is always open to him and drastic revisions are made in the governor's planned schedule so that he can spend time with a legislator who 'just dropped by to say hello.' " [8]

Governors frequently feel compelled to go to great lengths to win legislators over to their side. They may not only offer them various forms of patronage such as jobs, contracts, etc., but also often spend many hours simply socializing with them. As governor of California, Ronald Reagan used to invite groups of legislators to his home, where, among other things, they would play with the model electric train network that he had set up in the basement.[9] Thus, while a few governors have managed to bully their lawmakers, most governors have had to engage in continual and strenuous efforts to make friends with them.

When it comes to dealing with his state's own administrative agencies, the governor often has found himself in a still worse position. Even governors who have managed to boss their legislatures have frequently fumbled when dictating to their own bureaucracies. A study conducted in the mid-1960s asked 933 top level administrators in fifty states whether the governor or the legislature exercised the most influence over their agency's activities. Only 32 percent of the administrators named the governor, while 44 percent named the legislature. (Another 22 percent said each exercised about the same influence, and 2 percent either did not answer or named another source).[10] Thus, although the

8. Alan J. Wyner, "Gubernatorial Relations with Legislators and Administrators," *State Government* (Summer 1968).

9. Marshall Frady, "California," *Harper's Magazine* (December 1969).

10. Deil S. Wright, "Executive Leadership in State Administration," *Midwest Journal of Political Science* (February 1967).

governor is supposed to be the chief executive, less than a third of the states' other executives were willing or able to acknowledge him as such.

When it comes to serving as state leader of his party, the governor also frequently finds himself in trouble. The states' U.S. Senators, Congressmen, county leaders, mayors, ward bosses, and others often greatly limit his discretion. No Democratic governor of Illinois during the 1960s and early 1970s could override the voice of Chicago mayor and Cook County Democratic chairman Richard Daley. And no Democratic governor of Massachusetts could have superseded the will of Senator Edward M. Kennedy in his state's party affairs.

The problem plagues Republican governors somewhat less than Democratic ones, because they operate as a separately constituted unit within the Republican National Committee and enjoy a greater stature generally within their party. Yet Republican governors also suffer problems in trying to lead their state party organizations. For example, Florida's Claude Kirk went to the Republican 1968 Presidential Convention enthusiastically committed to Nelson Rockefeller's candidacy. But when the roll was called, the Florida delegation cast only one vote for Rockefeller. Although Kirk, as governor, headed up the state's delegation, he was unable to induce a single other delegate to support his favored candidate.

Thus, despite the near dictatorial domination some governors have wielded at least on occasion, the view of most observers is that governorship in the United States suffers more from too much weakness rather than from too much strength. The governor is not a master in his own house, lamented the Committee for Economic Development in its 1967 report, and it urged, "Governors should become chief executives in fact as well as name." [11] As we shall see, much has transpired in the decade since the report was written to bring attainment of that goal closer. But now let us delve a little deeper into the reasons why governors have so often lacked the powers to play their manifold roles.

WHY WEAK GOVERNORS?

Distrust of executive power has a long heritage in U.S. history. We won our independence by overthrowing the rule of a king, and, as we have seen, the chief *political* instrument our forefathers used in doing so was popular assemblies. So, early in our history, we became accustomed to considering legislative bodies as expressions of democracy and executives as devices of despotism.

This dislike of executive power registered an especially strong impact at the state level. There it was increased by the fact that the prerevolutionary

11. *Modernizing State Government* (New York: Committee for Economic Development, 1967).

95

governors had been appointees of the British king and therefore were considered by the colonists to be oppressors. When the colonies shook off British rule, they retained these misgivings about the gubernatorial function. Consequently, they established for the most part weak chief executives constrained by numerous checks. Most of the New England states kept the popularly elected governor's councils, which had been used to obstruct executive power when the executive was a royal appointee. North Carolina even refused to give its governor any veto power over legislation. As one American farmer expressed it after the revolution, we do not need "any Guviner but the Guviner of the Univarse."

State constitutions have reflected this heritage of hostility to the gubernatorial function. Their proliferation of detail, noted in the preceding chapter, has succeeded in sapping the strength of their chief executive. To begin with, most governors were elected for only two years. A governor elected for two years, it has been said, spends his first year learning about the job and his second year running for reelection. He usually has little opportunity to achieve any significant accomplishment.

Some states have granted their governors four-year terms but limited them to only one term at a time, with no right to succeed themselves. This limitation has been particularly popular in the South. Although many such governors have managed to acquire substantial authority, the one-term rule does in many ways tie their hands. In a sense, a governor elected under this restriction is a "lame duck" from the moment he is sworn in. Those that he has to deal with know that his days in power are numbered and shape their responses to him accordingly.

Another and probably more important curtailment of gubernatorial discretion arises from the fact that the governor must usually share his authority with other elected executives. At the beginning of the 1970s, forty-two states elected attorney generals, forty-one elected treasurers, thirty-nine elected their lieutenant governors, and an equal number elected their state secretaries. Auditors were elected in twenty-nine states and state superintendents of instruction were elected in twenty-three. In some states, voters elect highway commissioners, mining commissioners, state university trustees, and other officials. This situation sharply contrasts with that of the federal government, where the American president shares his power with only one other elected official, the vice-president, whom he has usually handpicked.

State elected executives are usually major political figures in their own right and have their own bases of support. Only rarely can a governor order them around. Indeed, in many instances they spend much of their time trying to impede the governor's actions, seeking to discredit him so that they can either run for his office or help someone else do so. This is especially likely to happen when an elected state official is of a different party than the governor. But even when they are members of his own party, such separately elected officials are likely to give the governor a difficult time.

As might be expected, the lieutenant governor often proves the most troublesome. In contrast to the vice-president, the lieutenant governor in most states does not run with the governor as a team. He has relatively few functions to perform other than to fill in for the governor when the latter goes out of state or to take over his job completely if the governor for any reason leaves office during his term. Many a lieutenant governor has used much of his ample spare time and whatever authority he may possess to undermine the governor. For example, when Colorado's voters elected Republican governor John A. Love to a second term in 1966, they also elected Democrat Mark Hogan as lieutenant governor. Hogan, predictably enough, spent most of the next four years attacking Love. Toward the end of his term, Love began expressing interest in a federal appointment. However, the Republican administration in Washington refused to give him one, for that would clear the way for a Democrat to become governor.[12]

That such problems are not limited to situations in which the governor and lieutenant governor are from different parties is borne out by what was occurring in Vermont during the same period. Governor Deane C. Davis found himself being opposed by Lieutenant Governor Thomas L. Hayes, a fellow Republican. The ostensible issue splitting the two Republicans was the Viet Nam War, which the governor backed but the lieutenant governor opposed. The latter began stumping the state to voice his opposition to the war and to his own governor who was supporting it.[13]

Even Louisiana's formidable Huey Long did not escape such problems. Long so feared his lieutenant governor, Paul Cyr, that he refused to leave the state and allow Cyr to take over in his absence. Long even declined to attend the dedication of a new bridge over the Mississippi River since the ceremony would have required him to stand on Mississippi soil for twenty minutes.[14]

Other elected executives have also managed to make life difficult for their governors. In Wisconsin a Republican treasurer refused to honor the salary vouchers for a member of a state commission whom the Democratic governor had appointed. In Massachusetts, a secretary of state backed the successful campaign of a lieutenant governor to defeat the reelection bid of the state's governor. In this case all three men were Democrats. But even when they do not

12. *New York Times*, 22 October 1970.
13. *Boston Globe*, 9 November 1969.
14. Williams, *Huey Long*, p. 514.

openly oppose the governor, these officials usually make governors meet them halfway. Their very existence may make a mockery of the governor's claim to be chief executive.

The functions these elected executives fulfill would not seem to provide them with any great sources of power. Many of their duties seem to be only routine. The secretary of state, for example, serves more or less as the state's chief clerk, keeping the records and archives, putting the state seal on papers, and printing up proclamations, ballots, and other state documents. However, John D. Rockefeller IV in serving as West Virginia's state secretary during the late 1960s achieved national prominence by exposing large patterns of registration fraud in West Virginia's elections. Other holders of this office have used their powers for less praiseworthy ends. When a state secretary of Illinois died in 1971, he left an estate valued at nearly three million dollars. Some of it consisted of wads of bills stuffed in old shoe boxes.[15]

The rationale for making these state offices elective rather than appointive includes not only the desire to curb the powers of the governor but also the more positive desire to permit the people to participate more fully in determining who they want to run their government. It is questionable whether or not this purpose has really been achieved. A Michigan poll, for example, showed that 73 percent of the voters could not name the incumbent secretary of state, 75 percent were unable to name the highway commissioner, 77 percent could not identify the superintendent of public instruction, and 81 percent were at a loss to name the attorney general. A full 96 percent could not come up with the name of the state treasurer even though he had served in office longer than any other official on the list. What seemed most remarkable was the fact that the poll was taken a short time after an election when, presumably, a majority of the poll's respondents had voted for the same people whom they now could not identify.[16]

Separately elected executives do not provide the only obstacles keeping the governor from exercising effective executive authority. More numerous and possibly more important are those administrators who, though not elected, nevertheless do not owe their appointment to him. About 20 percent of all state executives achieve their positions through civil service. Therefore, the governor can usually exert little authority over them. A greater number hold their appointments on a fixed-term basis. This means that on taking office the average governor finds himself confronted with a host of officials appointed by his predecessor. He must wait until their terms run out before he can replace them with his own appointees. Furthermore, once he has made his own appointment

15. *New York Times*, 15 January 1971.
16. Coleman B. Ransone, Jr., *The Office of Governor in the United States* (University, Ala.: University of Alabama Press, 1956), p. 376.

to a position he frequently loses all formal authority over the official who now holds his office for a fixed term.[17]

An example of how this situation handicaps a governor is provided by the experience of Florida governor Leroy Collins with his state's milk commission. The commission had been setting minimum prices for milk and Collins had campaigned on the issue of doing away with such price fixing. Abolishing such price setting would, it was hoped, lower the cost of milk to the consumers. However, each of the milk commission's five members was serving a five-year term on what is called a staggered term basis. This means that one member's term expires every year. Collins had to wait three years before he could get three of his own appointees on the commission, which presumably gave him a majority. However, it didn't work out that way. His third appointee decided, after looking into the matter, that the commission's price setting was a good idea that should be continued. And so the governor's efforts to carry out his campaign pledge were frustrated a while longer.[18]

Another factor that further compounds the governor's problems in carrying out the functions of chief executive is the extreme fragmentation of the state's administrative apparatus. The Committee on Economic Development found the number of state agencies more or less reporting directly to the governor to average eighty-five. This is only the average figure—in some states the number of separate agencies goes into the hundreds. This means that even if he could hire and fire his agency heads at will, and even if he could devote full time to the task of administration, the typical governor could still not properly supervise their activities. Experts on administration usually feel that twelve to fifteen constitutes the maximum number of people or units that should report to any single individual. Most of our state governors must oversee many times that number. It is an impossible task.

Finally, a host of other problems tend to whittle away at the governor's authority. In almost half the states at any one time he is likely to find one or the other of the legislative chambers under control of the opposite party. This puts added pressure on him to conciliate, cajole, and compromise in order to get his legislation passed and to ward off damaging attacks. Since one or more of the opposition party leaders may have their sights set on his own job, this makes dealing with them a difficult business indeed.

17. Writing in 1971, Joseph A. Schlesinger said that in only thirteen states was the governor able to appoint as many as one-half of the key officials in the executive branch. The Tennessee governor had the most power in this respect and the governor of Arizona seemed to have the least. (See Schlesinger's "The Politics of the Executive," in Herbert Jacob and Kenneth Vines, eds., *Politics in the American States* (Boston: Little, Brown and Co., 1965).

18. For an interesting case study of this event see: Harmon Ziegler, *The Florida Milk Commission Changes Minimum Prices*, Inter-University Case Program #107 (Indianapolis: Bobbs-Merrill).

Then, governors, especially in recent years, have found themselves increasingly faced with the necessity of increasing taxes in order to pay for growing state programs. Tax bills, as can be easily understood, are among the most difficult pieces of legislation to get through a legislature. Furthermore, they do little to increase the governor's popularity with the voters. Consequently, a governor may find himself neglecting other duties in an all-out effort to secure passage of a program that, if passed, will only cause him to lose favor with the electorate. Another pressure upon him comes in the form of patronage demands from those U.S. Senators and Congressmen from his state who are members of his party. He usually can ignore their requests only at his own political peril, but their demands, joined with those coming from legislators, other party leaders, and members of his own campaign organization, often place him in a position in which he ends up antagonizing too many powerful people. It is no wonder then that research indicates that governors lose their reelection campaigns much more often than do most other elected officeholders.

A trend of recent years has further tended to sap gubernatorial strength. This has been the growth of national concerns and the growth of national news media to cover them. People focus much more of their attention on national politics today than they did a half century ago, and the media, especially the network television news shows, tend to foster this phenomenon. As a result, U.S. Senators and Congressmen have gained in prominence. Governors have usually lost. It is interesting to note that while ten of the nation's presidents have been governors, Franklin Roosevelt was the last of them until Jimmy Carter.

Pointing out that governors do not hold interviews in the Kremlin or make tours of the Sinai defense lines, pollster Louis Harris has written, "Somehow in a cosmic, atomic, mass-media age, governors have shrunk to being seen all too often as local figures."[19] And another commentator, writing in the *New York Times* in 1970, asked, "Who are the nation's governors? Who knows? So far as power, prestige, and importance are concerned, all governors are 'underdoggers' in the American political system."[20]

Gloomy as the governor's situation seems to be, brightening signs began to appear on the horizon as American federalism entered its third century. We have already noted the signs of change stirring in state legislatures. Those symptoms of change also seem to be spreading to the state executive offices as well.

The modernization of state constitutions has provided much of the impetus for strengthening the governor's role. Thanks to such modernization

19. Louis Harris, "Why the Odds Are against a Governor's Becoming President," *Public Opinion Quarterly* (Fall 1959).

20. John A. Hamilton, "Who Are the Nation's Governors?" *New York Times*, 17 August 1970.

efforts, by the mid-1970s only four states still clung to a two-year gubernatorial term and only seven others still limited the governor to one four-year term. In other words, in nearly four-fifths of the states anyone elected governor can look forward to one four-year term and the possibility of a second. A further boost has been the move to make the lieutenant governor run with the governor as a team. Eighteen states had taken this step by 1976.

Another and perhaps even more important change growing out of the constitutional reform movement has been the reorganization of state bureaucracies. From 1965 to 1971 some twelve states reorganized their administrative branches and hardly a year has gone by since then without one or more states following suit. These reorganizations have almost invariably consolidated the number of administrative agencies, sometimes quite drastically. In Georgia, some three hundred agencies were merged into twenty-two units, while in Massachusetts an equal number of agencies were consolidated into eleven cabinet departments. Such reorganizations are designed to make the executive branch more manageable. To the extent that they do, they strengthen the governor's managerial power.[21]

Accompanying this trend is the move to give the governor more power over the people who head these agencies. Most of the new consolidated units that have emerged from these reorganizations are headed by officials serving at the governor's pleasure. This means that he can hire and fire them at will. At long last, the governor seems en route to becoming the master of his own house.

Salutary and sweeping as these reorganization schemes may seem, however, one must take care not to exaggerate their effect. They usually deliver less than they promise. In some cases the old units have been not eliminated but merely absorbed within the larger ones with many of the older ones preserving a good deal of their former independence. Furthermore, the governor often lacks the personnel and overhead agency staff to monitor them effectively. Finally, most reorganizations fail to touch those agencies headed by elected officials. The latter still retain much of their power to "pluralize" the executive function. Nevertheless, despite all these caveats, the governor's position has in most states grown somewhat more powerful in recent years.

Finally, the governor has benefited from the surge of the states generally. As we noted in Chapter 2, spending and employment have grown faster at the state level than at either the national or local levels. Governors now preside over

---

21. In 1974 Deil S. Wright again surveyed 1,600 state agency heads as to who exercised the most influence over their agency's activities. This time 46 percent of them named the governor, 26 percent the legislature, and 26 percent gave governor and legislature equal weight. This indicates that the governors are gaining strength though most of them apparently still have some way to go before they become masters in their own house.

a proportionately larger domain today than at any time in our history. Consequently, if they are failing to receive the recognition that U.S. Senators, Congressmen, and others are acquiring, they are nonetheless managing to make their impact felt.[22]

The 1976 presidential campaign saw former Republican governor Ronald Reagan of California and former Democratic governor Jimmy Carter of Georgia emerge as formidable contenders for their respective parties' presidential nomination, with the latter going on to win both the nomination and the presidency. This marked the first time in modern history that a representative from each party had used the statehouse as a springboard to national prominence. This development may be a result of the changes that have been occurring and a harbinger of other changes to come.

22. Robert Walters, "A New Breed of Governors Puts Zip into State Government," *Parade*, 27 July 1975.

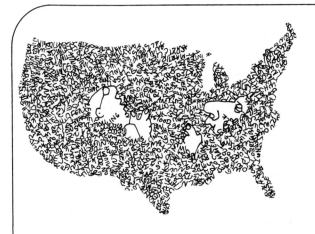

GOVERNMENT EMPLOYEES AND EMPLOYEE UNIONS

CHAPTER EIGHT

It is difficult to find activities that state government does not affect. State agencies regulate insurance companies, support national guard military units, and check up on the disposal of sewage. State employees police small outlying communities, drive buses and trains, and advise schools about their music programs. Louisiana has a state Blueberry Commission, Connecticut a Cuban Refugee Program Committee, and Minnesota an Indian Affairs Council. If you find that your local garage can't do certain work on your car even though it has the expertise and equipment, call the motor vehicles department for an explanation of their policy. If you are a college student, the chances are that you or some of your fellow students are being assisted by scholarships from different state agencies, including the labor department's vocational rehabilitation program. The states run programs ranging from agricultural experiments to zoos.

In short, state government does a lot. And these programs are not carried out by the legislature, and only in small part by the judiciary. It is the bureaucracy of the executive branch that is the action area of government, employing over four million workers. The number has grown 200 percent since 1950, compared to 44 percent for the total labor force in the U.S.A. This total exceeds the number of federal government employees, and it rose at a much faster rate than that for federal employees throughout the period 1946–1976.[1]

BUREAUCRACY: THE MOST ESSENTIAL BRANCH OF GOVERNMENT

The bureaucracy is the most essential branch of government because it is the branch that provides services and regulates behavior. Without bureaucracy, government ceases to function, for there is no one to carry out what legislatures and chief executives command. This obvious fact explains why bureaucrats are such important figures in any government, and certainly in American state government. Without a legislature, no new laws would be enacted, but the garbage would be picked up. Without a governor, there would be no state of the state messages and executive orders, but the machinery of government would continue to run.

First, legally and in fact, the bureaucracy is the most important policymaking branch of government. Most proposals for new legislation can be traced back to bureaucratic origins, whether they are put forward by legislators, governors, or interest groups.[2] When Governor Grasso of Connecticut proposed in 1975 that the fringe benefits of state hospital employees be drastically modified, she was advocating a policy that had been backed by one bureaucrat for twenty years. The creation of an extensive state university system in Florida in the 1960s did not spring full-blown from the heads of governors and legislators, but was taken by them from proposals put forth by the heads of Florida higher education.

Second, since bureaucrats actually implement the laws, they possess a great deal of discretion in deciding just how these laws will be implemented. When federal courts ordered that Charlotte, North Carolina schools implement a busing plan to further racial integration, state and local bureaucrats decreed that black children should sit in the back of the bus and white children in the front. This throwback to the days of full-fledged segregation was justified by the

1. John O'Riley, "Service Costs Skyrocket," *Danbury* (Conn.) *News-Times*, 19 June 1976, p. 1.
2. An empirical study demonstrating this point is Elisabeth Mck. Scott and Belle Zeller, "State Agencies and Lawmaking," *Public Administration Review* 2 (Summer 1942): 205–220.

bureaucrats as a way to minimize racial scuffling on board the bus. In fact, it flew in the face of the spirit of the integration order.

Citizens wishing to understand state policy cannot be content with merely reading the state statutes. They must also consult agency regulations in different policy areas. Legislatures have long delegated to bureaucrats the authority to write the "regs," acknowledging that there is no way the legislature could draft laws that would cover every contingency. The agencies must be free to draw up rules—hopefully consistent with the original statute—to cover details and to meet changing conditions. Unfortunately, sometimes these regulations and their implementation bear little resemblance to legislative intent. In the summer of 1975, New York State Environmental Conservation officials ruled that Daniel Markowski could not keep a deer he had found on his farm. The young animal was near death when Markowski found it, and he nursed it back to health. State officials took the deer away, supposedly to release it in the wild. But conservation officer Carlton Gay then decided the deer could not survive in the wild, so he "humanely destroyed it." This demonstration of bureaucratic authority left Mrs. Markowski with a desire for "someone to explain to my kids how they can trust the law." [3]

A third area of administrative authority is adjudication, or decisions made about legal challenges to a bureau's cactivities. Before someone can take an agency to court to try to get it to reverse its actions or pay damages for an alleged wrong, he must go through an appeals process within the agency itself. There are usually various stages within this process, culminating in a hearing that looks very much like a full-scale court trial, presided over by a hearing examiner, who acts as a judge. Many complaints have been made against administrative adjudication, in which agency employees function as both prosecutor and judge (there is no jury), but the system remains unchanged.

These three aspects of agency operations indicate why agencies are so influential. They act not only as policy implementers, but also as advocates of policy change and as judges of challenges to policy.

Line and Staff

Bureaucrats can be divided into two broad categories: *line* employees, who actually carry out services or regulate behavior, and *staff* employees, who perform activities that keep the agency functioning and that anticipate future changes. Line employees include teachers, welfare case workers, and police officers. Staff workers include employees within these agencies who are assis-

3. Lawrence Van Gelder, "Another Deer Killed by State Warden," *New York Times*, 18 June 1975, p. 1.

tants to the commissioner, personnel directors, and members of the budgetary office.

Line and staff workers typically have very different perspectives on their work. Line employees are usually concerned about the continued existence of their work activity, whether it be educating children or guarding reservoirs. Staff workers are more concerned about the continued existence of their agency as a whole rather than any particular line activity. In fact, they may recommend that certain activities be ended or replaced by others.

Employees of central staff agencies such as the departments of personnel or budget that serve an entire state government may be highly critical of line employee actions and may urge curtailment of line activities and functions in many fields. One example is the earlier mentioned modification of state hospital employee benefits advocated by Connecticut governor Grasso. An official in the state budget division urged the governor to end the free meals and cheap housing benefits given to the hospital employees, and she agreed. The vehement disagreement of the line employees with this step culminated in a strike, which led to a return to something very much like the original policy. As this case illustrates, staff and line perspectives often differ, and line employees do not necessarily have to take staff-initiated changes affecting them lying down (a theme we return to later).

A Profile of Top State Bureaucrats: The Rise of Experienced Experts

Several surveys of the three thousand state government agency and department heads were conducted between 1963 and 1974.[4] These studies enable us to sketch the characteristics of top state bureaucrats. They are predominantly white (90 percent) Protestant (70 percent) males (90 percent) of middle age (mean age fifty years). In most of these respects they resemble their equivalents in top business executive posts. Like the businessmen, they are people who have done well in the existing system and so are unlikely to want to make drastic changes in it.

State bureaucrats are also an extraordinarily well educated group, since half of them have graduate degrees, while another 16 percent have done graduate study beyond the bachelor's degree. This indicates that they are more

4. Richard L. McAnaw and Deil S. Wright, "Accentuate the Positive," *National Civic Review* (July 1966), pp. 380–384; Stanley B. Botner, "Personal and Career Characteristics of State Government Administrators," *State Government* (Winter 1974), pp. 54–58; data made available by Fred W. Grupp, Jr., from his 1970 survey of ten states; and Deil S. Wright, *Assessing the Impacts of General Revenue Sharing in the Fifty States* (Chapel Hill, N.C.: University of North Carolina, 1975).

than political hacks, unable to function outside the political party system. They are, rather, skilled personnel who could earn a living in a number of different types of organizations. Indeed, half of these executives have semipermanent tenure because of their skills or their close relations with interest groups that support them, thus allowing them to survive changes in the governor's office. Fully one-fifth are covered by civil service tenure, a system we will examine more closely later.

Top state bureaucrats, then, are persons of considerable expertise and experience who have not received their appointments primarily because they are loyal members of the governor's party. Further, their stay in office makes them a semipermanent part of government. Why is this the case? Why aren't these bureaucrats replaced wholesale when the governor's office changes hands?

The underlying cause of these characteristics is the increasing complexity of the tasks carried out by state governments. One hundred years ago the states built roads, operated agricultural colleges and insane asylums, and provided a few other services. Today states operate universities; mental hospitals and training schools for the retarded; and departments of environmental protection, transportation, and welfare; as well as a host of other services. There is increasingly less room for the amateur in these organizations if such services are to be carried out with maximum effectiveness. What is needed are highly skilled specialists to, for example, determine the purity of the air, train students to be chemists, and diagnose and treat illness. Government is increasingly a job for the specialist, and it will continue in that direction in the future. This is not to say that all government employees earn their posts through expertise, especially at lower levels—as the next section indicates.

Patronage and the Merit System

While all states employ thousands of workers, state hiring, firing, and promotion procedures differ greatly. Someone wanting a position with the Indiana state highway department, for example, is well advised to register as a member of the political party in control of the governor's office. A twenty-five-year-old veteran who recently applied for such a post was told that there was only one qualification: membership in the Republican Party. Since he was enrolled in the G.O.P., he filled out the application form, which asked him, "How long have you been a member of the Republican Party?" and, "Would you be willing to contribute regularly to the Indiana Republican State Central Committee?" Those who answer negatively to the second question can look for work elsewhere, while

107

those who respond affirmatively are expected to contribute 2 percent of their salary. If they fail to do so, they will be fired.[5]

This patronage approach to employment differs from the procedure followed in some other state agencies in Indiana. In the welfare department, for example, applicants take a written entrance test. Only those who score above a certain level are eligible for consideration. Promotion is also based on tests designed to measure employee competence. This is the merit system approach, which is concerned more with competence than camaraderie with political party officials.

The reason for this difference among Indiana agencies illustrates the power of the federal government. Since the 1930s, Congress has required state agencies of health, education, and welfare receiving federal funds to use the merit system or face a cutoff in funds. And now there is some anxiety in the Indiana state highway department, since President Ford signed a new law into effect in October 1976. The law prohibits kickback contributions by employees paid wholly or partially by federal funds. It will be interesting to see whether the intent of this new law can be sidestepped by astute state bureaucrats, or whether this patronage practice will be endangered.

In 1975, somewhat less than 60 percent of state jobs were governed by merit systems. Wide variations exist among the states. Most of California's employees work under merit systems, while most of Mississippi's and half of Pennsylvania's do not. But there are different types of merit systems. State officials have been masterful at maneuvering mechanisms to undermine the purpose of merit systems. One technique is to pack the civil service commission with appointees who will favor party members' applications. Another approach is to use the "rule of three" in a way contrary to the intentions of civil service reformers. The rule of three allows an agency executive to select among the three top-scoring applicants for a job. It is designed to allow for flexibility and executive leadership. But if arrangements are made for one of the three to be a party protegé or the boss's brother-in-law, there is not much merit in the system. This may be arranged by bullying tactics or blandishments to other applicants or by making the existence, time, or place of a merit system exam secret. It is also possible to write a job description so that only the candidate desired by the party can meet or would want the job. A final ploy is the rising use of "temporary" appointees, who don't have to be examined. These temporaries are then reappointed every few months until they retire at a ripe old age.[6]

5. John Kifner, "Kickbacks Still Thrive in Indiana," *New York Times*, 11 July 1971, p. 21.

6. See: John Blydenburgh, "Party Organizations," in Alan Rosenthal and John Blydenburgh, eds., *Politics in New Jersey* (New Brunswick, N.J.: Eagleton Institute of Politics, 1975), pp. 110–137.

The reader should not automatically assume that patronage is bad and the merit system good. Patronage at least has the virtue of responding to the popular will at election time. When the out party wins and takes over as the in party, it replaces state employees with its followers and friends. Whatever problems this practice promulgates, disloyalty to the chief executive and his party will not be among them.

A U.S. Supreme Court decision of June 1976 may change the practice of patronage somewhat. The case, *Elrod* v. *Burns*, followed the election of Richard J. Elrod, a Democrat, to the office of sheriff of Cook County, Illinois. Elrod replaced a Republican, Joseph Woods, and immediately moved to dismiss the patronage employees of the sheriff's office so he could replace them with his own. Four of the fired Republicans brought suit, charging that Elrod's action deprived them of their First Amendment right of freedom of expression. The Supreme Court agreed, holding that patronage employees of any level of government cannot be dismissed merely because they belong to another political party than that of the office holder. Again, the next few years will reveal whether this is a crippling blow to patronage employment, or merely a troublesome hurdle to be cleared.

In some merit systems, unfortunately, the guarantee of career tenure after a probationary period has caused real problems. Knowing that they cannot be easily fired, employees may become contemptuous of the clientele or customers of the agency. Until the 1970s, the Connecticut Motor Vehicles Department had the reputation of greeting the public with a sneer instead of a smile. After long waits, people would be told, in a tone that indicated they were childish incompetents, that they were in the wrong line.

Job Orientation versus Paycheck Orientation

There is a broad distinction among agencies that is probably more crucial than anything else, including the merit system–patronage division, in determining how well they serve the public. Some agencies are more concerned with their continued existence than with anything else. Others are more concerned with the task or function, whether it be law enforcement, welfare, or transportation, with which they are entrusted. While any agency will be concerned with both matters, there are noticeable differences in the degree of commitment different agencies have to each. One way to measure this commitment is to observe how much time is spent on coffee breaks and idle chatter. Another is to observe how often many professional staffers leave the office early or exactly at the official closing time. If employees do these things and counsel, ridicule, or ostracize the employee who works more than the necessary hours, they are not

109

committed to the work of the agency. Many field workers in the construction inspection division of the New Jersey Department of Transportation show this lack of commitment, doing as little work as they possibly can. They and other merit system employees following similar practices show little merit.

While most patronage-oriented departments are unlikely to be task-oriented, some departments outside civil service may be. A public works department staffed on a patronage basis, where employees receive jobs for working for the political party in power, will usually view the department's task as a matter second in importance to keeping the party organization going. On the other hand, intensive commitment to the task is a common pattern for newly created agencies. And these agencies often hire outside the merit system, looking for specially qualified professionals and people committed to agency goals. The agency heads do not want to wait for the slow workings of the merit system to churn up would-be employees. They want to start at once, with a handpicked crew in which they have confidence. Personnel in departments of environmental protection or energy often have not entered through civil service. Yet they may be more concerned about reducing pollution and energy waste than any other aspect of their jobs.

An Area of Bureaucratic Influence: The Budgetary Process

There is no better illustration of line bureaucratic influence in state government than the annual (in some states, biennial) budgetary process. The result of this process is the decision on how much each agency shall be allowed to spend in the coming fiscal year. The process begins with the submission of line agency budget requests to the central budget office, and thence to the governor and legislature. After the governor and legislature decide on the level of budgetary appropriations, the central budget office than allocates the funds to the line agencies, usually on a quarterly basis.

A more detailed scrutiny of how this process actually works indicates the key roles of the line agencies in budget making. First, these agencies initiate the process through their requests. They set the agenda for the decisions that the budget office, legislature, and governor make. In a real sense, these latter three budgetary participants *react* to the original requests of the line agencies.

Second, until very recently line agency budgets have not been given thorough scrutiny by the governor and legislature. That is, the assumption usually made by both is that the amount of funds the agency got during the present fiscal year should be the base upon which the budget for the next year is built. In most cases an amount is added on to this base for the next year; in the more rare event of cuts, the cuts are generally less than 5 percent of the base.

Traditionally, executive and legislative officials have not given the base a thorough examination to see whether or not the job the agency is doing is an appropriate one.

Zero-Base Budgeting and Sunset Laws. State government budgets and taxes have grown enormously since the 1950s. In 1954, state governments spent $12.8 billion, while their 1976 expenditures were estimated at $104 billion. Taxes have increased apace, and there is growing pressure on elected officials to hold down budgets.

One of the methods proposed to restrain spending was used by Jimmy Carter while he was governor of Georgia. President Carter pledged to implement this method—zero-base budgeting—in the federal government as well. Zero-base budgeting involves looking at all of an agency's budget each year to see if its programs are still justified. Hence its title: it is not assumed that there is any base figure which should not be tampered with. All programs are scrutinized to see how many people they are serving. Zero-base budgeting, if used correctly, is a tool to evaluate the performance of government agencies.

In 1976, twelve states were taking a zero-base approach to at least some agency budgets, and most budget officials were reportedly pleased with the results. New Jersey and Massachusetts used zero-base to cut budgets, while Texas and Georgia used it primarily as an information tool to help officials make more knowledgeable program decisions. Proponents of zero-base budgeting argue that it is a far superior way to cut budgets than across-the-board slashes, which cut effective and ineffective programs equally. A working zero-base approach identifies the weakest programs and recommends that they be trimmed to the greatest extent.[7]

Another attempt to control skyrocketing government growth and spending uses what are called "sunset" laws. Sunset is indeed what happens under this concept, for agencies and their programs are automatically ended after several years, unless renewed by the legislature. At present, it is a relatively rare occurrence for a state agency to die, as the Connecticut Research Commission did in 1971, when the governor refused to spend any of the funds appropriated for it. But Colorado passed a sunset law in 1976, and twenty-four other states followed suit by the end of 1977.

Colorado found that the passage of the sunset law brought immediate results in some agencies, even though none have yet been abolished. Regulatory agencies had severely restricted the number of persons eligible for professional licenses. Stenographers were in short supply, but only 2 percent of those

7. "Zero-Based Budgeting—A Way to Cut Spending, or a Gimmick?" *U.S. News and World Report* (20 September 1976), pp. 79–80.

111

applying were licensed by the responsible agency. After the sunset law was passed, 48 percent of the applicants received licenses.[8] This is why proponents of sunset laws argue that they will make agencies more responsive to public needs and desires.

Like any other decision, the decision to implement zero-base budgeting or sunset laws has both costs and benefits. Both require investigative and analytical staffs and a lot of paperwork to function. This is why most states that have adopted either technique have not begun these programs on a crash basis, but have singled out a few agencies with which to begin. Colorado, for example, applied the sunset law initially to only thirteen of twenty-eight regulatory agencies.

The next few years will tell whether zero-base, sunset, or other programs designed to hold down state government spending or make state agencies more responsive will actually work. Most of these programs face substantial opposition, directly or indirectly, from the groups we consider next.

GOVERNMENT EMPLOYEE UNIONS

In 1972, over half of the state and local government work force was unionized. (See Table 8.1). This meant that these state workers were organized to bargain collectively with state officials to determine wage levels, fringe benefits, and working conditions. Implicit in their unionization was the threat to strike if the unions did not get what they wanted, whether strikes were illegal or not. And strike they have, as actions closing down the eight New Jersey state colleges in 1974 and most of Massachusetts state government in 1976 show. In 1974, there were thirty-four state government strikes, idling 25,000 workers for 86,000 man-days.[9] (See Table 8.2)

But even more important than strikes or the threat to strike are the political activities of state employees. Acting on the adage that you can kill a lot more flies with honey than with vinegar, state employee unions and associations have made it a point to aid elected officials in their quest for state office. Campaign contributions and votes have made the unions an important influence in many state capitals. As Jerry Wurf, President of the American Federation of State, County, and Municipal Employees, remarked in 1975, "*We* elected Governor Michael Dukakis in Massachusetts." [10] (Italics added.)

In fact, most union leaders do not like strikes. They would prefer to see

8. Bob Cunningham, "Sunset Law–More Red Tape?" *Bergen Evening Record,* 2 August 1976, p. 1.

9. Neal R. Peirce, "Public Employee Unions Show Rise in Membership, Militancy," *National Journal* (30 August 1975), pp. 1239–1249, at 1245.

10. Ibid., p. 1249.

TABLE 8.1 LABOR ORGANIZATION MEMBERSHIP

The following table shows the number of members in unions and related organizations in the private and public sectors (figures are in thousands):

YEAR	PRIVATE SECTOR	FEDERAL	PUBLIC SECTOR STATE-LOCAL	TOTAL
1968	18,158	1,391	2,466	3,857
1970	18,478	1,412	2,668	4,080
1972	18,539	1,383	3,137	4,520
1974	18,830	1,414	3,919	5,333
% increase, 1968–74	3.7	1.7	58.9	38.3

SOURCE: U.S. Department of Labor, Bureau of Labor Statistics.

TABLE 8.2 EMPLOYEE WORK STOPPAGES

The following table gives the number of work stoppages by state and local employees from 1960 through 1974 (figures for workers involved and days idle are in thousands):

	STATE GOVERNMENT			LOCAL GOVERNMENT		
	NUMBER OF STOPPAGES	WORKERS INVOLVED	DAYS IDLE	NUMBER OF STOPPAGES	WORKERS INVOLVED	DAYS IDLE
1960	3	1.0	1.2	33	27.6	67.7
1961	—	—	—	28	6.6	15.3
1962	2	1.7	2.3	21	25.3	43.1
1963	2	.3	2.2	27	4.6	67.7
1964	4	.3	3.2	37	22.5	57.7
1965	—	—	1.3	42	11.9	145.0
1966	9	3.1	6.0	133	102.0	449.0
1967	12	4.7	16.3	169	127.0	1,230.0
1968	16	9.3	42.8	235	190.9	2,492.8
1969	37	20.5	152.4	372	139.0	592.2
1970	23	8.8	44.6	386	168.9	1,330.5
1971	23	14.5	81.8	304	137.1	811.6
1972	40	27.4	273.7	335	114.7	983.5
1973	29	12.3	133.0	357	183.7	2,166.3
1974	34	24.7	86.4	348	135.4	1,316.3

SOURCE: U.S. Department of Labor, Bureau of Labor Statistics.

binding arbitration installed as the mechanism to settle all differences and disputes. Binding arbitration was the law for *local* governments in eleven states in 1976. State union leaders are pushing for it also. Under binding arbitration, government and the unions submit their differences to a person both have agreed on as arbiter. The arbiter makes the final determination, which both sides have to accept. Government officials usually dislike binding arbitration, since it

113

removes their discretion and flexibility. Government labor leaders like it, because they feel they do better under it. As yet, there is no evidence to indicate who, if anyone, prospers under binding arbitration. Its impact, though, on elected officials is obvious. It removes decision-making authority from them and lodges it with a temporary appointed official. This reduces and fragments the power entrusted to the elected chief executive, further complicating the task of coordination.

Unions exacerbate the existence of elected officials in other ways. They are concerned not only with bread and butter wage and fringe benefits, but also with questions of policy. The New Jersey college teachers who struck in 1974, for instance, demanded among other things that student tuition not be increased and student enrollment not be reduced. Concern for working conditions, such as student-teacher ratios, number of police officers per patrol car, and social worker case load, also have policy implications. None of these is simply and purely a question of working conditions. They all raise basic questions about the policies and goals of the agency, and they are crucial factors in determining budget size. Unions are constantly more aggressive in their demands on working conditions and policy areas.

Unions have been stupendously successful in raising the compensation of their members. In 1955, state and local government employees averaged only 92 percent of the wages paid their counterparts in business. In 1973 they averaged *more* than their private sector equivalents—106 percent.[11] The big increases came in a period of unrivalled prosperity, 1965–1973, which indicates why the unions had a harder time of it during the lean years from 1974 through 1977. Both the New Jersey college teachers' and Massachusetts statewide strikes mentioned above were failures. In both cases, employees returned to work with nothing to show for their strikes except lost paydays. Jerry Wurf, who boasted that he had helped elect Massachusetts Governor Dukakis, had to add, ". . . and now he's killing us."[12] Many states imposed hiring and wage freezes, while others, like Connecticut, actually laid off employees. The Congressional Joint Economic Committee estimated total layoffs of 35,000–45,000 state workers in 1975.[13] The realities of recession overpower union edicts.

The future is always uncertain. Yet we can expect that hard economic times themselves will swell the ranks of the unions. Union power will vary with political and economic conditions, but it surely will not vanish. Employee organizations will remain important participants in state government.

11. Neal R. Peirce, "Public Worker Pay Emerges as Growing Issue," *National Journal* (23 August 1975), pp. 1198–1206.
12. Peirce, "Public Employee Unions," p. 1249.
13. Peirce, "Public Worker Pay," p. 1206.

114

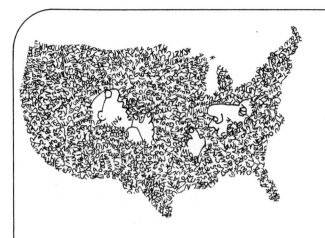

THE STATES
AND THE FEDERAL
NETWORK

CHAPTER NINE

While *every* one of our states possesses sovereignty, no state stands as an isolated island within the American political system. On the contrary, each state finds itself enmeshed in a complex and convoluted network involving relationships with the federal government, other state governments, and its own local governments. Furthermore, the lines that define and demarcate these relationships usually overlap and intersect. The pattern that emerges often confuses more than it clarifies.

The late Morton Grodzins used an apt analogy to describe this phenomenon. He noted that most people regard the federal system as a layer cake with each level of government snugly and securely spread over the other. This image conveys a wrong impression, said Grodzins. The system is really a marble cake with diffuse and diverse clusters of authority and contours of activity. "In virtually no field does the complete body of law with respect to a given governmental activity have its source in one of these so-called levels of government. In a typical case a *mixture* of federal, state and local regulation covers an area of regulation or activity."[1] (Italics added.)

So intricate and entangled has this federal network or marble cake become that it has given rise to a whole new subfield of study called intergovernmental relations. Many colleges and universities offer one or more courses in just this particular subject. In the limited space available to us in this book we can at best skim the surface, supplying only a sketch of this panorama of governmental activity. However, later chapters dealing with substantive issues will shed some additional light on just how the federal network operates.

STATES AND THE FEDERAL GOVERNMENT

The U.S. Constitution grants the federal government certain exclusive powers and prerogatives and gives it the right to protect these from encroachment from the states. As a result, Washington can stop a state from coining or printing its own money or from signing a treaty with a foreign power. It can also crack down on a state that is interfering with interstate commerce.

The Constitution also authorizes the federal government to regulate many of the relationships between the states. For example, the Constitution stipulates that "Full faith and credit shall be given in each state to the public acts, records and judicial proceedings of very other state." This means that a contract or another legal instrument such as a deed or a mortgage that has been legally signed or negotiated in one state must be upheld in another state. If two people marry in one state and then move to a state with more stringent requirements for marriage, the latter state can not declare the marriage to be null and void simply because it does not meet its own standards. And as with marriage, so with divorce. In the days when divorce was a difficult and drawn-out process in many states, many individuals would slip off to Nevada where they could secure a divorce almost automatically in six weeks. Many states frowned on this practice but the Supreme Court required them to accept such divorces as legal and binding.

Other constitutional provisions also give the national government jurisdiction in interstate relations. Any state harboring a fugitive from justice from another state must send the fugitive back to the state from which he has fled. Two or more states desiring to sign a compact with each other must first secure

1. Morton Grodzins, *The American System* (Chicago: Rand McNally, 1966), p. 80.

116

the consent of Congress. As we shall have occasion to see, these provisions are not always rigorously enforced. Nevertheless, they form part of the federal government's authority over state governments.

Enforcement of the federal government's constitutional authority over the states, however, forms only part of the interactions that go on between these two sovereign components of our political system. And it does not form the greatest part. The federal government enjoys only limited legal jurisdiction over the states and if it wishes to get states to do some things and to prevent them from doing others, it must often use other devices than legal power. The instrument it has made the most use of in working its will on state governments is a simple but very strong one, money. By giving the states funds to finance certain activities and refusing to give them funds for others, Washington has greatly expanded its influence in the statehouses of the nation.

The practice of funneling funds to the states goes back to the earliest days of our republic. Alexander Hamilton, as our first secretary of the treasury, saw to it that the new national government paid off all the debts that the states had contracted to wage the revolutionary war. However, it wasn't until 1836 that the federal government handed over to the states any revenues to spend for their own purposes. In that year the U.S. Treasury found itself with a twenty-eight-million-dollar surplus on its hands, and not knowing what to do with it—federal governmental functions being so limited in those days—it divided up the sum and gave it to the twenty-six states.

The first federal program to provide states with support for specific services did not come into being until 1862. Congress that year passed the Morrill Act, giving aid to the state-sponsored land-grant colleges. In 1886, grants were made for agriculture experiment stations and in 1916 the Federal Aid Road Act was enacted to supply funds to the states for highway construction.

The practice of providing money for specific purposes came into its own during the depression when the federal government began channeling resources to state governments for a variety of New Deal programs. Many of these programs continued after World War II, and several new ones joined them. However, the real boom in federal grant-in-aid programs did not occur until the 1960s, when Presidents John F. Kennedy and Lyndon Johnson sought to make the political system more responsive to what they deemed to be the nation's needs. In 1962 there were some 160 such grant-in-aid programs in operation. By 1969, the figure was approaching 800. The federal government meanwhile had begun publishing a semiannual catalogue listing the different types of grants available as the list kept on growing. The 1974 edition of this catalogue cited 975 assistance programs administered by fifty-two federal agencies.

The sum of money involved in such programs had grown proportion-

117

ately. In 1964 the federal government distributed slightly over $10 billion to the states and their local governments in grants-in-aid. By 1974, the figure had grown to $46 billion, and by 1976 it amounted to around $60 billion.[2] The latter represents a 30 percent increase in just two years. The states were now deriving more money from federal aid programs than they were from their own number one revenue producer, the sales tax. And that portion of the federal money that was being channeled, with state sanction, directly to local governments was having, if anything, an even more significant impact on their budgets.

Federal financial aid to states and their local governments assumes many forms. Essentially, however, such payments fall into three basic classifications: *categorical grants, block grants, and revenue sharing.*

Categorical grants transmit about three-quarters of the total amounts. These grants are earmarked for specific programs and are circumscribed by numerous regulations. They can only be spent for designated purposes and only in a defined manner. Usually, though not always, they require the receiving government to make some contribution of its own. Sometimes they are structured so as to encourage the governmental recipient to make more than the minimum contribution required. This is done by increasing the federal payment when the state or local government adds more of its own money to the pot. Welfare and highway construction programs are two major categorical grant programs.

Block grants differ from categorized grants by being much freer from federally imposed rules and regulations. In block grants, the federal government gives the money for a specified area of activity but allows the receiving government a good deal of flexibility in deciding how to spend it. Some general guidelines are customarily attached and some specific goals are usually defined, but the methods for achieving such goals within these broad guidelines are left open. Consequently, the specific programs operated under block grants may vary from state to state and from locality to locality. Much of the federal government's assistance to the states for criminal justice comes under the block grant classification.

Revenue sharing carries this flexibility feature still further. It dispenses federal funds to state and local governments to spend pretty much as they see fit. They are required only to make sure that the money is not used by any governmental agency that discriminates on racial or religious grounds in any way. As long as they meet that requirement, the 38,000 state and local governments benefiting from revenue sharing are free to spend the money as they wish. The money is allocated to these governments on the basis of a complicated

2. Advisory Commission on Intergovernmental Relations, *Intergovernmental Perspective* (Fall 1975), p. 17.

formula that takes into account their respective populations, their per capita income, their "tax effort" (how much they tax themselves), and other factors.

The fact that only 38,000 of the nearly 80,000 U.S. governments receive revenue-sharing funds results from the requirement limiting distribution to what are called general purpose governments. Thus, states, counties, cities, and townships qualify for such aid; educational and special districts do not. Of course they may benefit indirectly, for the general purpose government may turn around and reallocate some or all of the funds to one or more of these limited governments.

As might be expected, this spiraling trend of federal aid to the subnational system has suffered from growing pains at almost each stage of growth. Critics have had no difficulty in finding fault with all the ways and means used to direct these funds back to the states and their localities, and many have questioned the entire principle of such assistance regardless of how it is transmitted.

Federal Aid: Problems, Paradoxes, and Possibilities

The money state and local governments derive from Washington is not, strictly speaking, money that is given but money that is redistributed. The federal government can generally only give what it has previously taken. Grant-in-aid programs involve only a transfer of funds from one level of government to another, and the money transferred comes essentially from the inhabitants of the jurisdictions that receive it. The revenue first flows to Washington from the grass roots and then some of it flows back again.

This process necessarily involves considerable red tape, delay, and general expense. One small health center once spent over $50,000 in a single year just to apply for grants.[3] Indeed, the system has given rise to a new profession, that of the grantsman who specializes in preparing and negotiating grant applications. As a matter of fact, over half the states have seen fit to open up special offices in Washington to make sure they take maximum advantage of this federal largesse.[4]

Such developments as these have led some to say that it would be better for the federal government to reduce its own taxes and let the states and their localities raise and spend the money themselves. Why go through the cumbersome and costly process of transferring the revenues to Washington only to have Washington return them?

3. The executive director of a small hospital in Ashburnham, Massachusetts told a Senate subcommittee in 1972 that her staff had to deal with twenty-three federal and state agencies. (*Boston Record-American*, 19 November 1972).

4. The number of states with liaison offices in Washington rose from one in 1960 to twenty-seven in 1972.

One of the answers often given to this question is that in making the transfer, the national government can reallocate funds to those who need it the most. For example, the citizens of Mississippi, our poorest state, paid some $1.2 billion to the federal government in taxes in 1971. In the same year they received almost double this amount, some $2.3 billion, in federal aid. Uncle Sam paid nearly half the total governmental bills for Mississippi and its localities that year.[5]

As one might suppose, this answer fails to assuage many of the critics of these programs. First, they point out that it is unfair for some states to have to pick up part of the burden for other states. Furthermore, the transfer does not always take from the rich states and give to the poor ones. The state receiving the largest amount in per capita payments from the federal government in 1975 was Alaska. The $776.20 per capita payment in federal funds Alaska received that year was more than double that of the second highest recipient, New Mexico. Yet Alaska, with its immense oil reserves, is far from a poor state. Even wealthy New York State by the mid-1970s was receiving back from the federal government slightly more than its citizens were contributing in federal taxes.

Of course there are numerous reasons for these discrepancies. Alaska is a high-cost state and it requires more expenditure to maintain a federal facility there than it does on the mainland. Building a road in Alaska is especially expensive, and with its sparse and scattered population the state requires more road mileage per person than do most other states. There is also the large Eskimo and Indian population that needs and receives special attention from federal authorities. As for New York, this state was actually on the losing end of the federal aid process for many years. During the years 1965 through 1967, New Yorkers paid into the federal treasury nearly $7.5 billion more than they received in federal assistance programs. Only New York's burgeoning welfare rolls succeeded in tipping the balance in its favor a decade later.

The system's supporters also argue that the federal role is needed to insure the maintenance of proper standards and the achievement of national goals. To the national government must perforce fall the task of coordinating as well as catalyzing such activities. But the system's detractors remain unconvinced. One of these, former California governor Ronald Reagan, made a return of many of these functions to the states a key part of his campaign platform in his 1976 bid for the presidency.

Categorical grants have borne the brunt of the criticism leveled at the grant-in-aid program. This, to some extent, is to be expected since they are the most typical and traditional of the grant mechanisms and since they involve the

5. Neal R. Peirce, *The Deep South States of America* (New York: W. W. Norton, 1974), p. 206.

bulk of the funds. Many who generally believe in such federal aid disavow the categorical grant as a device for distributing it.

Many of the nearly 1,000 assistance programs that use the categorical grant approach overlap. A 1975 report by the Office of Management and Budget (OMB), for example, found that there were 22 separate programs for drug abuse alone. In the more general health area there were some 230 programs administered by ten separate agencies.[6] Some programs may duplicate each other while others may work at cross-purposes. A study of Richmond, Virginia found that federal grants in some instances had created new institutions to compete with existing ones.

The effect of all this has often been to weaken the hand of governors, mayors, and other local officials, as well as to deter their governments from making desirable reforms. Many of the moves that states and some local governments have sought to make to consolidate their sprawling bureaucracies have been stymied by the need to maintain separate agencies to handle grant money. For example, states must operate their mental health and mental retardation programs through separate agencies in order to make them eligible for federal help. In the face of all these federally imposed restrictions and regulations, it should come as no surprise to find that over one-half of all state administrators surveyed said they would have spent their federal grant money in other ways if they had been allowed to do so.[7] As governor of New York, Nelson Rockefeller castigated the categorical grant system, saying it "has weakened the ability of state governors to govern and it's getting worse all the time."[8] Bernard Hillenbrand, Director of the National Association of Counties, claims, "The categories are a floodgate of dollars which create an enormous distortion of local priorities."[9]

In an effort to calm some of these critics, President Johnson in 1966 issued a memorandum to federal officials directing them to consult as fully as possible with their state and local counterparts in developing and executing grant programs. The federal government also began organizing regional councils to bring together the regional directors of the major grant-in-aid agencies to coordinate their activities. And in 1968, Congress passed the Intergovernmental Cooperation Act, which allows state and local officials more authority in shaping federally aided programs.

Congress in 1968 also passed another bill that opened up new pos-

6. *Strengthening Public Management in the Intergovernmental System*, a Report Prepared for Office Management and Budget by the Study Committee on Policy Management Assistance, p. 9.

7. Deil S. Wright, "The States and Intergovernmental Relations, *Publius* 1 (Winter 1972).

8. *Strengthening Public Management*, p. 9.

9. Ibid.

sibilities in distributing grants-in-aid. This was the Omnibus Crime Control and Safe Streets Act. It provided, among other things, for the distribution of money to the states to improve their criminal justice activities. What was somewhat unique about the program was the fact that it contained few federal guidelines. Each state was to set up a special agency to draw up its own plan for administering the funds and once its plan was approved by the federal government, it would receive the money to implement its plan. In other words, funds under this legislation were to take the form of block grants. Although Washington had experimented with the block-grant device before, this marked its first use as the basic instrument for an entire program area. Congress created, in passing the act, the Law Enforcement Assistance Administration as a special agency within the Department of Justice to approve state plans and to parcel out the money. The initial results, at best, were mixed. Block grants, it was soon found, also provide problems.

For one thing, indications soon arose that some state agencies had misused the funds. Federal officials demanded the return from Florida of $35,000, which they said had been improperly spent. And they abruptly cancelled a $200,000 officer education program in Alabama, which, they claimed, had been largely used to send the sons of high-ranking state police officials to college with scholarships and stipends of up to $6,000 a year. An Alabama newspaper that investigated several alleged abuses in the way the state handled its allocated grant accused the state's planning agency of "handing out federal dollars in about the same manner that old John Rockefeller used to hand out dimes." [10]

More pervasive and persistent charges against the program focused on the way the states set up their priorities. A report by the Advisory Commission on Intergovernmental Relations in 1970 found that rural areas and small cities were obtaining too large a share of the funds while the big cities, with a disproportionate amount of the crime rate, were receiving too little. In Michigan, for example, the sheriff of rural Ogemaw County, with a total population of about ten thousand, obtained $1,500 for new radio equipment; Grand Rapids, a city of over two hundred thousand, received a mere $180 to purchase two cameras.

Other complaints centered on the fact that most of the money had gone to the police to the detriment of other components in the criminal justice system, such as courts and corrections; that citizens and locally elected officials were inadequately represented on the boards the states were supposed to set up to

10. There is an abundance of material on the misfunctioning of block grants under the Omnibus Crime Control and Safe Streets Act. See: *New York Times,* 19 June 1970, 7 August 1970, 22 February 1971, and 22 July 1971 for some of this material. See also: *Wall Street Journal,* 4 February 1970 for a comprehensive wrap-up of early abuses of this legislation.

supervise the program; and that in general the states had farmed out the funds on a scatter-shot basis, distributing a little here and a little there rather than using the money to launch fewer but more fundamental efforts toward improving their systems of criminal justice. In short, the early experience with the Safe Streets Act suggested that the block-grant approach provided no panacea to the problems generated by categorical grants. It indicated instead that it might only substitute one set of problems for another.

These objections notwithstanding, in 1972 Congress took a still stronger step toward expanding the subnational system's say in disposing of federal funds. It did so by passing the State and Local Government Fiscal Assistance Act. This measure brought to fruition long-time efforts to have the federal government share some of its revenues directly with state and local governments. The revenue-sharing bill authorized the transfer to these governments of over $30 billion over the next few years. One-third of this amount was to go to states, the rest to municipalities. As noted earlier, the recipient governments could not use the funds to foster racially discriminatory policies and programs. Otherwise they remained fairly free to spend them as they wished. (Actually local governments, but not states, had to spend the money within seven basic program categories. However, the categories were so comprehensive that most areas of local government activity were covered.)

How has the program worked out? As might be expected, it has not succeeded in satisfying everybody, including some of its organized backers. Many liberals have voiced discontent over the fact that although poorer areas tend to receive more money per capita than richer ones, only a small proportion of the funds has actually gone to social service and health care programs. Most of the money has instead been spent for law enforcement, street and road care, fire protection, recreation, or simply to reduce taxes. Furthermore, the program has failed to elicit more effective public involvement in local budget decisions. Finally, even its own basic restriction, that no funds be used for discriminatory purposes, may, in some jurisdictions, have been flouted. A U.S. District Court suspended payments to Chicago in 1974, claiming that the city's police department, which was spending 70 percent of all the city's revenue-sharing funds, was practicing discriminatory employment policies.[11]

11. As with the Omnibus Crime Control and Safe Streets Act, there is no dearth of critical material regarding the revenue-sharing program. Many of these criticisms are included in a story headlined "New Federalism Raises Some Old Problems" in New York Times, 6 January 1974. See also: National Civic Review (February 1975), p. 97 for a report on four cities from which the federal government withheld funds on charges that they were using them in agencies with discriminatory hiring policies. For an interesting critical perspective on the whole principle see: Max Frankel, "Revenue-Sharing Is a Counter-Revolution," in New York Times Magazine, 25 April 1971.

123

The plethora of charges and criticisms elicited by federal aid in all its forms notwithstanding, most American political leaders, and most American citizens, remain more or less committed to the basic principle. Only the national government, so the feeling runs, controls enough of the nation's resources to insure that needed and necessary governmental functions are maintained. Furthermore, only the national government can prescribe priorities and set standards for the nation as a whole. Federal aid is now a fixture of the American political system and seems destined to remain so, at least for the foreseeable future.

At the same time, however, such assistance may undergo changes in form and function. The emerging trend of the mid-1970s seems to be taking the form of a gradual shift away from categorical grants to what might be called modified block grants. Under this approach, many if not most of the restrictions that previously governed several grants-in-aid are being eliminated. They are being replaced with some more basic and general guidelines that allow state and local governments to work out their own programs within a fairly broad framework. Federal officials must advise and consent to their plans and must broadly oversee their implementation. But they do not dictate just how the money is to be spent. An added feature of this approach is the allocation of more authority to federal field officials to work out program details with state and local officials within their regions. Many health programs are now operating along these lines, while the Housing and Urban Development Act of 1974 authorized the Department of Housing and Urban Development to move even further in this direction. Under this act various categorical grant programs such as urban renewal and model cities were replaced by a community development program that devolves considerable discretion on each recipient community to determine what it will do with its aid money.

Revenue sharing, meanwhile, seems likely to continue. Without such financial nourishment from Washington many of our cities and towns and possibly even a few of our states might find themselves confronting the spectre of bankruptcy. At the same time, however, the federal government may exercise somewhat more supervision over the program, at least to the extent of making sure that its antidiscrimination provisions are obeyed. In one way or another the helping hand of Uncle Sam will continue to be felt in the statehouses as well as in the city halls of the nation.

STATES AND OTHER STATES

On May 19, 1970, the *New York Times* carried in its back pages the following dispatch from Little Rock, Arkansas:

124

> The Governors of seventeen Southern and border states and two territories have joined in an effort to fight pollution through multistate compacts and agreements.
>
> They formed on Thursday the Southern Regional Environmental Conservation Council, which will be an arm of the Southern Governors Conference.

The news story went on to relate how the council will, as one of its first steps, seek Washington's advice and approval in enacting an "umbrella compact." Such a compact would give them broad authority to enter into multistate agreements for the handling of various ecological problems. The governors had already received a tentative blessing from the national administration and would submit specific proposals following further study.

As this story suggests, relations between the states have come a long way since the difficult days of the Articles of Confederation. Although fairly intense competition continues to characterize interstate relations, the forces of cooperation and compromise have started to make themselves felt. The trend toward joint understandings and joint undertakings really got underway in the 1920s. New means of communication and transportation were bringing the states into closer contact with one another. Concomitantly, problems were becoming regional and even national in scope. These factors were forcing the states to consult and cooperate with each other. Two landmark interstate compacts took form during this decade. One was an agreement between New York and New Jersey to develop their joint port facilities at the mouth of the Hudson River. The other was a concord between the states bordering the Colorado River on how to use the resources of that vital waterway.

Since then the number of interstate compacts has grown apace. By 1971, some 160 of these agreements were in operation. They covered a wide variety of concerns, such as conservation, corrections, education, criminal justice, etc. Many of these compacts are regional. The Atlantic State Marine Fisheries Commission, the Kansas City Area Transportation Authority, and the Southern States Forest Fire Compact are examples of these. Others, such as the Interstate Workmen's Compensation Compact or the Interstate Compact on the Placement of Children, span the entire nation. Only a few, however, have managed to elicit the signatures and support of all or nearly all the states.

Interstate agreements often grow out of governors' conferences. Such conferences themselves take a variety of forms. There is the National Governors' Conference, which meets every year and which usually attracts the attendance of all fifty state chief executives. Then there are separate conferences for Republican and Democratic governors. As might be expected, these conclaves center on matters of party policy that affect the states. Most important, however, are the five regional conferences in which governors from the South, New England, the mid-Atlantic states, the Midwest, and the West sit down with their area colleagues to discuss problems and develop plans. Many of these regional groupings of governors meet several times a year.

The governors are far from being the only state officials who meet with their counterparts from other states to exchange information and to evolve proposals. Attorneys general, highway commissioners, welfare commissioners, and a host of other state officers belong to national and sometimes regional associations that bring them together on a periodic basis. Many of the compacts now in force between states have emerged from such gatherings. Similarly, local officials also join hands across state lines. There are national organizations for mayors, district attorneys, county executives, and others.

Many of these associations, and many of the compacts they have spawned, have created organizations with offices and full-time staffs. The New England Governors Conference runs a second office in Boston. There are also offices in Boston for the New England Board of Higher Education, the New England School Development Council, and similar compact-created agencies. The situation in many other regional centers is somewhat the same. Interstate relations has become in effect a growth industry. The Council of State Governments, meanwhile, acts as a clearinghouse and catalyst for interstate cooperation.

Despite all this thriving activity in establishing amicable alliances between states, problems yet remain. For one thing, the Constitution specifies that states must secure congressional approval before they can form a compact. In 1948, Congress refused to endorse an effort by southern states to set up a regional education compact, fearing that it would only reinforce school segregation. However, the southern states proceeded without Congress' consent. Subsequently, the Supreme Court narrowed congressional authority in this area saying that Congress could reject only those compacts that might tend "to increase the political power in the states, which may encroach upon or interfere with the just supremacy of the United States." [12]

A greater stumbling block to increased cooperation has been the reluctance of the states themselves. Our sovereign states tend to guard their independence quite zealously and do not easily surrender any of it until they become convinced that they have much to gain in doing so. On occasion the federal government has had to step in with a grant-in-aid program in order to gain the necessary unanimous consent most compacts need to become operational. Thus, when a prolonged drought hit the mid-Atlantic states in the early 1960s, and the four states bordering the Delaware River fell to wrangling amongst

12. *Virginia v. Tennessee* (1949).

126

themselves as to how to allocate the river's now precious water, President Johnson used the promise of federal assistance to prod them into an agreement.[13]

In general, examples of the failure of states to cooperate with each other vastly outnumber instances of their success in doing so. The 160 formal compacts, numerous as they may seem, still leave many areas of activity untouched. Furthermore, even these compacts are not always fully enforced. Consequently, any believer in the benefits of interstate harmony would have to conclude that though the states have come a long way in this respect, they still have a long way to go.

STATES AND THEIR LOCAL GOVERNMENTS

Anyone undertaking the study of local government in the United States soon comes across what is called "Dillon's Rule."[14] Named for the nineteenth-century judge who formulated it, Dillon's Rule simply states that local governments can exercise those powers, and carry on those functions, that their respective state governments have allowed—and that is it. Our counties, cities, towns, etc., possess no inherent power even to exist let alone to do anything for which they have not obtained at least implicit state approval. Indeed, it is no exaggeration to say that in a legal sense local government is merely an extension of state government.

Since the states have created our local governments one might assume that the states would take care to nourish them. Traditionally, however, such care and protection have fallen far short of what many would expect. States have often been accused of giving their localities too many responsibilities while withholding from them the resources needed to discharge such responsibilities. A city or town all too often has to go to the statehouse to beg humbly for permission to hire an additional dog catcher, dispose of a piece of surplus land, or even advertise its charms in a tourist brochure. Meanwhile, the state may require the local government to undertake a new and costly program, or to improve an existing one, while giving it no new revenues to carry out such a mandate.

It is indeed no wonder then that local governments have often looked upon their state overseers as rather bossy on one hand and as neglectful on the other. Local officials continuously complain of the things their states require

13. Richard A. Hogarty, *The Delaware River Drought Emergency*, Inter-University Case Program #107 (Indianapolis: Bobbs-Merrill).

14. John F. Dillon, *Commentaries on the Law of Municipal Corporations*, 5th ed., vol. I (1911), p. 448.

them to do as well as of the things their states will not let them do. They tend to look upon their state governments as parents who are neither protective nor permissive.

If the states have not been as supportive of local government generally as the latter would have liked, then they have been especially remiss in helping the larger cities. Frequently cities have fared less well then rural communities or even affluent suburbs in obtaining state assistance. Surveys show that city officials regard the federal government as being more helpful to them than their state governments. The figures indicate they are right to believe so. By 1975, the federal government was giving the cities about three times more aid, on a per capita basis, than it was giving surburban communities.[15]

The reasons why states seem so often to have given their larger cities the short end of the stick are many. For one thing, our political culture tends to be biased against cities. Most of our founding fathers were countrymen and many of them, such as John Adams and Thomas Jefferson, positively detested cities. The whole ethos of our country, with its emphasis on rugged individualism and an expanding frontier, betrays an antiurban (and possibly antiurbane) flavor.[16]

State government has tended to foster such feelings. The predominance of rural influence in state legislatures has been previously noted and the gradual replacement of the "squires" by the suburbanites has not automatically altered the situation. In a book describing his experiences as mayor of New York City in the late 1960s, John V. Lindsay wrote, "When I prepare for the Albany journey, I think of Henry Hudson who began his own journey as captain of the stately *Half Moon* and ended it in a rowboat somewhere off the coast of Canada."[17] State capitals do have a way of dispiriting and derailing even the mightiest of metropolitan mayors.

Yet in this situation, as in so many others on the state political scene, the winds of change are beginning to stir. In 1960 only two states found it worthwhile to maintain a separate state department to aid and assist local government. Twelve years later some thirty-two states were operating such agencies. The amount of financial aid the states give to their grass root governments also has gone up precipitously. It amounted to only $5 billion in 1952. By 1962 it had risen to $10.9 billion. In 1972 the figure reached $32.8 billion. And by 1974 the states were supplying $46 billion to their local governments in one form or

15. *National Civic Review* (November 1975), p. 543.
16. For an informative analysis and review of this cultural attitude see: Morton White and Lucia White, *The Intellectual and the City* (New York: New American Library, 1965).
17. John V. Lindsay, *The City* (New York: W. W. Norton, 1970), pp. 189–190.

128

another.[18] New York State was actually devoting nearly 60 percent of its budget for this purpose.[19]

This surge in state support has also brought with it a slight shift of the balance wheel in favor of the cities. A government study based on 1970 data disclosed that in the largest metropolitan areas, the average central-city resident was receiving slightly more state assistance or state-administered federal assistance than was the average suburbanite.

The states had also started to loosen some of the fetters that had frustrated local officials for so long. During the period from 1920 to 1972, at least twenty-two states granted greater home rule to their communities, thereby giving them much more discretion to do things on their own. Some states had already taken such a step prior to this period; others have done so since. The results have not always seemed so salutory. The increase in home rule has led many localities to set up more special districts, a form of government many political scientists, for reasons we will examine in Chapter 11, frown upon. And New York City's brush with bankruptcy in 1975, and the fact that many other municipalities seemed to be courting similar danger, has made many wonder if state governments should not exercise more rather than less supervision over their governmental offspring.

Nevertheless, the situation is changing and though it may change still more, and in other ways, it will probably never go back to the days of disinterest. As one observer has noted, "There are some indications to suggest that the more significant developments emerging in intergovernmental relations as gauged by lobbying activities of subnational chief executives may not emanate solely from Washington during the decade ahead. Instead, they may well reside at the state level in the working between state capitals, city halls and other local governments."[20]

18. Advisory Commission on Intergovernmental Relations, *Intergovernmental Perspective* (Fall 1975), p. 17.

19. *New York Times*, 5 January 1975.

20. Donald E. Haider, *When Governments Come to Washington* (New York: Free Press, 1974), p. 299.

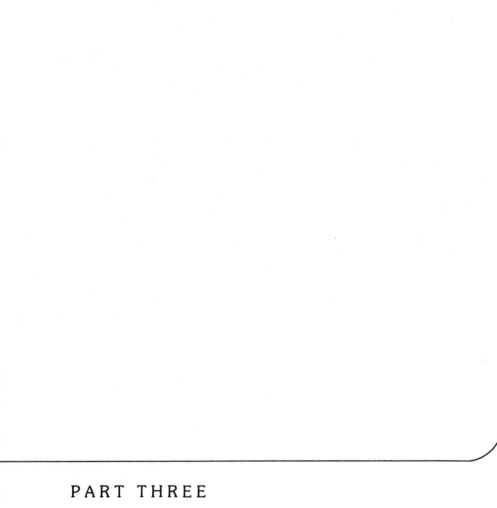

PART THREE

LOCAL GOVERNMENT

THE MAZE OF
LOCAL GOVERNMENT:
MUNICIPAL AND
TOWNSHIP GOVERNMENTS

CHAPTER TEN

According to Greek legend, King Minos of ancient Crete built a labyrinth so complex that it served as a prison for a monster called the Minotaur. Those who have felt imprisoned by the labyrinth of American local government structures can't be blamed for wondering if King Minos had a hand in building our system of local governments. Like the Minotaur, many of us are baffled when we try to penetrate this maze. Should we go to an office of municipal government for the problem that ails us—or to the county government, or to a special district? Once we have determined the government we think we should go to, *where* in that government do we go—to which office? However impressive King Minos' labyrinth, it was a plaything compared to our local government maze.

Consider first the aggregate figures: the U.S.A. has 3,000 counties, 16,000 school districts, 24,000 special districts, 17,000 townships, and 18,000 municipalities. As Congressman Henry Reuss put it, "Nowhere but in America have so few ever been governed by so many." [1] This works out to an average of one local government for every 2,750 residents of the nation. This average can be misleading, since the majority of local governments is found in rural areas, where only 30 percent of the population lives. But there is still a vast proliferation of governments in our urban areas. The Philadelphia metropolitan area, for example, has over 900 governments. (A metropolitan area is defined by the U.S. Census Bureau as a city of 50,000 or more with surrounding suburbs that are economically integrated with the city.) See Figure 10.1, which shows the many governments of the St. Louis area.

Consider next the case of Whitehall, Pennsylvania, admittedly an extreme example but indicative of what our system can produce. In 1972, Whitehall (population: 16,000) housed all or parts of fourteen local governments within its boundaries: the borough of Whitehall, Baldwin-Whitehall School District, Baldwin-Whitehall Schools Authority, Pleasant Hills Sanitary Authority, South Hills Regional Planning Commission, South Hills Area Council of Governments, City of Pittsburgh, Allegheny County Sanitary Authority, Allegheny County Soil and Water Conservation District, Allegheny County Criminal Justice Commission, Allegheny County Port Authority, Allegheny County, Western Pennsylvania Water Company, and Southwestern Pennsylvania Regional Planning Commission. Had King Minos been around to see Whitehall, he would have had to tip his crown in tribute to this maze. Many of these governments levy taxes, so an individual resident of Whitehall pays taxes or user charges to several different governments at once. [2]

Fragmentation flourishes, but there are wide variations among the states. While the average number of local units per state is over 1,500, Illinois's 6,500 units contrast with Hawaii's 20. Population alone does not explain these differences, for Illinois would have only 320 governments if the Hawaiian ratio of residents to government held in Illinois. Nor is our fragmentated system caused

1. Henry S. Reuss, *Revenue-Sharing* (New York: Praeger, 1970), p. 41.

2. See: Advisory Commission on Intergovernmental Relations, "Regional Decision Making: New Strategies for Substate Districts," A-43 (Washington, D.C.: U.S. Government Printing Office, October 1973), pp. 3–4.

FIGURE 10.1 The St. Louis Urbanized Area—One Example of the "Governmentally Crowded" Modern Metropolis (as of 1970)

SOURCE: Advisory Commission on Intergovernmental Relations, *Improving Urban America: A Challenge to Federalism* (Washington, D.C.: U.S. Government Printing Office, 1976).

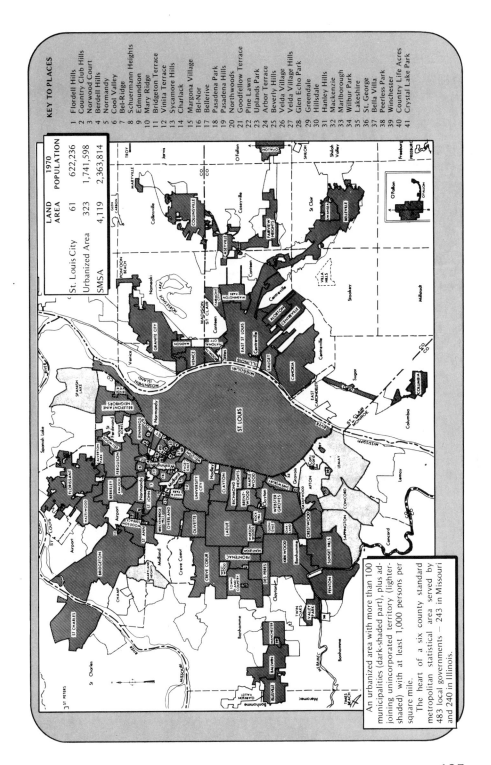

	LAND AREA	1970 POPULATION
St. Louis City	61	622,236
Urbanized Area	323	1,741,598
SMSA	4,119	2,363,814

An urbanized area with more than 100 municipalities (dark-shaded part), plus adjoining unincorporated territory (lighter-shaded) with at least 1,000 persons per square mile.

The heart of a six county standard metropolitan statistical area served by 483 local governments — 243 in Missouri and 240 in Illinois.

KEY TO PLACES

1 Flordell Hills
2 Country Club Hills
3 Norwood Court
4 Berdell Hills
5 Normandy
6 Cool Valley
7 Bel-Ridge
8 Schuermann Heights
9 Edmundson
10 Mary Ridge
11 Bridgeton Terrace
12 Vinita Terrace
13 Sycamore Hills
14 Charlack
15 Margona Village
16 Bel-Nor
17 Bellerive
18 Pasadena Park
19 Pasadena Hills
20 Northwoods
21 Goodfellow Terrace
22 Pine Lawn
23 Uplands Park
24 Arbor Terrace
25 Beverly Hills
26 Velda Village
27 Velda Village Hills
28 Glen Echo Park
29 Greendale
30 Hillsdale
31 Hanley Hills
32 Mackenzie
33 Marlborough
34 Wilbur Park
35 Lakeshire
36 St. George
37 Bella Villa
38 Peerless Park
39 Winchester
40 Country Life Acres
41 Crystal Lake Park

135

by divine edict, since a number of governments have been able either to substantially reduce fragmentation or to avoid it to begin with.

TYPES OF LOCAL GOVERNMENT

Local governments can be divided into two broad types: *general* governments, which carry out a number of different functions, such as health, welfare, highways, police, fire, etc.; and *single-purpose* governments, which carry out only one, or perhaps two, closely related functions, such as water and sewerage, education, or public safety. No matter what the formal name of a local government may be, it is necessary to look at what it actually does before we can conclude whether it is a general or specialized government. Two localities that are called townships, for example, may actually differ greatly in government work load. In the sections that follow, we examine the general governments called municipalities and townships.

MUNICIPALITIES

The term "municipality" derives from the Latin word *municipium*, a label given to Roman cities allowed special privileges. The 18,500 U.S. municipalities, which are usually called cities, towns, or villages, were originally established as providers of local services, such as police and fire protection and public works. Municipalities are legally public corporations, with a charter from their state legislature that spells out what they can and cannot do.

The city is one model of a municipality. Cities are specially chartered by the state legislature so that they can provide more services and security for their residents than other forms of local government. They are usually the most densely populated and commercialized-industrialized areas, and for these reasons need to provide more services. In New York State, for example, cities generally are responsible for streets, police and fire protection, water and sewers, garbage disposal, parks and recreation, hospitals, jails, planning and zoning, licensing of trades, and inspection services and may also provide mental health, airport, and library services.

Other types of municipalities include the town, the village, and the borough. Towns typically take a general charter from the legislature, rather than having one tailor-made for them. This situation reflects the fact that there are many more towns, villages, and boroughs than cities. Furthermore, these units of government do not serve the densely populated industrial areas that cities do, so they usually do not provide as many services as cities. Using New York State as our example again, we find that there are 62 cities and 930 towns. There are

136

only 7 cities under 10,000 population, while the majority of towns are under 10,000 population. Unlike cities, New York towns and villages do *not* provide hospitals, public parking, jails, mental health facilities, airports, or libraries.[3]

These legal restrictions, of course, are just one factor in determining what these local governments actually do. Wealthy communities whose residents feel that local government should provide many services, such as recreation and special education, will offer a number of programs that poorer towns cannot even begin to think about. Many towns, even those within densely populated regions like the Chicago and Los Angeles metropolitan areas, are very small in population and may not even have full-time police and fire protection, relying instead on volunteer services.

TOWNSHIPS

The township furnishes far fewer functions for its residents than municipalities do for theirs. It lacks the degree of discretional authority municipalities have.

The township usually has responsibility for roads, and this may be its only function. (In these cases, it amounts to a *de facto* single-purpose government.) In remote rural areas, townships may become rudimentary forms of local government. Here they provide more services to residents than does any other local government.

The 17,000 townships in the United States are found principally in the north-central states of the Midwest and mid-Atlantic areas. This land was originally part of the national domain, and townships often evolved from federal surveyors' maps (which explains why many of them have neat, geometrical boundaries). Townships declined by 2,000 from 1942 to 1972, the only form of general government to decrease in number.

GRASS ROOTS GOVERNMENT

Our 35,000 townships and municipalities average out to one general government per 6,000 citizens. Since the biggest cities have millions of residents, this means that many towns have only paltry populations. Over half our local governments had fewer than 1,000 residents in 1960, and 85 percent had less than 5,000. One such town is Story, Indiana—population: 112. In 1973 all of Story's seven buildings, including its feed mill, were put up for sale for $34,000.

Grass roots government is not fading away. In 1970, 38 percent of U.S. citizens lived in towns of under 25,000 population outside suburbanized met-

3. See: "Local Government in New York State" (Office for Local Government, June 1973).

ropolitan areas. Polls indicate that these people are envied by many citizens, who list small rural towns second after suburbs as the type of place in which they would most prefer to reside.[4] Indeed, some residents of suburbia try to create their own grass roots governments. Elmwood Park, Wisconsin, with one-sixth square mile of territory and 432 residents, legally incorporated itself as a village in 1960. Not about to sell out its birthright for a sewerage system, Elmwood Park retained its independence even after home septic tanks and the school drainage system failed. The village could have solved its problem by merging with neighboring Racine and tapping its sewer lines, but preferred to live free rather than see its independence die.[5]

There is an interesting relationship between population density and proliferation of governments. The less populated the metropolitan area, the larger the number of units of local government. In other words, the King Minos effect is at its maximum in rural areas. This fact has several important consequences. For one, grass roots government has to be part-time government. Roscoe Martin recounts a visit to a Kentucky village council meeting. The mayor was forced to adjourn the meeting at 4:00 to allow council members to get home to milk their cows before dark. Whatever problems New York city government has, this is not one of them. Writing in 1957, Martin reported that only 37 percent of the employees of towns under 5,000 worked full-time for the town.

Grass roots government is also a government of amateurs. It usually lacks a civil service merit system, a regularized budget system, competitive purchasing, and double-entry accounting. Martin tells the story of a small town mayor who listened to a lecturer advise town officials that a mayor's secretary should control the boss' appointment calendar. The mayor leaned over to the man in the next chair and murmured, "That's very interesting, but what do you do if you don't have a secretary?"[6]

The inevitable outcome of these conditions is the incapacity of grass roots government to perform the increased services demanded of it today. Small towns are increasing in population and are being affected by the wide-scale social changes we discuss in the sections on the economy, social welfare, and criminal justice. These changes make the old ways of doing government business hopelessly inadequate. For instance, small town officials are often unable even to understand and fill out forms requested of them by state environmental protection agencies, much less implement programs in these areas. And lack of

4. Wayne King, "The Small Towns: They Didn't Disappear at All," *New York Times*, 11 November 1973, Section E, 8.

5. Reuss, *Revenue-Sharing*, p. 43.

6. Roscoe C. Martin, *Grass Roots: Rural Democracy in America* (New York: Harper & Row, 1964), pp. 33–41.

138

professionalism is illustrated by the tax assessor of a small New England town who would respond to complaints about his assessments by raising them.

LOCAL VARIATIONS ON FRAGMENTATION: GOVERNMENT STRUCTURE AND SERVICE DELIVERY

The King Minos approach can be seen in the many cases where there is more than one local general government affecting residents of a certain area. In some states, township governments may have villages or cities within them, serving the most densely settled areas of the township. These cities have their own charters and are thus legally independent of the township. Such a city may leave the township precious little to do, since the city provides most services to most of the population. Another pattern is found in Windham, Connecticut, a rural town government which runs the school system for itself and for the city of Willimantic, which is located within the boundaries of Windham. Willimantic residents are thus directly affected by two local governments, the city and the town. A third variation is for the central, more populated part of a municipality, often called a borough, to provide certain services, such as water or sewerage, only to residents in that part of town. Its residents receive the bulk of their local services from the larger municipality of which they are also a part.

As if these practices were not puzzling enough, the same labels are often used to mean different things. A New England town often has far more authority than towns in other regions. A township in Pennsylvania may carry out all the services of any city, while a midwestern township may have only a few minor functions. The same holds true for boroughs in New Jersey, which may be very active compared to their specialized New England namesakes. Cities with different types of charters may be legally able to do very different things. The distinctions among types of general local government are fading slowly, but at present you almost need a program before you can figure out the local government game.

Local government fragmentation can be exploited in ingenious ways. Ludowici, Georgia was for years a notorious speed trap for winter tourists en route from northern climes to Florida. The tourist would be driving along a road with posted limits of 45 miles per hour and then suddenly find himself in Ludowici with a posted 10 m.p.h. limit. With enviable efficiency, a Ludowici police car would pull the tourist's vehicle over at the instant it crossed the town line, and escort it to traffic court, where a substantial fine would be levied. Traffic fines were, indeed, Ludowici's chief source of revenue. In 1970, Governor Lester Maddox, angered at these conditions, erected billboards warning drivers to slow down before they hit Ludowici.. Local officials were so irate at this

139

interference in their affairs that Maddox felt it necessary to assign state troopers to guard the billboards.[7] This example makes one ponder the case of Puerto Rico, comparable in population to our average state. The Puerto Ricans have only one police, fire, and school department, all of which are reported to work fairly well.

MUNICIPAL AND TOWNSHIP EXECUTIVES AND LEGISLATURES

Further confusing the beginner trying to master the maze of local government are the myriad forms and functions of chief executives and legislatures. In this chapter and the next one we will briefly review some of the general characteristics of these different forms, and in Chapter 12 we will discuss their political dynamics.

Executives

Cities, townships, and towns over 25,000 population usually have one of three types of chief executive: a mayor, a manager, or a commissioner.

Mayors may be elected directly or chosen from among the members of the local legislature; they may have much or little formal authority. The mayor of New London, Connecticut, for example , is the councilman who gets the most votes in the election. He presides over council meetings, cuts ribbons to open new buildings, and gives up the job after one year to another councilman. Contrast the mayor of New London with the mayor of Paterson, New Jersey, who is elected by the voters to his post, and who has the authority to replace all department heads in the city government. Until recently, he had the authority to draw up the budget without interference from the city council. It is no coincidence that the Paterson City Hall has stained glass windows with pictures of past mayors rather than the saints.

The mayoralty is the foremost form of chief executive in cities over 500,000; over 80 percent of these cities have mayors. Political writers have surmised that this is so because these socially and economically diverse cities need a political leader who can act as a broker among different groups. Certainly this is the way the late Mayor Richard Daley of Chicago defined his role as mayor.

Only 40 percent of cities of 10,000 to 500,000 have the mayoralty. More popular than the mayoralty in these localities of 10,000 to 500,000 is the city or town manager form of executive. Conversely, only one-fifth of cities over

7. *Newsweek* (27 April 1970), p. 35.

140

500,000 are run by managers. The city manager is a full-time professional employee appointed by the local legislature to be the chief executive officer of its government. The legislature can remove the manager at any time, by majority vote. The manager usually has full legal authority over administrative matters such as personnel, purchasing, or budgeting, but has no formal voting or veto powers.

Adding to the confusion of local government is the presence of mayors in most manager governments. For the most part, these mayors are limited to the kind of ceremonial tasks performed by the mayor of New London, which is a manager city. But in some manager localities, such as Hartford, Connecticut, the mayor is a more important figure, elected in his own right, with authority to veto ordinances passed by the council. In this book, we use the term "mayoralty" to mean the office of mayor in a mayor-council form of government, not the office of mayor in manager-council government.

The rationale behind the manager form of government, and related reforms like nonpartisan (no party labels on the ballot) local elections, is that it is best to keep politics separate from administration. By letting the manager administer, say the advocates of manager government, we will get the most efficient, economical, professional, and honest administration. By letting the politicians or elected officials develop policy, the manager will be left free to devote all his time to deciding how best to implement these policies.

Regardless of whether or not one feels that this policy-administration dichotomy would be a good thing, the fact is that no one has yet been able to compartmentalize politics and administration so neatly. Most politicos are interested in influencing both phases of policymaking, and many do influence both, regardless of whether or not a manager is running things. Complicating the picture is our inability to distinguish politics and administration in a way that would satisfy everyone. For example, the mayor of Oakland, California argued in 1968 that police department policy on use of weapons should be changed by the city council. The city manager disagreed, stating that a *policy* decision would be that police officers should carry guns, but the questions of when, where, and how they should use their guns constituted *administrative* decisions.[8] No matter how they label it, most managers will become involved with policy questions. Indeed, city councils expect them to do so more often than not. In fact, many localities would start to look for a new manager if their manager consistently refused to come up with suggestions for new policies.

City manager government has enjoyed a slow but steady rate of increase in all but the largest cities, at the expense of the mayoralty and the third type of

8. Jeffrey L. Pressman, "Preconditions of Mayoral Leadership," *American Political Science Review* (June 1972), pp. 511–524.

141

executive form, the commission form. The commission is a fusion of the executive and legislative branches. Elected commissioners make up not only the local legislature, but the executive department heads as well. In addition, one commissioner serves as mayor, usually receiving this post because he got the most votes in the election or on the basis of rotation. Thus, one commissioner can simultaneously be mayor, commissioner of public works, and a city councilman.

The commission form spread rapidly after it was judged to have been effective in helping Galveston, Texas deal with the emergency created by a catastrophic hurricane in 1902. Since 1945, however, the number of commissioner municipalities has declined steadily. Today, less than five percent of localities of 10,000 to 500,000, and none of those over 500,000, use the commission form. Moreover, cities that use this form are characteristically older industrial cities declining in population and tax base, so the future of the city commission does not look particularly rosy.

Many small localities use other plural executive forms that lack the legislative authority of commissions. These include the board of selectmen, found in New England towns, and the boards of trustees, supervisors, burgesses, or wardens, as they are variously called, in northeastern and midwestern townships. These elected boards of three or more members are the chief executive authority in their governments. One of their number usually has the primary executive role. In the New England town, for instance, he is called the *first* selectman. But since these boards consist of several executives, there is nothing to stop the other selectmen (or commissioners, trustees, supervisors, burgesses, or wardens) from disagreeing with and stymieing the primary executive. Since he usually needs a majority vote of the board before he can act, the other board members can hamstring him. And this they will assuredly do at least part of the time if they are members of the opposing political party. In 1976, Newtown, Connecticut residents were witness to the edifying spectacle of the Democratic first selectman and the Republican second selectman branding one another "crybaby" and "sore loser." Government business often proceeded at a snail's speed, since the first selectman was the only member of his party on the board.

In addition, chief executives in both small and large localities often have to face competition from other independently elected executive officials. In the New England town, not only the selectmen, but also the town clerk, treasurer, and tax assessor are often elected in their own right. In New York City, the comptroller, who is the chief financial officer of the city, is elected. Comptrollers not only have substantial authority to defy the mayor, but also often eventually run for mayor themselves. During the post–1973 fiscal crisis, Comptroller Harrison Goldin kept up a steady stream of criticism against Mayor Abraham Beame for his fiscal management. Whether he is in the right or the wrong, the local chief

142

executive's ability to manage his government is weakened by independently elected officials.

Legislatures

There is just as much variety among local legislative bodies as there is among executives. In most cities over 25,000, though, the legislature is either a city council (sometimes called a board of aldermen) or the commission.

City councilmen or commissioners can be elected in one of two ways: from a specific geographic area, usually called a ward or a district, or on an at-large basis, by all the voters of the city. Many councils use both methods, as does Newark, New Jersey, where five councilmen are elected by wards and four at-large.

The municipal reform movement, which pushed both the manager plan and the idea of nonpartisan elections (which we will examine in Chapter 12), also supported at-large elections. The reformers believed that legislators oriented to specific districts and neighborhoods could never take a broad view of what was best for the city as a whole, but would always put the narrow interests of their ward above all else. As a result of the reformers' work, we now have many more at-large elections than we did at the turn of the century.

There is some evidence that the reformers' expectations about the effect of at-large elections were accurate. In Boston, the city council switched from district to at-large representation in 1949. Before the switch, hundreds of resolutions requesting street improvements in specific neighborhoods were passed; after the switch, only about twenty a year passed.

That at-large contests have a centralizing impact is probably correct; whether or not this is desirable requires a value judgment. We do have representative government, and how representative is a government that ignores requests for needed street repairs? We also have a system that values minority rights as well as majority rule. Under the district system, Irish Boston's city council had a membership that was 11 percent Jewish, 9 percent Yankee, 4 percent Italian, and 1 percent black. But of the first forty-five councilmen elected after the switch to at-large districts, thirty-nine were Irish and six Italian, with no Jews, Yankees, or blacks.[9]

The New England town's traditional legislature was a town meeting of all voters and property owners, and this form survives in hundreds of smaller New England localities today. Its procedures recognize the right of any voter or taxpayer to speak as well as to vote, and the town meeting represents a true form

9. Edward C. Banfield and James Q. Wilson, *City Politics* (Cambridge, Mass.: Harvard University Press, 1963), pp. 94–95.

143

of grass-roots democracy. (Some townships also have township meetings, but usually these lack the full authority or guaranteed right to participate of the New England town meeting.)

In theory the town meeting sounds akin to the glory and greatness of ancient Greek democracy. But a closer inspection of the town meeting reveals flaws (just as Greek democracy had flaws, such as slavery). All studies report a very small proportion of the electorate participating in the town meeting. Even when a red-hot issue arises, such as a decision whether or not to impose zoning controls, or to cut the budget in a recession, it is rare for as many as 10 percent of the electorate to attend. In Stoneham, Massachusetts, attendance was so low in 1973 that it did not constitute a quorum, and the meeting could not proceed. The selectmen then decided to award door prizes—turkeys and free dinners—to encourage future attendance.[10]

One group that *is* faithfully in attendance consists of town officials and employees. Often, they pack meetings so that the budget can be gavelled through with impressive efficiency. One of the authors once arrived five minutes late for the annual town budget meeting in Montville, Connecticut, to find that it was over.

As towns and townships grow larger, they usually evolve from the town meeting to a form called the representative town meeting (RTM). A large number of elected legislators (usually 50 to 150) have the sole right to vote, but townspeople can still speak their piece from the floor. The RTM usually evolves into a council form of government as the community grows larger. The council has fewer members and no guaranteed right for townspeople to be heard from the floor.

These, then, are some of the varieties of municipal legislatures. We will examine the politics and power of some of these legislatures and their executive branches in Chapter 11.

10. Gary Kayakachoian, "Town Meeting for the Birds," *Boston Globe*, 8 November 1973, p. 1.

144

THE MAZE OF LOCAL GOVERNMENT: SPECIAL DISTRICTS AND COUNTIES

CHAPTER ELEVEN

SPECIAL DISTRICTS AND SCHOOL DISTRICTS

Special districts usually supply only one specific service of government, such as mosquito control or soil conservation, although some special districts provide closely related services, such as water supply and sewerage. We have lumped special districts together with school districts in this discussion, because both are *single-purpose governments,* usually providing only one service instead of the range of services a municipality offers. There were a total of nearly 40,000 single-purpose governments in 1976, meaning that they outnumbered municipalities and townships by about 5,000.

145

The growth rates of these two single-purpose agencies are very different. There has been a drastic reduction in the number of school districts, from 108,000 in 1942 to 16,000 in 1975. This has not been caused by a reduction in the number of schoolchildren, but by the combination of many of the smaller districts into larger ones. Special districts, on the other hand, are the fastest-growing type of local government, more than doubling in number from 1952 to 1972. In 1976, there were over 24,000 special districts, making them the most numerous form of local government in the U.S.A. Eight of the fourteen governments of Whitehall, Pennsylvania, listed at the beginning of the previous chapter, are special districts.

Special districts provide almost every type of local government service. In 1972, according to the federal Advisory Commission for Intergovernmental Relations, the most popular type of special district was the fire protection district; there were almost 4,000 of these. Other popular functions were soil conservation, housing and urban renewal, water supply, drainage, cemeteries, and sewers, but there were also special districts for electric and gas supply, libraries, transit, and health. Less than 4 percent of the districts had more than one function, and two-thirds of these were in the related areas of sewage and water supply.[1] Table 11.1 shows the functions of special districts in three different years.

As we shall see in more detail in the chapter on education, school districts have historically had independence from the rest of local government. A separate board of education runs the schools, and its budget and personnel are insulated from the control of the general government's legislature and executive. School districts make the coordination of local government services more difficult by their very existence. Just as it is more difficult to get a group of three people to decide how they want to spend an evening than it is for one person to make that decision, it is more difficult to coordinate the efforts of several independent governments operating in the same geographical area than to coordinate the various departments of one government. Since special districts are structured in the same way as school districts, the problems created by single-purpose governments rival the difficulties involved in escaping from King Minos's labyrinth.

We have already remarked that special districts are the most numerous and fastest-growing form of local government. Why is this so? One cause is the legal restrictions on the ability of local governments to tax themselves or accumulate debt. Since the states set tax and debt limits, many cities cannot bond or tax

---

1. See: Advisory Commission on Intergovernmental Relations, "Regional Decision-Making: New Strategies for Substate Districts," A-43 (Washington, D.C.: U.S. Government Printing Office, October 1973), pp. 19–47.

TABLE 11.1 TYPES OF SPECIAL DISTRICTS: 1962, 1967, 1972

TYPE OF DISTRICT	1972	1967	1962	PERCENT CHANGE 1967–72	1962–72
SINGLE FUNCTION DISTRICTS					
Cemeteries	1,496	1,397	1,283	7.1	16.6
School Buildings	1,085	956	915	13.5	18.6
Fire Protection	3,872	3,665	3,229	5.6	19.9
Highways	698	774	786	−9.8	−11.2
Health	257	234	231	9.8	11.3
Hospitals	655	537	418	22.0	56.7
Housing and Urban Renewal	2,270	1,565	1,099	45.0	106.6
Libraries	498	410	349	21.5	14.0
Drainage	2,192	2,193	2,240	−0.0	−2.1
Flood Control	677	662	500	2.3	35.4
Irrigation and Water Conservation	966	904	781	6.9	23.7
Soil Conservation	2,564	2,571	2,461	0.3	4.2
Other Natural Resources	231	209	309	10.5	−25.2
Parks and Recreation	749	613	488	22.2	53.5
Sewers	1,406	1,233	937	14.0	50.1
Water Supply	2,323	2,140	1,502	8.6	54.7
Electric Power	74	75	76	−1.3	−2.6
Gas Supply	48	37	30	29.7	60.0
Transit	33	14	10	135.7	230.0
Other	889	622	488	42.9	82.2
MULTIPLE-FUNCTION DISTRICTS					
Sewer and Water Supply	629	298	138	111.1	355.8
Natural Resource and Water Supply	67	45	56	48.9	19.6
Other	207	110	120	88.2	72.5

SOURCE: U.S. Bureau of the Census.

themselves to provide new services. Another cause is the great expense of some of these services, such as water supply, sewage treatment, or trash incineration. If the cost can be spread over a wide area, economies will result. For these two reasons, the appeal of a single-purpose agency extending over a broad geographical area, unhampered by debt and tax limits, is substantial.

Since special districts are surging so spectacularly, they pose even more problems for coordination of services than do school districts. Paradoxically, while special districts were created in part to overcome problems of service delivery caused in the first place by governmental fragmentation, they have increased fragmentation. An example should make the point clear. In the postwar period, many rural towns quickly became suburbs when city residents moved out to the country. These towns eventually found it necessary to install

147

municipal water supply systems, because there were too many houses for each to have its own well. Yet how was a small town to develop its own reservoir system? A typical solution to the problem was the creation of a water supply special district, which would provide water to several towns, thereby sharing the costs of a reservoir system among them. Thus, the problems caused by the fragmentation of local government into small units were overcome in this one policy area. However, at the same time, *fragmentation* was increased by the creation of yet another local government—the independent water district, which generated its own revenues through the sale of water to users in the district. While the immediate problem was solved, then, future attempts to coordinate policy with related areas like sewerage disposal and flood control were inevitably complicated by the existence of additional units that would have to be coordinated. For this reason, many specialists in public administration look askance at the spread of special districts.

An example of the problems that can be created by the spread of special districts is a situation that occurred in Bridgeton Terrace, Missouri, in October 1963. The telephone operator who received word of a residential fire called the Community Fire Protection District, which advised her it was not their jurisdiction. The operator then called the Pattonville-Bridgeton Volunteer District, which went to the fire. These volunteers couldn't enter the burning house immediately because their masks did not work. Once in the house, they operated their inhalators incorrectly. As a result of the delay and incompetence, two girls died of smoke inhalation. In the wake of the furor over this incident, upset citizens and officials made a serious attempt to merge the county's fifty-two fire districts into one unit. But the jurisdictional jungle remained intact in the face of opposition from many individual fire districts.[2]

The Governance of Special Districts

As mentioned previously, school districts are almost always run by a multi-member board separate from the local general government. In the chapter on education, we will examine the operation of those boards in more detail.

Boards are also the usual bosses of special district business. In 1967, 58 percent of the members of these boards were elected, while 42 percent were appointed by local officials. The usual pattern is to have chief executives of general governments appoint members representing their government to special districts that operate in their areas. In practice, more than 42 percent of board members are appointed, for often election turnouts are so low that the elections must be cancelled under the law. Rather than hold another election, the law may

2. Henry S. Reuss, *Revenue-Sharing* (New York: Praeger, 1970), p. 77.

call for appointments, or vacancies may go unfilled. A study of the San Francisco area found that median turnout at special district elections was 27 percent, compared to 45 percent in county and 67 percent in city elections. Elsewhere it is often far lower, as the 4 percent turnout for all special district elections in Oregon from 1954 to 1964 shows.[3] Most students of the subject believe that this low turnout occurs because voters are overwhelmed by the great number of governments they confront, and simply have neither the inclination nor the time to follow all the issues and candidates.

The net effect of this low turnout in elections and the alternative appointment mechanism is to make special district government more autonomous. As John Bollens has written, "Appointed governing-body members are at best twice removed from the voters, and residents can seldom legally bring a direct recall action against any of them."[4] In other words, even though special districts are originally created by local action, once they are formed, there is often little lingering local control.

Other reasons for autonomy include less stringent debt and tax limits, one of the reasons the districts are created in the first place. Often taxpayers are not even aware of the taxes they pay to special districts, since these taxes are frequently collected by the county along with its own general taxes. Many special districts raise revenues through user charges, such as water and sewage fees, further liberating them from fiscal constraints. And certainly the customer who doesn't like his bill can't go to the competition—the water or sewer district is the only show in town.

While special districts have often supplied essential security and services, and have done so efficiently, Bollens's indictment seems to hit the nail on the head: "Simply stated, there are too many separate governments, and special districts are largely responsible. If 'grass roots government' means broadly based public control, it is frequently an illusion in special districts. A very important way to improve citizen control and to solve the problem is to have fewer special districts. . . . Many of them should be absorbed into other types of government."[5]

A Case Study: An Empire of Special Districts

The extremes of independence to which special districts and those who direct them can go is illustrated by the forty-year career of New York's Robert Moses.

3. Advisory Commission, "Regional Decision-Making," pp. 33–34.
4. John C. Bollens, *Special District Governments in the United States* (Berkeley: University of California Press, 1957), p. 251.
5. Ibid.

149

In the 1920s, Moses was director of the Long Island State Park Commission, a special district designed to serve the masses of metropolitan New York. He was able to persuade the state legislature to set up other special highway districts, which he also headed, to get people to his parks. At one point, Moses was simultaneously head of many state and city agencies, including New York City's departments of housing and parks, the Triborough Bridge and Tunnel Authority, the Henry Hudson Parkway Authority, and a host of others. He had accumulated so much power that he was able to keep New York mayor Fiorello LaGuardia waiting in his office, fuming with anger at Moses' tardiness, but unable to do anything about it. Once a visitor entered Moses' office and heard him call the speaker on the other end of the telephone "a goddam son of a bitch," after which he hung up. When his visitor asked to whom Moses had been speaking, Moses replied that it was New York's Governor Dewey. And like LaGuardia, Dewey found it impossible to rid himself of Moses.

Moses was able to act this way in impunity because of the vast revenues produced by the tolls on his highways, bridges, and tunnels. He used them to lend money to the city of New York and to provide patronage jobs for followers of party chieftains. He thus cemented his support in city and state so strongly that he could operate independently of elected chief executives and legislatures. His power was impressive enough that onlookers wondered if he was about to emulate his biblical namesake by rolling back the waters of the Hudson River. Moses had admirers, to be sure, but his accomplishments did not include increased coordination of policy in New York government. He was rather head of a vast state within a state, which went in a direction all its own.[6]

Prospects for the Special District

The poet William Blake once wrote, "Mock on, mock on . . . you throw the sand against the wind, and the wind blows it back again." This is the experience of the critics of the special district, for all their diatribes and denunciation do not seem to have slowed the growth of special districts one iota. Most special districts are found outside urban areas, where population is too small to support functions performed by the district unless they are shared among several localities. Yet one-third of special districts are found in urban areas, and the growth rate of urban districts has been just as high for those in rural areas since 1945, indicating that the increasing urbanization of the country is not going to slow down the rate of special district increase. Unless there are major changes in our governmental

6. Robert A. Caro's *The Power Broker* (New York: Alfred E. Knopf, 1974) is a massive and monumental analysis of Moses' career.

structure, then, fragmentation caused by the proliferation of special district governments should continue to increase.

COUNTIES

The county is, fittingly, the final form of local government we examine, because it encompasses all the other forms of local government within its boundaries. Counties, a form of general government, are easily the largest local governments in area, which explains why there are far fewer (3,000) of them than any other type of local government. King County, Texas, for example, is larger than the state of Rhode Island. It is not uncommon for there to be a hundred or more municipalities, townships, school districts, and special districts within the confines of a county. In addition, there may be unincorporated areas over which the county does not share its jurisdiction with any other local governments.

Counties are important units of government in all parts of the country except the six New England states. In New England, the town existed prior to the county and assumed a vigorous role early in its history. This did not leave the New England counties much to do after they were formed beyond electing a sheriff and operating jails. In the twentieth century, Rhode Island completely abolished its counties, and Connecticut left its counties with sheriffs who do little more than officiate at the opening of the state legislature. The other New England states have continued to operate marginal county governments, whose functions could easily be absorbed tomorrow by the state or by other local governments without much trouble.

The explanation for the relative insignificance of the township is to be found in the importance of the county. New England towns were important because counties were inactive. Conversely, the township of the north central states never attained the significance of the New England town, because it always dwelt in the shadow of the county.

Counties are more subject to state regulation than towns and cities, for they were originally designed as local branches of the state government. Counties were to keep the peace, through the operation of criminal justice systems, and do the paperwork, whether it involved birth certificates, licenses, or deeds. Road building was another common task. This subordination to the state explains the symmetrical boundaries of many counties, especially those of the West and Middle West. The state governments simply divided the state into rectangular districts, for administrative convenience, and called them counties. City boundaries were more irregular in shape because they reflected the way people had settled.

151

The county has changed more than other forms of local government. Historically limited in the scope of their powers and responsibilities, many counties have greatly expanded their regulatory activity and service delivery. In 1976, fully two-fifths of the states had granted increased home rule or decision-making authority to the counties, allowing them greater discretion in determining both the form of county government and the scope of activity of county agencies. The National Association of Counties reports that counties offer fifty-eight different types of services, ranging from fire protection through rehabilitation of crippled children to operation of museums, airports, and zoos. See Table 11.2 for a government compilation of county functions. By any measure, counties are spending a larger relative share of each local taxpayer's income each year, and they already account for over one-fifth of the money spent by all local governments. Nassau County, N.Y. has a vigorous consumer protection program, involving both educational and publicity efforts and investigation of complaints. The four services on which counties spend two-thirds of their total budgets are welfare, education, highways, and hospitals. Highways, a traditional county function, have not kept up with the three other functions or with a host of other services in rate of growth, indicating that counties are expanding and diversifying their services.[7]

TABLE 11.2 RANK ORDER OF FUNCTIONS PERFORMED BY 150 URBAN COUNTY GOVERNMENTS

FUNCTION	NUMBER	PERCENT OF TOTAL
1. Jails and detention homes	145	97
2. Coronor's office	130	87
3. Courts	130	87
4. Tax assessment collection	125	83
5. Public health	120	80
6. Prosecution	120	80
7. Probation and parole service	119	79
8. Police protection	117	78
9. Roads and highways	117	78
10. General assistance public welfare	114	76
11. Planning	114	76
12. Agricultural extension services	112	75
13. Medical assistance	105	70
14. Mental health	104	60

7. Susan Walker Torrence, *Grass Roots Government: The County in American Politics* (Washington, D.C.: Robert B. Luce, 1974), pp. 21–44.

FUNCTION	NUMBER	PERCENT OF TOTAL
15. Libraries	86	57
16. Veteran's affairs	86	57
17. Parks and recreation	83	55
18. Zoning	82	55
19. Crippled children	78	52
20. Public defender	77	51
21. Subdivision control	77	51
22. Animal control	75	51
23. Data processing	65	43
24. Code enforcement	63	42
25. Hospitals	61	41
26. Central purchasing	60	40
27. Soil conservation	59	39
28. Secondary schools	58	39
29. Special education programs	57	38
30. Mosquito abatement	56	37
31. Elementary schools	56	37
32. Solid waste disposal	55	37
33. Air pollution	55	37
34. Personnel services	52	35
35. Flood and drainage control	51	34
36. Sewers and sewage disposal	50	33
37. Fire protection	47	31
38. Water pollution	45	30
39. Junior colleges	40	27
40. Airports	36	24
41. Livestock inspection	34	23
42. Ambulance service	34	23
43. Industrial development	32	21
44. Refuse and garbage collection	31	21
45. Water supply	31	21

SOURCE: Advisory Commission on Intergovernmental Relations, *Profile of County Government* (Washington, D.C.: U.S. Government Printing Office, 1972), p. 23.

Counties also regulate human behavior. Almost all of them have a law enforcement officer, usually the sheriff. In addition, urban counties may maintain standards for restaurant cleanliness, drug abuse, and air pollution. Perhaps the key county regulatory activity today is zoning, which determines how land will be used—whether for commercial, industrial, residential, or park and forest development. Zoning practices can be very controversial; few homeowners want to see a factory, town garage, or landfill dump near their homes, while those supporting such actions may argue that the location is best for the county as a

153

whole. Developers will seek the smallest possible residential lot size; those who want to keep the tax rate down and have the community change as little as possible will argue for larger required size lots. Those who want to keep the property tax down will support industrial and commercial zoning, while those who want to preserve a semi-rural character will fight these changes.

The area of zoning provides a good illustration of another facet of the local government labyrinth. County zoning authority usually stops at the city line, preventing consistent zoning policy for the county as a whole. Black Jack, Missouri, an area of 2.7 square miles, became a city in 1970 to avoid coming under the county's zoning authority. The county wanted to zone Black Jack for a multi-family, moderate income housing development. Black Jack residents wanted no part of this, and by incorporating as a city were able to stymie the county. (As of 1976, the matter was in federal court.)[8]

On the other hand, many contemporary counties have come a long way in accumulating both legal authority and political muscle. This enables them to fight the incorporation of new municipalities. DuPage County, Illinois has fought for years to frustrate new incorporations. It encouraged municipalities with which it was friendly to expand into areas antagonistic municipalities might also wish to acquire. It supported municipalities that used their legal power to zone 1½ miles into bordering unincorporated areas for the same reason. Several other techniques, including the *quo warranto* lawsuit, which puts the burden of proof on a municipality to show that it gained its incorporated status precisely according to law, were also used. The result in one case was the destruction of the village of ˙ Weston, which had dared to oppose the construction of a massive atom smasher in its territory. (The county was even able to persuade the U.S. Post Office to locate the mailboxes of Weston residents several hundred feet from their homes.)[9]

Friction between county and other local officials is not limited to the area of zoning. In Bergen County, New Jersey, police officers of one township made it a practice to follow county police cars when they drove on county highways through the township. The township police would turn on their overhead blinker light, making clear they did not appreciate the presence of the county police in their bailiwick. (The county police solved this particular problem by turning off the traffic lights on county highways in the township and hopelessly snarling traffic, thereby inducing the local police to end their tailing practice.) In Fayette County, Kentucky, a man with four bullets in him lay in the street while city and county police debated their jurisdiction in the case.[10]

8. *Time* (26 April 1971), pp. 19–20.

9. Theodore J. Lowi et al., *Poliscide* (New York: Macmillan, 1976), pp. 175–194.

10. Torrence, *Grass Roots Government*, p. 66.

Since the county is much larger in area than other local governments, and encompasses a large number of municipalities and single-purpose districts, some reformers have argued that the county affords a fine way to finish off fragmentation, through consolidation of local governments. We will explore this topic further in Chapter 13.

The Governance of Counties

Most county governments use the commission form, which we have already described in the section on local government. In addition, some 350 counties have an appointed manager to handle administrative duties. Another 50 have a directly elected county executive, analogous to a municipal mayor.

In most counties commissioners (sometimes called supervisors, and referred to as freeholders in New Jersey) share authority with various boards and special districts, as is the case in most municipalities and townships. In addition, they must share authority with officers responsible for functions ordered by the state. Sometimes elected and sometimes appointed by the state, these officials often hold the posts of sheriff, clerk or recorder, treasurer, auditor, and coroner. These officials are free to cooperate with or defy the commissioners, as they see fit. Susan Walker Torrence, author of one of the best introductions to county government, contends that this lack of control by the commissioners is not a serious problem today. She argues that these positions are not policy oriented and often not even necessary, but exist only because state constitutions and statutes mandate them.[11] Perhaps this is true most of the time, but this host of independent officers cannot help coordination or lighten the load on the tax-payer's wallet. Moreover, as the section on criminal justice indicates, both the sheriff and coroner often perform disastrous disservices to the citizenry. And Torrence admits that the lack of stipulated qualifications for becoming assessor and treasurer are serious problems, since these officials determine how much income is required for the county each year. In 1968, only four states had statewide criteria for the occupants of these highly technical posts.

In the 2,600 counties without managers or elected executives, the commissioners function just as city commissioners do, serving as both department heads and legislators. Faced with rapid growth, which has turned them into urban areas, 350 counties have adopted a county manager system. These counties number about 12 percent of the total, but contain 28 percent of the population of the nation.

Managers, who are called chief administrative officers, county adminis-

---

11. Ibid, p. 72.

trators, or appointed county executives in some counties, vary in formal responsibility. More than is the case with municipal managers, there are "weak" county managers who act primarily as staff consultants to the commission and who do not supervise departments or hire and fire employees. "Strong" managers, such as the one in Dade County, Florida, have authority over budget preparation, personnel decisions, and departmental supervision. In strong manager forms, the commissioners no longer act in an executive capacity, but function only as legislators. Full-time department heads under the supervision of the manager take on administrative responsibilities. The commissioners will often rubber stamp the proposals of these administrators. Such a case occurred in 1971, when Los Angeles residents suddenly discovered that Jefferson Boulevard was being decorated with $74,000 of plastic trees. This proposal by the head of the road department had been automatically accepted by the commission.[12]

The fifty elected county executives, like the manager, are found in densely populated urban areas, such as metropolitan Maryland and New York State. Most of them are strong full-time executives, comparable to the county manager in this regard. In addition, they are able to play the partisan political game in a much more uninhibited fashion than the manager. This can help skillful executives get the support they need for major controversial changes. Commissioners are elected independently of the executive and function only as a legislature.

Even managers and executives often confront independently elected officers, semi-autonomous commissions, and special districts. In Baltimore County, for example, the departments of education, health, libraries, and social services have varying degrees of independence from the county executive. While internal fragmentation in counties is on the decline, then, we still have a long way to go to achieve widespread coordination. And even if such fragmentation were ended, this is not equivalent in itself to increased county authority to coordinate other local governments within the county, as we shall see in Chapter 13.

12. Ibid, pp. 78–80.

POWER IN LOCAL GOVERNMENT

CHAPTER TWELVE

STUDYING POWER

There are almost as many definitions of and dissertations on power as there are political scientists. Power is defined in this chapter as the ability to get what one wants from other people, even when they oppose giving it. We call those people who try to get power politicians. These definitions would not please all political scientists, but are adequate for our discussion.

Since there is no case on record of any human being getting everything he wanted from others, no one has yet enjoyed complete power. Some politicians, though, such as Philadelphia's Mayor Rizzo, have much more power than most of the rest of their fellow citizens. Political power, then, is a comparative relationship among human beings, not an absolute.

People often make statements about who the most powerful persons in a community are. But just as often, finding a community's controllers is about as easy as finding the pot of gold at the end of the rainbow. Why is this so?

Power is a puzzle because the perceptions of political participants and onlookers color their judgments about it. One person, for example, may define the powerful as those who hand out government jobs and patronage, while others are primarily interested in policy questions, such as the shape of the local highway system or school curricula. One's perceptions will vary with his vantage point: a member of a local party committee watches town politics with a different perspective from the member of a school board. If there are variations in policymaking and power relations between these areas, one observer may conclude that the mayor, for example, is weaker than the other observer thinks. Finally, one's personal values may influence his conclusions. Strong positive or negative feelings about a politician may influence the onlooker to believe that he or she is stronger or weaker than is actually true. For example, those who strongly dislike a mayor may make him a scapegoat for the city's problems, thereby implicitly attributing more power to him than he actually wields. Many New Yorkers made such a judgment of Mayor John Lindsay in the late 1960s and early 1970s, attributing to him a measure of power he surely wished he had.

The study of power is an imprecise and impressive task. But since the obstacles observed above have never stopped human beings from being fascinated with political power, they will not stop us from looking at power relations in local general government in this chapter.

COMMUNITY POWER STRUCTURE

The term *community power structure* has been used by social scientists who have done research to see who really runs things in localities. Communities in which power is shared by a relatively large number of individuals, groups, and institutions are defined as *pluralistic* power structures. Those in which power is in the hands of a small group are said to have an *elitist* structure. Included in these definitions is the notion that there is a diversity of opinion about political issues under pluralism, while the opinions of leaders in an elitist structure are similar. Pluralism denotes *competition* in both ideas and political factions. Elitism indicates a *monopoly* of opinion and leadership by a small group.

These different types of power structure are illustrated by two of the most important studies in the field. In the early 1950s, sociologist Floyd Hunter

158

examined Atlanta, Georgia in detail.[1] He concluded that it was dominated by a small number of businessmen who thought alike and worked together to resolve the major issues confronting the city. Whether these issues were economic development or racial relations, Hunter reported that the same names and faces kept turning up in his investigation. This is the kind of power structure we call elitist. Perhaps the most extreme example of elitism yet uncovered is that of Muncie, Indiana in the 1920s.[2] Researchers found that just one family, to whom they referred as the X family, dominated almost every aspect of local life, from the X plant to the X bank, the X college, the X hospital, the X political party, the X charities, the X YMCA, the X newspaper, and the X airport.

In the mid-1950s, political scientist Robert Dahl studied New Haven, Connecticut and found a very different pattern of power.[3] Rather than being dominated by a small, like-minded group, New Haven politics were the playing field of a wide variety of disparate politicians. In education, for example, the key movers were school officials and parent groups; in urban renewal, the mayor and his personal staff; and in nominations to political office, party officials and workers. Furthermore, the nature of agreement on the issues varied with the issue and the area. In some cases, consensus on what to do was reached quickly and easily; in others, bargaining over a protracted period was necessary. This type of power structure we call pluralistic.

The reader should be aware that our description is a simplification of several hundred sophisticated studies. For example, a battle rages over the methods used by researchers, which are different. There seems to be a connection between the methods and academic disciplines and the findings of power researchers. Political scientists focused on decisions and found pluralistic structures, while sociologists probed for those who had a reputation for power, and found elitism. However, enough research has been done to indicate that there are indeed different types of power structures. Take contemporary Jersey City, New Jersey. Mayor Paul Jordan shared power with the local legislature, party leaders, and interest groups in 1977. His influence was a good deal different from that of "Boss" Frank Hague, whose party organization ruled Jersey City with an iron hand from the 1920s until 1949. Hague once listened to some complaints from local businessmen, who threatened to organize themselves against him. He responded by telling each businessman what favors he had received from the organization, which laws he was violating, and the money he owed to banks of which Hague was a director. He also noted that some

1. Floyd Hunter, *Community Power Structure* (Chapel Hill, N.C.: University of North Carolina Press, 1953).

2. Robert S. Lynd and Helen M. Lynd, *Middletown* (New York: Harcourt and Brace, 1929).

3. Robert A. Dahl, *Who Governs?* (New Haven, Conn.: Yale University Press, 1961).

159

businessmen had relatives on the city payroll, while others engaged in business practices they would not want made public. He then walked out on his stunned and stupefied audience.

Another caveat to be considered is the oversimplification inherent in discussing only two types of power structure. There are in reality scores of different types of relationships. For example, in some pluralistic systems, five groupings share power; in another, only two do so. The possible and actual variations are almost unlimited. We have already discussed two types of elitist structures, one run by businessmen and the other by the party organization. But since our concern is less with the fine details of power studies and more with the broad features of local government, we will stick to our two-fold distinction.

Some social scientists have raised a crucial question about the significance of power structure. How important is it, they argue, unless you can show that the type of power structure has a direct effect upon government policy? That is, what difference does it make if businessmen or labor or the mayor and his staff run the town, or if they share power? Do different types of power structures result in different policies for the schools, police, and welfare department in the community? Is money being allocated to different programs and projects in different types of power structures? Or do policies continue to be basically the same no matter who is in charge?

While there is not sufficient research to make strong conclusions about this question, one study examined the participation of communities in federal housing, antipoverty, renewal, and model cities programs. It found that cities with a pluralistic structure were more likely to participate in these federal programs than cities with an elitist structure.[4] While the authors caution us not to generalize from their study, it does dicate that different power structures do affect policy outcomes. And they certainly affect the access of different groups in the community to patronage. Jobs, favors, exceptions, and contracts in and from government are handed out by choice, not chance. One's friends and allies will usually be in a better position to get these rewards than enemies or neutrals.

Factors Affecting Power Structure

The evidence from hundreds of community power studies has found a number of prevailing patterns. Several of these are examined below.[5] Suffice it to say here that there are many individual exceptions to these patterns.

4. Michael Aiken, "The Distribution of Community Power: Structural Bases and Social Consequences," in Michael Aiken and Paul E. Mott, eds., *The Structure of Community Power* (New York: Random House, 1970), pp. 487–525.

5. This section is based on C. W. Gilbert, *Community Power Structure: Propositional Inventory, Tests, and Theory* (Gainesville, Fla.: University of Florida Press, 1972).

The larger the population of a city, the more likely it is to have a pluralistic structure. This condition is no doubt related to the greater social and economic heterogeneity of larger cities. St. Louis and Cleveland are pluralistic cities of over 700,000. There, different business, labor, ethnic, and political party groupings share power. These cities contrast sharply with "Springdale," the pseudonym given to an upstate New York village of 2,500 by those who studied it. Springdale was run by a tiny, like-minded clique.

Conversely, cities of smaller and more homogeneous population are most likely to have an elitist structure than are other types of towns. This holds true both for middle-class suburbs and working-class factory towns. Montville, Connecticut, an example of the latter, had very cohesive leadership by a small group within the Democratic Party from 1940 to 1960. Members of this ruling group were related by blood and marriage, and they kept the business of government tightly in their own hands. After the town's population became more diverse, with the influx of middle-class commuters, governmental control shifted away from the hands of this group and became more pluralistic.

The greater the number of political parties and factions within parties, the more likely the power structure is to be pluralistic. New Haven, Connecticut had a history of vigorous two-party competition at the time Robert Dahl concluded it was a pluralistic structure. New Haven contrasts with San Antonio, Texas in the 1950s and 1960s. San Antonio's Good Government League dominated city elections. No other local electoral or party organization had any clout at the polls. And San Antonio's power structure was an elitist one dominated by business.

Another conclusion from the power studies is that the more economically diversified a city is, the more likely its power structure is to be composed of elected officials and party leaders. Such is the case in diversified cities like Philadelphia, a city with many different types of industry and employers. Less diversified cities are more likely to have "informal" leadership by members of interest groups who do not hold formal office. San Diego, whose economy is heavily dependent on the federal government through both military installations and defense contracts, is regarded as a bastion of political elitism. A power study of San Diego concluded that the business sector monopolized local public decision making. A further example is Muncie, Indiana, mentioned earlier, which in the 1920s was a one-industry town completely dominated by the owners of the industry. City government officials were used politically and otherwise ignored by the informal power structure of Muncie.

These findings indicate that socioeconomic diversity seems strongly related to political pluralism and leadership by elected and party officials, and that active political party competition is related to pluralism. The opposite holds for the elitist structure. One implication of these findings is that a politician who

161

holds the same title and formal-legal powers in two cities may find he has markedly different power when he moves from one city to another. As we shall see below, a city manager in one city may be a very influential leader; in another city, he may be just an administrative clerk.

The following section lists the types of politicians one usually finds on the local scene. Our concern is with the actual power of these politicians under different conditions. The list is not exhaustive. Some politicians are not discussed here because they are examined in other sections of the book. (Judges are examined in the criminal justice section, while some analysis of the role of minority ethnic groups is found in the section dealing with social welfare.) And others are ignored not because they are never important, but because this is not a comprehensive survey of every aspect of community control.

A CATALOG OF LOCAL POLITICOS

The reflective reader will note a number of similarities between Part Two of this volume and this section. In Part Two, participants in state politics were discussed, and many of the points made there apply equally well here. For example, chief executives are often weak in formal and legal authority, legislatures are often part-time endeavors, and political parties often proliferate patronage. At the same time, there are often important differences in structure, style, subtleties, and substance between the two levels of government.

The Chief Executive

The Mayor and the County Executive.   The first question to ask about the power of a mayor or county executive is what kind of formal authority does he have? For example, can he veto the actions of the city council or county commission and be upheld in this act unless the council musters a two-thirds majority to override him? Is he the only elected *executive* official? Is he elected to his job, or is he simply the councilman who got the largest number of votes or whose turn it is to be mayor this month? Does he serve for four years, or for a lesser period? Does he have authority to appoint and remove the major department heads? Does he have the authority to draw up the budget and reorganize governmental structure? Does he have sufficient personal staff to gather information and "trouble-shoot" for him? Does he get a salary sufficient to support himself?

If the answer to all these questions is yes, we can say that the mayor is a strong mayor, the term used to describe a mayor with this kind of formal authority. Most mayors lack this authority; a 1971 study of cities over 50,000 population found that only 39 of 151 mayor-council governments had a strong mayor form.[6] We do not have similar data for the 53 counties with executives, but most of those have other elected executive officials outside the county executive's chain of command.

Mayors without this formal authority may be handicapped, but this does not mean that in reality thay cannot be very strong. For there are three additional dimensions to mayoral leadership beyond formal authority: the way the mayor defines his role, his leadership skills, and the extent to which he is leader of his political party.

A strong mayor may not be much of a leader, regardless of his formal authority, if he does not pay attention to these other dimensions. Perhaps the most important factor is the mayor's own definition of his role: does he see himself as a leader in policymaking, or is he content to confine himself to ceremonial and formal duties? Mayor Walton H. Bachrach of Cincinnati loved giving out keys to the city, making welcoming speeches, and cutting ribbons. He was heard to say that if Cincinnati switched to a strong mayor form, he'd retire immediately.[7] Conversely, a formally weak mayor who wants power may be able to become a leader. The key element in determining his success, given his inadequate authority, will be his personal political skill. The case of Oakland, California in the 1960s shows how a politically adept weak mayor can exercise leadership.

First, Oakland's mayor was able to influence some people on the basis of his prestige and legitimacy as the symbolic leader of the community. Those he asked for support and favors, especially in the private sector, often found it hard to refuse a request made by "his honor." Further, since the mayor presided at city council meetings, he had the chance to guide debate and thus subtly influence some outcomes. In addition, he appointed council members to council committees, and thus was able to cultivate councilmen like the legislator whose chief interest was an airport golf course. The mayor made this councilman chairman and only member of a special golf course committee, winning his gratitude and support in return.[8] Paying attention to councilmen and other actors at social occasions also may help. And even weak mayors may have the authority to name members to many city commissions, which can be especially valuable if the mayor stays in office long enough to make a large number of

6. Russell M. Ross and Kenneth F. Millsap, "The Relative Power Position of Mayors in Mayor-Council Cities" (Iowa City: Laboratory for Political Research, University of Iowa, 1971), p. 16.

7. John P. Kotter and Paul R. Lawrence, *Mayors in Action* (New York: John Wiley & Sons, 1974), p. 88.

8. Jeffery L. Pressman, "Preconditions of Mayoral Leadership," *American Political Science Review* (June 1972), pp. 511–524.

appointments. Will and skill, then, are ultimately more important than formal authority, since one can't lead without them.

There are different kinds of leadership skills.[9] When Hubert Humphrey was mayor of Minneapolis in the 1940s, he had the knack of getting groups to support him without promising them anything. Humphrey would speak to a meeting and tell those in attendance how *they* felt about several issues. When he was done, his audience would be happy, feeling that Humphrey sympathized with them, since he understood them. The mayor would then go to another meeting, held by bitter opponents of the group to which he had just spoken. He would follow the same procedure—equally successfully.

Anton Cermak, mayor of Chicago in the 1920s, was adept at another technique of leadership. He created scores of citizens' advisory committees, made up of the city's social and economic leaders. Procedures followed in the committees were impeccably democratic, but Cermak controlled the results. He was able to do so by appointing a few key supporters and committee staff and by controlling the agenda. This charade earned the mayor widespread support.

George Christopher, mayor of San Francisco in the 1950s, was particularly skilled at cutting committee and bureaucratic red tape. He was able to do so because he had a thorough knowledge of bureaucratic procedures and budgeting. Previous mayors had failed for fourteen years to build a needed branch library in the North Beach section of town. They had appointed study committees, which split into factions after they began work. If they did come up with a recommendation, some North Beach residents were bound to protest the choice. Christopher appointed a committee and gave it a three-week deadline. He asked it to name several possible sites, and then made the final decision himself. This site, located in a city park, drew protests from the Park Commission. Christopher responded by "ordering" the commission to turn the site over to him for construction, which it reluctantly did.

Two other related resources of enormous importance are the mayor's status as a leader in his political party and the extent to which the bureaucracy is *not* covered by civil service regulations. If the mayor is the undisputed leader of an activist local party, he may be able to short-circuit all the restrictions on his formal authority. For example, if a majority of the city council belongs to his party and is responsive to the wishes of their party's leader, he doesn't need to worry about not having a veto. The same relationship may hold true with other elected executive officials. If his party has a lopsided edge in most elections, a two-year term will not worry the mayor very much.

Civil service merit systems require that government job applicants pass

9. The examples of Humphrey, Cermak, and Christopher that follow are drawn from Kotter and Lawrence, *Mayors in Action.*

certain objective tests for entrance and promotion. If such a system does not exist, the mayor can decide who is going to work for the city by appointing his faithful followers to office and removing those who do not support him. This mayoral "patronage" will make the bureaucracy much more responsive to the mayor's wishes than would otherwise be the case.

These two variables—strong mayoral party leadership and a patronage system—often occur together, as in the case of Providence, Rhode Island. Joseph Doorley, mayor from 1964 through 1974, was both the party leader and head of the personnel system throughout the city's government, the school system excepted. In any city where the mayor is formally strong, is not personally reluctant to exercise power, and is skilled at this exercise, mayoral power resources are at a peak. The same held true for Mayor Richard A. Daley of Chicago. As a Chicago Alderman once said, "I don't even go to the bathroom with checking it out with His Honor first."

Perhaps the most important thing to remember about power is that it is a relationship. If a mayor or any other politician encounters strong opponents, he will be less powerful than if he confronts weak ones. In the sections that follow, we examine some of the conditions under which other politicians wield various amounts of might.

The Manager. As in the case of the mayor, the manager's power varies widely from locality to locality. One key factor is the actual nature of manager government in the community. Is the council really committed to the goals of professional, expert management? One easy way to tell is if the council consistently selects local talent without substantial training or experience in management over more technically qualified outside applicants. If so, this indicates that the council is more concerned with its own ability to influence the manager than with whether or not the manager is an independent, qualified administrator. Such was the case in Elmwood, New Jersey, in 1974. Councilman John Guadagnino, who had voted against the creation of the manager form the year before, was named manager. Guadagnino, owner of a grocery store, replaced Victor Shapiro, who had a master's degree in public administration and several years experience in various governmental posts. Mayor Richard Mola exclaimed, "My God, I can't believe it . . . we are witnessing a return to cronyism." [10] But in spite of his disbelief, the change took place, just as similar shifts in managerial status occur every year.

Another clue to whether the council prefers influence over expertise is frequent turnover in the manager's post, indicating that the council and manager

10. "Elmwood Democrats Give Chairman Major Post," *Paterson News*, 13 December 1974, p. 15.

165

are unable to cooperate. Turnover was terrific in Norwich, Connecticut during the 1950s and 1960s. At one point, five managers had served during an eight-year period. The Norwich scene was more reminiscent of musical chairs than good government.

The professional manager usually spends his career in several different localities, moving from smaller to larger ones as he gains experience and expertise. His power is based primarily on this expertise, since he is not elected and is not a party leader. The most powerful managers, however, are politically skillful. Such skill consists in large part of knowing that politics is the art of the possible, and thus not pushing for projects that are unlikely to be popular enough to be passed. An astute manager may be as much of a leader as any mayor. In fact, he usually will have the edge over a mayor in the bureaucratic arena because of his administrative expertise. An example of managerial power can be found in Los Angeles County. In 1972, the county manager noted with pride that fully 95 percent of his recommendations were accepted by the county commissioners.[11] A survey of forty-three manager cities in the Southwest found the manager to be almost exclusively dominant in the areas of personnel and budget. All forty-three managers agreed that regardless of their personal preferences, they *had* to lead the council most of the time. Otherwise, they felt that there would have been no leadership at all.[12]

But, naturally, not all managers are as dominant as these southwesterners. The factors of will, skill, and competition from other strong politicians vary with the individual manager and community. In addition, the orientation of the locality is a crucial factor. Managers are usually most influential in homogeneous upper-income suburbs, where residents tend to share a value system that prizes the efficient, professional approach to government over the provision of patronage to party loyalists and friends. Residents of these communities are usually economically secure enough not to be concerned about whether or not the local government can help them in putting bread on the table. For the same reason, managers are to be found to the greatest extent in smaller middle-class towns. In more heterogeneous, lower-income cities, on the other hand, a government job, favor, or contract may be the only thing standing between a resident and the welfare department. In Providence, Rhode Island in the 1960s, one could find an illiterate city file clerk. Manager government in Kansas City, Missouri was installed in the 1930s by Democratic Party "Boss" Tom Pendergast, who decided it would be good public relations. Kansas City government did not

11. Susan Walker Torrence, *Grass Roots Government: The County in American Politics* (Washington, D.C.: Robert B. Luce, 1974), p. 79.

12. Jack V. Hough, Jr., *et al.*, "The Relationship of Political and Personal Variables to the Roles of City Managers" (Norman, Okla.: Bureau of Government Research, 1973).

become efficient and professional overnight. Instead, managers who would be responsive to the Pendergast machine were selected.

Legislators

Councilmen. However formally weak the average mayor may be, the members of the city council are usually even weaker. In fact, legislatures at all levels of government and in all countries have lost power relative to chief executives over the past century. This change has been brought about primarily by the growth of government and the increasing difficulty of governmental tasks. A hundred years ago, localities were primarily concerned with technical problems like road building and fire fighting. Today, local government confronts a vast array of social problems, including those in welfare, health, and education. Programs designed to tackle them often become exceedingly complex and convoluted. This naturally makes it harder to understand both the rationale and running of these programs. And most city legislators are hampered still more by the nature of the conditions under which they work.

These conditions include low salary levels, insufficient to support the councilman; sessions of limited duration; and lack of clerical and professional staff assistance. This means that the municipal legislator is usually a part-time government official, unable to devote the hours necessary to understand how programs work and thus to rationally evaluate proposed changes in policy. There is a great deal of turnover in city legislative posts from one election to the next, because many council members decide they can no longer afford the job. A survey of Connecticut councilmen showed that one-quarter of them complained about the way their office robbed them of time and of money they could have earned elsewhere.[13] The most vivid illustration of the part-time nature of council work is the hour most councils meet in formal session. Neither state legislatures nor Congress meet primarily at night, but city councils do, because this is the most convenient time to convene a body whose members are working elsewhere during daytime hours.

Small wonder, then, that the mayor or manager is usually more likely to be an initiator of legislative proposals than the council. In study after study, the council emerges as a passive factor, reacting to proposals made elsewhere. An example is a 1973 survey of 179 Texas city managers. Sixty-five percent of them said their councils did not initiate new programs, while forty-eight percent reported that the council did not check up on the way the manager handled his

13. Rosaline Levenson, "Municipal Legislators: A Study of Attributes, Attitudes and Job Satisfactions" (Doctoral dissertation, University of Connecticut, 1971), pp. 220–237.

167

administrative duties.[14] Councilmen seem to be more interested in patronage concerns, in who will get that job or contract, than in the nature of the job or contract itself.

The causes of this situation are similar to those that lead most chief executives to be less than activist policymakers. Most council members do not seem to think of themselves as activist policymakers. When they do, they can change the working conditions that doom them to a backseat role. This has actually happened in Seattle, where well-paid council members have set up standing committees that exercise substantial control over executive agencies. Committee chairmen maintain close contact with department heads, who frequently consult with them on policy matters.[15] After all, it is the council which passes the laws, and if it decides to make itself a full-time, adequately staffed body, it can do so. A study of twelve manager-council cities in the San Gabriel area of California showed that councilmen had the means and tools to check up on the manager's job. Their failure to monitor the manager was caused by a lack of desire to do so, rather than an intrinsic impossibility of the assignment.[16]

In addition, *individual* councilmen can become leaders in policy areas of particular interest to them. Intensity of concern for an issue may overcome the handicaps listed above. For instance, some Hartford, Connecticut councilmen average over forty hours a week on the job, travelling through the city to examine different programs, whether they be in the area of schools, law enforcement, or public works. But they are exceptions. Neither individual nor institutional leadership is characteristic of the council. What are the causes of this?

There are two likely reasons. One is our tradition that the government that governs least governs best. While this orientation no longer characterizes American government as a whole, as the impressive array of programs discussed in this book indicates, it has left its mark on certain areas. The citizenry of a town may not be able to control school board spending as much as it would like, since many school programs are required by the state, but it can much more easily determine the salaries and staff levels of the local legislature. The relatively minor costs involved in creating a full-time legislature may not be politically acceptable to irate taxpayers, so the council remains a part-time operation.

14. Jerry L. Yeric and Charldean Newell, "Texas City Managers: Some Professional Characteristics" (paper presented to the annual meeting of the American Society for Public Administration, Los Angeles, 1973).

15. Edward C. Banfield, *Big City Politics* (New York: Random House, 1965), p. 82.

16. Cortus T. Koehler, "Policy Development and Legislative Oversight in Council-Manager Cities: An Information and Communications Analysis," *Public Administration Review* (September/October 1973), pp. 433–432.

Another probable cause is the nature of political party leadership in this country. In many sections of the United States, especially the urban Northeast, council members are likely to be loyal party followers of the mayor or the party chairman, and as such are unlikely to play an independent role in policymaking. Their primary concern will more probably be patronage for themselves, their campaign workers, and their friends and families. The New Haven Board of Aldermen has traditionally been a rubber stamp for the mayor, since he dispenses patronage. Most board members either work for the city, have a relative who works for the city, or do business with the city. It is no accident that the most activist councils are found outside the Northeast, in areas like California and the Southwest, which have a history of extremely weak local parties.

Commissioners. We have lumped city and county commissioners together with other legislators, even though almost all of them (except those in some counties with county executives or strong managers) carry out administrative duties as well.

The factors causing the job of city councilman to be a part-time one also hold for most jobs as commissioner. The average salary for a commissioner in a metropolitan area was under $10,000 in 1971, while rural commissioners averaged less than $4,000.[17] In today's inflated economy, such salaries will only support those with the most abstemious life-styles. Likewise, most commissions lack adequate staff, and while city governments are restricted by state statutes, such restrictions are much more severe in counties.

Thus, most of the remarks made earlier about the limitations on the power of council members to make policy hold for commissioners, with one very important difference. This is the executive or administrative authority wielded by the commissioner, who usually acts as department head for one or more county agencies. This means that a county welfare commissioner is both department head and legislator, able both to directly administer the department and to vote in commission sessions on policy affecting the department. A politically skilled commissioner who stays in office a long time can parlay these resources into strong leadership of whatever policy area of which he is in charge. This authority is reinforced by the fact that there is no one who can veto the actions of the commission. All commissioners are equal in formal authority. One serves as presiding officer at a given time, but that is the only legal distinction among them. Commissioners with the will and the skill, then, may be better able than other local legislators to have policymaking impact, especially on administration.

Unlike the scene at the state level, there has been no municipal or county

17. Torrence, *Grass Roots Government*, p. 25.

169

legislative reform movement. While state legislatures have been making earnest efforts to get out from behind the eight ball, local legislatures seem locked into lethargy. We may have to wait for the decline of local parties and of the narrow taxpayer mentality before local legislatures start to live up to their potential.

Government Employees and Employee Unions

Government Employees. We have already given a sketch of state employees in Chapter 8. Rather than reiterate the common features of state and local bureaucracy, we will focus here on dimensions that determine employee power.

While government employees do not enjoy the popularity of a film celebrity, they rate higher than some other local politicians. A Harris poll showed that confidence in local government had sunk from 43 percent in 1965 to 14 percent in 1975. But the public figures enjoying greatest esteem were garbage collectors, with 51 percent.[18]

Bureaucratic power rests primarily on two bases: specialized expertise or knowledge and the existence and support of a strong agency clientele. The case of Harry D. Ross, San Francisco controller in the 1950s and 1960s, illustrates the importance of expertise. Ross knew the intricacies of the city's budgetary system as no one else did, and he was once able to expedite the construction of a city convention center because of this knowledge. The city was in a jam because the low bid for the project was $700,000 more than the government's estimate. If the mayor had to submit the new figure to the voters in another bond referendum, the final figure would float even higher. But Ross discovered that the new sewer lines necessary for the center could be paid for from surplus sewer funds on hand. The same was true for the sidewalks involved. Ross drew up a perfectly legally package that enabled the center to open without a hitch at the earliest possible date.[19]

An agency's clientele is that group (or groups) most directly affected by the work of the agency. A welfare department's clientele is made up of welfare recipients, while a transportation department's is made up of those who ride the department's vehicles. An agency with a politically powerful clientele that supports the agency will have a lot going for it. A school system that can turn out large numbers of the members of its parent-teacher associations to vote for its budget enjoys an enormously helpful clientele relationship.

Conversely, agencies with a politically weak clientele, such as welfare departments, cannot bank on much help from it. The very fact that a person is

18. John Kifner, "Pollster Tells Mayors that Public Doesn't Trust Them," *New York Times,* 8 July 1975, p. 13.
19. Kotter and Lawrence, *Mayors in Action.*

170

on welfare indicates that he lacks most of the resources necessary to participate successfully in any area of our society. Sit-ins by welfare recipients at city council meetings are unlikely to persuade local legislators to vote more funds for the welfare department. If anything, such activity would probably have exactly the opposite effect.

Several other factors relate to the power of specific agencies. One is the extent of consensus in support of the agency's goals. If an agency's employees strongly support the same values, the agency will be stronger than if their ranks are divided. If a housing agency's employees, for example, believe very strongly in aggressive inspection for building code violations, it is more likely that the agency will be able to carry out such assertive policies than if there were no such agreement.

Another factor is formal-legal independence. An agency not directly under the control of budgetary and personnel systems run by the chief executive will have an advantage in policymaking over bureaus that are within the chain of command. Local school systems that are run by a separate board and raise their own revenue, for example, enjoy a significant power resource that many agencies lack.

A third factor is the technical complexity of agency functions. The more an agency relies on advanced technology to carry out its task, the more likely it is to be powerful in policymaking. It is much harder for a layman to understand and evaluate the procedures of a county hospital, for example, than it is for him to understand what the highway department is doing.

An additional factor is the structure and size of the executive branch as a whole. The larger the government, the more likely it is that bureaucrats will influence policymaking. In a large government, both the chief executive and legislature will find it harder to monitor executive agencies, because there are so many of them. Even an organization chart may boggle the mind with its complicated detail. Thus bureaucrats in Chicago have the advantage over their counterparts in Peoria.

Finally, political will and skill are crucial determinants of power. These qualities, already discussed in connection with other politicians, are no less crucial for bureaucrats. The desire to influence policy and the talent to do so are necessary before any of the resources listed above can be cashed in at the political gaming table. A study of two welfare departments found that one constantly—and often successfully—asked for more funds and proposed new programs, while the other drifted from one year to the next without change.[20]

20. Rufus P. Browning, "Innovative and Non-Innovative Decision Process in Government Budgeting," in Robert T. Golembiewski, ed., *Public Budgeting and Finance* (Itasca, Ill.: Peacock, 1968), pp. 128–145.

Employee Unions. Government unions have been better organized, more successful, and more militant in our larger cities, counties, and school systems than at the state level. In 1974, for instance, there were thirty-four state government strikes compared with ten times that number at the local level, which idled 135,000 workers for 1,316,300 man-days. Local employees have succeeded in gaining binding arbitration in eleven states. New York City employees were able to win pensions that let them retire in some cases with more than they earned while they were working.[21]

But what goes up must come down. Local workers were hurt much more by economic conditions in 1974 through 1976 than state workers. New York City became financially dependent on the state and national governments, in large part because of its huge public payroll. Thousands of New York employees were laid off in 1975 and 1976. Cleveland, Baltimore, and Detroit shrank their payrolls by 30 percent from 1970 to 1976. A thirty-eight day strike in 1976 by San Francisco employees failed completely. In Seattle in 1975, Mayor Wes Uhlmann turned back a recall election which that city's firemen called when he wanted to decrease the fire department's budget.[22] Like their state counterparts, unions will remain as important factors in local politics. But times will be tougher for them when taxpayers want thrift.

Political Parties

Units of the Republican and Democratic Parties are found in most U.S. localities, but their importance in local politics varies greatly. In some areas they are second to none; in others, they may be less of a factor than the local birdwatchers society.

Even more than is the case at the state level, many localities have experienced one-party dominance for what seems like countless generations. In the larger cities, Democratic domination is typical, as it is throughout the Southland. In smaller communities of the Northeast and Middle West, Republican rule is equally common. Often the minority parties are resigned to their lot, since the majority buys them off. The ruling party provides just enough patronage to the minority party in such cases to assure that it won't mount a serious challenge at

21. Neal R. Peirce, "Public Employee Unions Show Rise in Membership, Militancy," *National Journal* (30 August 1975), pp. 1239–1246.

22. Lee Dembart, "The Public Disdain of Public Employees," *New York Times*, 27 June 1976, Section E, p. 3.

the polls. This lack of competition, whatever the reason, encourages corruption, as the recurrent scandals in one-party fiefdoms like Chicago underscore.

One important structural difference between state and local politics is the predominance of local nonpartisan elections, in which no candidate's party affiliation is identified on the ballot. Over 60 percent of cities and towns over 5,000 as well as many school and special districts and counties use nonpartisan elections. Nonpartisan elections are used in races for state legislative office in only two medium-sized states, and not at all for federal office, so local government is practically unique in this respect.

Nonpartisan elections came about as a result of a reform campaign by organizations such as the National Municipal League, which argued that local government should be made free of politics and more businesslike in its operation. The manager plan and at-large elections were other parts of this program. Another aspect was the attempt to shield local government from the contaminating influence of state and federal elections by holding elections for local government in different years.

The effectiveness of nonpartisan elections varies widely. Chicago's nonpartisan elections for the board of aldermen have not changed Chicago politics at all. Commentators talk about the board of aldermen's forty nonpartisan Democrats and its ten nonpartisan Republicans. But elections in other communities have weakened the local parties. There seem to be several factors that determine the impact nonpartisanship will have. One is the heterogeneity of the community. If a city or county is made up of diverse ethnic, social, and economic groups, the chances are that a switch to nonpartisan elections is unlikely to have much immediate impact, as the case of Chicago indicates. In relatively homogeneous middle-class suburbs, however, nonpartisanship may definitely weaken or even destroy the local activities of parties. Another key factor is the traditional strength of local parties. In the urban Northeast, for example, local parties have always been important, but such has not been the case in the younger cities of the Pacific Coast and Southwest. In many of these newer cities, like Los Angeles, the local parties are nearly impotent, and thus nonpartisanship works as it is supposed to. But in Seattle, a city with one dominant party, nonpartisan elections have strengthened the dominant Democratic Party.

In addition, of course, party labels remain on the ballot in many large and small localities. But just as the presence of nonpartisanship is not equal to weak parties, the presence of partisanship does not automatically mean that local parties are effective, well-organized units. In 1973, Edward Hanna was elected mayor of Utica, New York on the Rainbow Party ticket. His election was viewed as a fluke, but after unconventional accomplishments such as firing large numbers of city employees, putting "Please walk on the grass" signs in city parks, and building a bell tower that plays "I Did It My Way" every half hour, Hanna was reelected by a vast majority.[23] Again, socioeconomic factors, tradition, and dynamic personalities are likely to be more important than the form itself.

Party leaders are usually less interested in policy than they are in the material benefits of government, such as jobs, contracts, or favors. The one policy area in which they maintain a continual strong interest is election laws, changes in which may affect their position as party chiefs. And occasionally party leaders will try to get elected officials to change their stance on an issue, if they feel that this stance is so unpopular it will cost the party votes at the next election.

Party officials, then, are primarily concerned with winning elections. To do so, they need to reward their followers. In "reformed," nonpartisan systems these rewards may be primarily of a symbolic sort, such as praise for help in winning the election. Or they may be directly policy-related, such as appointment to a part-time government post, which usually pays little or nothing in this type of government.

But where party leaders are important in local government, they are usually more likely to be interested in material rewards for their followers. A local government in a city of even 150,000 is likely to have hundreds of jobs to which the party faithful can be appointed, millions of dollars in contracts to award, and the chance to grant favors to hundreds of people. For example, Mayor Erastus Corning of Albany, New York is president of a firm that does $100,000 business a year insuring buildings in Albany County. He also appoints scores of patronage employees to city government posts.[24] Jersey City's Frank Hague once justified his system of kickbacks to a reporter. As the "Boss" put it, "I think 3 percent—the rate for city employees and contractors—is a bargain for getting good service."[25]

The focus of party leaders on patronage makes them much more important figures in administration than in policy formation. Policy as such is a secondary concern to most of them, but their desire to influence jobs and contracts and to get favors and exceptions for their friends invariably affects administration. The choice of a building contractor, for example, will determine the quality of the structure; the choice of personnel will determine the agency's ability to effectively perform its job; and granting exceptions to policies will determine whether or not there is anything consistent enough to be called a

23. Bruce Porter, "I'll Do Things My Way," New York Times Magazine, 19 September 1976, pp. 45-63.
24. Martin Tolchin, "Political Patronage Rising at Fast Rate, Study Finds," New York Times, 17 June 1968, p. 1.
25. "Weeding the Garden State," Time (19 July 1971), p. 38.

174

policy at all in existence. Because of their priorities, then, party leaders operate under an unusual set of constraints, which do not apply to other politicians when they become involved in the policy process.

This century has seen a slip in the status of party leaders. Most of the party machines of the past, with their boss leadership, are gone. A city like Chicago is now the exception, rather than the rule. This is not to say that party leaders are unimportant. Patronage jobs and favors still abound in many localities. The point is that the number of strong bosses like Jersey City's Frank Hague, who could say, "I am the law," has decreased notably. The party leader is now usually just one of numerous contestants for power in American cities, where in the past many a boss was the most important leader in a city.

The Communications Media

Specialized media reach relatively small groups especially interested in certain topics. Our concern here is with the role of mass media, including newspapers, radio, and television, that reach large audiences.

As the political scientists Edward C. Banfield and James Q. Wilson have pointed out, one can understand the media only by realizing that they are businesses, established to make a profit through the sale of advertising. Media executives are usually careful not to run stories that would upset their leading advertisers. This is true whether these stories are directly critical of their advertising customers or so controversial that certain groups would stop reading or listening to the media, thus missing the ads. Media executives may go easy on fellow businessmen because they identify with them and their problems. They may also play down news such as poor housing and traffic conditions, racial strife, pollution, and declining school test scores, which gives the city a bad image.[26] Examples of papers that have slanted the news to reflect the political and social interests of their owners are the *Wilmington* (Delaware) *Morning Post* and *Evening Journal*, owned by the DuPont Company, the most powerful corporation in the state, and the *Jackson* (Mississippi) *Clarion-Ledger* and *Daily News*.[27]

At the same time, reporters and editors define the most newsworthy stories as the ones involving conflict, great change, or the unique.[28] Thus, if a conflict or scandal involving some of a medium's biggest advertisers occurs,

26. Edward C. Banfield and James Q. Wilson, *City Politics* (Cambridge, Mass.: Harvard University Press, 1963), pp. 314–315.

27. Bill Boyarsky and Nancy Boyarsky, *Backroom Politics* (Los Angeles: J. P. Tarcher, 1974), pp. 209–210.

28. On this point, see: Delmer D. Dunn, *Public Officials and the Press* (Reading, Mass.: Addison-Wesley, 1969).

there will be pressures both to emphasize and to play down the story, and different editors will handle the matter differently.

Today, in most of those big cities with more than one paper, one corporation owns the newspapers. And in many cases, it owns the local television station as well. Most cities with daily papers have just one paper. This lack of competition enables the medium to decide what kind of local news it will cover, without feeling it has to keep up with its rivals. Reporter Bill Boyarsky feels the *Los Angeles Times*, with only one small rival which cannot match it in coverage, ignores much important local news in a way the more competitive Chicago newspapers do not.[29] On the other hand, Banfield and Wilson conclude that when competition reduces profit margins, papers neglect local news in favor of sensationalism and features (sports, comics, and columns) they feel will build circulation more rapidly. All of these conditions cut down on the amount of local news coverage.[30]

A contrary trend some observers think is developing stresses greater coverage of local news. Again, economic causes are crucial. Larger papers trying to save money can save more by reducing the Washington or state capital staff instead of cutting back on local reporters. Rising production costs, from labor to newsprint, have led papers of all sizes to reduce the number of pages they print. And when editors cut back, they do not usually trim local news, but international, national, and state news. As Burdett Stoddard, assistant managing editor of the *Detroit News*, said in 1975, "We do ourselves a lot of good with more local coverage. It's pretty much our bread and butter, especially in bad times."[31]

While most news media do not devote most of their attention to local news, studies of what readers desire agree that they probably give the average reader more of it than he wants.[32] Presumably this is because media executives feel some kind of civic duty to do so, and they receive rewards in the form of pride and recognition as well as profits.

Even so, local news is low in prestige and priority. Higher salary and recognition are attached to covering state and national politics, rather than city hall, and the highest status and salary are those of an editor. There is thus strong pressure on the most capable and ambitious reporters to leave local news behind as their careers take off. If the city hall reporter remains on his job for a number of years, he is likely to develop a close, cooperative relationship with local officials. Rather than probing deeply into their operations, he will take the

29. Boyarsky and Boyarsky, *Backroom Politics*, pp. 211–212.

30. Banfield and Wilson, *City Politics*, pp. 321–322.

31. Martin Arnold, "Newspaper Trend: Stress Local News, Cut National and Foreign Coverage," *New York Times*, 8 July 1975, p. 18.

32. Cf. Dunn., *Public Officials*, and Banfield and Wilson, *City Politics*.

information they choose to give him, which will be enough to make his editor happy.[33] This kind of reporter becomes a watchdog with rubber teeth.

But not all city hall reporters become soft, for much the same reason that news executives do not always suppress views they feel might upset their advertisers. The reporter and government official are by nature adversaries. The news reporter has the incentive to get as much information about government as he can get, so he can file interesting stories. The official wants as little news as possible that is not written from his viewpoint to get out, because this may make him look bad and affect his work adversely. For these reasons, the local media, even though they may be unaggressive most of the time, tend to go on periodic "crusades," probing scandals or questionable procedures in local government.[34] There are tensions, then, between both the economic basis and career patterns associated with the media, on the one hand, and the reporter's definition of news and the executive's sense of civic duty, on the other. These strains may cause inconsistent news policy over a period of time.

What is the nature of media power? The media are not as able to change people's opinions about different subjects as they are able to get them to think about these subjects in the first place. In other words, the media *set the agenda* about which their average reader or viewer thinks. For example, a survey of St. Louis found that most of the population had heard of a plan for Metro government backed by the St. Louis press, but could not identify the stand the paper had taken on the issue.[35] This power to set the agenda should not be downgraded: it is a power most other politicos would love to have.

It also is a resource that the astute politician can often use to his own advantage. The politico who is controversial, unique, or an advocate of sweeping changes is newsworthy in the eyes of the media. He can force the media to cover him even when they dislike him, as Louise Day Hicks proved in Boston in the 1960s. Mrs. Hicks, an opponent of school desegration plans, actually welcomed media editorial attacks and unsympathetic news coverage, for she knew that instead of adversely affecting the way people felt about her, they shined a spotlight on her so she could not be ignored. In effect, she put herself on the agenda and made herself a strong candidate for the mayoralty.

Richard Lee, mayor of New Haven during the 1950s and 1960s, was also aware of how to use media power in his own behalf. Lee carefully courted the press, paying close attention to editors and reporters. He created a press office that cranked out reams of releases about his programs, in convenient packages

33. Banfield and Wilson, *City Politics*, p. 318.
34. *Ibid.*, p. 317.
35. Scott Greer, *Metropolitics* (New York: John Wiley & Sons, 1963), p. 113.

of just the right length for news stories. This policy paid handsome dividends, for no one who followed the media could avoid noticing Lee and his administration.[36]

The extent of media influence in local politics varies with local conditions. The absence or weakness of other actors on the political scene means the media are likely to be more powerful than would otherwise be the case. In nonpartisan cities, for example, the media may assume much of the role played by political parties in providing the most important cue voters use in selecting candidates. Banfield and Wilson argue that the *Los Angeles Times* is the most powerful single political participant in Los Angeles, and that in Detroit the press is also extremely influential. But in Chicago, where nonpartisanship exists only on paper and power is centralized in the machine, the media are not as important.

Interest Groups

Business. The business community is not monolithic. There are small, middle-sized, and large businesses. Some businessmen manufacture goods, while others provide services. Competition among businesses exists in many areas, while in others the names of the game are collusion and cooperation. Banfield and Wilson argue that certain kinds of businesses—department stores, utilities, real estate operators, and banks—are more directly affected by what goes on in the city than are other businesses and are thus more likely to participate in city politics.[37]

Department stores want to increase their business by attracting middle-class customers and discouraging low-income shoppers. To achieve this end, they may support new highways and parking facilities and urban renewal designed to remove the poor from the vicinity of their stores. In Hartford, Connecticut, there are four exits in one mile of Interstate Highway 84 that take suburban drivers into the downtown shopping area.

Utility companies, such as electric, gas, and water suppliers, favor steady, predictable growth because of the large fixed costs (water mains, power stations, etc.) involved in their businesses. This makes them supporters of city planning, land-use control, and consolidation of local government units.

Real estate operators include brokers, on the one hand, and owners and managers of office buildings. The former tend to back any kind of plans for large-scale changes involving buildings in the city, because they make their living by arranging transactions. The latter are concerned with the stability of the

36. Allan R. Talbot, *The Mayor's Game* (New York: Harper & Row, 1967), pp. 92–97.
37. Banfield and Wilson, *City Politics*, pp. 261–264.

property tax rate and assessment practices. They like to see new buildings placed where they will increase the value of their own properties, and they work to keep city budget expenses down.

Banks are concerned with the general economic health and growth of the city. If the city begins to decline, banks are not able to lend as much money as they would if the community were thriving, so they are interested in government plans for renewal and development, as well as the property tax rate.

Coversely, most local branches of national corporations, as well as absentee-owned companies, usually do not participate in local politics. These businesses are more concerned with a national market than with conditions in a locality, and will move if they feel those conditions are becoming troublesome. But Ypsilanti, Michigan's two largest employers—Ford and General Motors— exercised substantial influence in local affairs in the 1960s. The three top political offices in the county and township were held by Ford employees. These officials helped in getting the access roads to the Ford plant paved, while company public relations officers worked to minimize conflict between the auto companies and other residents in town.[38]

What resources does business have to influence local politics? First is the direct use of money. Business wealth may be used legally to finance attempts to influence policy through advertising, community service projects, and political party contributions. Or it may be used illegally, for bribes and kickbacks. Second, business may assgn employees to work for a local government project, like urban renewal. Third, and probably most important, is the business's contribution to the economic health of the community. A corporation that employs a large percentage of local residents and with ownings that make up a sizeable portion of the taxable property is listened to by local officials. These officials know that businesses may leave the community if they feel they can make more money elsewhere. This pattern has been repeated over and over in the last thirty years, as industries have left the urban Northeast and Middle West for the cheaper labor markets of the South. Local governments often give tax breaks and make efforts to provide superior services to businesses, to keep them or to attract them from elsewhere. New York City paid over $100 million in 1976 to rebuild Yankee Stadium, to stop the baseball Yankees from following the football Giants across the Hudson River to their new stadium in New Jersey.

A less tangible business resource is its perceived legitimacy as a participant on the local scene, something one of its rivals, organized labor, often does not enjoy. Examine local "blue ribbon" study groups or community service drives, like the United Fund, and you will find that they are dominated by

38. Paul E. Mott, "The Role of the Absentee-Owned Corporation in the Changing Community," in Aiken and Mott, *Community Power*, pp. 179–180.

179

businessmen more often than not. The United States has the most capitalistic economy in the world, for we never had a feudal structure or nobility to displace. It should come as no surprise, then, to find that more prestige attaches to business in the United States than is the case in any other country, and this prestige is a very useful tool for gaining influence. Government officials too busy to see others will often make time to meet with a leading local businessman.

A key factor affecting business influence is the relationship of the internal power structure of the business community with that of government. Banfield and Wilson distinguish six types of interrelationships, each of which has different implications for business power.[39]

One pattern is elitist power structures in both business and government, with business controlling government directly. Dallas is usually given as an example of this type, with its Citizens' Council speaking for business, and its city council dominated by business members.

Another pattern is elitist power structures in both business and government, with business controlling government indirectly through a political boss. The Vare machine in turn-of-the-century Philadelphia is an example of this kind of relationship. Big business interests like the Pennsylvania Railroad and the city's largest bank were the powers behind the throne.

A different relationship involves elitist power structures in both business and government, with both sharing power. This has been the pattern in Pittsburgh, with a strong Democratic machine and a united business community.

Some localities have an elitist power structure in government and a pluralist one in business, with government dominating. Chicago, whose size and diversity preclude a centralized power structure for business, is the city where the Democratic machine generally holds political power. Since business usually cannot speak with a single voice, the mayor is free to ignore it.

Other localities have an elitist business power structure and a pluralistic government power structure, with businessmen hampered in trying to exercise political influence. This is the case in Los Angeles, where many issues are decided not by the mayor and council, but through referenda, which are more expensive and difficult for business to influence.

A final pattern is pluralism in both business and government, with minimal influence on business. This is the case in Boston, where there is neither a boss to deal with business, nor one spokesman for business.

While business power is clearly to be reckoned with in local politics, then, numerous factors affect its importance from place to place. Of all the "informal" power groups in U.S. local government, however, business seems to be the most

39. Banfield and Wilson, *City Politics*, pp. 272–276.

important. An examination of the power of its principal opponent, organized labor, should make this clear.

Organized Labor.   Labor unions come in as many different shapes and sizes as do businesses. Craft unions recruit membership on the basis of a particular skill or trade, such as carpentry or hod carrying. Industrial unions organize an entire industry, like automobile manufacturing, regardless of the various skills of different workers in it. Craft unions usually negotiate their contracts on the local level. The industrial unions, on the other hand, negotiate contracts on a national level. This fact accounts for the greater orientation of craft unions to local government. Their members are licensed by local government, which controls apprenticeship programs. For the building trades, which are the largest grouping of craft unions, local housing and building codes are crucial considerations. Local governments also provide work for these unions, since they need to construct and repair buildings for their own use.

Local labor leaders, as Banfield and Wilson point out, are usually less ideological than national leaders.[40] They must be concerned with the day-to-day details of enforcing contract agreements, supervising work conditions, and bargaining for new contracts. These leaders are more concerned with friendly treatment from the police and courts, especially during strikes, than with any other function of local government.

Some unions, especially industrial ones, like the United Auto Workers, go beyond these concerns to participate in local political campaigns. Since industrial unions are usually more nationally oriented than craft unions, their involvement in these campaigns can probably be explained as the result of their work in state and national elections. Once they have set up a local campaign organization, it makes sense to use it in all elections, thereby maximizing power in our complicated system of intergovernmental relations. Since labor supports the Democratic Party almost exclusively, craft unions tend to stay away from campaign activity. With their greater concern for local government, they want to stay on good terms with Republicans as well. The craft unions usually rely on lobbying, rather than election campaigning, to maximize their influence. Thus we have the paradox of more activity in local elections by those unions that are less interested in local government.

Labor is not usually so influential in local government as is business. We mentioned above the "legitimacy" of business in American society, which labor does not enjoy. Further, unions usually have neither as much money nor as much manpower to devote to pushing policy proposals in local government as

40. *Ibid.*, pp. 277–292.

do businesses. In addition, labor tends to be more preoccupied with labor goals—wages and benefits—than are businesses, which define their business concerns more broadly, to include projects like urban renewal. There are exceptions, such as Detroit, where the unions are the dominant factor in the party system. But overall, labor lags behind business, because of its definition of priorities, the nature of its resources, and its problem of perceived legitimacy.

State and Federal Government Officials

While we examined intergovernmental relations in more detail in Chapter 9, we pause here to repeat the point that officials of the state and federal governments are important in any locality. Most community power studies have ignored these governments, something mayors often wish very much they could do. The influence of officials from "higher" levels of government is based primarily on the grant monies they dispense, as well as on legislation that often gives them regulatory power over local government. The 1970 Federal Clean Waters Act, for example, has made it possible for the "feds" to direct local governments to clean up their waterways.

A study of Syracuse, New York, systematically analyzed the power of state and federal actors in local politics. The authors found that 16 percent of the key decision makers in Syracuse were federal officials, and 28 percent were state officials. They concluded that local government officials were important figures in their own right, with 56 percent of key decision makers and only one policy area, water pollution control, under the control of "outsiders." [41] But their study graphically illustrates what all local officials know: state and federal officials are powerful figures in local government.

CONCLUSIONS

There are two matters of primary concern as we conclude this chapter. First, those resources (money, votes, high position in an organization perceived to be legitimate, staff, and political skill) that are most important in affecting decisions are not available to the average citizen, or even to the average group. To the extent that these people lack these resources, they are handicapped in trying to get government to do something they want. This is especially true for people below the middle-class economic level, since numerous studies show that they are often looked at with disgruntled disdain by government officials when they

41. H. George Frederickson and Linda Schluter O'Leary, *Power, Public Opinion and Policy in a Metropolitan Community* (New York: Praeger, 1973), pp. 92-96, 153-157.

make requests or demands. This situation may change in the future, for a number of younger leaders in public administration are concerned that "social equity," or treatment of the less powerful on an equal basis, be given top priority by government officials. To do this, however, the very currency of power will have to be changed. Money and social status will have to cease to be important. Since this has not yet happened in human society, it would be naive to expect it to happen tomorrow. Some observers feel that participation in all kinds of organizations is growing, so that the future will be a very different and more democratic place, but that future is not yet here. The very notion of a "power structure" leaves the average citizen out.

Second, when a pluralistic power structure exists, it is harder for government to get anything done. Pluralism, or the distribution of power among differrent governmental and nongovernmental politicians, reinforces and exacerbates our fragmented governmental structure to the point where it is often nearly impossible for government to do more than function on a day-by-day basis. A new master plan for a community, for example, requires cooperation from all agencies and powerful groups if it is to be implemented. Very few such plans are ever carried out in their original form. Those that are tend to be found in communities with elitist power structures. Likewise, policy coordination among related functions, such as public health, education, housing, and welfare, is next to impossible under pluralism. Analysis of urban renewal programs shows that the more citizen participation in the program, the less likely it is to get off the ground. It is much easier to veto policy initiatives in a pluralistic system than to achieve their enactment. Those who want change have to clear a whole race-track of hurdles. Those who oppose change have merely to trip their opponent at one hurdle, and the race is over. The community power studies indicate that there is more pluralism in community politics today than there was thirty years ago.[42] With increasing pluralism, coordination and change will be even harder.

These two conditions constitute a cruel dilemma. If greater democracy (pluralism) causes policy paralysis, wide-scale change may depend on undemocratic (elitist) power structures. And as the next chapter argues, some changes at the local level are badly needed.

42. Gilbert, *Community Power Structure*.

THE METRO MESS
AND MEANS TO
MODIFY IT

CHAPTER THIRTEEN

CITIES IN CRISIS

In the mid-1960s, when some of our central cities were put to the torch, many commentators concluded that something was wrong. They labelled the existing unease the "urban crisis." Although President Nixon declared in 1973 that the urban crisis was over, city problems did not vanish with this pronouncement. Most definitions of the urban crisis boil down to the belief that most of our largest central cities are no longer viable and are steadily declining compared to their suburbs and the rest of society.

One aspect of the decline is economic. The cities, once the center of the nonfarm economy, are losing out to their suburbs as jobs migrate from the

185

center to the periphery. In the fifteen largest metropolitan areas, jobs in the suburbs increased by three million, or 40 percent, between 1960 and 1970. Meanwhile, jobs in the central cities dipped by 800,000, or 7 percent. This trend has continued unabated since 1970 and spells eventual disaster for the cities, whether they depend on property or sales taxes for revenue.[1] (See Table 13.1.) With less business property and fewer retail transactions, government revenues will decline. Attempts to raise these taxes are counterproductive, encouraging business to move to the suburbs, so the cities are stuck in a bind.

TABLE 13.1 HOW JOBS HAVE SHIFTED TO THE SUBURBS (IN THE 15 LARGEST METROPOLITAN AREAS)

YEAR	REPORTED METROPOLITAN AREA WORKERS	THOSE WHO WORK IN THE CITY	THOSE WHO WORK IN THE SUBURBS	THOSE WHO LIVE AND WORK IN THE SUBURBS (FIGURES IN 1,000s WORKERS)		CITY'S SHARE OF METROPOLITAN AREA JOBS
				NUMBERS	PERCENT	
1960	19,132	12,060	7,072	6,227	67.8%	63.0%
1970	21,382	11,224	10,158	8,699	72.3	52.4

SOURCE: The *New York Times*, 15 October 1972, p. 58. © 1972 by The New York Times Company. Reprinted by permission.

Probably the most persuasive picture of urban decline is that of the city blocks burned out in the riots of the 1960s. Many of them remain wasteland today, since business will not rebuild on these properties.

Cities can ill afford to lose taxable property for another reason. The percentage of their area containing tax-exempt territory, such as highways; colleges; hospitals; museums; clubs, and county, state, and federal offices, is much greater than that found in the suburbs. Close to half the area of Newark, New Jersey, a city on the brink of bankruptcy, is tax-exempt.

Middle- and working-class residents have been able to leave the city for the same reason businesses have. Modern transportation and communication have made it unnecessary for people to live closely grouped together next to their jobs, shopping, recreation, and service areas. City residents have availed themselves of these resources, moving out in droves. The population of the older central cities of the Northeast and Midwest has steadily declined since 1945.[2] (See Figure 13.1.) Our citizens travel billions of aggregate miles annually,

1. U.S. Bureau of the Census, *Census of Population and Housing*, General Final Report PHC (2)-1 United States Demographic Trends for Metropolitan Areas, 1960–1970 (Washington, D.C.: U.S. Government Printing Office, 1971).

2. Ibid.

186

San Francisco-Oakland Area ①

	Percent Change	
	1960-'70	1970-'73
San Francisco	−3.3%	−3.8%
Suburbs:		
Alameda	18.2	1.7
Contra Costa	36.5	2.7
Marin	40.3	1.2
San Mateo	25.2	1.5

New York Area ⑥

	Percent Change	
	1960-'70	1970-'73
New York City	1.5%	−2.3%
Suburbs:		
Rockland	68.1	4.4
Westchester	10.5	−0.4
Bergen, N.J.	15.1	0.1
Putnam	78.7	12.0
Nassau	9.8	−1.1
Suffolk	68.7	6.2

St. Louis Area ②

	Percent Change	
	1960-'70	1970-'73
St. Louis	−17.0%	−8.7%
Suburbs:		
Franklin	23.7	10.8
Jefferson	58.6	9.5
St. Charles	75.5	11.5
St. Louis County	35.2	
Madison, Ill.	11.7	1.1
St. Clair	8.6	0.6

Philadelphia Area ⑤

	Percent Change	
	1960-'70	1970-'73
Philadelphia	−2.7%	−3.5%
Suburbs:		
Bucks Co., Pa.	34.5	6.1
Chester Co., Pa.	32.1	3.2
Delaware Co., Pa.	8.5	−0.3
Montgomery Co., Pa. . . .	20.7	0.7
Burlington, N.J.	43.9	0.1
Camden, N.J.	16.4	3.9
Gloucester, N.J.	28.1	5.0

Baltimore Area ③

	Percent Change	
	1960-'70	1970-'73
Baltimore	−3.6%	−3.8%
Suburbs:		
Anne Arundel	44.0	8.0
Baltimore County	26.1	2.8
Carroll	30.7	10.2
Harford	50.4	11.9
Howard	71.3	29.5

Washington Area ④

	Percent Change	
	1960-'70	1970-'73
Washington	−1.0%	−1.4%
Suburbs:		
Montgomery Co., Md. . .	53.5	7.3
Prince Georges Co., Md. . .	84.8	5.1
Arlington Co., Va.	6.7	−6.0
Fairfax Co., Va.	74.1	13.0
Loudoun Co., Va.	51.3	12.2
Prince William Co., Va. . .	121.5	16.2
Alexandria, Va.	21.9	−5.4
Fairfax City, Va.	61.7	−1.6
Falls Church, Va.	5.7	−4.8

mostly by car, which means they can live in suburbs. At the turn of the century, when neither the automobile nor cheap mass transportation was available, only the rich could live outside the city. But after 1945, the suburban exodus reached new heights, drawing the middle class out of the city. Those left behind were increasingly the poor, who could afford to live only in the city. City populations today are disproportionately black, Hispanic, and elderly. (See Figure 13.2.) Thus, another potential city revenue source—the income tax—yields propor-

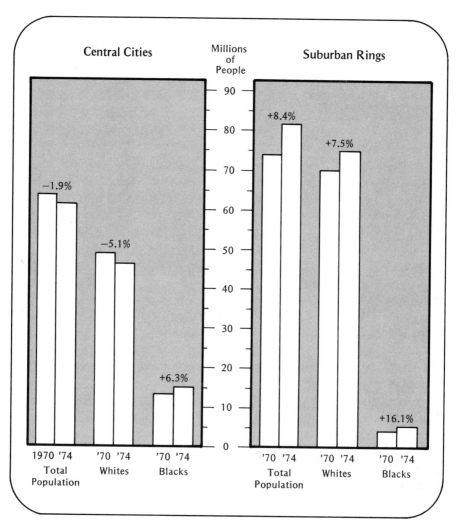

FIGURE 13.2 Where the People Are Going
SOURCE: U.S. Bureau of the Census.

tionately less from this increasingly inpoverished population. At the same time, the poor need more services from government, especially in areas like health and welfare, because they do not have the money to buy them themselves. While the revenue potential of the cities declines, service expenditures are forced up.

Cities declining in population, and then losing their capacity to raise revenue, have the highest per capita costs for governmental services. Why should this be so? Two costs directly related to the economic impoverishment of the city are increases in crime and in the false alarm rate for fires. Both of these correlate with the increase in poor, minority residents of the city. Both of these are costly, since more police must be hired and expensive fire apparatus used more frequently. Other costs that are understandably higher in older cities than in newer or less-populated areas are those for traffic control and for maintenance and firefighting in older buildings.[3]

The most serious spending drain of all has been rapidly rising compensation for city government employees. Increased militance and union activity has led to great gains for municipal workers—but these gains may come at the peril of the city itself, as New York's economic collapse indicates. Public school teachers' salaries *doubled* in cities like New York, Chicago, Los Angeles, Washington, and San Francisco, during the 1960s. In New York City, the 1961 municipal work force of 235,000 became 381,000 by 1971, while large increases in the work force also took place in cities like Detroit, Philadelphia, Los Angeles, and San Francisco. While layoffs have occurred since then, they have been caused in large part by the strain of increased wages on city budgets.[4]

Between 1950 and 1975, aggregate annual state and local government payrolls swelled by a factor of ten, from $915 million to over $9 billion.[5] To be sure, inflation accounted for 150 percent of this increase. But the other 850 percent is due to increased numbers of workers (four million in 1950 versus twelve million in 1975) and increased compensation, described in Chapters 8 and 12. Small wonder that Frederick O'R. Hayes, former New York City budget director, is on record as saying that unions made his job "almost impossible." He could not predict the outcome of wage bargaining, which had enormous impact on his job of financial planning.[6]

Since the evidence we have indicates that higher wages have not led to

3. Thomas Muller, *Growing and Declining Urban Areas: A Fiscal Comparison* (Washington, D.C.: Urban Institute, 1975).

4. Frances Fox Piven, "The Urban Crisis: Who Got What and Why," in Robert Paul Wolff, ed., *1984 Revisited* (New York: Alfred A. Knopf, 1973), pp. 165–201.

5. John O'Riley, "Service Costs Skyrocket," *Danbury* (Conn.) *News-Times*, 19 June 1976, p. 1.

6. Frederick O'R. Hayes, "Collective Bargaining and the Budget Director," in Sam Zagoria, ed., *Public Workers and Public Unions* (Englewood Cliffs, N.J.: Prentice-Hall, 1972), pp. 85–105.

better services, the cities are in even more trouble. Private garbage firms can do the same job as New York City's sanitation department for one-third the cost. The Boston Metropolitan Transit Authority's operating costs are almost twice those of other major transit systems. Norton E. Long has summed up this problem:

> The most important, the best organized, the most concerned, and the most destructive of the city are the public employees and their unions. With no intention to bankrupt the city, they lack any structured incentive to do otherwise. The low productivity of the service industry would by itself ensure that in their simple effort to keep pace with comparable wages in the private sector the employee unions would face the city with staggering, mounting costs. But in addition, there is no incentive to reward efficiency. Manpower is used instead of technological advance to improve working conditions, and such technology as already exists is ignored or, when used, rendered ineffective. This is bad enough, but there is little reason to doubt that much of the city's expenditures in education, health, and police, to name three of the largest city services, are not only unproductive but counterproductive.[7]

At its most basic level, then, the urban crisis is economic in nature. The central cities are going broke, with some of them, such as Newark and New York, already on the brink of bankruptcy. In April 1976, fiscally desperate Detroit had a giant "garage sale" of fifty years of surplus inventory.

There is a social dimension to the urban crisis as well. While it is not by any means limited to the central cities, vandalism has increased most noticeably there. Destruction of streetlights and private property, proliferating graffiti, and other forms of damage to the physical and esthetic environment cost us not only money but also peace of mind and body. Many of our cities have become centers for dope addiction, and they have much higher rates of homicide, suicide, and violent crime per capita than does the nation as a whole. Because of more permissive court decisions, pornography and prostitution are now much more visible in the cities, adding to an unsavory image and contributing to the crisis in the eyes of many urban residents. It is now impossible for an unaccompanied man to walk down Eighth Avenue in midtown New York, or its equivalent in other cities, without being accosted by prostitutes. Marauding teenagers terrorize Detroit's East Side residents with gang attacks.

Not all central cities are subject to the urban crisis to the same degree. In fact, some of the newer, rapidly growing cities of the West and Southwest are thriving. These cities—Houston, Tucson, Phoenix, San Diego, and others— began their growth in the era of the automobile. They are much larger in area

7. Norton E. Long, *The Unwalled City* (New York: Basic Books, 1972), pp. 188–189.

than the older cities of the Northeast, and much less densely populated. Some are still expanding in area through annexation of the unincorporated areas on their borders. At the same time, even these newer cities house a disproportionate number of the poor and minorities within their borders. In the long run they will probably develop the same problems the older cities have. Los Angeles can be used as evidence for this assertion, for that first city of the automobile is gradually becoming a city of minorities, and it is losing jobs to its suburbs. But for many of the newer western cities, urban problems do not yet constitute the crisis they do for the older cities.

SOME POSSIBLE CITY SCENARIOS

The Sandbox

George Sternlieb has argued that these crisis conditions have turned the cities into a sandbox. In his definition, a sandbox is a place where children are dumped by their parents to play so the parents can tend to more important affairs, intervening occasionally to break up strife and provide more toys and sand to the youngsters. In this analogy, the children are the impoverished residents of the city, and the toys and sand those (increasingly federally financed) government programs aiding them. No one is evaluating the success of these programs, universally accepted as failures, as we shall see in later chapters, but the sandbox approach continues nevertheless. This approach is a bandage rather than a basic cure, since the root problem is that the core areas of our cities lack economic value. Elsewhere in the world central cities are gaining population, while ours are declining.[8]

Indeed, one can argue that the central city is outmoded. With the advent of rapid communication and transportation, there is no further need to cluster homes, businesses, and government services in one small geographic area. The urban areas of the future will be like Los Angeles, a city without a really distinct center and downtown. Even the traditional recreational attractions of cities, such as opera houses, zoos, museums, and the like, can now be located in the suburbs, and surely will be in coming years. Athletic facilities are already relocating, as the construction of suburban stadia outside Boston and New York proves.

But even if the older central city is outmoded, it is an undeniable fact that our system of subnational government savages the city. Differences in regional welfare and local housing policies, which we explore in later chapters, have

8. George Sternlieb, "The City as Sandbox," *Public Interest* (Fall 1971), pp. 14–21.

made the older cities poorhouses. James Q. Wilson has compared them to Indian reservations, for they are the only asylum open to the poor.[9] The cities now carry an unfair burden compared to their suburbs. Our crazy-quilt fragmented system does not only impose efficiency and effectiveness costs on local government. It also threatens the very life of our centers of population and culture. The city can avoid becoming an economic and social shell only if the suburbs assume their fair share of the costs of services that benefit the entire metropolitan area.

In a word, then, the economic function of U.S. cities has become outmoded. They will thus continue to decline, and perhaps they should. After all, why fight dominant economic trends? Why prop up a structure that should be abandoned? The best argument for doing so is that the poor, who are stuck in the cities, cannot abandon them for the suburbs, as we explain in the chapters on housing and welfare. Something, and hopefully something more than a sandbox, has to be provided for the millions of urban residents of our underclass.

The Job Bank

Political scientist Norton E. Long has made a series of provocative proposals for the rescue of the city. Long argues that the loss of jobs is at the heart of the city's illness. Policies intended to benefit the poor, such as the minimum wage, have the opposite effect. Existence of the minimum wage makes it impossible for employers to hire as much unskilled labor as they could use. Instead, the poor get welfare, and learn dependency instead of how to earn their bread. Since 40 percent of urban black teenagers seeking work were unemployed in 1976, Long's recommendations merit serious study.

The schools share a lot of the blame here. A native of the boondocks probably knows how to build a house, even if it's not a very good one. But the product of our elaborate and expensive educational system is hard-pressed to unplug a stopped-up toilet. Education must be linked closely to the world of work, or it becomes irrelevant. This does not mean that all school subjects should be narrowly vocational. It does mean that the schools must become more concerned about the utility of what their students learn, if they hope to serve them. An unskilled eighteen-year-old will not find knowledge of history very useful when he tries to support himself.

The central element of Long's plan for action is a systematic inventory of

9. James Q. Wilson, "The Urban Unease: Community vs. City," *Public Interest* (Summer 1968), pp. 25–39.

192

the job skills of the population. In his view, a city's "job bank" is its most important asset. The nature and extent of its residents' employment is the most crucial resource of a city. In 1976, Long was hired by the city of Hartford, Connecticut to direct a survey compiling this information.

Long is also concerned because industry has not made clear what skills it really needs. He accuses it of asking for academic credentials like the college degree rather than specifying the actual skill requirements for jobs. Changes in both the attitude of industry and the approach of the schools, then, are needed if the situation is to improve.

Long does not minimize either the political or technical barriers to change. The chapter on education in this book discusses the political monopoly certain groups have over schools. As far as the techniques and technology of problem solving are concerned, we now simply lack the answers to questions like "How do we teach children to read better?" and "How do we train the hard-core unemployed to work?" As Mayor Carl Stokes of Cleveland said in 1969, "Money will help us do the things we know how to do. But what do you do about the things you don't know how to do?" It is not that we cannot learn the answers, but that we have not yet invested enough effort to learn them.

Long does not have, or claim to have, all the answers. Yet he is surely right when he says that if current trends continue, the older cities will soon be little more than poor farms. Only serious and sustained effort will ward off this disastrous decline.[10]

Planned Shrinkage

Roger Starr, head of New York City's Housing and Development Administration from 1974 to 1976, advocates a policy of planned shrinkage for New York. This policy would seem to have as much relevance to other older central cities losing population and jobs as it does to New York, so it merits attention here.

Starr views his controversial proposal as an attempt to come to terms with the inevitable. Since New York is shrinking demographically and economically and there is little that can be done to halt the trend, he advocates making the best of it.

Starr argues that a New York with a population of less than 5 million, compared to its present 7.5 million, could still be a great world city and a good place to live. But such will be possible only if the pattern of costs remains the same in the smaller city as it is in the larger. There will have to be a reduction in

10. Long, *The Unwalled City*.

the number of miles of streets patrolled, cleaned, repaired, and served by public transportation. The key to this reduction is consistent density of population, so that buildings and blocks are full. Otherwise social cohesion is impossible and economic return so low that the buildings will be abandoned. Even more crucially, the city government can provide services much more efficiently to the fully populated areas. Currently, the South Bronx of New York is a sparsely settled area of abandoned buildings, yet the city must still provide services to the survivors, whether fire protection, education, or public transportation.

In short, the population must be relocated to the sections that remain alive and densely populated. In the abandoned sections, buildings must be razed and all service centers closed down. Planning must focus on ways to do this in the most humane manner possible, such as using relocation subsidies rather than eviction notices. As Starr concludes, "Better a thriving city of five million than a Calcutta of seven million, destroyed by its internal wrangling." Surely his proposal deserves serious consideration in all the declining central cities of this country.[11]

THE SURGING SUBURBS

In 1889, the British political commentator James Bryce wrote about the American suburbs: "Taxes are so much higher in the larger cities than in the country that there is a strong tendency for rich men to migrate from the city to the suburbs in order to escape the city collector."[12] While the reason Bryce cited is just one of many motivations causing city dwellers to move outward today, the quotation shows that suburban living has been on the minds of our citizens for a long time. With the advent of new methods of transportation and generous housing mortgage terms, the suburbs have grown enormously since the end of World War II.

It was not until 1920 that over half of the U.S. population lived in urban areas, with most of these residents located in the central cities. Fifty years later, in 1970, a majority of those living in urban areas lived in the suburbs. The total for urban areas as a whole in 1970 was 68.6 percent of the population, with 37.2 percent of the population in the suburbs.[13] If 1920 marked the statistical advent of an urban United States, then 1970 marked the coming of the suburban age. This trend has continued unabated since 1970. Between 1970 and 1974, cities

11. Roger Starr, "Making New York Smaller," *New York Times Magazine*, 14 November 1976, pp. 32–33, 99–106.

12. James Bryce, *The American Commonwealth* (New York: World Publications, 1889), p. 228.

13. U.S. Bureau of the Census, *Census of Population and Housing.*

lost 4.6 million net population to the suburbs, and this population had higher average incomes than those who moved into the cities.[14]

The stereotype of the suburb as a dwelling place for upper-income residents never has been totally accurate, and it is less so today when almost 40 percent of the nation's population lives there. One can find blue-collar working-class suburbs, and exclusive suburbs for the very wealthy. There are industrial suburbs with few residents and many jobs, and residential suburbs with many residents and few jobs. Some suburbs are socially and economically diverse in both business and residents. Others are astonishingly homogeneous, with the same type of person or business to be found in all neighborhoods. And some of the older suburbs, such as White Plains, New York, twenty miles from New York City, have succumbed to a "suburban crisis" identical to the urban crisis.

While some suburbs, such as White Plains, have substantial black populations, most suburbs are predominantly white. Blacks composed 27 percent of the population of urban areas as a whole in 1974, but made up only 5 percent of the suburban population.[15] As we shall see in the chapter on housing, there are a number of reasons for this, but the fact remains that while blacks and Hispanic Americans are already a majority of the population in Newark, Atlanta, Baltimore, Washington, and Detroit, they make up only a very small proportion of the suburban population. These racial and ethnic factors are basic to an understanding of the differences between the cities and their suburbs.

Some writers have argued that the suburbs are parasites of the cities, since most cities (but no longer Los Angeles, Philadelphia, Detroit, Washington, and Boston) contain more jobs than their surrounding suburbs. The cities contain as well central business districts and recreational facilities like museums, theatres, zoos, and professional sports stadia, which are used by residents of the entire metropolitan area. The city government must provide services, whether water, sewerage, or police protection, to enable these institutions to function. The suburbs do not share in helping the city foot the bill. Quite the contrary, in fact. Attempts by state legislatures to spread the tax burden for these facilities fail in the face of surburban opposition. In 1970, the Utah legislature killed a tax bill needed by Salt Lake City for increased fire and police protection. In the 1950s the city of Boston searched surrounding suburbia to find a new landfill dump location. The only sites it found were offered at an outrageously exhorbitant price. The suburbs knew they had the city at their mercy, and they took full advantage of it rather than try to help alleviate its problems.

14. U.S. Bureau of the Census, *Social and Economic Characteristics of the Metropolitan and Nonmetropolitan Population—1974 and 1970* (Washington, D.C.: U.S. Government Printing Office, 1975).

15. Ibid.

Some suburban observers might disagree with the brunt of this analysis. They argue that most cities now tax the payroll earnings of all who work in the city, and that suburbanites who spend their money on anything in the city benefit the city's economy and thus its government, which taxes the economy. But it is clear that the cities must bear an unequal share of services like public housing and welfare, because a greater proportion of their residents are poor.

ARE THERE WAYS OUT OF THE MAZE?

Theseus, a Greek prince, finally succeeded in entering King Minos's labyrinth, killing the Minotaur, and escaping from the maze. But it is going to be harder to emerge from our local government labyrinth than it was for Theseus to escape from the maze. While Theseus had the assistance of Minos's daughter, Ariadne, who gave him a ball of string to unwind as he entered, so he could follow it back out later, there is no Ariadne around to help us today.

Our principal concern in this section is with attempts to coordinate governmental functions under a new level of general government. More specifically, we focus on the consolidation of the range of service and regulatory activity offered by several localities into a new and necessarily larger unit of general government. This approach, of which there are several variations, is different from another one that has enlisted growing support in a number of areas: unifunctional regionalization or consolidation of services. There are, for example, some regional police and fire governments. When unifunctional consolidation is implemented by the creation of a new special district, as we have already noted, one kind of fragmentation is exchanged for another. When regionalization of one service takes place under a new government, on the other hand, fragmentation is reduced. Our focus here will be on the attempt to create and enlarge the responsibilities of general governments that are geographically larger than the local governments they take over.

Alternative Escapes from the Maze

Creation of a larger general government is not the only way to increase coordination of local government services. Rosceo Martin lists a total of sixteen approaches, including unifunctional regionalization.[16] Some of these alternative approaches warrant inspection before we begin our examination of enlarged general government.

A good deal of *informal cooperation* (mutual aid in fire fighting, sharing of

16. Roscoe C. Martin, *Metropolis in Transition* (Washington, D.C.: Housing and Home Finance Agency, 1963).

police teletype information) occurs among local governments. Of course, its effectiveness and its very existence depend upon the desire of governmental units to cooperate.

A number of cities and counties buy and sell local services through a *service contract*. Los Angeles County, for example, through what is called the Lakewood Plan, offers a range of services, including police protection and water supply, to municipalities within the county. (Chapter 22 examines the operation of the Lakewood Plan for police protection.) A 1971 survey of 2,000 cities found that 62 percent of them contracted with their counties for services.

Annexation of unincorporated areas into cities and counties has slowed in recent years because most areas surrounding large cities are now incorporated. This gives them a legal life of their own, so that they cannot be absorbed by cities. Some cities have used their practical monopoly on vital services to force annexation. In the 1960s, Mayor George Sensenbrenner of Columbus, Ohio informed those suburbs that bought water from Columbus that their days of independent existence were over. Unless they allowed annexation, the water supply would be shut off. Annexation began at once. But growing suburban power has prevented other cities from using this approach. Milwaukee's attempt to emulate Columbus failed when the suburban-dominated state legislature forced it to supply the suburbs with water at low cost.[17]

Functional consolidation of city and county services has occurred in a number of areas. For example, the city of Rochester, New York has combined its welfare department, airport, civil defense, health, mental health, and park programs with those of Monroe County.

COUNCILS OF GOVERNMENT (COGs)

The first Council of Government (COG)–type organization was the Detroit Area Supervisors' Inter-County Committee, formed in 1954 by the supervisors of the six area counties. The committee was established to deal with common problems in water supply, sewage and waste disposal, and transportation. This COG, like the hundreds of others that later sprang up around the nation, can be defined as a voluntary regional association of local governments, which is concerned with a broad range of government services and problems. Each member government is represented in the COG by elected officials, who meet to exchange information, discuss problems, and develop policy on matters of common interest. COGs usually also formulate a comprehensive plan for the area, review applications from members for federal grants to see if these applica-

17. Long, *The Unwalled City*, p. 79.

tions are consistent with the plan, and serve as liaison groups with federal bureaus.

The COG's limitations lie in its lack of authority. A confederal body, it lacks governmental powers and operating responsibilities. It cannot compel participation, attendance, or acquiescence in its decisions. President Harry Truman once said about his job that all he had was the power to persuade, to convince others that what he wanted was in their best interest as well. Such is quite literally true about the power of COGs.

Since COGs lack formal authority, why have local governments bothered to create them? First, government officials have supported COGs because they see them, however imperfect, as a start towards coordination and as the only mechanism available for such coordination. Second, officials have feared that if they do not take regional action, they might lose authority to the state and federal governments or to proposed metro governments. Third, the federal and some state governments have given local governments incentives to form and join COGs. In 1965, the federal housing act passed that year entitled COGs to "701" planning funds, which made them eligible for the first time for significant income sources.

In 1966, the federal Model Cities Act required cities and counties to clear many grant applications with COGs or regional planning agencies in their area. The Intergovernmental Cooperation Act of 1968 reinforced and extended this grant-clearing provision. The increase from 35 COGs in 1965 to 352 by 1972 indicates the importance of these federal incentives.

While COGs are growing in number and importance, they remain, as the Advisory Commission on Intergovernmental Relations has said, "essentially a device for incremental adaptation to changing needs."[18] No major or sweeping changes are likely to come from an institution that can only make decisions by consensus. COGs find it relatively easy to agree on a common approach to purchasing, whereby all governments will benefit from lower prices resulting from larger orders. But more controversial matters, such as busing central-city schoolchildren to the suburbs, or deciding where to place low-income housing, are not going to be resolved by COGs. The very different perspectives of the central city, the county, and different types of suburbs preclude this type of decision making.

COGs are further limited because of their often conflicting relationships to the federal and local governments. They have to assure the "feds" that they are

18. Advisory Commission on Intergovernmental Relations, *Regional Decision Making: New Strategies for Substate Districts*, (Washington, D.C.: U.S. Government Printing Office, 1973), Chapter 3.

worthwhile investments and simultaneously reassure local governments that they are not a threat. Federal insistence on common area approaches to problem solving will be resisted by the desire of local governments to approach these problems in their own individual ways.

At the same time, the probable prospect for the future is an increased role for COGs. The "New Federalism" emphasized by Presidents Nixon and Ford stressed "decentralizing" federal programs to state and local elected officials. If it is continued in the late 1970s and in the 1980s, it will probably put more grant-implementation authority into COGs as it evolves. COGs are more active and robust now than ten years earlier. The reasons for their establishment—service coherence and coordination—will probably cause them to become increasingly important in the years ahead.

METRO GOVERNMENT

There have been two basic approaches to the creation of metropolitan area-wide government in the U.S.A. One is consolidation of a central city's government with that of the surrounding county. The other is the two-tier approach, which strengthens an area-wide government while retaining all or most existing municipalities. Neither has been very popular, but both have been used more frequently in recent years than ever before.

Examples of city-county consolidation in the nineteenth century include New Orleans, Philadelphia, New York, and Boston. Since 1945, there have been consolidations in Baton Rouge, Louisiana; Nashville, Tennessee; Jacksonville, Florida; and Indianapolis, Indiana, among others. For each of these successful efforts, there are scores of failures.

City-county consolidations usually involve one major city in a rapidly urbanizing county in a moderate-sized metropolitan area. No postwar consolidations involved a city over 500,000. The seven consolidations occurring between 1969 and 1973 were limited to cities under 200,000. The smaller municipalities are free, through a referendum, to join or stay out. The new government is divided into different tax districts, depending on the level of services provided in each area. The consolidated government has an elected chief executive, who usually confronts a fairly large legislature.

The two-tier approach has been carried out in Miami and Minneapolis-St. Paul. Such an approach may or may not involve a reallocation of functions, in whole or in part, from one level of government to another. All of the metro area, as in the case of Atlanta, or only part of it, as in the case of Miami, may be involved.

199

In the sections that follow, the experiences of cities with different types of metro will be examined.[19]

City-County Consolidation: The Cases of Indianapolis and Nashville

In 1961, the city of Nashville, Tennessee and Davidson County were consolidated into one government, after a referendum election in which all voters of both jurisdictions were able to vote. The merger came after demands for greater cooperation among Nashville localities following the end of World War II, a failure to consolidate in 1958, and the annexation by the city of Nashville of fifty square miles of unincorporated area with 87,000 residents between 1958 and 1961. Perhaps the key factor creating Metro was the failure of suburban septic tanks. Awash in their own waste, suburbanites sought a solution in Metro.

Metro Nashville has a mayor-council form of government, with all the powers of a municipality. It is divided into two service districts, the general services district (GSD), which consists of the entire county, and the urban services district (USD), which consists primarily of the area of the former city of Nashville. Each district has its own tax rate. Residents of the USD pay more because they receive additional services, including water, sewers, garbage collection, and fire protection. GSD areas that desire these services can be annexed into the USD.

The 1969 merger of Indianapolis, Indiana with Marion County was accomplished not through referendum, but by an act of the state legislature. This makes the Indianapolis situation unique, and it may remain so for quite awhile. This merger was not as complete as Nashville's. Both the city and county continue to exist as separate legal units, and the eleven school districts were left untouched. Further, three municipalities of over 5,000 population were left outside the merger, as was the judicial system, and the mayor was given no authority over the county welfare board. These exceptions were felt to be the necessary political price if any merger went through. Like Nashville, metro Indianapolis (referred to as "Unigov") has different taxation and service districts.

The Two-Tier Approach: Dade County and the Twin Cities

In 1957, Dade County, Florida, in which Miami is located, adopted a new home rule charter giving the county government the authority to take over many of the functions carried out by the county's municipalities. Those who live in

19. These sections are based on Advisory Commission on Intergovernmental Relations, *Regional Governance: Promise and Performance* (Washington, D.C.: U.S. Government Printing Office, 1973).

municipalities live under two-tier (county and city) government, while the half-million residents of unincorporated areas are governed only by the county. The continuation of two-tier government is guaranteed by the charter, which does not allow municipalities to be abolished unless a majority of their voters so desire.

Dade County's charter is unclear about which governmental functions belong to municipalities and which to the county. This has made comprehensive metro planning impossible. In addition, the charter does not provide strong, unified leadership; there are only a weak mayor and a professional manager who has not been allowed to play a strong leadership role by the council. The county also lacks strong, flexible fiscal power, still relying principally on the property tax and user fees to raise its own revenue.

At the same time, county activities are gradually increasing. Functions taken over by the county include the traffic courts, air and water pollution control, subdivision control, and tree removal. Most new county services resulted from transfers from city governing bodies to the county. Examples include traffic engineering, the Miami seaport, urban renewal, and a number of police functions.

A different approach from that taken in Dade County was used in the Twin Cities area of Minneapolis–St. Paul, Minnesota to create its Metropolitan Council. In 1967 the state legislature established the Council, a fifteen-member body appointed by the governor, which represented several counties in the metropolitan area. The Council's authority includes the areas of sewerage, solid waste disposal, highways, creation of parks, transit, air pollution, and COG-type review of federal grant applications. (As this last responsibility indicates, multi-jurisdictional Metro governments may be designated as COGs by the federal government. At the same time, as in the case of Nashville, a consolidated county-city government may also belong to a COG that includes the other counties in the metropolitan area.) The Twin Cities approach has been labelled the state-supported umbrella regional council. It differs from Miami metro government in that the Metropolitan Council is strictly a policy-determining group, like a city council. It relies on previously existing agencies to implement the policies it approves, rather than creating a new layer of government and directly supervising the execution of policy itself.

Metro Politics

There have been only a handful of new metro governments created since 1945. Further, as we have seen previously, most of these do not wield strong authority.

201

With the crying need for coordination of services, why has metro failed to spread?

The answer to this question lies partly in the attitudes of suburban residents, who tend to oppose the various forms of metro. As we mentioned earlier, they left the city to escape its problems, and they don't want to find that their suburb is suddenly part of the city. Another cause lies in the nature of our political system. Most mergers of governments have to be approved by referendum, so the suburban voters and other opponents can express their opposition directly. In the exceptional cases of Indianapolis and the Twin Cities, whose metro approaches were enacted by the state legislature, one wonders what the outcome would have been had a referendum been the decision-making mechanism instead. And even when the state legislature makes the decision, substantial local influence is felt, as the failure of Indianapolis's "Unigov" to assume all governing authority proves.

Usually, state legislatures are as anxious to get involved with the creation of metro government as they are with bubonic plague. In Indianapolis and the Twin Cities, strong local sentiment for the change led to state action. Remember that state legislators are elected from local districts, so they will heed the desires of their constituents. And most suburban constituents are not interested in metro government. The example of the reaction of Milwaukee suburbs to a proposed metro government illustrates the point. The following statements were made by suburban enemies of Metro:[20]

> West Allis will resist any program of step-by-step functional consolidation which will eventually emasculate cities and leave them mere hollow shells.
> Wauwatusa doesn't want to end up in Milwaukee's stomach.
> St. Francis's local government is necessary to maintain the freedom of action and spirit among citizens.

Neither are many central-city politicians and government officials interested in metro. The mayor of the central city may well not win reelection to the chief executive post in an enlarged metro government. And who will be police chief or health director? A host of existing officials will vie for each job in the new government, and only one will succeed. Majority party leaders, usually Democrats in the central cities, may be reduced to minority status when Republican suburbs join them in metro.

Our system is one, then, that largely leaves it up to the local governments themselves to decide whether or not they want metro, and at this time they do not. Of the 127 single-county metropolitan areas, only four are city-county

20. Henry S. Reuss, *Revenue-Sharing* (New York: Praeger, 1970), p. 75.

consolidations, while there are only three two-tier approaches (Miami, Atlanta, and the Twin cities) that have accomplished anything of substance.

That more comprehensive metro plans can be enacted under different political conditions is illustrated by examining our neighbor to the north, the Toronto, Canada area. Toronto's two-tier government was created in 1954 by the provincial (equivalent of our state) legislature. From the beginning, Metro was entrusted with more substantial authority than has been the case in the U.S. The reasons for this United States–Canadian difference are explained at greater length in Chapter 27. Suffice it to say here that they have to do with the different political culture, traditions, and power relationships found in Canada, which make the provincial level of government more powerful relative to local government. This independence was underscored in 1967, when the legislature consolidated Metro Toronto's thirteen-member government into six units. In 1972, as a further example, metro government in the Winnipeg area was established by abolishing the cities in the area and vesting full authority in the metro government.

Such dramatic breaks with the past are unlikely to occur in the U.S.A. Rather, the simultaneous growth of unifunctional special districts and of COGs will probably continue, until the day when these two forms will have to confront each other. At some point in the future, it seems safe to assert that COGs will evolve into metro governments—but this is a long way off, and may not even occur in our lifetime. Changes will likely be evolutionary in nature, with COGs slowly gathering more authority over time.

Metro Accomplishments

The reader may have suspected that an implicit assumption of this book is that the various mechanisms for coordination discussed here will partially alleviate the urban crisis. It is now time to examine this assumption more critically, because we shall find, as usual, that reality is more complex and complicated than any generalization.

As is true of all political situations, preference for metro government is a matter of values. Suppose that a person would prefer to see a variety of local governments continue to exist, just as he would like to see a variety of new car models. This selection would give him a wide choice in picking the area in which he wanted to live. Perhaps some people would like to live in low-tax, low-service areas, while others would prefer the opposite. While metro government would not wipe out these kinds of differences among localities, it would tend to level the extremes and increase homogeneity. And there is no question that most people prefer heterogeneity over service coordination today. One could argue that they

203

feel this way out of selfishness, parochialism, or ignorance, but even if these are the reasons, they are irrelevant. If we live in a democracy, regard for the wishes of the majority is essential.

Suppose further that you belong to a minority group, such as the blacks or the Hispanic-Americans, who are about to become the majority in a central city and take over the government through their voting power. Certainly your feelings about metro will be mixed. While you may recognize that the city and whole area have problems that only metro can help to solve, the creation of metro will deprive your group of much political power. Under city-county consolidation, the minorities will lose out to the white suburban majority; under a two-tier approach, they will have to share power with the metro government. Opposition to metro in this context is understandable. Certainly black mayors like Cleveland's Stokes, Gary's Hatcher, and Newark's Gibson have not been ardent advocates of metro.

What has metro's record been? Has it led to more efficient and effective service delivery? Is money being saved as a result? These questions are harder to answer than one might think. The only way to adequately answer them would be to duplicate a metropolitan area, leaving one area with its old form of government and providing one with the metro form, and then compare service delivery and costs in each. Since this is impossible, we have to use more indirect methods of analysis. It is not surprising that different studies report different findings. Asking the following questions will enable us to examine the results of these studies.

Does metro spend less on government services? Daniel Grant argues that it does, by eliminating duplication and introducing "economies of scale."[21] Economies of scale are the lower per-unit costs of providing services and goods that result when production is increased to an optimal level. For example, General Motors, with its huge plants, can make the same type of car more cheaply than smaller manufacturers that turn out only a few hundred cars a day. Likewise, it is argued that bigger government departments, which can create specialized units a small government cannot afford, will be more effective and more economical. Grant admits that spending has risen in Nashville and Miami since the advent of metro, but argues that it would have risen at a far higher rate without it. This may be so, but it is impossible to test.

Grant's argument is disputed in a provocative analysis carried out by

21. Daniel R. Grant, "Political Stability in Metropolitan Government," in F. Gerald Brown and Thomas P. Murphy, eds., *Emerging Patterns in Urban Administration* (Lexington, Mass.: D.C. Heath, 1970), pp. 39–63.

Steven P. Erie, John J. Kirlin, and Francine F. Rabinovitz, who argue that research shows that above a population level of 15,000 there are no further increases in economies of scale.[22] In other words, governments serving more than 15,000 people do not necessarily function more efficiently and economically than those serving fewer.

More research in this area is badly needed. Very little has been done, so one cannot draw definite conclusions about the relationship between size and spending. But at this point we cannot conclude that metro is a money saver. And even Grant feels that metro causes higher spending, because metro residents demand more services after metro is passed. Note, again, that it is impossible to prove this assertion, because we do not know what would have happened had metro not been created in these places.

Does metro reduce taxes? While the ACIR has found that metro governments almost always spend more than was the case before, in a number of instances taxes have declined. This happened in Jacksonville and Indianapolis, but ACIR concludes that these tax decreases do not necessarily stem from greater efficiency. Rather, they are a result of the creation of a larger property tax base through metro.[23]

Does metro lead to greater tax and spending equity? Proponents of metro, such as Grant, argue that metro brings about a more equitable distribution of taxes by eliminating the free ride of the suburbs. Suburbanites who did not pay before for many of the services of the central city that they used now share the costs. Erie, Kirlin, and Rabinovitz, on the other hand, argue that metro governments often do not provide services any more equitably than was true before metro. They point to the continued existence of different tax and service districts, which we mentioned earlier. Again, one would like to see additional in-depth studies of this subject because existing evidence is only fragmentary.

Does metro facilitate the solving of area-wide problems? Grant, in a survey of Nashville and Miami, believes this to be true, as do we. As the sections on Miami and the Twin Cities pointed out, area-wide problems are being tackled where before they were not. While not everyone would give high grades to the efforts of the metro governments, the point is that they are doing considerably more than was done previously.

22. Steven P. Erie, John J. Kirlin, and Francine R. Rabinovitz, *Reform of Metropolitan Governments* (Washington, D.C.: Resources for the Future, 1972).
23. Advisory Commission, *Regional Governance*.

It seems safe to conclude, then, that metro governments and COGs can contribute to solving area-wide problems. On the other hand, one should not expect them to lower taxes and spending. In the long run, though, they will probably lead to more effective service delivery, since any mechanism that cuts through the jungle of fragmentation is going to make it easier to get a job done. But note that coordination cannot in itself solve the urban crisis. That solution will depend on other factors, discussed in the following chapters dealing with specific policy areas.[24]

24. The best general discussion of these factors is William Gorham and Nathan Glazer's *The Urban Predicament* (Washington, D.C.: The Urban Institute, 1976).

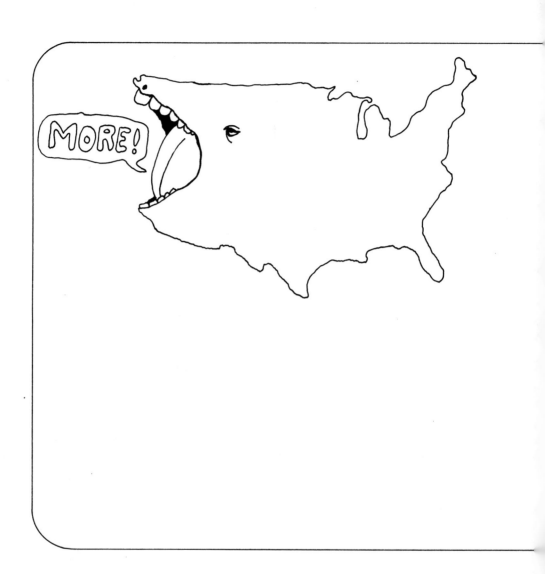

PART FOUR

THE SYSTEM IN ACTION: ECONOMICS

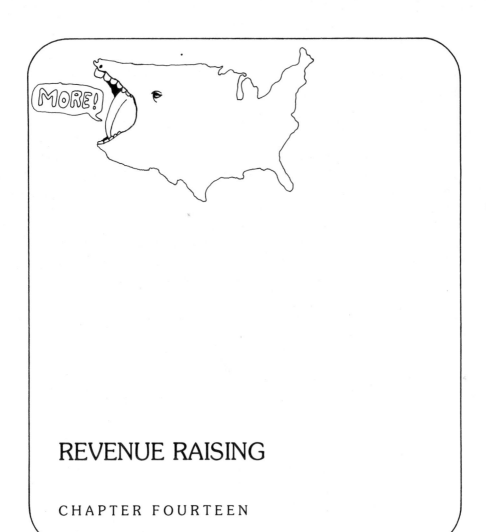

REVENUE RAISING

CHAPTER FOURTEEN

A little over a hundred years ago a noted English writer named Walter Bagehot commented that the United States would probably never have any tax problems. "America is not a country sensitive to taxes," he wrote. "America is too rich, daily industry there is too common, too skillful and too productive for her to care much for fiscal burdens."[1]

Although Bagehot still is held in considerable esteem by political scientists, their admiration for his perceptions does not extend to his prophecies—at least insofar as they deal with American public finance. For, as anyone who reads newspapers or hears newscasts knows, we have become a country extremely

1. Walter Bagehot, *The English Constitution and Other Political Essays* (New York: D. Appleton & Company, 1907), p. 324.

sensitive to taxes. And this has registered a strong impact on the state and local system.

WHERE THE SYSTEM GETS ITS MONEY

Although state and local governments are receiving heavy injections from the federal government, and in the case of local governments increasing financial support from the states as well, most of these governments must raise a good deal of money on their own. To accomplish this purpose they have created a wide variety of taxes as well as other revenue-producing measures. No state's revenue-raising pattern duplicates another state's and even within any given state the strategies of the individual communities will differ. Nevertheless, certain general patterns emerge, and certain generalizations can be made.

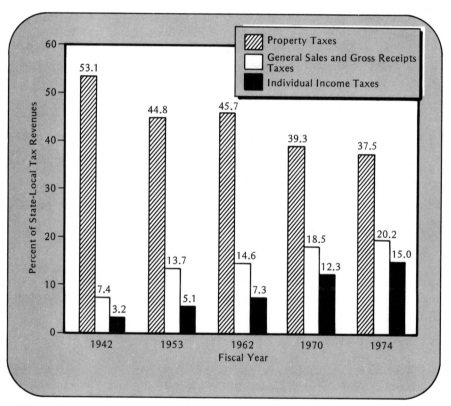

FIGURE 14.1   The Big Three's Contribution to State-Local Tax Revenue, Selected Years: 1942–1974

SOURCE: ACIR, *Trends in Fiscal Federalism* (1975) based on U.S. Bureau of the Census data compiled by the ACIR staff.

Sales Taxes

The sales tax has long served as the bulwark of state financing. Although, as we shall see, it no longer occupies the prominent position it once did in the state financial picture, it still produces more money for state governments than any other revenue source. In 1972, sales taxes poured over $17.5 billion into state treasuries, making up about 40 percent of all the money the states received. Forty-five states today impose sales taxes, ranging up to 7 percent.

Although the states have made the most use of the sales tax, local governments have not remained oblivious to its attractions. More and more of them in recent years have asked for and received permission from their state governments to use it. Such local sales taxes usually take the form of an "add-on," with the local government tacking its tax onto the state impost. Anyone shopping in New York City, for example, pays an 8 percent sales tax, with 5 percent going to the state and 3 percent going to the city. However, while such local sales taxes are becoming increasingly common, the tax does not constitute a major source of municipal revenue.

The reasons why states have relied so heavily on the sales tax are not difficult to discover. First, it is an area of taxation the federal government has left largely untapped. Beyond certain selective taxes on such things as liquor, cigarettes, and gasoline, Washington has chosen to raise most of its money through other means. This gives the states something of a clear field.

Then, although no tax is ever painless, the sales tax seems less painful than many others. People pay it only a little at a time except when they buy substantial items such as new cars. And even when it comes to these items the tax does not seem to bulk large in the overall price. Furthermore, taxpayers feel they have more discretion over just how much tax they must pay since they pay the tax only when they decide to make a purchase. This discretion may be somewhat illusory, especially when the tax applies to many necessities, but nonetheless they can usually modify their purchases, if they cannot forego them, and this gives them the feeling that they are paying only those taxes that they consent to pay.

One final factor in favor of the sales tax is that it enables the state or the local government to reach into the pockets of its nonresidents. Sales taxes are assessed on all those who buy taxable goods, regardless of their residence. Consequently, out-of-state visitors, including students, contribute to its proceeds. It is no surprise then that states with large tourist industries have made the most use of sales taxes. Florida, for example, derives over three-quarters of its income from such revenues.

Despite its relative popularity—and we must keep in mind that almost no tax is ever really popular—the sales tax is not without its critics. Liberal groups and labor unions usually oppose it on the ground that it hurts the poor the most. This does not mean that they pay out more than the well-to-do in sales taxes. They do not. But what they do expend is a greater proportion of their income. The sales tax is *regressive* since it absorbs a smaller and smaller *proportion* of a person's income as his income increases.

Many states have moved to reduce this regressiveness by exempting certain necessities from the sales tax. Food and medicines are the most customary items excluded from sales taxes, with fuel and clothing next. Since poorer people tend to spend a larger share of their income on such goods, exempting such goods from taxation helps the have-nots more than the haves. However, such limited sales taxes, as opposed to general sales taxes, pose problems of their own. They lend themselves to a form of cheating called *leakage*.

An example will illustrate how such leakage occurs. A person buys an apple for a quarter and a pack of razor blades for a dollar from the corner grocery store. Let us assume that food is exempted from the sales tax but razor blades are not. The storekeeper charges the buyer the tax on the razor blades but then rings up both items as food. This allows him to pocket the tax himself as an extra profit. If all items were taxed, however, it would not be so simple. Then, the tax inspectors would only need to check the storekeepers's gross sales receipts to find out how much tax he should pay. The merchant cannot switch receipts from taxable to nontaxable categories when the sales tax is a general one and covers them all.

Another problem with limited sales taxes, i.e., sales taxes that exempt certain kinds of commodities, is that they rarely succeed in eliminating the problem of regressiveness altogether. They do make the tax less regressive then it would otherwise be, but they fail to make it *progressive*, which means that it would take an increased proportion of a person's income as his total income increased. Consequently, sales taxes of all kinds continue to draw criticism from those committed to taxing the rich at a higher rate than the poor.

Income Taxes

Until fairly recently, states tended to shy away from using income taxes. At least three factors underlie such skittishness. First, the federal government seemed to have more or less preempted this area of taxation for itself. Second, income tax encounters more resistance from the people than do sales taxes. Since income taxes take chunks of money directly out of their pay envelopes, workers often disagree with their union leaders by preferring sales taxes. Meanwhile, higher-income receivers usually regard state income taxes as absolute anathema.

214

The fact that higher-income people, including employers, tend to oppose such taxes with particular vigor introduces the third factor for their relative unpopularity. States have often felt that adopting an income tax would drive business and highly taxed individuals away or discourage new businesses and high-income groups from settling in the state. So for all these reasons state income taxes were slow in coming.

However, the surge in state spending that has occurred since World War II has forced one state after another to abandon its antagonism to such revenue-raising measures. By the mid-1970s some forty states were collecting income taxes.

How do state income taxes compare with the federal income tax? As might be supposed, they take a much smaller share of the citizen's income. If they were as steep as the natonal income tax, many people would have little left in their pay envelopes. State income taxes usually absorb less than 10 percent and some take no more than 2 percent.

Such taxes are also, for the most part, far less graduated than the federal income tax. In other words, their rates do not increase so sharply as one moves up the income scale. Yet some degree of difference in their rates is usually present. The rich generally pay a somewhat greater proportion of their income than do the poor, so that state income taxes, unlike the sales tax, are at least modestly progressive.

The federal government has sought to encourage states to link their income taxes with its own. This would not only increase the progressiveness of these state taxes but also cut down on administrative costs for the state governments and reduce the confusion for the taxpayers. In 1970 Congress passed legislation allowing states to "piggy back" their income taxes onto that of the federal government.[2] Under this system the taxpayer makes out only one tax form and, after determining his federal tax, adds a percentage of it for his state income tax. Just what percentage is used is up to the individual state. The federal government then returns the added amount to the state. Such a system means that the state does not have to process and audit its own income tax and the taxpayers do not have to make out two separate and often quite different tax forms.

The piggy-back plan was to become operative in 1974 providing at least two states having between them at least 5 percent of the U.S. population signed up for it. Three states, Nebraska, Rhode Island, and Vermont, accepted the offer and some observers believe that it is only a question of time before many other states take advantage of its provisions.

2. Robert Metz, "'Piggyback' Tax Collections in the Offing," *New York Times,* 7 January 1973.

Income taxes, like sales taxes, have begun to attract the interest of many municipalities, particularly the usually hard-pressed major cities. Many have obtained their state's permission to level income taxes of their own. However, such taxes are usually limited to salaried income and are imposed at flat rates, which are usually no more than 1 percent. Confining such rates to wages and salaries and imposing them without graduated rates would normally make such taxes regressive. However, since they are levied on all wage earners in the city, they force the usually better-paid commuters to shoulder some of the burden for the usually less-well-off city residents. Hence, a measure of progressivity may be found.

By 1972, some thirty-five hundred municipalities and other local governments were collecting about $2.2 billion in income taxes. This represented less than 2 percent of all local government revenue for the year. However, for many of these local governments, the tax was providing substantial benefits.

Property Taxes

While few taxes ever achieve popularity, possibly no tax has managed to arouse more animosity than the property tax. What is more, this hostility emanates from the entire political spectrum. Conservatives and liberals, Democrats and Republicans, large property owners and small property owners, tax specialists and average taxpayers all tend to react to the property tax with revulsion.

"It has been said," observes one economist, "that the property tax has only two faults: first, it is wrong in theory and second, it does not work in practice. Others have said that the administrative defects of the tax somewhat compensate for its conceptual shortcomings."[3] Those who pay it usually agree. Polls have persistently shown that the American people regard the property tax as the most unfair and undesirable levy thay have to pay.[4]

Before going on to examine some of the reasons why the property tax has succeeded in currying so much disfavor, let us first briefly see what it is. Essentially, it is a tax on real estate. Anyone owning a commercial building, a home, or even just a garage receives a bill each year telling him how much he has to pay. Two factors determine just how much this bill is. One is the value the levying government has placed on the property. The other is the tax rate the levying government has set for all property in its jurisdiction.

3. Harold Groves, *Financing Government*, 6th ed. (New York: Holt, Rinehart & Winston, 1964), p.248.
4. For a report on one such poll see: *National Civic Review* (November 1975), p. 543.

216

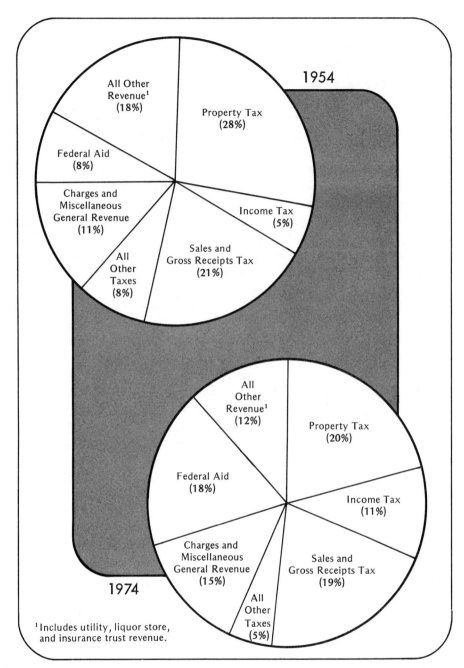

FIGURE 14.2   The State and Local Revenue System Becomes More Diversified with the Relative Decline in Property Taxes and Relative Increase in State Income Taxes and Federal Aid, Fiscal Years 1954 and 1974

SOURCE: Advisory Commission on Intergovernmental Relations, *Improving Urban America: A Challenge to Federalism* (Washington, D.C.: U.S. Government Printing Office, 1976).

Here is how it works: Suppose the resident of a city owns his own home. If the city assesses the value of this house as $10,000, and if it has set a tax rate for the year of $100 for each $1,000 of value, then the homeowner must pay a tax bill of $1,000. Suppose the following year the city decides that the value of his home is really $15,000. Then, if the tax rate remains the same, he will have to pay $1,500. On the other hand, if the city does increase his assessment to $15,000 but at the same time cuts its tax rate to $50 per thousand, the lucky homeowner will see his tax bill drop to $750. Thus, the tax bill on a piece of property depends on (1) how much the taxing jurisdiction thinks the property is worth and (2) the tax rate which the jurisdiction has set for the year.

The tax rate itself may be expressed in other ways than in dollars per $1,000 valuation. Some jurisdictions set it in the form of cents or even mills. (A mill is worth one-tenth of the cent.) Thus a rate of $100 per $1,000 could be expressed as $10 per $100 or one hundred mills per dollar. The citizen would pay the same amount of money in each case.

Property taxes constitute the chief source of revenue for municipal governments. Although their reliance on this levy has gone down somewhat in recent years thanks to increased revenues from Washington and state governments as well as increased use of other taxes, they still depend on it for over half of all the money they receive. The actual figure varies, however, from municipality to municipality. Philadelphia, with a city income tax, derives less than one-third of all its funds from property taxes. Boston, without a city income tax, depends on property for over two-thirds of its financing. Counties, educational districts, and special districts also tend to lean heavily on property tax revenues. States, however, make little use of it.

Aside from the fact that it is a bit more complicated than other taxes, what makes the property tax place so low on the popularity poll? To begin with, it is rather expensive to collect. The jurisdiction using it must periodically, sometimes even annually, assess the value of all property within its borders. This is usually a herculean task. To do it correctly means that each piece of privately owned real estate must be inspected and then its value must be computed based on a good deal of complicated data. In practice, as we shall see, few, if any communities, actually do this on a regular basis. But even limited efforts in this direction can be quite costly. Then, individual tax bills must be sent out for each piece of taxable property. And if the property owner doesn't pay the bill on time, collection costs start to mount.

Second, the property tax tends to discourage community improvement and growth. Of course, it can be argued that all taxes tend to do this, yet the property tax seems to strike with a heavier hand. The problem here is that the tax tends to "punish" people for improving their property since if they do so

218

they increase its worth. And, as we have seen, the worth of a piece of property, as determined by the tax assessors, is one of the two factors that determine how much tax its owner must pay. Property taxes, by penalizing improvements, may thus tend to promote slums. Certainly, they provide little incentive for people to upgrade their real estate. When real estate owners do make such improvements, they do so in spite of, rather than because of, the property tax.

But more disheartening than these problems are the many inequities and even iniquities it produces. These come about in a variety of ways and take a variety of forms. For one thing, the property tax is a legacy from colonial days when most wealth took the form of real estate. This, of course, is no longer true. As a result the property tax does not necessarily take the most money from those who can most afford to pay it. Those who have put most of their net worth into property pay more proportionately than others. Among these are elderly couples who through their working years have used their savings to pay off their mortgages rather than to buy stocks and bonds or maintain bank accounts. When their incomes are reduced through retirement, they frequently cannot meet their property tax payments and so must sell their homes. The steep rises in property tax rates in most jurisdictions during the early 1970s forced many retired couples to take this step.[5] In general, property taxes discourage people from putting their savings into home ownership.

Another widespread source of unfairness is the difficulty involved in administering the tax. As we noted earlier, it is almost impossible for the taxing government to make a thorough evaluation every year of the value of each piece of property it taxes. Consequently some property may be improved without being evaluated upward by the assessors. Other properties may fall into disrepair without experiencing a lowering of their assessed value. Whole neighborhoods may increase in value without any commensurate change in valuation. (There are, however, ways in which property owners who believe their property to be overvalued can appeal for a lowering of their assessment.)

Sometimes such discrepancies in valuations are deliberate. For example, some municipalities tend to underassess single-family homes and maintain a much higher assessment rate for commercial property. In this case the authorities may be trying to placate those who cast the most votes in the municipal elections. In other jurisdictions, certain favored industries may benefit from underassessment. Here the government involved may be trying to encourage the industry to stay put and possibly expand, rather than move to a lower-tax locality.

This brings us to another problem. The property tax, more than almost

5. Robert Lindsey, "Property Taxes Soar in Nation," *New York Times*, 23 November 1975.

any other, lays itself open to outright corruption. Property owners frequently find ways of offering inducements of various kinds to tax assessors or to the elected officials who oversee these assessors. And instances where such inducements have been accepted are far from rare. But even where money has not changed hands, favoritism, nepotism, and other unacceptable practices may play a part in determining the valuation placed on a piece of property.

Some of the worst inequities of the property tax involve intergovernmental relations. For example, two cities lie side by side. In one city there are many churches, colleges, hospitals, and government office buildings. The other city has few such structures. Offhand, one would envy the former city with all these institutions to enrich both its social and spiritual life and its economy. However, probably it is the other city that benefits most. Governmental and nonprofit organizations do not have to pay taxes. Consequently the first city must yield up often valuable land and provide services to institutions that pay no part of the city tax bill. Yet the services these institutions provide are often as available to residents of the neighboring city as they are to its own citizens.

As might be suspected, central cities tend to suffer most from the problems of the property tax. They usually house most of the region's government agencies, hospitals, schools, charitable agencies, churches, etc. The suburban or satellite communities make use of these institutions without having to incur any of the costs they impose. A 1970 study estimated that the revenues lost on such tax-exempt property amounted to nearly $12.5 billion every year.[6] This would come to well over $300 per family if distributed uniformly throughout the nation. However, since the central cities bear the brunt of the problem, their losses on a per capita or per family basis are much higher.

The property tax results in another and probably more serious imbalance in the finances of local governments. This occurs because some communities simply contain much greater amounts of taxable property than do others. An example will show how this works.

Inkster and Dearborn are both suburbs of Detriot; the two communities adjoin each other. Yet a 1969 study showed that Inkster had a tax rate of $32.90 while Dearborn's tax rate was only $23.15. Immediately, one would suspect that Inkster was raising more money per capita than was Dearborn. But this was not the case. As a matter of fact the reverse was true. Although Inkster was taxing its property at a 25 percent greater rate than was Dearborn, it was raising and spending only about one-quarter as much per school child as Dearborn.

6. This estimate is provided by Alfred Baulk in his detailed study of the problem. See his *The Free List* (Los Angeles: Russell Sage Foundation, 1971). For an account of how some communities have sought to exact some money out of untaxable colleges and universities see: "Boston Not Alone in College Push," *Christian Science Monitor*, 5 August 1970.

Two factors account for this anomaly. First, Inkster was a poorer community than Dearborn. This meant that its homes and other properties were generally worth less. This, of course, meant that the city had to impose a higher tax rate to make up for the lack of total valuations. (Remember: the proceeds from the property tax depend on both the tax rate itself and the values of the property taxes. Lower valuations require higher tax rates to raise any specific amount of money.)

The second and related factor was the fact that Dearborn was the home of the Ford Motor Company's River Rouge works. This plant provided substantial tax revenues, but though both Inkster and Dearborn residents worked in it, the property taxes it paid went solely to Dearborn. Thus, Dearborn residents were able to spend substantially more money educating their children, while taxing themselves at a substantially lower rate, than were their neighbors in Inkster.[7]

This fiscal tale of two cities is far from unique. Similar situations have sprung up elsewhere in Michigan and in nearly every state of the nation. Such problems are bound to occur when state governments allow local governments to use the property tax to raise local revenue. In California, for example, residents of Baldwin Park in Los Angeles County paid in 1970 a tax rate of $5.48 per $100 of assessed property. This gave them only enough to spend somewhat less than $600 per school child. In plush Beverly Hills, also in Los Angeles County, residents were taxing themselves only at a rate of $2.38 or less than half that of Baldwin Park. Yet, thanks to their much more substantial valuations, Beverly Hills' residents were able to spend over $1,200 per child for education.

This discrepancy, though it only duplicated numerous others throughout the nation, became the basis for a court case that ended in a decision one newsmagazine called "potentially . . . the most far-reaching court ruling on schooling since *Brown* v. *Board of Education* in 1954."[8] The case was brought by the parents of Tony Serrano of Baldwin Park. They claimed that the disparity in educational expenditure between the two communities violated the California Constitution. On August 30, 1972, the California Supreme Court said they were right. In a six to one decision the court outlawed the use of locally collected property taxes as the determining factor in school spending. Said the court in its *Serrano* v. *Ivy Baker Priest* decision, "We have determined that this funding scheme invidiously discriminates against the poor because it makes the quality of a child's education a function of the wealth of his parents and neighbors."

7. *Wall Street Journal,* 15 January 1971.

8. *Time* (13 September 1971). See also: Tom Wicker, "Equalizing the Schools," *New York Times,* 12 March 1972.

The *Serrano v. Priest* decision sent shock waves reverberating through the ranks of local government. Soon similar suits were coming before other state courts. Some states, however, could see the writing on the wall and began to head off such suits by taking steps to rearrange their school expenditure patterns.[9] (It should be kept in mind that neither the California court or any other court has claimed that property taxes per se are discriminatory. What is discriminatory is allowing any community's school spending to be determined by the value of its property. Communities and educational districts may continue levelling property taxes and using the proceeds therefrom for schools. However, the state government must see to it that this practice does not give appreciable advantages or disadvantages to any child.)

The decision thus produced a flurry of activity in many states largely aimed not at eliminating the property tax but at supplementing it or reapportioning it in order to even out the highs and lows in educational expenditure. This does not mean that we can expect all states to move in this direction—at least not immediately—nor can we expect all state judges to find the state's present school spending pattern in violation of the state constitution. In 1975, the Idaho Supreme Court rejected a suit similar to the one brought in California. Furthermore, the U.S. Supreme Court has ruled that using local property tax for educational purposes does not violate the U.S. Constitution.[10] However, after taking all these qualifications into account, we can still expect to see the shift away from the property tax gradually gather momentum in the years ahead.

Other Taxes, Other Revenues

Numerous other taxes as well as nontax sources of income round out the subnational revenue picture. In terms of taxes, state and local governments levy duties on inheritances and large gifts. Although the federal government also taxes such items, most, though not all, states add their own levies to them. States fortunate enough to contain raw materials tax their extraction. And many states also tax business corporations.

Then there are the so-called "nuisance taxes." They include such imposts as a tax on restaurant meals or on hotel rooms. These are fairly popular for some of the same reasons that sales taxes are: they seem comparatively painless and they reach into the pockets of out-of-staters. In some instances the hotel tax costs almost as much to collect as it nets, yet no state that has adopted it has ever given it up since it imposes little hardship on the taxing state's own residents.

9. See: "Who Pays the Bill," *Time* (7 February 1972). Also: "New Jersey Now Must Find a Different Way," *New York Times*, 28 October 1973.

10. *Rodriquez v. San Antonio Independent School Board* (1973).

Licenses provide another source of revenue. States license motor vehicles and their drivers, plus many professions and trades. Local governments give out licenses for taxi cabs, restaurants, amusement parks, parking garages, and other facilities. All told, licenses brought in approximately $6 billion in 1972, with motor vehicle registration supplying the biggest share.

Their often desperate search—some would say scramble—for more revenue has led many state and local governments to embark on business enterprises of their own. North Dakota has gone the farthest in this direction. It operates a bank, a grain elevator, a casualty and bonding insurance company, a land-sales agency, and other businesses. Sixteen states run their own liquor stores, deriving considerable revenues by exercising a monopoly on all liquor sales within their jurisdiction. It is somewhat ironic that many of the most conservative states, such as New Hampshire and Vermont, have never shown any qualms about engaging in such a socialist endeavor.

In recent years more and more states have turned to lotteries as a way of not only raising revenues but also, they hope, curbing organized crime. So far such lotteries have failed to swell the state treasuries appreciably but they do bring in some money. In fiscal 1975 the thirteen states conducting such lotteries netted $500 million from the proceeds. The Illinois lottery was apparently the most successful that year; it netted over $64 million.

Many local governments have found public utilities such as power plants a rewarding source of revenue. Such government-owned utilities brought in $8 billion in gross receipts in 1972. New York City blazed a new trail in the late 1960s by setting up, with state permission, a city-run off-track betting system. It has brought in some substantial earnings and does seem to have put some pressure on local bookmakers. However, it has certainly not ended illegal betting on horse races and it did not save the city from its close call with financial catastrophe in 1975.[11]

PROBLEMS AND PROSPECTS: COMPETITION

The patchwork pattern, that subnational revenue raising presents, results from numerous problems. One particularly persistent difficulty reflects the competitive factors we examined in Chapter 1. Fear of losing out to another jurisdiction continually guides state and local government financial policies. This, as we have already seen, helps explain why states prefer sales taxes to income taxes. But

11. In the spring of 1976 Connecticut launched an off-track betting system that included eleven parlors in ten cities. Despite the fact that the network did not include Hartford, and despite the fact that the system suffered a computer breakdown that delayed its opening, it took in $270,000 in the first two days.

even with sales taxes, the competitive factor often emerges. No state wishes to raise its sales tax too high lest it induce its residents to shop, either by mail or in person, in other states. Merchants in communities bordering another state that has no sales tax will often strongly oppose any sales tax in their own state for fear that it will spur shoppers to cross over to the neighboring state. The same elements play a role in local sales tax policy as well. Although many municipalities now have adopted local sales taxes, they have done so reluctantly. Many other cities and towns have spurned offers from their state governments to allow them to impose such taxes.

This fear of competition also influences income tax policy. It has kept many state and local governments from using income taxes and has caused those who do to keep their taxes small and only slightly graduated. A similar situation curbs states from taxing inheritances too heavily. Some states, such as Florida, have no inheritance tax whatsoever and this is one reason why the sunshine state attracts so many well-to-do retired people. No state wishes to add to this exodus, at least from its own jurisdiction.

This competitive element of our political system also curbs the use of nuisance taxes. When New York City raised its taxes on stocks and bonds in August 1975, one New York Stock Exchange firm moved one-third of its staff and operations to Jersey City. It expected to save about one million dollars a year on its total tax bill. Since then, many other firms have made similar moves.[12]

This incident indicates that raising taxes too high can actually result in less rather than more revenue for the taxing government. When New York State doubled its tax on cigarettes in 1965, cigarette sales dropped by almost one-quarter. Did that many New Yorkers give up smoking? By no means. The increase simply touched off a boom in bootlegged cigarettes. Soon underworld elements had started smuggling tobacco from North Carolina, which at the time had no cigarette tax, to New York. By 1968, its tax increase was costing the Empire State between $40 and $60 million a year.[13]

As with taxes, so with nontax revenues does competition cause endless complications. Agents of the Pennsylvania Liquor Control Board frequently "stake out" certain Maryland liquor stores to catch Pennsylvanians suspected of stocking up on Maryland's cheaper alcoholic wares. They must wait, however, until the suspects return to their home state before making any arrests. Mean-

12. *New York Times*, 12 October 1975.

13. The problem persists and has become worse, judging from a news item in the *New York Times* of 5 December 1976. It pointed out that bootlegging of cigarettes from North Carolina into New York State was costing the latter $85 million in lost taxes plus the costs of maintaining a squad of sixty-five investigators in its effort to stop the smuggling. The bootleggers counterfeit New York State cigarette tax stamps and place them on the contraband goods, thereby making them harder to spot.

while Maryland itself experiences the same trouble with the District of Columbia. The District's prices are still lower, and so many Marylanders seek to replenish their supplies in the nation's capital.

Some states take advantage of this competitive situation in order to export, in effect, their tax burden. Probably no state has succeeded so well in doing so as New Hampshire. The New Hampshire state-owned liquor system purposely keeps its prices low to attract buyers from adjoining states. As a result, nonresidents purchase half of all the goods the system sells. Maine, which also has a state-owned system, has been forced to lower the prices on its one store near the New Hampshire border in order not to lose customers and revenues to the Granite State.

A low cigarette tax has also helped enrich New Hampshire's governmental coffers. It costs Massachusetts alone between $5 and $10 million a year in lost revenue from its own cigarette tax. Through these and other means, New Hampshire has become the only state in the union to avoid having to levy either a sales tax or an income tax. The shrewd Yankees of New Hampshire have managed to make others pay for a good share of their tax bills.

PROBLEMS AND PROSPECTS: COSTS

As we noted in Chapter 1, a piecemeal political system tends to run up bills—lots of bills. And, as we also pointed out, these bills are becoming increasingly burdensome. Not only has state and local spending risen faster than federal spending but state and local debts have soared even more. State debt was well under $4 billion in 1948. By 1972 it had reached nearly $55 billion, an increase of approximately 1,500 percent. Local debts, meanwhile, had gone from $15 billion to $120 billion in the same period. By 1975 spending by our subnational governments was rising by 12 percent a year, while their debts were increasing by about $10 billion annually.

But 1975 was the year when, so to speak, the chickens came home to roost. The system began to show signs of financial breakdown. Most spectacular of all was the threatened collapse of New York City, which required not only state but also federal aid to keep going, but the spectre of bankruptcy was haunting other jurisdictions as well. Only a few miles away from New York City, Yonkers found itself unable to meet its costs and had to go to the state to avert insolvency. And early in 1976 Mayor Coleman Young of Detroit told a committee of Congress that his city was confronting the same crisis. Even though the city had cut its payroll by 18 percent, it faced a deficit of over $44 million during that fiscal year and a deficit of well over $100 million the following year. Said Young,

225

"Detroit may find itself in the same situation as New York. . . . Philadelphia will not be far behind, nor will Boston, San Francisco and some others." [14]

State governments were also starting to show signs of severe strain. Many were experiencing great difficulty not only in meeting their basic needs but also in marketing their bonds. Restraint and retrenchment became the order of the day. One state after another cut out some programs and curtailed others. Governors elected under liberal banners began expressing conservative concerns. As one of these governors, Edmund Brown, Jr., of California put it, "We are entering an era of limits." [15]

Meanwhile, storm clouds on the financial horizon pointed to further trouble ahead. The biggest threat concerned pensions. State and local governments had become quite generous in bestowing pension benefits on their employees. In some cities, policemen and firemen had obtained pension benefits equalling almost half of their salary costs. The problem was that the cities were not budgeting for these expenditures. Indeed, few municipalities and none of the states had set up a fully funded pension system; i.e., none of them were setting aside every year enough money to take care of the pension obligation accumulated during that year. [16]

Further aggravating their financial plight was the fact that the taxpayers were growing increasingly annoyed with what they regarded as too great a burden. Resistance to new revenue measures was on the rise. In 1975, voters throughout the country voted down over 90 percent of all proposed bond issues put before them in referenda. "The art of taxation," a wise Frenchman once noted, "consists in plucking the goose in such a way as to get the most feathers with the least hissing." [17] As American federalism entered its third century, increasing numbers of its citizens were apparently feeling that they had been plucked too much and so were emitting vigorous hisses. State and local governments could afford to ignore these signs of protest only at their peril.

Just what steps the system will take to deal with these developing difficulties remain uncertain. However, some possibilities warrant consideration. Undoubtedly, pressure will mount to have the federal government assume, in one way or another, a growing part of this increasing burden. Most probably such

14. *Washington Post*, 26 February 1976.

15. Douglas W. Gray, "The State of the States Turns Lean," *New York Times*, 8 February 1976.

16. Congress passed a law requiring full funding of corporation pension plans but the law did not affect state or local governments. However, by late 1975 Delaware and Connecticut had adopted plans that would make their pension systems fully funded in forty years.

17. This statement has been attributed to the seventeenth-century statesman Colbert. In Number 7 of *The Federalist Papers*, Alexander Hamilton also said something worth noting when we view the financial pressures now besetting our state and local governments: "There is, perhaps, nothing more likely to disturb the tranquility of nations than their being bound to mutual contributions for any common object that does not yield an equal and coincident benefit."

efforts will involve Washington taking over more and more activities from state and local hands. Welfare seems to be one of the more likely candidates for such a shift. The federal government already pays half the nation's welfare bill and many governors and mayors have urged the federal government to take the program out of their hands completely.

But the fiscal problems now plaguing them will require more action by the states and local governments themselves. Undoubtedly they will seek to find more and more areas in which they can raise revenues with the least resistance. This may lead many of them to plunge more deeply into legalized gambling. State lotteries, as we have seen, have not yet yielded the profits their proponents promised. But they do make some money, and enlarging such operations may provide even more. By the mid-1970s, most states with legalized gambling were mulling plans to extend it.

Finally, subnational governments will come under increasing pressure to cut their costs. There is little doubt that many of these governments could easily do so. New York City's brush with bankruptcy may have resulted in large part from factors beyond its control, but the city itself must bear some of the blame. From 1960 to 1975, the number of its school department employees doubled while the number of pupils remained the same. (The reading scores, meanwhile, went down.) The city also added 10,000 employees to its health and hospital department although the latter's patient load actually dropped 25 percent.[18] And while the city's officials were pleading poverty in Washington, some of the city's bus drivers and sanitation men were retiring at the age of fifty with pensions of $15,000 or more per year.[19]

But although our state and local governments may succeed in cutting some of their costs, in raising some new revenues, and in transferring some of their troubles to the national government, financial pressures and problems seem likely to haunt them for many years to come. The fiscal squeeze will undoubtedly influence the course of their development in ways which no one at the present time can accurately predict.

18. *U.S. News and World Report* (10 November 1975). (Interview with Treasury Secretary William E. Simon.)

19. New York City is apparently not the only city with such a problem. See: "Public Pension Game Makes Cities Losers," *National Civic Review* (February 1976).

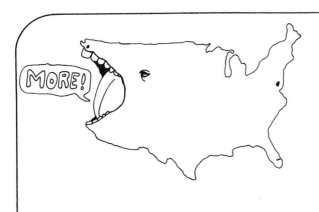

THE FEDERAL ECONOMY

CHAPTER FIFTEEN

The United States, it can be said, was born out of economic exigency. The framers of our constitution converged on Philadelphia in the spring of 1787 with one essential idea in mind: to establish a system that could correct the chaotic economic conditions the Articles of Confederation had created. It is no wonder, then, that the constitution they drafted, and which the country eventually adopted, conferred onto the new central government certain basic economic powers.[1]

Most important, perhaps, of these new powers was the exclusive right to coin or print money. This gave the national government nearly complete control

1. This does not necessarily mean that the U.S. Constitution was strictly designed to solve only economic problems.

over monetary policy. The national government was also given the power to tax and spend to promote the national welfare. Unlike the right to regulate the supply of money, however, this was not to be a federal government monopoly. The states retained the right also to tax and spend as they saw fit. But since the federal government could impose taxes throughout the United States, while no state could tax anyone or anything beyond its borders, the Federal Government soon became predominant in determining fiscal policy as well.

The founding fathers also furnished the new federal government with the authority to regulate all commerce between the states as well as all trade with foreign nations. And they empowered the new national government to make sure that the states upheld each other's laws, contracts, etc. Over the years these powers, under increasingly broader interpretations by the U.S. Supreme Court, have made Washington the overriding force in the federal economy.

But this fact notwithstanding, the states still play a most important role in our economic life. They control certain chunks of the economy almost completely and they heavily influence almost all the rest. Anyone hoping to obtain a complete picture of the complex and often confused relationship between government and the economy in our country today must understand the influence of the states.

To begin with, state governments charter all corporations. Every corporate company in the United States, no matter how extensive its operations may become, must hold a charter from a state government. And every individual proprietorship, no matter how large or how small, must usually be registered with its local city or town hall. Thus, it is nearly impossible to start a business in the United States without in some way receiving permission from some subnational governmental agency.

To obtain its state charter, a corporation must meet certain stipulations and standards. And to retain its charter it usually must make periodic reports on its conditions. The requirements vary from state to state. In some states, they are minimal. In others, they may be stricter but, at the same time, may not be strictly enforced. But each state establishes some rules and regulations regarding the corporations it charters and each state retains the right not only to enforce them but also to change them as it sees fit.

Certain businesses must operate under more rigorous regulations. These include banks, public utilities, liquor stores, sewing establishments, racetracks, and others. Somewhat less scrutinized but still heavily subject to state control are such industries as insurance, small loans, real estate, and stock and bond sales. Again, we will find that the scope and intensity of all this regulatory activity varies from state to state, and within any one state, from one administration to another.

Yet, virtually all states set the rates public utilities may charge, the maximum interest which small loan companies may levy, and the costs of certain kinds of insurance. In some areas where state regulation overlaps with federal regulation, such as in the issuance and sale of stocks and bonds, some states set stricter standards than does Washington.

Labor unions also come under state regulation. Most states have some legislation circumscribing the tactics striking workers can use. Some states, for example, specifically forbid sit-down strikes. About one third of the states have passed "right-to-work laws," which outlaw the union shop. (A union shop means that every employee must join a union if a majority of his fellow employees choose the union to represent them.) On the other hand, two pro-labor states, New York and Rhode Island, have enacted laws giving striking workers the right to draw unemployment compensation if their strike continues beyond a certain period of time. Since unemployment compensation is largely funded by employers, such laws mean they may have to finance strikes against themselves.[2]

Many other matters of vital interest to both labor and management are determined, at least in part, at the statehouse level. These include workmen's compensation, safety and health protection, child labor, and many others. To be sure, in several of these areas the states must share authority with the federal government. But this does not necessarily mean that the states lack substantial discretion. In unemployment compensation, for example, each state decides, within certain broad limits, how much it will pay unemployed workers and what conditions such workers must meet to qualify.[3]

Finally, the states exercise almost exclusive control over the fastest-growing segment of the economy, the professions. Doctors and lawyers are licensed solely by the states in which they practice. So are architects, engineers, and numerous others. And so are a wide variety of other occupations such as hairdressing, barbering, undertaking, plumbing, etc. Some states even license television repairmen. As we can see, the subnational system plays a real role in the operations of our national economy.

2. In the 1971–1972 New York Telephone Company strike, some $43 million was paid out in unemployment benefits to the striking employees. However, striking workers only become eligible for such benefits if the strike lasts six weeks or more.

3. Eighteen states allow those who voluntarily quit their jobs to collect benefits after a certain period of time. Nineteen states permit workers to collect after earning less than $500. In Ohio in 1975 a sixteen-year-old high school student, laid off from his evening job, collected $1,500 in tax-free benefits.

PROBLEMS AND ISSUES

As might be expected, state and local involvement in the economy has not been viewed as an unmixed blessing. And in keeping with our approach, which is to focus on the problems the system presents, let us examine some of the more controversial aspects of state and local activity in this arena.

The overlap by the states and the federal government in many economic matters provides a fertile field for sowing seeds of discord. State and local officials are concerned with state and local problems. National officials are concerned with national ones. And though their interests do not always diverge—indeed they may more often coincide—some conflicts are bound to occur. Each is likely to have different priorities, time frames, etc. The national government, for instance, may adopt certain policies designed to encourage certain types of farmers to leave the land. But states containing sizeable numbers of such farmers may inaugurate policies designed to keep them on the land.

State and local spending policies, to take a more pervasive example, generally tend to aggravate rather than ameliorate the business cycle. When the economy is experiencing a boom, subnational governments tend to spend heavily. After all, the money is now flowing into their treasuries so the time seems propitious for undertaking some hitherto-neglected projects. However, this only intensifies the boom, driving up both the interest rate and the inflation rate and thereby making the subsequent dip in the cycle deeper than it would otherwise become.

In times when business is slow, subnational governments tend to curtail their spending plans. But this comes at a time when the federal government is often planning to spend more in order to perk up the economy. Consequently, state and local spending tends to move counter to national policy and often gets in the way of Washington's plans to moderate the business cycle. In general, state and local financial policies have weakened the ability of the public sector to stabilize and strengthen the nation's economy.

Another illustration of how our piecemeal political system may adversely affect our economic welfare is in the area of unemployment services. The U.S. government set up a national employment service during the depression of the 1930s. However, after World War II, the states managed (through their congressmen) to retrieve this function for themselves. The federal government still has some say over the operations of state employment agencies. But, in the view of some observers, its authority is insufficient. As a result, state employment agencies generally list and try to fill only those jobs that lie within their own borders. An unemployed welder in Kansas, for example, might never learn of the jobs in his field that might be available in Oregon or Tennessee. By concen-

232

trating too exclusively on finding local jobs for the jobless, state employment services reduce labor mobility, limit the options available to the unemployed, and damage the national economy.[4]

Unemployment compensation benefits might also benefit from greater federal involvement. A national system, say some, could spread the risks of unemployment more widely, eliminate much administrative duplication, enhance worker mobility, and free the states and their employers from payroll tax competition with each other. Others, however, claim that moving in the direction of greater federal control in these areas would centralize more power in Washington and would lead to less flexibility and experimentation in the entire system.

The question of payroll tax competition brings us to another fundamental problem of our federal system. This is the competition that continually goes on between jurisdictions. We saw earlier how this influences the revenue-raising policies of the states; we should not wonder then at finding that it affects their economies as well. Indeed, economic competition and tax competition are directly related. For example, New York has experienced a severe exodus of business firms into neighboring Connecticut and New Jersey. Some twenty-seven major corporations moved from Manhattan to New Jersey in the first half of the 1970s and a greater number may have relocated in Connecticut. Neither New Jersey nor Connecticut has an income tax. Southern New Hampshire, meanwhile, has become one of the great growth areas of the Northeast, thanks to an influx of industry from high-tax Massachusetts.[5] And two foreign firms, one German, the other Japanese, chose South Carolina as the site of their American plants in part because of the state's low tax.[6]

Tax policies and problems constitute only one component of this economic rivalry between states, and probably not the most important one. The two foreign firms who found South Carolina so appealing said that low labor costs were an even greater factor in their decision. The lower wage structure of the South has caused much of New England's textile industry to pack up and move there. Other industries have also found the southern states, with their low wage structures and low tax policies, to be hospitable.

In their continual search to support their economies, states often issue industrial development bonds. In this manner a state borrows money to finance new buildings and plants for industries that will choose to relocate, expand, or

4. Federal Reserve Board Chairman Arthur F. Burns points out that electronic computers could match up available jobs with available workers anyplace in the nation within a matter of hours or even minutes. However, such matching usually does not occur because of the lack of a truly federal, i.e., national, employment service. See his *The Business Cycle in a Changing World* (Washington, D.C.: National Bureau of Economic Research, 1969).

5. Daniel J. Corcoran, "Business Discovers New Hampshire, *Boston Globe*, 20 July 1975.

6. Neal R. Peirce, *The Deep South States of America* (New York: W. W. Norton, 1974), p. 119.

start up operations in the state. The industry must usually pay back the costs but the terms under which it must do so are customarily most lenient and generous. Sometimes it does not have to pay back all the costs, so hungry has the state become for its economic benefits. This practice began in the 1930s and by 1967 some forty-two states were engaging in it.

The Advisory Commission on Intergovernmental Relations has condemned the use of industrial development bonds, pointing out that it causes industries to switch from state to state in a manner that is counterproductive for the entire economy. Furthermore, such bonds cannot be taxed by the federal government, for the Supreme Court has ruled that the states and the federal government cannot tax each other's instrumentalities. Consequently, the issuance of such bonds by the states results in a tax loss to the federal government.[7]

Southern states were the first to adopt such schemes but most other states have since joined them. For example, an advertisement in the *New York Times* of February 20, 1972 reads, "You Can Finance a New Plant in New York State for as Little as $00.00 Down." The ad then goes on to state, "No state can equal New York's capacity for industrial loans—from both private and public sources. In fact you can actually get 100 percent financing for new facilities and equipment, in certain circumstances." The advertisement also lists certain other advantages of establishing or expanding industrial operations in New York, including a 1 percent investment tax credit (since doubled to 2 percent).

The states themselves have often expressed misgivings over extending such inducements—some would call them bribes—to industry. But as long as some states pursue this practice, other states feel compelled to follow suit simply to protect themselves from industrial loss. North Carolina, for example, enacted a bill in 1967 permitting its communities to issue industrial development bonds. But in doing so the state said it was acting "reluctantly as a defensive measure with reservations" and the legislature, in approving the bill, also passed the resolution calling upon the President and Congress to outlaw such practices nationwide.[8]

Many states conduct full-scale and on-going campaigns to entice industry. Many have set up special agencies to spur such activity. Governors are frequently pressed into service (or join voluntarily) in this endeavor. They act as brokers and salesmen and, when successful, run for reelection on their records of how many new industries thay have brought to their states. What has developed is a system of what might be called perpetual piracy. When a

7. *Ninth Annual Report*, 1968, p. 11.

8. Donald E. Harder, *When Governments Come to Washington,* (New York: Free Press, 1974), p. 148.

hurricane ravaged much of Connecticut in 1954, industrial development "experts" from Virginia showed up in the storm's wake seeking to persuade Connecticut's hard-hit industries'to resettle under favorable terms in Virginia, a grim example of the extent to which the practice of interstate scavenging may go.

Another example of the zealousness with which states pursue industrial development occurred in Mississippi in the late 1960s. Litton Industries was considering either Pascagoula, Mississippi or Tampa, Florida as the site for its new shipbuilding company. The operation would provide approximately twelve thousand jobs. The Mississippi legislature, with only two negative votes, passed a $130 million bond issue to finance the facility, with Litton to repay the cost over thirty years at a modest 5 percent interest. The state's labor unions agreed to sign a five-year contract. But Litton still hesitated. A gubernatorial campaign was underway and it feared that these generous terms would be made a campaign issue. The state's outgoing governor solved the problem by summoning all seven candidates for governor to his office and there, with a Litton representative observing and a tape recorder whirring, made each candidate pledge to go along with the agreement if he won election. Since none of the candidates wanted to be accused of sabotaging the deal, they all agreed.[9]

As might be assumed, if states show few scruples over pirating industries from their fellow states, they also demonstrate little devotion to policing their own industries that draw business from other states. Thus, a land development corporation may offer land for sale through advertisements in out-of-state newspapers and fail to say that the proffered acreage is swampland. The host state often has little interest in cracking down on such a practice, though the federal government may do so if the land is deliberately misrepresented.

At best, policing is uneven. Some states, such as New York and California, regulate their insurance industries quite intensely. Others are much more lax. As a result, at least 127 automobile and fire insurance companies turned out to be insolvent in the decade that ended in 1968. Of these, 20 were in Illinois and 19 were in Pennsylvania.[10]

When it comes to policing the professions, the record becomes still more uneven. Educators with dubious credentials are often free to set up schools to issue diplomas that are still more dubious. Of course, such schools may not gain accreditation from any recognized accrediting body but this does not necessarily prevent them from holding classes or, in some instances, simply conferring degrees by mail upon receipt of a sum of money. Only eighteen states exercise any control over such mail-order degrees.

9. Peirce, *The Deep South States*, pp. 209–210.

10. See: "Patchwork of Regulation Causes Insurance Woes," *New York Times*, 30 November 1969.

One such institution, which calls itself Jackson State University, operates in California, Arizona, and Mississippi. It has no affiliation with the fully accredited Jackson State in Mississippi though it undoubtedly benefits from the similarity in names. Jackson State University issues a catalogue saying, "Our approach to education is considered by many as unusual because we require no courses, books or forms of study for our degree applicants. . . ." The catalogue then goes on to state that for "tax-deductible donations" it offers the following: "high school diploma, $75; bachelor's degree, $125; master's degree, $150; Ph.D., $180; 20 percent discount if more than one degree ordered simultaneously." [11]

Aggravating this situation is the fact that many states have been sluggish in setting up certification procedures for several quite important professions. For example, most of them have not yet gotten around to licensing psychotherapists. Thus, someone equipped with a mail-order doctorate could set himself up in business as a therapist or marriage counselor and begin treating patients.

Fortunately, the states have established registration processes for most professions and for a good many trades as well. But even here their activities have evoked increasing criticism. State governments usually set up a board or commission to certify an applicant's credentials for a particular profession. All too typically the regulating body is filled largely with present members of the profession. This means that the professions largely police themselves.

Self-policing does have distinct advantages, for it allows those who should know best what is required for practicing the profession to set the requirements for doing so. But it also presents distinct drawbacks. Too often, the regulatory body sets standards that are unnecessarily high in order to restrict entry into the ranks of its constituency.[12] This protects the practices as well as enhances the prestige of those already in the profession. More importantly, perhaps, these boards and commissions fail to take disciplinary action against errant members of the profession and do not even see to it that the practitioners keep up to date with new developments. Once a person has obtained the right to practice a particular profession in a state, he usually never need fear losing his license.

Bar associations, for example, have constantly tended to increase their admissions standards above what many practicing lawyers admit is necessary. Many states require graduation from a three-year law school though lawyers themselves often concede that a person can learn all he needs to know in two years or less. At the same time, bar associations exhibit great reluctance to

11. *Boston Globe*, 31 December 1975.

12. To take one example, Colorado's Board of Cosmetology requires hairdresser trainees to undergo 1,650 hours of instruction, including a full 100 hours of supervised shampooing.

236

discipline any of their misbehaving members. Usually it takes a felony conviction for a lawyer to lose his license.

Medical associations perform little better than bar associations when it comes to controlling their errant colleagues. The Federation of State Medical Boards estimated in 1976 that 5 percent of all practicing physicians were unfit to practice.[13] This means that 16,000 doctors who were treating patients should not have been doing so. Yet, only 66 M.D.'s a year throughout the United States had been having their licenses revoked. It was believed that this incompetence was causing thousands of deaths and an incalculable amount of human suffering every year.

RECENT DEVELOPMENTS

In 1929, Mississippi's per capita income came to only 41 percent of the national average. Connecticut, at the other end of the scale, had a per capita income that was 146 percent of the national average. By the mid-1970s, Mississippi and Connecticut were still the nation's poorest and richest states respectively, but Mississippi's income per person had risen to 69 percent of the national average while Connecticut's had dropped to 119 percent.[14]

These figures point up a significant trend. The economic distinctions that differentiate one state from another are continually shrinking. This, in turn, tends to modify and mitigate some of the economic problems our segmented political system poses. It means an ever-narrower gap in labor costs, living costs, and even in tax costs. As such, it may eventually result in somewhat less competitiveness between the states in economic development.

Already we are seeing signs that states are becoming less fearful of cracking down on certain economic abuses. Regulatory commissions, for example, are doing more regulating than they have ever done in the past. In 1975 alone, at least a dozen state public utility commissions took steps to protect citizens against abuses in utilities' deposits and to insure "lifeline" supplies of gas or electricity at reasonable rates. So strict has regulation become in some states that a few economists have started to wonder whether or not the utilities will be able to finance their necessary growth.[15]

Several states have also started to bear down on long-neglected abuses in

13. *New York Times*, 26 January 1976. The *Times* claimed that doctors knowing of the poor and/or harmful practices of other doctors showed great reluctance to complain of such practices or even talk about them.

14. *Intergovernmental Perspectives* (Fall 1975), p. 18.

15. *Boston Globe*, 2 February 1976.

nursing homes. Furthermore, four states passed laws in 1975 allowing pharmacists to substitute less expensive generic drugs and six eased up their restriction on drug advertising, with the goal of getting more competitive pricing. And many states had already outlawed fair trade laws before Congress enacted legislation prohibiting such laws nationwide. (A fair trade law allows a manufacturer to set a price on a product and every merchant who sells the product must charge the stipulated price.)

This first wave of consumerism in the states left most professions and regulated trades pretty much unscathed. But there are indications that they too are in for more rigorous regulation. Early in 1976, for example, a committee of the New York City Bar Association condemned the association's own policing procedures. "A disciplinary system that moves slowly, and in secret, then ends up publicly disciplining a miniscule percent of those whose conduct is complained about can be neither effective nor credible," said the committee.[16] It recommended, among other things, that nonlawyers be allowed to participate in disciplinary proceedings and that the proceedings themselves be opened to the public in later stages. No state or local medical society has as yet demonstrated any determination to improve its own policing process but increasing indications of the need for such stricter review was making such improvement more likely. It is perhaps significant that it was the Federation of State Medical Boards that came up with the estimate that 5 percent of the nation's doctors were unfit to practice medicine.

Despite all these developments, the demand for stepped-up consumer protection understandably continues. Increasingly it is bringing the federal government into the picture, HEW, for example, has asked hospitals to set up what it calls "peer review." Under this system committees of doctors evaluate the work of their colleagues. (This has engendered remarkable resistance from physician groups.) Ralph Nader has called for the federal government to charter the country's seven hundred largest corporations. This, he claims, would make them "more democratic, efficient and law-abiding."[17] Meanwhile a bipartisan group of senators has filed a bill calling for the federal government to take on the function of economic planning. Such a step would obviously have great impact on the states and their role in the economic process. There seems little doubt that the complex relationship between the economy and the state and national governments will provide controversy for many years to come.

16. *New York Times*, 2 February 1976.
17. *New York Times*, 25 January 1976.

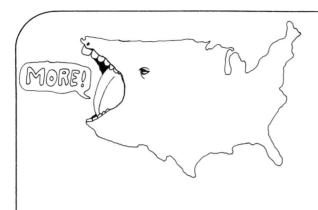

TRANSPORTATION

CHAPTER SIXTEEN

No country in the world spends more of its national income on transportation than does the United States. It adds up to more than a tenth of our Gross National Product, as compared, for example, with Japan, which devotes less than 4 percent of its national income for the same purpose. Though most of our transportation expenditure comes directly out of the pockets of the citizenry, government picks up a substantial share of the bill. In 1975, government spending for transportation amounted to $26 billion, with one-third of this sum consisting of grants from one level of government to another.

In the face of such figures as these, it should come as no surprise that, excluding education, state and local governments spend more on transportation than they do on anything else. All told, they devote some 12 percent of their budgets for the purpose of conveying people and goods from place to place. Two fundamental features characterize this pattern of expenditures: (1) it is split among a vast number of governmental units, and (2) it is heavily concentrated on highways. Let us examine each of these features in turn.

FRAGMENTED POLICYMAKING

When it comes to transportation, it can truly be said that nearly everyone has gotten into the act. The federal government, the state governments, cities and towns, counties, and special districts—all have managed to make some input. Only the educational district has remained excluded from the transportation picture and yet with their busing programs even they manage to exercise at least a slight influence.

A 1973 study by the Advisory Commission on Intergovernmental Relations throws into bold relief the degree of fragmentation that pervades the nation's transportation picture. The ACIR studied 218 planning regions in the country. It found that the number of governmental units handling transportation within each of them ranged from a minimum of 11 to a maximum of well over 500.[1] As should be obvious, such a mixture makes the emergence, let alone the execution, of a cohesive transportation policy nearly impossible.

The impact of such fragmentation on central cities is particularly severe. Boston offers an example. The flow of traffic in and out of the city is influenced by a wide variety of agencies. A regional transit authority operates the public transportation network; a turnpike authority operates a toll road from the west as well as two toll tunnels to the north; the local port authority has custody of a toll bridge into the city from the north. A special district called the Metropolitan District Commission builds and maintains certain other routes into and through the city and the state department of transportation controls the city's central artery. Another state agency operates a huge garage under the Boston Common.

All of this means that Boston can exercise little control over the traffic that pours in and out of it every day. Nor, for that matter, can the state itself, since most of these agencies are run by boards and commissions whose members hold their appointments on a fixed-term basis. Each agency, naturally enough, tends to pursue those policies that advance its own interests and these interests often run counter to those of the city that must suffer from their impact. Thus the turnpike and port authorities have set up fee structures designed to encourage

1. *Intergovernmental Perspective* (Fall 1975), p. 8.

suburbanites to drive their cars to work. This drains revenues from the city-subsidized public transit authority and compounds the city's traffic congestion.

As with Boston, so with most of the country's other major metropolises. And as with the metropolises, so with the nation as a whole. A piecemeal transportation system results all too easily from a piecemeal political system. One can expect one with the other.

ACCENT ON HIGHWAYS

Road construction has dominated state and local transportation policies from their inception. In 1891 New Jersey established the first state highway agency. By 1917, every state in the nation had such a bureau. In 1962, California's highway budget alone exceeded the entire state budget of forty-two other states. And as of late 1971, the states as a whole were still spending 98 percent of all their transportation funds on the building and maintenance of highways.

Local governments have also devoted many of their energies and resources to this end. Although four states—North Carolina, Delaware, Virginia, and West Virginia—have divested their local governments of all control over roads, the other forty-six states permit, and in some cases require, their subnational governments to participate in such programs. Many special districts such as turnpike authorities have been set up exclusively to operate road facilities. All told, the subnational system had built nearly four million miles of public roads and streets by 1975. As a result, over 80 percent of all citizens were driving to work everyday. This compares with the 6 percent who were commuting by bus and 3 percent who were commuting by train. (Other forms of transportation, such as walking and bicycling accounted for the remainder.)[2]

This partiality to cars has become especially pronounced since World War II. Before the war, for example, the Long Island Railroad ran fifty to sixty trains an hour into New York City's Pennsylvania Station. By 1975, the Long Island commuter population had grown 200 percent but less than thirty Long Island trains an hour were lumbering into Manhattan.

The near slavish devotion states have showered on automobiles was somewhat shockingly illustrated during the National Governors Conference of 1970. The governors were asked to endorse a resolution that would allow each state to spend part of its federal highway aid for other forms of transportation if it saw fit. The measure would not, it should be stressed, require them to do so;

2. These figures are based on a Gallup Poll taken in 1971. The oil embargo of 1973–1974, followed by a quadrupling of the price of oil, did not, however, significantly alter the country's commuting habits.

241

rather, it would simply give each state more discretion in how it wished to use such funds. Yet when the resolution was introduced, the governors voted it down. Since what they were doing was, in effect, rejecting more authority for themselves, their negative vote was amazing. The then Secretary of Transportation, John A. Volpe, a former governor himself, observed that he certainly could not ask Congress to give them more control over how they wanted to use their federal aid if the governors themselves rejected such a move. Many newspapers blasted the governors for apparently being so deeply beholden to highway interests. The outcry caused the governors to reverse themselves forty-eight hours later and to endorse the idea.

The reasons for this intense involvement with the building and operating of roads are fairly obvious. For one thing, such activity is easy to finance. The state simply earmarks its gasoline tax money for such purposes. Special districts may collect tolls on their facilities for motorists. Either way, the motorist usually feels he has made a good buy. After all, what is a cent or two more a gallon on gasoline or a bridge or tunnel toll of twenty-five or fifty cents compared to the convenience such expenditures seem to provide. Politicians have usually found road, bridge, tunnel, and other such programs to be quite popular with the people. And politicians like to vote for popular programs.

The fact that the federal government has often been ready to support such endeavors has only increased the desire of state and local governments to launch them. In 1916, the federal government made $75 million available in grants to the states over a five-year period to spur road construction. In 1955, Congress passed the Federal Highway Act providing up to 90 percent financing for all state and local road building that would fit in with the federal government's proposed national network. This network today covers approximately one-fifth of all non-urban roadways. The federal government's disbursements, it should be noted, came out of the proceeds from its own gasoline tax.

Many critics have protested that this method of financing highways is actually deceptive. Road construction generates many more "spill-over" costs, such as the loss of taxable revenue from land taken for road construction, the loss of revenues to government-subsidized public transit systems, the costs stemming from the car congestion and pollution such facilities encourage, etc. Nevertheless, since these costs fail to show up in the calculations of highway engineers they are usually omitted from consideration when road-building bills are put to a vote.

Other factors only enhance the appeal of highway programs to political leaders. Such programs often present excellent opportunities for patronage. There are, first of all, the contracts to be awarded for their construction. Highway contractors constitute one of the most politically active groups in many states and often head the list of a candidate's contributors. This form of patronage has many ramifications. For example, a highway contractor, upon receiving a government contract, must post what is called a performance bond to compensate the governnent if he for any reason cannot complete the contract. Customarily, such contractors pay insurance companies to post such bonds for them—and many state legislators are agents for insurance companies.

Highway construction also affords such lower-level but still valuable patronage. Since most highway construction as well as highway maintenance takes place during the warm-weather months, at least in the northern half of the country, it affords many jobs for high school and college students. Many a college graduate has worked his way through school thanks to highway jobs secured through his family's connection with a state legislator or other political figure.

There are all kinds of interests that benefit from highway programs: the numerous trucking companies and their powerful union, gasoline companies, certain real estate interests and, of course, the motorists themselves. This last-named group may be the most important, for it is unlikely that accommodating the automobile would ever have attained such a high priority in the United States if it had not reflected popular desires. Chicago, for example, sought to balance the two huge highway arteries it built into the heart of the city by establishing rapid transit tracks down the median strips. But it did not work. Over two decades, the highways became increasingly clogged with cars while transit authority ridership sank more than 50 percent.[3]

Thus, in ascribing blame for the faulty balance in state and local government transportation policies and priorities, we need not search for scapegoats. Instead, as Pogo said, "We have met the enemy and they is us."

TRANSPORTATION TRENDLINES

As it became increasingly apparent in the early 1960s that highway construction had antagonized rather than alleviated transportation problems in urban areas, the federal government began to shift its focus of attention. In 1961, Congress passed legislation authorizing the federal government to pay up to two-thirds of the costs for certain "pilot projects" to test new techniques in urban transportation. Three years later Congress passed the Urban Mass Transportation Act of 1964, allocating $375 million over the next three years to improve mass transportation in urban areas. The allocated sum hardly bestowed a bonanza on the nation's hard-pressed transit systems but it did mark a significant breakthrough.[4]

3. "The Agony of the Commuter," *Newsweek* (18 January 1971).
4. Michael N. Danielson, "Cities in Trouble," *National Civic Review* (December 1965).

243

In 1970 Congress swung the balance still more toward public transportation by authorizing one billion dollars a year for its support. And late in 1974 President Ford signed into law the National Mass Transportation Assistance Act, providing nearly $12 billion over the next six years for urban public transportation. Meanwhile, the federal government had set up a public corporation named Amtrak to operate and, hopefully, improve and increase intercity passenger train service. Aside from its subsidies to Amtrak, in 1976 Washington allocated about two-fifths of all federal transportation aid in urban areas to public transport.[5]

Responding to this new emphasis, many of the nation's metropolitan areas plunged ahead with public transportation. In 1972, San Francisco unveiled its Bay Area Rapid Transit System (BART). The first major rapid transit system to be built in the United States in half a century, it included thirty-four stations situated along seventy-one miles of track. Washington itself was preparing to open the first segment of a ninety-eight mile system in 1976, while other systems were under construction in Baltimore and Atlanta, and under consideration in a host of other cities.

Unfortunately for public transit's growing number of backers, the initial results of these efforts were not uniformly reassuring. BART was plagued with numerous technological failures. Operated by automation, its trains sometimes bypassed stations and stopped in the middle of the line, or they stopped at the station but their doors did not open or opened on the wrong side of the car. The system cost $1.6 billion to build—some 70 percent more than its projected costs—and was running up a yearly deficit of $45 million by 1975. Most important of all, perhaps, was the fact that it was attracting only 125,000 passengers a day and had reduced downtown traffic into San Francisco by only 4 percent.[6]

The BART experience, together with the findings of certain research studies, suggests that the problems of public transit involve more than a lack of funding. More and more of the travel in urban areas, so it seems, does not follow the spoke-hub concept under which people live outside the city and journey to downtown and back every day. Actually fewer than 10 percent of employed residents in metropolitan areas now work in central business districts. Unfortunately, most public transit systems are oriented to funneling people in and out of downtown. The rest go to work elsewhere in the metropolitan area.

---

5. *New York Times*, 2 August 1975.

6. There have been numerous articles criticizing BART's performance. Material used here is taken from "BART: Wave of Tomorrow or Folly of Today?" *Boston Globe*, 8 February 1976. The article also noted that the salaries of station agents and train attendants averaged $23,800 a year. Pay for maintenance workers was somewhat higher.

Then, the building and operation of public transit systems has become inordinately expensive. Land taking, construction, equipment, and labor operating costs have all soared in recent years. BART'S station agents and attendants averaged $23,400 a year in salaries and fringe benefits by 1976.

Finally, our citizens still show a strong preference for their automobiles. In Boston, the Massachusetts Bay Transportation Authority cut its fares in 1973 from twenty five to ten cents between 10:00 A.M. and 2:00 P.M. weekdays and all day Sundays and holidays in an effort to attract more riders to the system. Two years later it abandoned the idea, saying that all it had achieved was to give a boon to its already small core of confirmed patrons. (Others pointed out that though the Transit Authority's own employees have always had the right to ride free of charge, the parking lot at the transit system's headquarters was always full. Public transport had become a commodity that, in some instances at least, one could not even give away!)

This does not mean that public transportation backers need throw up their hands in dispair. Some claim, for example, that by making it more difficult for commuters to drive and park downtown, one can prod them into taking public transportation. It is folly, they maintain, to build expressways and parking garages and then expect downtown drivers to leave their cars at home. To encourage people to board trolleys and trains one must first discourage them from using their cars

Another way of dealing with the problem would be to concentrate more on building up bus service. Bus systems are much cheaper to set up and operate than rail lines. They also provide much more flexibility and therefore can more easily accommodate the vast majority who commute into parts of the metropolitan area other than the central city. Some states have begun setting aside certain expressway lanes exclusively for buses as an initial step toward increasing their use.

The states have also begun tackling the other major problem beleaguring state and local transportation, namely the overabundance of agencies involved in its delivery. In 1960 Hawaii established the first state department of transportation. By 1971, some fourteen other states had followed suit and more have joined the trend since then. To be sure, many of these new transportation departments are much like the old highway departments, simply with a new name. But a few have moved to coordinate and balance the myriad transportation functions within their states. Most exemplary, perhaps, is the Maryland Department of Transportation. It receives all the state's transportation revenues, such as gasoline taxes, bus fares, etc., and then allocates the money in terms of what it believes to be the correct priorities. In 1975 it began building a rapid transit system for Baltimore and creating berths for new cargo vessels as well as building and maintaining roads and highways. It has, to some degree, begun to impose a unified and balanced transportation system on the state.

At local levels moves are also afoot to coordinate transportation with the aim of promoting more public facilities. In Minnesota, the Metropolitan Transit Commission was created to serve seven counties in the Minneapolis-St. Paul area. In Greater Chicago, voters in 1974 gave narrow but certain approval to the creation of a regional transportation authority with the power to draw on several forms of revenue, including a tax on parking facilities, in order to develop public transportation.

Consequently, those who have long lamented the system's lack of coordination, accompanied by its overconcentration on automobiles, have started to gain heart. Progress may be slow, but, at least, the wheels are now turning in the right direction.

246

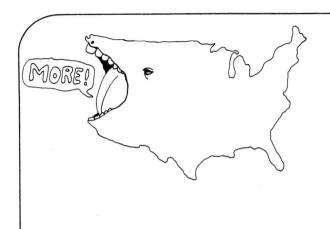

ENVIRONMENT

CHAPTER SEVENTEEN

Nowhere, perhaps, do the inherent forces of federalism tend to produce so many problems and activate so many antagonisms as in the area of environmental control. Considerations of cost and competitiveness seem to place economic concerns and ecological concerns on a collision course. In the past, economic considerations have usually won.

Take, for example, the question of pollution. As we saw in Chapter 1, if one state cracks down on a polluting industry, it may not merely encourage but actually force the industry either to move to another state or shut down. For as long as other states take a go-easy approach, an offending industry seeking to comply with a more zealous state's requirement will experience great economic difficulty. Profit margins of U.S. business are, on the whole, much more limited

247

than many people realize. (They average less than five cents on each dollar of sales.) Any control program that seriously shrinks this margin may well make an industry unable to compete with other companies. And effective pollution control programs can prove quite costly.

Industry, however, is not the country's major polluter. Average citizens are. The single greatest source of water pollution is human waste and the greatest single source of air pollution is the automobile. But here again economic factors have tended to ride roughshod over environmental desires. Building waste treatment plants can be expensive. Curbing auto traffic can prove extremely difficult. Here, too, commercial concerns enter into the picture. The taxes and inconveniences control programs impose can make a state or community a far less desirable place in which to do business, even for a business which does not, in itself, cause pollution.

Faced with such forces, the subnational system responded only slowly to the growing threat of pollution. As a result, the federal government began to intervene. During the 1960s Congress passed a good deal of legislation designed to cope with the growing threat. The bills included the Clean Air Act of 1964, the Water Quality Act of 1965, and the Clean Rivers Act of 1966. These measures largely confined themselves to offering inducements to the subnational governments to take action on their own. They produced only limited results.

In the field of water pollution, for instance, efforts got underway during the 1960s to set up interstate compacts for the Hudson, Potomac, and Susquehanna Rivers as well as for the Great Lakes. However, by 1973, only the Susquehanna compact had been approved. And although many other compacts were already in operation, they were often quite limited in scope and even more limited in effect. The Delaware River Basin Compact in 1965 may have succeeded in meeting the crises of the time, namely the severe drought that affected the middle Atlantic States during the early 1960s, but it has failed to make much further progress. As Martha Derthick has observed, "After more than ten years, it is still seeking to develop a set of functions that will be stable, serve important public purposes, and not be fatally undermined by the non-cooperation of members." [1]

Similar problems are evident in efforts to reduce air pollution. The Clean Air Act, while it set up air planning and control regions, continued to give primary responsibility to the states. It did result in some progress. The air in most of our cities stopped getting worse and in many places became noticeably better. However, accomplishments fell far short of expectations. In November of 1969, for example, Chicago was blanketed with a greyish cover of pollutants because

1. Martha Derthick and Gary Bombardier, *Between State and Nation: Regional Organizations of the United States* (Washington, D.C.: Brookings Institution, 1974), p. 55.

of an unusual weather pattern. Hospital admissions for respiratory disorders rose 10 percent. Some physicians estimated that the five-day smog blanket took at least one hundred lives. Yet the Chicago city administrators, fearful of alarming the people and discouraging business, refused to declare an emergency and take any forceful action.[2]

State and municipal governments not only showed hesitation in cracking down on industrial and automotive air pollution but also frequently continued to produce a good deal of pollution on their own. By 1970, there were 300 municipal incinerators in the United States and a full 70 percent of them operated without any pollution controls whatsoever.[3] In many a U.S. city, the biggest and blackest smoke spirals on the skyline were coming from the municipality's own facilities.

Trash handling has brought other environmental concerns to the fore. Municipalities that do not burn their rubbish customarily dump it, and by 1970 the cities were running out of dump space. This was forcing them to seek dumping grounds outside the city limits and many were encountering all sorts of additional problems. Boston in 1965 had to pay an enormous sum to the private owner of a dump in a suburban community. The city, however, had no other choice since its power to take property by eminent domain did not extend beyond its own limits.[4] A few years later San Francisco faced an even worse situation. One nearby town with a dump site used a cordon of police to turn back San Francisco's garbage trucks.

When it comes to other conservation concerns, the subnational system's policies and practices have also left a lot to be desired. Those states blessed with substantial mineral resources have often failed to protect these resources. Extractors of raw materials have encountered few impediments. Regulations have not been very rigorous nor rigidly enforced. Strip miners, for example, have in the past been allowed to tear huge chunks out of the countryside without having to take any substantial steps toward repairing the damage thus created. Oil regulations, however, have been something of an exception to the policy of profligacy. Texas began instituting what is called *proration* many years ago. Under proration the state determines how much oil is to be drilled and delivered each year. The purpose is to keep a glut of oil from depressing the price. Other oil states have gradually begun following suit.

States have also shown a good deal of vigor in wildlife development. New

2. Patrick J. Sloyan, "The Day They Shut Down Birmingham," *Washington Monthly* (May 1972).

3. *Newsweek* (29 June 1970).

4. One of the authors (Berkley) was then serving as chairman of the Boston Finance Commission and protested bitterly when the contract was sent to him for approval. However, when the city's Public Works Commissioner challenged him to find another dump, he bowed to reality and signed the inflated contract.

Hampshire created a fish commission during the Civil War and after the war set up a game commission as well. Today all states have fish and game agencies. States have also taken steps to protect their woodlands, tidal marshes, and other natural preserves. New York and Pennsylvania, for example, have each set aside one million acres in public forests. Yet the overall record remains spotty. South Carolina, for example, has more tidal marshland than any state on the eastern seaboard—some 450,000 acres in all—but at the dawn of the current decade it had not passed a single law to protect this vital resource.

All in all, then, America's subnational system has in the past failed to support and sustain adequate environmental controls. But, as with so many other problem areas that we have been examining, the situation has started to change. Indeed, in few areas has the present decade produced a greater turnabout in policies and practices.

SHIFTS OF THE SEVENTIES

On November 18, 1971, Birmingham, Alabama confronted a smog condition somewhat similar to the one that had hit Chicago two years before. This time, however, the federal government rapidly intervened. It shut down all the city's industries for thirty-one hours until the pollution levels subsided sufficiently to place the city's residents out of immediate danger.[5]

The federal agency that took this decisive step was the Environmental Protection Administration, which had been created the year before. It had been given substantial powers to control pollution. As the 1970s proceeded it began exercising these powers more and more.

This does not mean that the federal government, acting through the EPA, has become the sole policymaker and enforcer in environmental matters. Rather, the federal government seeks to work with state and sometimes local governments in establishing and implementing rules and standards. It distributes funds to these governments to help them do so. It also possesses the power to act when any of these 80,000 governments face problems. Hence its shut-down of Birmingham in 1971.

Thus, although pollution control continues to be a shared responsibility, the balance of power has passed to the federal level. Washington now wields a big stick in this vital area, and though its enforcement programs have not succeeded in satisfying all those concerned, they have produced something of a new era in pollution control. States are free to set higher standards than those approved by the EPA but they cannot set lower ones. And though the federal agency has frequently granted extensions in the time required to meet these

5. Sloyan, "Birmingham."

250

standards and, on occasion, has even modified them—the upsurge in oil prices in 1974, for example, caused some slowdowns in the anti-pollution fight—nonetheless it has brought new vigor to the environmental cause.

However, perhaps the most interesting development has been the growing tendency of the states themselves to take steps toward conservation. The conservation movement has succeeded in enlisting liberals, moderates, and even some conservatives in its ranks. In many states it has become one of the most powerful lobbies in the state, buffeting not only state but local officials as well. Political leaders of all persuasions have found the conservation cause to be one they can ignore only at their peril.

Oregon has led the way. It has banned billboards and nonreturnable bottles and containers. And when the Oregon legislature refused to pass a bill designating 500 miles of the state's rivers as scenic, and hence untouchable waterways, conservationists launched a referendum. The voters approved the measure by a two-to-one margin. Furthermore, Oregon has banned all construction below the vegetation line along the state's spectacular coast.[6]

Other states have not lagged far behind in responding to this new surge of support for environmental protection, though the oil crisis and the recession of 1973 to 1975 may have slowed down their efforts. In 1975, fourteen states passed laws controlling strip mining. West Virginia outlawed such mining in twenty-two of its fifty-five counties. Hawaii became the first state to adopt a comprehensive land use plan. Florida, Wyoming, and Idaho began moving in the same direction.[7]

Of course, these developments, salutary as they may seem to supporters of conservation, do not spell the end of the problem. Many a battle remains to be fought and many a solution remains to be found. Further, some of the steps already taken may prove to be undesirable or unworkable. For example, Minnesota passed a strict anti-smoking law that required businesses to provide smoking breaks in designated areas so that smokers would not pollute the air of their nonsmoking fellow workers. This provision was threatening to cost some companies up to half-a-million dollars a year.

Yet, despite all the problems that continue to plague the system, and despite the new problems that continue to emerge, most observers would concede that state and local governments, often at the behest of the federal government but more and more often on their own initiative, have broken new ground. In the area of environmental protection the system has begun to display some of the resourcefulness and resiliency that characterize it at its best.

6. Earl Selby and Miriam Selby, "How One State Fights to Stay Livable," *Reader's Digest* (April 1975).

7. Neal R. Peirce, "States Bid to Streamline Government," *Boston Globe,* 2 February 1976. Also see: *Book of the States, 1974–1975* (Lexington, Ky.: Council of State Governments, 1974), p. 9.6.

251

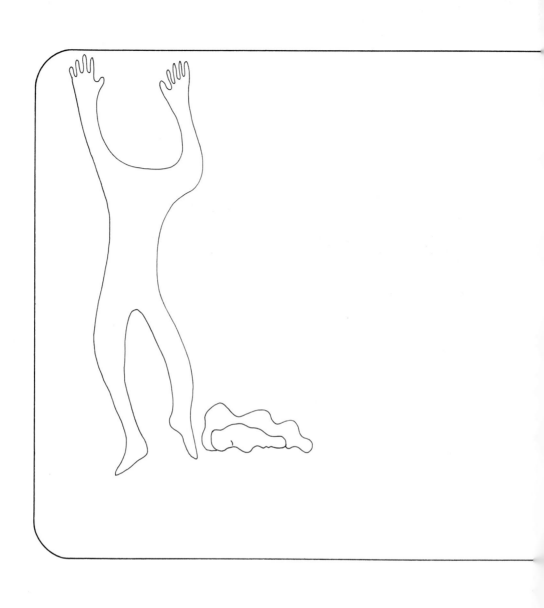

PART FIVE

THE SYSTEM IN ACTION: SOCIAL WELFARE POLICY

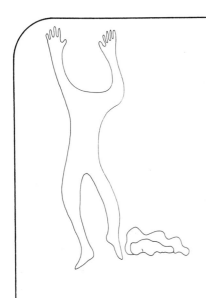

ELEMENTARY AND SECONDARY EDUCATION

CHAPTER EIGHTEEN

Public elementary and secondary education consumes almost half of the total budgets of American local government and employs one-third of the total employees of local *and* state governments. Forty-five million students were educated by 2.6 million teachers at a cost of $60 billion in 1976. This figure is expected to rise to over $80 billion by 1981. This spending dwarfs that for any other function of state and local government, and it rose over 300 percent from 1961 to 1976,[1] but there is no indication that American children are now any better educated. Indeed, there has been a steady decline in the reading ability of

1. *Rankings of the States* (Washington, D.C.: National Education Association, 1976), pp. 16, 23, 26, 50–53.

255

school children, as measured by nationally administered tests. At the same time, a furious racial conflict rages in the schools, making this policy area easily the most controversial one on the domestic scene today.

EDUCATION: A FUNCTION OF LOCAL GOVERNMENT

French national ministers of education have been able to boast that they could tell what page of what book French schoolchildren were reading on a given day. It is impossible for our secretary of Health, Education and Welfare to do this, because elementary and secondary education has been and remains today primarily the business of local government—though state and federal funding and influence have increased over the years. (Public higher education, which is not examined in this book, is also primarily the concern of subnational government: the states and the counties run almost all public institutions of higher learning.)

The number of school districts—16,000—indicates that there is place for much local variety. There are numerous cases from the late 1800s of American school districts that taught classes in a language other than English. German immigrants in Ohio and Texas, for instance, used their native tongue as the language of instruction for some years. Even today, some big city systems use a bilingual approach for students of Hispanic background, teaching some subjects in Spanish and others in English. In practice, this has often amounted to a Spanish-language education.

Some school districts have abolished certain subjects others have embraced. In 1925, a Tennessee teacher named Richard Scopes was not only fired from his job, but also brought to stand trial for what he had done in the classroom. His crime? Teaching Darwin's theory of evolution, which had been studied in thousands of other school districts across the nation without a fuss.

Attempts to censor reading materials occur constantly. In some inner cities, black groups want to remove older volumes like *Little Black Sambo*, which they claim embody vicious racial stereotypes. Some suburbs, like Ridgefield, Connecticut, on the other hand, want to get rid of books like black writer Eldridge Cleaver's *Soul on Ice*, on the grounds that it is both sexually impure and unpatriotic. A West Virginia school district was paralyzed for several weeks in 1973 by the protests of evangelical Christians who denounced a number of textbooks on the grounds that they were irreligious. Angry confrontations between picketing parents and skeptical school officials took place, and several bombings were apparently related to the protest. Yet these same books were used in many other school districts with no problems.

In 1962, the U.S. Supreme Court ruled that spoken prayer could not constitutionally be part of public school exercises. While most school districts went along with the ruling, hundreds of schools in the southern and mid-western "Bible Belt" continued the practice of spoken prayer. Likewise, some southern school districts ended legal segregation with a minimum of fuss; in others, there was violent controversy, and a few actually moved all white children into "private" schools to bypass the ruling. Clearly, then, the 16,000 districts have about 16,000 different approaches to education.

SCHOOL DISTRICTS AS INDEPENDENT POWERS

Local school districts have been isolated from the rest of local government since the late nineteenth century. In fact, no other function of subnational government is as autonomous as is education. This autonomy translates into substantial political power and authority for those who run the schools.

Almost all school districts are formally governed by boards, four-fifths of which are independently elected, with the other one-fifth appointed by the chief executive. (The total number of board members in the nation is 90,000.) Even where the chief executive appoints a board member, he usually cannot remove him from office without good cause, such as drunken behavior at board meetings. Unless he is a strong electoral party leader, the chief executive has minimal influence in selecting the members of an elected board. And in many cities, including Boston, Cleveland, Detroit, Los Angeles, Milwaukee, and St. Louis, even the school superintendent is elected.

This division from the rest of government is true on the state level as well. In 1970, all but three states had a state board of education, for which elections were held in eleven states. State commissioners or superintendents of education were chosen directly by five of the governors; in twenty-four cases, the board selected the superintendent; and in twenty-one cases he was an independently elected official.

In many districts, the nominating procedure for board members is designed to delight those who want to make it easy for people to run for the board; school board elections are held separately to ensure that voters can concentrate their energies on school matters alone; and elections are nonpartisan, to keep out the "politicians." Whether these procedures are "good" or "bad" is a matter for decision by the reader, but he should know their consequences.

First, board members are not drawn in a representative way from the population as a whole, but come from the social and economic elite. In Indianapolis, for example, school board nominations were controlled for three years by a self-appointed citizens' committee of under 200 people. Second, separate school elections almost always have a much smaller turnout than general local elections, ensuring control by those who are most intensely interested in the schools. Third, nonpartisan elections do not take politics out of the schools. Sometimes they result in boards of "nonpartisan" Democrats and Republicans; in others, the politics become those of one of the groups most interested in the schools, whether parents, teachers, or administrators. The cumulative impact of these electoral procedures is to reinforce the independence and insulation of the school board.[2]

Other factors further support and solidify school district autonomy. Almost all school boards have a measure of fiscal autonomy that other types of agencies envy. In New England, for example, while city and town legislatures can cut school budgets, they cannot cut particular items. This means that if the town fathers want to slash the school bowling alley and swimming pool from the budget, they may find instead that they have cut out hot lunches and bus transportation. If the school board is able to achieve its own end in a manner skillful enough to shift the responsibility to the local legislature, these lawmakers will have to take the blame for the board's actions.

Yet the New England boards do not compare with those school districts, to be found in greatest number in the West, that have complete fiscal autonomy. Idaho school districts, for example, raise their own revenue through taxation, just as a general government does. They do not need the approval of the county or any other local government in drawing up a budget.

Why Do the Schools Have Such Independence?

American public education began in the seventeenth century with the Massachusetts Bay Colony's "Old Deluder Satan Act," which sought to fight the devil through education. For most of our history, the schools were not so segregated from the rest of local government. In our largest cities, up until the twentieth century, the schools were closely integrated with the city's political system. While the schools existed in a separate administrative structure with their own boards, members were selected by the city council or by ward elections. In this period of strong local party machines, the machine served to unite all agencies of local government, regardless of their formal administrative structure.

Two changes that occurred in the late nineteenth century served to undermine this governmental unity. First, antiparty reformers were able to substitute at-large elections, in which board members were elected on a city-wide basis, for ward elections. This weakened neighborhood control of the schools by cutting the close tie between board members and the different

2. Roscoe C. Martin, *Government and the Suburban School* (Syracuse, N.Y.: Syracuse University Press, 1962).

258

communities within the city. The second development was the creation of the post of superintendent of schools, made necessary by the growth of the school system. If some coherence was to emerge in these big-city systems, centralized, coordinated direction from the top was needed. The position of superintendent was filled more and more often by "professional" educators, or those who came by their credentials through higher education and working experience in school systems, rather than through their ties with party leaders or different ethnic and community groups in the city.[3]

The professionals in education pushed and propagated the kind of message that professionals in all fields do. They argued that their function of government was too crucial to entrust to amateurs and politicians. Policymaking should be left to those who know the policy area best, the educators held. In this way, children would get the best possible education, and practices that interfere with education, like political appointments and log-rolling, would be ended.

The professionals' viewpoint can be labelled the "unitary myth." This sees the local community as an organic whole with a single public interest in education. That is, there is one best way to educate all children, regardless of their ethnic, social, or economic backgrounds. Different groupings in the community, such as labor or Italo-Americans, should not have seats on the board representing them *as groups*, because there is no such thing as a meaningful labor or Italian perspective on education.

In practice, this myth's acceptance early in the twentieth century resulted in school government by professional educators and school boards made up predominantly of middle-class white businessmen. With some variations, these are the types of people who run local education today.

THE NATURE OF PROFESSIONAL CONTROL

Almost all U.S. public schools are dictated to by the educational professional in numerous ways.[4] First, the only way to become a teacher, administrator, or auxiliary staff person, such as a guidance counselor, is to be certified by the state for this work. To earn certification, would-be pedagogues must attend classes at state teachers' college in subjects like teaching methods and theory. Regardless of their other qualifications, only after they have taken such a program of courses will they be allowed to teach. A college professor who has earned a reputation as one of the country's great educators would not be allowed to teach junior high

3. Robert H. Salisbury, "Schools and Politics in the Big City," *Harvard Educational Review* (Summer 1967), pp. 408–424.

4. The following section is based principally on: Thomas H. Eliot, "Toward an Understanding of Public School Politics," *American Political Science Review* (December 1959), pp. 1032–1051.

unless he were certified, nor would the President of General Motors be allowed to apply for a superintendent's job without certification.

Second, once the educator passes a probation period, he earns *tenure* and cannot be fired except for cause or unless budget cuts drop his position. Causes for being fired may include socially unacceptable behavior such as heavy drinking or philandering. In some cases, identification with unpopular political or social causes may cost a teacher his job, though professional educators are increasingly able to fight such attempted ousters.

However, tenured teachers are not usually fired for being poor teachers. At worst, when they are notoriously and embarrassingly inept in the classroom, they are given a sinecure elsewhere. The fact that it is well-nigh impossible to remove tenured teachers indicates the clout of the teaching profession, which has been able to win a form of job security not found in many state and local government agencies.

In the area of personnel, then, the professionals dominate. They are almost as important in determining the curriculum, or what shall be taught in the schools. Here the key resource of the professionals is their knowledge or expertise in the details of courses taught. Only rarely does a board member have similar expertise in any given area, whether physics or physical education, so he has to leave the "details" up to the professionals. Only rarely is there criticism of specific textbooks or courses, and then only when they offend community morals. Complaints about assigning a book like *Lady Chatterly's Lover* obscure the fact that there are probably no other complaints about any other texts used, whose selection is left up to the professional. Likewise, while a film series entitled *Man* earned much criticism in some school systems in the late 1970s because it discussed the different attitudes of other societies toward sex and illness, protesting groups simply wanted the film removed and replaced. They had no suggestions for a substitute.

Decisions about facilities, on the other hand, are not completely in the hands of the professionals. Residents in a school district get more involved in school building politics than in other areas, for two reasons. First, a substantial amount of money is involved, necessitating bonding, which is usually subject to approval by referendum. Second, since buildings are visible and inspectable, and since the distance children must walk or ride to school is measurable, most residents feel more confident about voicing their opinions about the schoolhouse and school transportation than on what occurs inside the facility.

Decisions on personnel, curriculum, and facilities are all related to school financing. Here, local boards and voters have to share power with the state and federal governments, which make substantial contributions. And as in the case of facilities, the professionals must act as salesmen, hoping to persuade others to support their budget proposals. Sometimes the professionals are unsuccessful and must deal with large cuts in their budget proposals. Indeed, every year there are cases of local school districts that have closed down because the electorate refused to appropriate enough funds to keep the school system operating. In the 1970s, schools have closed in Missouri, Ohio, Pennsylvania, Illinois, and Oregon for this reason. And in a time of recession and inflation, school budgets have come under increasingly heavy scrutiny, since they are the largest expenditure of local government. The percentage of school bonding proposals approved in referenda dropped from 72 percent in 1961 to 57 percent in 1969.

The professionals, then, do not demarcate the overall size of the budget, but they do decide its *shape*. Most of the decisions about how the money appropriated is spent are made by the board and the professionals. Personnel costs usually make up three-quarters of the budget and, with the increasing growth of collective bargaining, are essentially a fixed expenditure. This leaves supplies, equipment, and maintenance to be cut, with the board and professionals determining where the cuts will be made. Do we repair the roof or the floor? Do we cut bus transportation or school lunch? The decision is up to the board, not the local legislature.

Professional influence in education is not omnipotent. But, as this section and the one which follows show, it is more important than the competition.

Professional Clout in the Classroom

Professional educators are organized into several national orders and associations. The Council of Chief State School Officers is composed of the 56 state and territorial heads of education, while the American Association of School Administrators includes 21,000 superintendents and principals. Until recently, these administrators held the whip hand over employees in the hierarchical organizations typical of education, but this situation has changed greatly. Now the teachers' organizations, notably the 1.8-million-member National Education Association (NEA) and the 500,000-strong American Federation of Teachers (AFT) wield increasing power.[5] This power comes from unity, and from willingness to use trade union tactics such as the job action and strike to bargain for what they want. Nor are strikes limited to big cities like Chicago and San Francisco any more. Numerous small towns have seen shut-down schools and teacher picket-lines.

5. For a discussion of these groups, see: Norman C. Thomas, *Education in National Politics* (New York: David McKay Co., 1975), pp. 137–141.

While the teachers' organizations are primarily concerned with the bread-and-butter issues of pay and benefits, their concern for their working environment gets them involved with other matters as well. Teachers' groups take stands on subjects like class size and special education programs, which are central policy issues. New York City teachers went on strike in 1967 to protest the establishment of two experimental decentralized school districts, which they saw as a challenge to the traditional assignment and tenure systems. They won the fight, and the experimental districts were terminated.

Two examples from the Johnson administration Great Society years of the 1960s underscore the power of the pedagogues. Efforts by those active in federal antipoverty programs to change local school systems failed, because the education professionals resisted them. The federal antipoverty agency, the Office of Economic Opportunity, sponsored a federal Teachers' Corps, designed to infiltrate the schools and establish new programs for minorities. Instead, local educators took over the program themselves, and changed it to conform with other existing programs. An attempt to use local antipoverty Community Action Programs to pressure the schools into change met with the same lack of success.[6]

Study after study of big-city systems, including those of New York, Baltimore, Chicago, Philadelphia, Detroit, and St. Louis, show the educational bureaucracy very much in charge of policy.[7] While professionals do not have as much power in smaller jurisdictions, which are often less professionalized and never as bureaucratically complex, they are still almost always a force to be reckoned with. The professionals have power because the entire inter-governmental network of education—federal, state, and local—is their creation, operating under rules they have drawn up.

As we have already seen, the states mandate standards and procedures for local agencies in almost every policy area. This is certainly the case in education, where reams of regulations govern every aspect of local education. Yet both state departments of education and the U.S. Office of Education are staffed by professional educators. Since the educators are writing the regulations, rules which really restrict local educators are extremely unlikely.[8] While it is not completely insulated, education is as much of a closed system as will be found in state and local government.

6. Paul E. Peterson, "The Politics of Educational Reform," in Stephen M. David and Paul E. Peterson, eds. *Urban Politics and Public Policy*, 1st ed. (New York: Praeger, 1970).

7. Marilyn Gittell and T. Edward Hollander, *Six Urban School Districts* (New York: Praeger, 1967).

8. See: Thomas, *Education in National Politics*, pp. 199–215; and Harry L. Summerfield, *Power and Process: Formulation and Limits of Federal Education Policy* (San Francisco: McCutchan Publishers, 1974), pp. 140–165.

The Consequences of a Closed System

So what if local education is in the hands of the professionals? Is this not a good thing, keeping out the politicians and those with special axes to grind? Not really; such would be true only if the professionals themselves had no axes to grind, and if the unitary myth discussed earlier were really true. But there is ample evidence that it is indeed a myth; that the teaching methods used for middle-class white children don't work for lower-class inner-city minority children; that citizens may have perfectly valid complaints or valuable suggestions about their schools; that, in short, the pros aren't perfect, which is the unspoken assumption upon which the myth is based.

In fact, educational autonomy can mean unresponsiveness to community groups, as thousands of frustrated parents who have tried to protest policies have found. It can mean policy fragmentation, as anyone who has ever examined the area of manual skills training (industrial arts in the local school systems) and looked for a logical tie-in of this program to state vocational education schools, or for any governmental job-training program, has found. And, ironically, autonomy may eventually mean vulnerability, since the schools will not have the legislative and executive support they could otherwise expect as agencies within the chain of command if they should lose popularity. In St. Louis, for example, the schools have long suffered because they lack close relationships with city councilmen and state legislators.[9]

In 1927, Big Bill Thompson ran for mayor of Chicago, thundering, among other things, that he would sack the school superintendent, whom he alleged to be a lackey of King George and the British. While his rhetoric was obviously an attempt to get the Irish vote, since Ireland had just won her independence from Britain through a bloody war, Big Bill was not attacking a paragon of virtue. He was criticizing an administrator who had antagonized organized labor, community groups, and teachers. Thompson was really saying that the unitary myth was only a myth; that conflict raged around the school system; and that he, as mayor, should have as legitimate a right as anyone to influence school policy.[10] We may see many mayors take this position in the future, but, at present, most leave education to the educators.

FRAGMENTATION

The proliferation of school districts leads to the same kind of variety in education as is found in other policy areas. The city of Boston maintained a policy of

9. Salisbury, "Schools and Politics," p. 419.
10. Ibid., pp. 410–412.

263

corporal punishment for unruly students long after most cities ended it. Racial segregation never existed in many northern communities, while it did not begin to disappear in the South until the 1960s. Teachers in New York were paid almost twice as much as Mississippi educators in 1974, and wide variations in salaries and programs exist among communities within the same state or even the same county.[11] Many suburbs of some of the largest cities with the heaviest concentration of minority children spend much more per pupil than do these central cities. Hundreds of other examples could be given, but what they add up to is that U.S. schoolchildren are not getting an equal educational break. Even if we exclude the elite private institutions, enormous differences exist among schools. Money spent per pupil is only a rough guide to quality, since money can be poorly spent or founder on social problems, but the many spanking new schools in the wealthy suburbs, equipped with highly trained faculty and professional staffs, contrast with run-down inner-city and/or rural schools in the South or northern New England with minimal facilities and low teacher pay. Naturally, most of the best-trained teachers compete for the highest-paying jobs, leaving what is left to those not so well trained.

Fragmentation in education, then, not only constitutes a hindrance to good service delivery, as fragmentation does in the other policy areas we examine in this book. It also makes equality of educational opportunity impossible, and therefore makes a mockery of our stated aspirations for an equal opportunity for every citizen.

In addition, there are several thousand school districts with fifty or fewer pupils. This means that the only way these students could ever get an equal educational break is through a grossly wasteful lavishing of resources. These systems are too small to afford educational specialists.

Some of the statements made in Chapter 10 about small units of government hold for small school districts. Election turnouts are smallest in these districts, and the least-qualified teachers and administrators are found here. An additional problem for small *school* districts is the much greater likelihood of interference with academic freedom of expression in the classroom, and greater vulnerability of school officials to the influence of extremists. The John Birch Society, a group that equates almost all government activity with Communism, has had its greatest success in removing books it doesn't like from the schools in the smallest districts.

However, fragmentation in education has decreased more than is the case in most other policy areas, as a look at the record shows.

11. *Rankings of the States*, pp. 62–64.

Forces for Centralization

The 16,000 school districts of 1976 represent a dramatic decline from the 108,000 of 1942. The impetus for this consolidation has come primarily from state departments of education, which have often informed school districts that they will not get state financial aid until they combine their operations. Here we have another example of how effective state governments can be in decreasing fragmentation when they want to.

The state education departments always have imposed requirements on local school districts. These relate to minimum teacher salaries, length of the school year, teachers' educational backgrounds, and shape of the curriculum. This "floor," however, in most states, remains barely above the level of the ground; it is not stringent, and a large percentage of school districts exceed their state floors. There is also the question of enforcement. In Connecticut, for example, while the state education department mandates that three school periods a week be spent on physical education, it does not have the manpower to enforce this provision, much less to prescribe the content of these classes.

While many state constitutions stipulate that education be a "perpetual object" of state government, only the state government of Hawaii has taken over public elementary and secondary education. Yet all states make substantial financial contributions to local school systems, giving them the power to bring about changes such as school district consolidation. In 1976, the states paid an average of 44 percent of the bill for local education. (This average covers a range from 85 percent in Hawaii to about 9 percent in New Hampshire.)[12]

Aware of the example of Hawaii, numerous educational groups are pressing their preference for additional state aid as a way of equalizing local education expenditures. Chief among these are the professional educators, like the NEA and AFT, who see state assumption of financing as a way of ending the wide disparities in local education support.

Here the professional groups confront not only local practices, but also a state legislative tradition of discriminating against the big cities in doling out the state dollar. In New York City, for example, the aid formula is tied into the pupil attendance record. Since truancy, like other social problems, is higher in the city than elsewhere, rural and suburban areas get more state aid per capita, even though there is unanimous agreement that the educational problems facing the city are greater than those elsewhere. In Michigan, the suburban schools get 25 percent more state aid per student than do cities, and this pattern is repeated

12. Ibid., p. 52.

across the country. Those who want state assumption and equalization have a formidable battle ahead of them.

But help has come from an unexpected source—the state courts. The California case of *Serrano* v. *Priest* was discussed in Chapter 14. This 1971 decision ruled that the wide disparities in support of local education were an unconstitutional infringement of the equal opportunity guaranteed by the state constitution. In 1976, the New Jersey Supreme Court ordered the public schools closed until the legislature passed a state tax to produce the "thorough and efficient," or uniform, level of support for education guaranteed by the state constitution. The legislature soon complied. Similar cases have been decided by the Connecticut Supreme Court and are pending before lower New York and Maine state courts and numerous other courts throughout the country. Since all the decisions handed down so far have ordered the states to devise more equitable financing, it seems likely that there will soon be major changes in local education, alleviating the most discriminatory and destructive aspect of fragmentation in this area.

But even if all the states enforced equal financing for education, there still would be great gaps among them, since rich states like Wyoming spend twice as much per pupil as poor states like Arkansas. The federal government did not begin to spend substantial amounts of money on local education until LBJ's Great Society programs of the late 1960s. But while it contributed 4.4 percent of the total local education budget in 1959, its level of support in 1976 was 7.8 percent.[13] And this support, after an initial period of confusion, has been directed in large part to the poorest school districts. Title I of the 1965 Elementary and Secondary Education Act provided $1.5 billion a year for compensatory education for poor children. Unfortunately, for at least the first five years of its existence, the funds did not get to their target very effectively. In Yakima County, Washington, for instance, these funds were spent on equipment, while special programs for poor Indian and Mexican-American children never came into existence. A 1971 study financed by the Ford Foundation found that rural areas got far more federal aid per pupil than urban areas, where educational and social problems are greater.[14] Since then, the U.S. Office of Education has moved to end abuses and get the funds where they belong, but it faces the usual enforcement problem of monitoring 16,000 school districts.

As is the case with state government, the federal judiciary has produced greater changes and challenges in education than have the legislative or executive branches. In 1954 the U.S. Supreme Court ruled, in the case of *Brown* v.

13. Ibid., pp. 52–53.
14. Joel S. Berke et al., *Federal Aid to Education: Who Benefits?* (Syracuse, N.Y.: Policy Institute, Syracuse University Research Corporation, 1971).

Board of Education, that legally required racial segregation in the schools was unconstitutional. While it took quite a while to implement this decision, most such separation had ended by 1970.

This change constituted a revolution in public policy, since almost all the school systems of the southern states were segregated, and governors like Alabama's George Wallace had built their careers on a cry of "segregation forever." For the imposing edifice of school segregation to crumble so completely is ample evidence of the far-reaching authority of court decisions (provided they are backed up by litigation from the U.S. Justice Department, as they were in the 1960s and 1970s). In addition, congressional statutes and Department of Health, Education and Welfare guidelines decreased segregation further.

In the 1970s, the fight for school integration moved north of the Mason-Dixon line. It began with a 1971 Supreme Court case, *Swann v. Charlotte-Mecklenburg County [North Carolina] Board of Education.* Here the court went beyond outlawing legally required segregation to state that all-black and all-white schools were unconstitutional, even if they were caused only by residential housing patterns. Transportation by bus was prescribed as the remedy for such racial imbalance. In the 1973 case of *Keyes v. School District #1 [Denver]* the Supreme Court ruled that *intent* to segregate must be shown. Since then, the federal courts have found again and again that such intent does exist in many northern cities, where poor and minority schools have not received the same amount of resources to educate as have schools in white neighborhoods. The court-prescribed remedy, again, is busing. Probably the most controversial of these conflicts is that of Boston, where a 1974 lower federal court ruling mandating busing was upheld by the United States Supreme Court in June 1976. Large-scale violence, including rioting, murder, and arson, followed the 1974 decision.

The pros and cons of busing are too complex a topic to delve into in this chapter. Our focus here is on the federal impact on fragmentation in education. If busing were to lead to a more equal distribution of educational resources, it would clearly reduce the most crippling consequence of fragmentation. While busing may have accomplished this goal in Charlotte, North Carolina, and other southern communities, where it has been accepted with a minimum of violence, such has obviously not been the case in Boston. There, the city school system has had to close down for periods of time, truancy has increased, and students are constantly on guard for violence. It is difficult to imagine a worse environment for learning than one charged with fear.

Indeed, one might well ask why anyone would want to persevere with busing under these circumstances. One reason given by advocates of busing is the survey done by sociologist James S. Coleman in 1966 to determine the key factors in learning. Coleman found that the things the professional educators had touted as important for so long, like smaller numbers of students per class, more highly trained instructors, and expensive equipment, had no evident impact on student learning as measured by standardized tests. The only variable Coleman could find that was related to achievement was the proportion of middle-class children in the schoolroom. The Coleman Report concluded that lower-class children performed markedly better when mixed with a larger middle-class group of children.[15]

Since most black and Hispanic inner-city schoolchildren are not middle-class, backers of busing have argued that busing is necessary if these children are ever going to do better in schools. Since most middle-class children are white, and since the black middle class tends either to leave the central city or to send its children to private schools, integration through busing has been advocated as the way to improve learning for lower-class children.

With all the transportation and integration that has occurred, we should have an idea of whether or not the Coleman Report's conclusions are valid—but we do not. Many of the busing experiences are not comparable, because of the different situations in which they have taken place. In addition, no attempt has been made to evaluate many busing programs, such as that of New York City.[16]

In 1975, Dr. Coleman said he opposed busing, because it contributes to white flight to the suburbs and thus is counterproductive in the attempt to foster integration.[17] Coleman had to admit that he had no data on this point, but his thesis seems reasonable. A bitterness toward busing is found in most northern cities where it is used, and this animosity is perhaps an inevitable result of the clash of ghetto and middle-class ways of life. White liberals who formerly backed integration are now heard to say that they can't send their kids to the city schools. Taunting, beatings, forced payment of lunch money to use the toilet, and theft are daily occurrences in many big city schools. One New York City junior high school about to integrate and become mostly white installed ultrasonic detection and alarm systems, required students to carry identification cards and eat lunch at the school, made students arriving by bus enter the school immediately, and fenced in the playground so that the only access to it is through the school.[18]

15. James S. Coleman, *Equality of Educational Opportunity,* Report submitted to the U.S. Office of Education, 1966.

16. Leonard Buder, "Findings Are Thin on Educational Impact of Busing on Children," *New York Times,* 20 June 1976, p. 1.

17. Edward B. Fiske, "Scholar Eases Criticism of Study of White Flight," *New York Times,* 3 September 1976, p. 13.

18. Nathan Glazer, *Affirmative Discrimination* (New York: Basic Books, 1976), p. 110.

A leading social critic, Nathan Glazer, argues that we should bus only children of low achievement, rather than racial groups as a whole.[19] But the amount of change such a policy would create in the older central cities, whose school populations are largely lower-achievement black and Hispanic children, is questionable. This fact introduces another uncertain aspect of busing: the relation of city to suburb. So far, no large-scale scheme integrating a large city with the school districts of its surrounding suburbs has been ordered. The Supreme Court, to the contrary, struck down a plan to bus Detroit children to the suburbs in 1970. Without such action, busing cannot achieve racial or class balance, since the central cities are becoming increasingly populated by minority groups. But if the courts move to sweep into the suburbs, the consequence may well be a constitutional amendment banning busing, as suburbanites react with rage.

While the outcome of busing is unclear, the cumulative impact of many state and federal actions has indeed led to a decrease of educational fragmentation. Yet there is vigorous activity to increase fragmentation—in the name of citizen participation in and control of education.

THE DEMAND FOR SCHOOL DECENTRALIZATION

The hottest issue in education is the racial one, of which busing is one manifestation. Blacks, concentrated in the cities, have demanded different programs and approaches to counter a century of discrimination and segregation. The most noticeable of these demands is for neighborhood or community control of schools, generally referred to as decentralization. Those who desire decentralization want a return to the neighborhood-based orientation of city schools that held sway before the triumph of the professionals and the unitary myth.

Decentralization's basic goal is different from that of integration and busing. Decentralization stresses control of neighborhood schools by those whose children attend these schools, because the professionals who run the schools are believed to have done an inadequate job. While black groups have been the most noticeable proponents of decentralization, they have not been alone. Members of other ethnic groups, including white groups in the Canarsie area of Brooklyn, New York, have also demanded community control. Nor is community control a phenomenon that must be limited to the largest localities. There is no reason that a community with only three schools could not move from centralized control to a decentralized school district for each neighborhood school.

Certainly those who complain about the performance of the schools have

19. Ibid., p. 136.

269

a legitimate gripe. A 1969 study found that 300,000 high school graduates were "functional illiterates," unable to read at a fifth-grade level. A survey of one hundred New York City corporations made about the same time found that 30,000 clerical jobs were unfilled because of "the demonstrated inability of public high schools, at present, to turn out sufficient numbers of qualified graduates." European educational systems can often teach in nine years what takes twelve years in the United States. A steady nationwide decline in student scores on reading and mathematics tests over the last fifteen years indicates that there are indeed problems in the schoolhouse.[20]

It would be unfair to blame all these educational failures on the teaching profession alone. Teachers today sometimes confront a more difficult task in educating black and Hispanic minorities, because many of these children come from troubled homes were no great value is placed on education. This is a very different situation from the one prevailing among earlier city immigrants, like the Jews, Italians, Irish, and Slavs, who wanted to see their children do better than they had done. A child who does not come from a home environment that stresses learning is handicapped in school and must be unusually motivated and/or have unusually good teachers to overcome this handicap.

Professional educators also often are faced with demands by parents of all social classes and ethnic backgrounds that their children be allowed to pass or graduate even if they do not meet the qualifications. One can sympathize with educators who knuckle under to this pressure, but disagree with the solution they have chosen. Graduating children who cannot read is a betrayal of all the highest goals of the professional educator, and one can see why some parents want to take over their schools in the attempt to get their children to learn more, rather than be happy with meaningless diplomas.

Certainly the response of professional educators to attempts to evaluate their job performance and productivity makes one wonder how interested they are in education. Since the early 1970s, many school districts have established evaluation systems for their faculty. These systems are usually based on the achievement of students, on standardized tests administered at the beginning and end of the school year. Some teachers whose students do not do well are penalized or fired, and one such case in Iowa was appealed all the way to the U.S. Supreme Court in 1974 by the National Educational Association. Regardless of the right and wrong in any individual case, it is noteworthy that these evaluation plans are almost never proposed initially by teachers' groups. Instead, these groups usually fight such plans tooth and nail—all of which makes onlookers wonder how genuinely teachers are interested in education. The Michigan

20. *Christian Science Monitor*, 25 November 1969, p. 13; Gene I. Maeroff, "Aptitude Test Scores Continue to Decline," *New York Times*, 12 September 1976, p. 27.

270

Education Association denounced a 1975 state evaluation plan as "ill-conceived" and "counter-productive," but had never proposed any alternatives beforehand.[21]

To date, there has been no case of complete decentralization, in which total control of neighborhood schools has been turned over to a neighborhood board, so it is impossible to assert that decentralization would result in better or worse education. But since New York City has implemented a limited scheme of school decentralization, we can examine it to see some of the consequences. Thirty elected district school boards were established in 1969, sharing power over budgets and personnel with the central city school board. Although the district boards are most noticeable when they decide to fire a principal, or to change the name of Fiorello La Guardia School to that of a Puerto Rican revolutionary, they do get into more fundamental matters. Many of the boards are forums for fights among different groups over which school is going to get what programs, personnel, and services.

In elections for the boards, less than 15 percent of those eligible turned out, even after substantial publicity. Sixty-four percent of those elected in 1970 were middle-class professionals, while only 28 percent were black and Hispanic, even though 57 percent of the pupils were black and Hispanic. Most noteworthy were the 53 percent of board members with children in Catholic parochial, not public, schools. These Catholic members were drawn to the boards because the boards administer state and federal aid to parochial schools.[22]

Advocates of decentralization argue that the New York case is not an example of true decentralization, any more than was a similar Detroit scheme of 1970, which resulted in the same patterns as those described above.[23] It is true that much if not most authority still remains with the central board. So perhaps a thoroughgoing decentralization *might* produce real educational benefits of a kind not yet found in New York or Detroit. But we can be sure it would also entail some of the following costs.

Decentralization, by definition, will result in another layer of government, and thus in increased fragmentation. The usual complaints about variations in programs, competence of government employees, and financial and manpower resources devoted to different subjects will be voiced, while coordination and consistency will decline. In addition, the creation of another layer of government will both cost more money to pay the bureaucrats working in it, and result in

21. Gene I. Maeroff, "Accountability Plan Angers Teachers, with Many Foreseeing Threat to Job," *New York Times*, 6 July 1974, p. 20.

22. Mario Fantini and Marilyn Gittell, *Decentralization: Achieving Reform* (New York: Praeger, 1973), pp. 48–52.

23. Ibid., *passim*.

more delay, with another layer for communications and decisions to penetrate.

It is probable that while non–central-city school districts will be gradually reduced and reformed by consolidation, central-city districts will expand because of the demand for improvement in educational results. While fragmentation will decrease outside the central cities, it will increase inside them. And it remains an open question whether decentralization will end the autonomy of education or merely exchange the insularity of educational professionals for the insularity of different neighborhoods in the city. What is needed above all is well-planned coordination of education with attempts to alleviate all other related human problems, such as poverty, housing, health, and crime—but education remains as isolated from this kind of program integration as it ever has been.

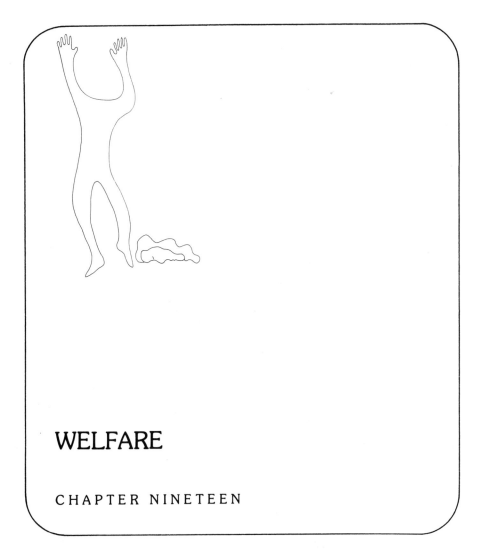

WELFARE

CHAPTER NINETEEN

One out of eight Americans is legally eligible to receive some kind of welfare payment from government, but at least one-third of those eligible do not get welfare. Twenty-five billion dollars in annual welfare payments are siphoned through a bewildering intergovernmental maze that makes the fragmentation of other policy areas look like the epitome of efficiency. Everyone agrees that our welfare system is a disaster, but it remains unchanged. In this chapter, we will examine how welfare works and why we are stuck with a system everyone despises.

THE FRAGMENTATION OF WELFARE

Our focus will be on public Aid to Families with Dependent Children (AFDC), the welfare program that serves the most people—over eleven million in 1976.[1] We will also briefly examine the food stamp program, but we will not scrutinize other welfare programs, such as public housing (discussed in the chapter on housing); veterans' benefits; or aid to the elderly, blind, and handicapped. Suffice it to say that each of these programs is administered by a different federal agency, and often by different state and local agencies as well, and the inevitable frustrations of fragmentation can be imagined.

This fragmentation is increased when related programs, financed by special payroll taxes, also enter the picture. Strictly speaking, these programs are not welfare programs, which we define as those that provide benefits only to those in financial need. Rather, they are available to anyone who is a paid-up member of the program, whether it be Social Security or unemployment compensation, regardless of their nonemployment income. It is commonplace for elderly residents of public housing to be given eviction notices when Social Security benefits are increased, because their income is raised over the ceiling for the housing project. Congress and federal, state, and local bureaucrats then have to provide new and workable legislation. Since many of those on welfare have little knowledge of the ways of government, these intersections of different programs often result in terrible problems.

FROM PRIVATE CHARITY TO PUBLIC WELFARE: THE SHIFT TO AN INTERGOVERNMENTAL NETWORK

Before the great depression of 1929–1941, assistance to the impoverished was the work of private charity and local government. The state governments were only minimally involved, and the federal government not at all.[2]

The natural result of this system was the variety we have discovered again and again in subnational government. Some towns provided food; others poorhouses; others put the poor to work; and many others did nothing. Moves to get federal aid for the unemployed in the serious depressions of 1893–1894, 1914, and 1921 failed. Opponents of federal aid argued that such aid would undermine the desire to work and lead to a federal takeover of local government.

1. Department of Health, Education and Welfare, *Public Assistance Statistics, March 1976* (Washington, D.C.: U.S. Government Printing Office, 1976).

2. This section is based primarily on: Frances Fox Piven and Richard A. Cloward, *Regulating the Poor: The Functions of Public Welfare* (New York: Pantheon Books, 1971), pp. 45–119.

The great depression gradually but greatly altered this welfare system. By 1932, private and local government "relief" to the unemployed had increased seven-fold since 1929—during a period of *deflation*, with the dollar worth more in 1932 than in 1929. Yet the rise of relief was incapable of stemming the problems created by mass unemployment. Thousands starved, hundreds of thousands lost their homes, and the Communists and others who argued that nothing short of revolution would cure these problems gained strength.

Franklin D. Roosevelt, elected president in 1933, immediately began to implement new relief programs. Most of these were work relief programs, under which the unemployed planted trees and cleared trails in forests, constructed highways, built dams, and worked on a multitude of local projects. At the same time, the Federal Emergency Relief Administration (FERA) provided direct relief, which totalled $3 billion by 1936, to state and local governments for distribution to the poor. This direct relief program is the ancestor of today's federal welfare programs.

The response by the states to FERA set a pattern that continues today. Some paid as much as 50 percent of the relief bill; others continued to spend nothing. By 1936, FERA had been phased out in favor of work relief programs. By 1940 the work relief programs were also ended. What remained were provisions of the 1935 Social Security Act that provided aid for children who lacked one or both parents. While the federal government provided funds, these funds were administered by state and local government. This program is now what is known as AFDC.

The usual place of the states in welfare administration is illustrated by a 1961 amendment to AFDC. In that year, Congress gave the states the option of allowing families with *both* parents at home to receive AFDC if the parents were unemployed. But by 1976, a majority of states had not exercised this option, and they continued to deny AFDC benefits to families with a present but unemployed father.

As with FERA, subnational responses to the AFDC program varied greatly. In 1939, Arkansas gave $8.10 a month to families with dependent children, while Massachusetts provided $61.07. These differences endure today. A 1972 study of families with a nonworking mother and three children found that annual AFDC payments ranged from $6,136 in Boston to $2,181 in Bolivar, Mississippi.[3] One reason the poorest states, like Mississippi, pay so little, is that the federal formula gives them the incentive to do so. In low-benefit states, the federal government picks up a higher proportion of the AFDC tab than in high-benefit states. In Mississippi, Uncle Sam pays about 83 percent of the cost;

3. "Effects of Welfare Studied," *Congressional Quarterly Weekly Report* (27 July 1974), p. 1977.

in New York, 50 percent. States that want to pay at a higher level have to assume a greater proportion of the cost themselves. Federal government policy, then, spurs local variety and fragmentation, rather than restraining it.

While the states in general pay the most substantial subnational share of welfare, there are numerous exceptions to this rule. Both New York City and San Francisco are required to pay 25 percent of their local welfare costs, but Baltimore pays only about 8 percent, and Boston and a number of cities pay

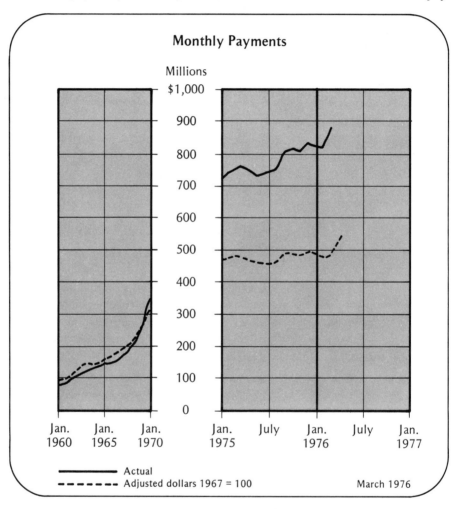

FIGURE 19.1   Aid To Families with Dependent Children

SOURCE: U.S. Department of Health, Education and Welfare, *Public Assistance Statistics* (Washington, D.C.: U.S. Government Printing Office, March 1976).

nothing. (While these big cities are made to foot some of the bill, it should be noted that the county is the unit of government that most frequently administers welfare.) This financial arrangement leads to different approaches on the part of welfare departments. In Baltimore, it is easier to get on welfare than in San Francisco; in San Francisco, welfare department employees place obstacles in the way of welfare applicants, while Baltimore welfare bureaucrats are more accommodating.[4]

Today about half of the total AFDC tab of some $15 billion annually is picked up by the federal government, with the states and localities dividing the other half. (The states pay 75 percent and the localities 25 percent of this half). Yet this does not mean that the federal government makes most welfare decisions. At any time, one can be sure that some states are not conforming with all the federal regulations they are supposed to accept as the conditions for their federal grant. The federal government is aware of these state failures to fulfill obligations, and it can cut off welfare funds if the states do not fall into line, but often states that do not conform still receive their funds. In 1971, California refused to make cost-of-living adjustments in welfare payments, even though federal law requires this. John J. Twiname, administrator of the federal Social and Rehabilitation Service, moved to suspend $684 million in federal funds. But California did not simply surrender. Negotiations began between state and federal officials including "summit" negotiations between California Governor Ronald Reagan and Secretary of Health, Education and Welfare Elliot Richardson. The result was not federal dictation of terms, but a compromise between the state and federal positions.[5] Such procedures are typical in welfare matters, and they reflect the political strength of subnational government in our federal system. They also indicate the nature of the stakes in this issue. If federal funds had been cut off in California, Governor Reagan would not have suffered directly—but welfare recipients would have.

Welfare Categories

AFDC is characterized by an abundance of categories. The handbook for the program is nearly a thousand pages long, and categories include those for rent, furniture, medicine, food, and many more. This approach to assistance means that the welfare bureaucracy must employ thousands of paper shufflers in order to function. Indeed, trained social case workers often must spend their time filling

4. Sharon Perlman Krefetz, "City Politics and Public Welfare" (Paper presented at the 1971 Annual Meeting of the American Political Science Association, Chicago).
5. Paul Delaney, "California Wins Welfare Accord," *New York Times*, 23 June 1971, p. 24.

out forms, rather than advising families in desperate need of information about how to budget money, how to keep house and care for children, and where to go to get assistance from other government programs for the poor.

These categories not only cause confusion because of red tape delays, but also irritate because they intersect with the other welfare and insurance programs described earlier. The following hypothetical case illustrates the point. Drawn from Paul Jacobs' book *Prelude to Riot*,[6] it uses 1966 payment levels, but the categories remain about the same.

Podunk Welfare Department
Family X receives $337.00 a month, based on:

1. The $25.25 allowance per child for their three children under six.
2. The $35.30 allowance for their two children seven to twelve.
3. The $48.00 allowance for their one child twelve to seventeen.
4. The $41.60 allowance for an adult female.

These funds, together with the monthly allowance for utilities, rent, and household operation of $91.35 and the new $10.00 cost-of-living increase, total $337.00.

However, since Mr. X is working, and earning $412.00 gross income a month, we deduct $220.00 of that income from the monthly allowance, since we regard it as applicable to meeting family X's needs. *This leaves $117.00.*

However, school expenses for family X total $175 monthly (tuition, child care, and transportation), which we add to the $117.00, giving a total of $292.00.

However, since the maximum the state will pay a family with three eligible children is $221.00, $71.00 must come from federal EOA funds. (Family X used to get $54.00 from EOA funds before last month, when the amount that Mr. X earned which could be deducted from the monthly allowance decreased by $17.00).

If you are confused, imagine yourself to have, like many welfare recipients, little formal education and knowledge of bureaucracy. As former Los Angeles County Welfare Commissioner Ellis Murphy once remarked, "It's disgraceful that we have no master plan to direct this monumental spending."

Another outstanding and arbitrary quality of this system of categories is its "sudden death" nature. While welfare recipients can earn some money up to a certain ceiling, they have to be careful, because if they exceed that ceiling by only a few dollars, they will lose *all* their benefits. This usually means a reduced standard of living, because their benefits, unlike their paychecks, are tax-free, and entitle them to related benefits like Medicaid, food stamps, and public

6. (New York: Random House, 1967), 86–92.

housing. Since the alleged purpose of welfare is rehabilitation, enabling the recipient to become gainfully employed, sudden-death stipulations are counter-productive. The situation is exacerbated by the schedule of reduced payments applied when a recipient gets a job. Usually, recipients are allowed to keep so little of their welfare payments when they go to work that they lack strong incentive to find a job or keep working, since most jobs open to them pay low wages. One study found that, given taxes, work expenses, and reduction in benefits, the net increase in income for welfare mothers who went to work averaged as little as 20 percent.[7]

In addition, in 1972, nonworking mothers with three children received tax-free benefits, including AFDC, food stamps, and Medicaid, totalling $400 more than the median wages of all working women.[8] In some cases, then, benefits may be too high to provide incentive to work. In *all* cases, the schedule of benefits retained by a working welfare recipient is too small to make a mother leave her children and work unless she is strongly motivated to do so.

Another counterproductive condition of welfare is that it works against stable families. While there is no evidence that provisions of the law actually cause desertion, the incentive is there, for in most states, a family whose father deserts stands to gain over a thousand dollars a year in benefits. Further, an unemployed, childless woman can double cash and food benefits by having a child. While the gain drops to 30 percent for the second and 20 percent for the third child, the incentive does exist to produce the first one.[9] A policy which *encourages* the birth of children into poverty should be seriously questioned.

Recently, pressure to change AFDC has grown, in part as a result of the fragmentation built into it. But as we shall see, a quick change from this questionable system seems unlikely.

THE CRISIS IN WELFARE

AFDC was originally conceived as a program constructed to help a small minority of children without parents. But by 1976 it had burgeoned to the point where it was given to 11.5 million Americans, over 5 percent of the total population. Another 8 million are eligible, but do not participate for various reasons. Why have the welfare rolls swollen so?

Part of the reason lies in the flight of farm workers from the country. New and better farm machinery has made these farmers and migrant workers unable to compete in selling their services to a national market, so they have had

7. "Effects of Welfare Studied."
8. Ibid.
9. Ibid.

to leave the farms. They migrate to the cities, where they lack the skills for all but the most menial jobs. Many thus end up on welfare, since it gives them a better living than the lowest-paid jobs.

As mentioned previously, much of this migration has been to the North. Black (and to a lesser extent, white) southern farm workers have moved north in great numbers, cutting the AFDC rolls of the southern states, but swelling those of the North. At times they have been assisted in this move by white southerners who have given them one-way tickets north. From 1959–1968, these rural southern areas succeeded in shifting about one-tenth of the AFDC load to the North.[10] This is understandable and inevitable, since northern AFDC payments are so much higher than those in the South.

A 1975 survey in New York City found that two-thirds of the heads of welfare households were born outside New York State. This compared with a national average of 48 percent of welfare household heads receiving AFDC in states other than that of their birth.[11] Another survey, in 1973, found that while southern-born blacks were less likely to be on the welfare rolls than their northern-born counterparts, blacks who had moved from the South since 1965 were more likely to be on welfare than any other group of blacks.[12] What this survey indicates is that the tendency of migrants to end up on welfare is accelerating. While there is no evidence that poor southern blacks move to wealthy states to get higher AFDC payments, since blacks not on welfare move to these states at the same rate as those on welfare, there is no question that the migration patterns result in a greater burden for northern states.

During the 1960s and 1970s other factors, when combined with these migration patterns, swelled AFDC rolls to the bursting point. In 1964, 4.1 million people received AFDC; in 1976, the number was 11.5 million. What caused this enormous change? Ironically, much of the increase seems due to the urging by a federal program (the War on Poverty) that the poor apply for welfare, which forced the federal government to spend more money on AFDC.

Local community action programs, set up under the War on Poverty, sponsored a number of services for the poor. These included counselling, legal advice, and information and leadership in the mounting of protest demonstrations, whether picketing, sit-ins, or other types. The leaders of the antipoverty programs knew that fewer than half of those entitled to AFDC were receiving it. They knew that one of the reasons was lack of information about the program,

10. Peter Kihss, "South Fostering Relief Rise Here," New York Times, 14 October 1968, p. 31.

11. Peter Kihss, "City Studies Out-of-State Roots of Relief Families," New York Times, 16 November 1975, p. 27.

12. Douglas E. Kneeland, "Welfare Study Minimizes Impact of Migrant Blacks," New York Times, 6 May 1973, p. 1.

so they worked to spread this information around through the communities. The Community Action Program's activities were reinforced by the rise of the National Welfare Rights Organization, made up of welfare recipients determined to get their legal entitlement.[13]

One might ask why welfare agencies had not promoted their benefits this way. The answer seems to lie in an ambivalent attitude toward welfare recipients. On the one hand, welfare agencies are responsible for helping the poor, and indeed depend on them for their continued existence. On the other hand, studies have shown that welfare workers come predominantly from middle-class backgrounds, which often means they take a patronizing attitude toward the poor.[14] If a social worker or welfare clerk disdains the poor for not getting work, he is unlikely to broadcast all the benefits available to the poor. In innumerable instances, welfare recipients have had to fight, through protests and in the courts, for benefits to which they are legally entitled. In Providence, Rhode Island, a sit-in by welfare recipients once closed the welfare offices until a furniture allowance that had been withheld was disbursed.

Besides the northern migration and the aggressive tactics of antipoverty agencies, it is likely that the welfare rolls also have risen because many families have been on welfare for a long time. Some poor families have been on welfare for three generations and know no other way of supporting themselves. There seems little question that a welfare environment is unlikely to encourage independence and self-confidence in a person. Rather, it conditions him to a passive dependence on government support. While it is impossible to prove this assertion, a number of scholars who have studied poverty and welfare believe that this atmosphere of dependency does exist.[15] It may be that the very act of providing welfare insures that the welfare rolls will increase in the future.

The rate of growth in the number of poor receiving AFDC slowed in the 1970s. But another social welfare program, food stamps, has increased so greatly that many politicians urged measures to trim it in 1976. The food stamp program began in 1964, sponsored by the U.S. Department of Agriculture as a replacement for its surplus food distribution to the needy. Under the program, recipients buy food coupons worth several times their purchase price and can use them to buy food in most grocery stores. In 1965, the program had 424,000 participants and cost $36 million. By 1976, it had exploded to over 19 million recipients and a cost of almost 6 billion dollars. Forty-five percent of these

13. See: Piven and Cloward, *Regulating the Poor*, pp. 285–340.

14. Virginia B. Ermer and John H. Strange, eds., *Blacks and Bureaucracy* (New York: Crowell, 1972), pp. 54–154.

15. Daniel P. Moynihan, *The Politics of a Guaranteed National Income* (New York: Random House, 1973), pp. 17–60.

281

recipients were on welfare; 15 to 20 percent were "working poor" who did not receive welfare; 10 percent were elderly, blind, and disabled recipients of Social Security. The remainder were the elderly, the unemployed, and students. Eighty-seven percent of the households receiving food stamps earned a gross annual income under $6,000.[16]

How did this enormous expansion take place? As is true of AFDC, changing events outstripped the expectations of those who created the program. Food stamps were designed to help farmers at a time when farm surpluses were the rule. Today, those surpluses, because of growing foreign demand, no longer exist. And when the economy goes into recession, as it did in 1974 through 1976, an estimated 750,000 recipients are added to the food stamp program for every percentage point increase in the unemployment rate. Congressional and public furor at this vast increase will no doubt cause some cutbacks, but the food stamp program is likely to continue because it fills a need for the severely economically strapped poorest 10 percent of our population.

Any social program as extensive as AFDC is bound to include errors. One of the most frequent criticisms of welfare is the allegation of fraud, or the assertion that a large proportion of recipients who are not entitled to it are receiving money. How extensive *is* welfare fraud? While no one is quite sure, a 1973 survey by the U.S. Department of Health, Education and Welfare found that over 30 percent of AFDC recipients were actually ineligible or overpaid. (The survey also showed that 8 percent of recipients were underpaid.)[17]

Such findings have led to attempts to tighten up eligibility requirements, which we will examine below. But attempts to discover fraud are often fore-stalled by our fragmented system of government. A recent case of fraud involved two welfare families, one in Holyoke, Massachusetts, and the other in Hartford, Connecticut. The families pooled their children when they made their original claims, so they would each receive more benefits than they were entitled to. Discovery was made more difficult because each family lived in a different state and was served by a different welfare department.

The existence of state boundaries swells welfare rolls for another reason. Every year, married men simply leave their families. Such "abandonment" is illegal, for these husbands are legally required to support their families if they are working. But by moving to another state, they can often escape retribution. Bringing them back requires an extensive search and costly litigation, so many mothers simply apply for welfare as a simpler option. One Chicago resident with

16. Joel Solkoff, "Food Stamp Program, As It Is, Has Very Few Friends," *New York Times*, 18 April 1976, Section E., p. 3.

17. "H.E.W. Study Finds Welfare Errors," *New York Times*, 21 December 1973, p. 22.

a good income abandoned his family and moved to Indiana, where he had his business. His wife continued to allow her child to visit with his father on weekends, believing that this was good for the boy. But, discouraged by the complications of going into the Indiana courts to sue her husband for support, she instead applied for and got welfare in Chicago.

Expanding welfare rolls may also occasionally be the result of local politics. The administration of New York Mayor Lindsay, in office from 1965 to 1973, increased the welfare rolls shortly before elections, clearly hoping that recipients would pay back this favor at the polls.

All of the factors discussed in this section have combined to create a crisis in welfare. Attempts to confront this crisis have taken different forms.

Responses to the Welfare Crisis

State governments responded to the rapidly rising welfare rolls of the early 1970s in a predictable manner, by moving in several ways to retrench. Some states redoubled the search for cases of fraud. The Texas legislature refused to appropriate enough money for welfare in 1972, while a Colorado county moved to drop its welfare program altogether. Benefit reductions of as much as 20 percent went into effect in ten states in 1971.[18] Several states imposed a one-year residency requirement for anyone receiving welfare. One of these, Hawaii, had a particularly good reason for doing so. Every year, thousands of young people flock to the island, looking for carefree days in a tropical paradise. These newcomers then go on the welfare rolls. The influx of "welfare hippies" had caused the rolls to grow at 25 percent a year, compared with a national average of 20 percent.[19]

These cutbacks resulted in a type of success, for the welfare rolls stabilized in 1972. They did not follow the pattern of the 1960s, when they rose even when the unemployment rate was dropping. (Welfare recipients still increase in economic downturns, such as the recession of 1974 to 1975.) The states and localities, then, continue to play a key role in our intergovernmental welfare system.

But so does the federal government. Federal courts ruled welfare residency requirements unconstitutional in 1971 and 1973, on the grounds that the poor have as much right to travel as more affluent citizens. They also ruled that an Alabama technique used to cut AFDC funds—paying AFDC families only a

18. Bill Kovach, "States Move to Reverse Wide Welfare Expansion," *New York Times*, 15 August 1971, p . 1.

19. "Hawaii Votes Law Curbing Welfare," *New York Times*, 13 June 1971, p. 14.

fraction of what blind, elderly, and disabled welfare recipients got—was unconstitutional.[20]

Since Uncle Sam prints money, something the states can't do, numerous state and local officials have advocated a total federal takeover of welfare as a way of relieving state and local government from a heavy burden. The U.S. Conference of Mayors has argued for this policy change for several years, a position adopted in 1976 by the National Governor's Conference. Advocates of change point out that welfare is a *national* rather than regional problem. And since half of all AFDC recipients are not natives of the states in which they live, it is difficult to deny the charge. In 1971, New York City sued both the state and federal governments in federal court to try to be relieved of the requirement that it pay 25 percent of city welfare costs. The city lost the case, but continues to press its case with Congress. Federal takeover, however, will be difficult, as an examination of abortive attempts in 1969 and 1971 shows.

From Welfare Categories to a Guaranteed National Income

The growth of the AFDC rolls in the 1960s created a more attentive audience for those critics who argued that our entire intergovernmental, fragmented, and categorized approach to welfare should be junked in favor of a more consistent and comprehensive system. The critics made several telling points.[21]

First, the U.S. is the only major industrialized nation that does not have a family allowance system. Under such a system, all families in the country are entitled automatically to a payment for each child. The system works much as our Social Security system does, mailing out monthly child support checks just like the ones the retired, widows, orphans, and disabled persons covered by Social Security get. This family allowance is considered a right, and receiving it is not dependent on the mood or whims of a welfare bureaucrat or the vagaries of a particular local welfare office. Every family gets the allowance, regardless of income, and the wealthy are taxed at a higher rate to compensate for their family allowance.

Second, the lack of uniformity in our system may well encourage migration that is not in the best interests of either individuals or the nation as a whole.

20. "Court Orders Alabama to Halt Welfare Payment Disparities," *New York Times*, 5 August 1975, p. 29.

21. This section is based on Moynihan, *Guaranteed National Income*; and Theodore R. Marmor and Martin Rein, "Reforming 'The Welfare Mess': The Fate of FAP, 1969-72," in Allan P. Sindler, ed., *Policy and Politics in America* (Boston: Little, Brown and Co., 1973), pp. 2-29.

When poor rural southern blacks have to move to big cities to survive, they encounter a totally different and often threatening environment that can weaken family ties and draw family members into crime and drug addiction. If these individuals were able to remain in their stable rural environment, they and the cities might be much better off. Programs to improve their health and education could be mounted in the country, and might enjoy far greater success than similar programs in the city.

Third, lack of uniformity imposes suffering on those in areas with low welfare payments who do not wish to move.

Fourth, the sudden-death nature of AFDC discourages attempts to find work, since workers can lose all their welfare by working, or make only a pittance more for working all week than they would by doing nothing but collecting welfare.

A longtime champion of change in welfare is Daniel Patrick Moynihan, who worked for Presidents Kennedy, Johnson, Nixon and Ford. Moynihan, whose own father abandoned his family when he was thirteen, persuaded President Nixon that the welfare system should be revamped. He argued in 1969 that the reason AFDC was a problem was not the $10 billion spent on it annually, which is not a huge sum in a trillion-dollar economy. Rather, the problem was a *social* one. Moynihan noted that in the 1960s the welfare rolls had increased in a time of increasing prosperity, something which had never before happened. Thousands of families had lived on welfare for three generations. AFDC was becoming a way of life to them, creating a large dependent lowerclass separated from the rest of society. This lower class had much higher incidences of social problems, including crime, suicide, mental illness, and drug addiction. In short, AFDC was *creating* social problems instead of solving them.

Moynihan was able to sell this analysis to President Nixon, a practical politician. Nixon had nothing to gain by advocating the solution Moynihan proposed, which amounted to a guaranteed annual family income. The outlines of the plan included a federally financed income floor for a family of four of $2,400 in 1971; a "workfare" requirement that all able-bodied adult recipients register for work or job training; and substitution of a new sliding rate of benefit reductions for the working poor designed to provide more incentive for those on welfare to get or keep jobs.

This proposal was called the Family Assistance Plan, because the term "guaranteed annual income" was a dirty phrase for many politicians. Mostly conservative, they felt such a program would lead to a large-scale breakdown of the urge to work. Far better to keep the present system, which at least discouraged some welfare seekers with its variety, red tape, and requirement that applicants prove they were destitute. These conservatives, including many congressmen of both parties and members of the U.S. Chamber of Commerce, normally supported President Nixon. Since it was hard to imagine welfare recipients and liberals backing Nixon, since they usually vote Democratic if they vote, the program seemed a net political loss for the president. For this reason, Vice-President Spiro Agnew urged him to reject it. Also for this reason, Nixon included the "workfare" section, even though he was convinced by studies that it would not lead to a significant amount of employment. He felt it absolutely essential to stress "workfare" to get conservative support for the program, and the tactic worked to some extent, enlisting the reactionary National Association of Manufacturers, among others, on his side.

But liberal opposition also endangered the proposal. Liberal critics like Senator Eugene McCarthy argued that the $2,400 floor would result in much lower payments in northern industrial states, some of which were paying more than twice this amount in AFDC. The administration's assurances that the bill included provisions requiring the states to pay no less than they had previously was met with suspicion. The National Welfare Rights Organization demanded a floor of $6,500, while denouncing workfare as a form of enslavement.

In addition, conservative southern congressmen opposed the $2,400 floor because it would provide a measure of independence to poor rural blacks. In the new system, the blacks would automatically get *more* money than they were currently getting in any southern state, and they would get it without being dependent on county welfare offices. This threatened to give southern blacks a good deal of economic independence, for while $2,400 would not take one very far in the North, it would go a good deal farther in the balmy weather of Mississippi farm country.

Another objection to the Nixon plan was the strong likelihood of greatly increased expenditures for welfare, at least in the short run. While Moynihan and other Nixon aides argued that the increased cost would be minor, evidence mounted that the annual cost of AFDC might well increase by 50 percent, or five billion dollars annually. While Moynihan argued that these costs would decline over time, there is no question that the financial prospects of the plan hurt its chances for passage.

While the Nixon proposal passed the House of Representatives in both 1969 and 1971, it was smothered in the Senate by a liberal-conservative coalition. George McGovern's proposal for a welfare system of "Demogrants," almost identical to the Nixon scheme except for its $4,000 floor, proved highly unpopular in the 1972 primaries. Nixon quietly junked the Family Assistance Plan and lambasted the McGovern welfare scheme in the 1972 election.

THE CARTER RESPONSE

In August, 1977, President Carter outlined a fairly bold attempt to reduce, if not resolve, the nation's growing welfare problem. In essence, the President's program would provide job opportunities, including federally funded public service jobs, "for those who need work." In so doing, it would tighten up AFDC eligibility rules by requiring all women with children aged seven to fourteen to accept employment. At the same time, however, it would offer some income benefits to all persons "who work but whose incomes are inadequate to support their families." And it would provide a minimum income, on a base of $4,200 a year for a family of four, to those single-parent families with children under seven. (The aged, blind, and disabled would qualify for similar stipends.)

How would the Carter proposal affect states and communities in regard to welfare? The President gave assurances that each state "will save at least ten percent of its current welfare expenses in the first year of the program" and that "substantially increased" savings would occur thereafter. Not only would the states receive higher basic grants for their welfare cases, but every state that chose to add some of its own money to the federal government's minimum payment could count on some additional federal aid.

Carter's plan elicited considerable initial favor from many governors and big-city mayors, since it offered them some financial relief. But, like Nixon's scheme of eight years earlier, it also aroused some animosity on both the right and the left. Many liberals felt it provided too little, while many conservatives felt it provided too much. Whether or not Carter's plan will suffer the fate of Nixon's remains to be seen. In any case, state and local welfare agencies are likely to continue to play key roles in providing relief to the poor of America.

HOUSING

CHAPTER TWENTY

The U.S.A. has two distinct housing problems: we do not have enough housing and much of it is bad. While the federal government plays an active role in funding attempts to alleviate both these problems, subnational governments have determined the way these funds will be used. Indeed, they have determined whether they will be used at all.

The most detailed study ever made of the housing problem, completed in 1973, concluded that one out of every five households lived in physically substandard or overcrowded conditions, or was forced to spend an excessive amount of its income for rent.[1] Throughout most of the postwar period, this

1. Joseph P. Fried, "Thirteen Million Families Are Held Housing-Deprived," *New York Times*, 12 December 1973, p. 64.

country successfully solved the housing shortage by producing enough new housing units to satisfy demand. But since the early 1970s, inflation and recession have made housing much more expensive. For the first time since 1945, large numbers of middle-class households cannot afford to buy single-family homes. There is now too little housing of this type at a price the average household can pay.

Attempts by the federal government to deal with these problems run into numerous local government regulations, which vary from place to place under our system of fragmented government.

FEDERAL-STATE-LOCAL RELATIONS: THE CASE OF PUBLIC HOUSING

The federal government has made energetic efforts in housing policy since the New Deal of the 1930s. Between 1933 and 1937, it constructed and operated subsidized public housing projects. These federal housing programs were free from local control, just as field offices of the Social Security Administration today carry out their business independent of local government. But local advocates of public housing, bolstered by some favorable court decisions, were able to change this method of operation in 1937. The Wagner-Steagall Act of that year provided for local housing authorities to plan, construct, administer, and own public housing in their jurisdictions. While the federal government continued to control funding and the right to approve site selections, plans, rentals, costs, and the regulations governing the operation of housing projects, it had to share its powers with state and local government. This situation has existed ever since.[2]

Although most states have not played an active role in housing policy, their approval is needed before local government can establish public housing authorities and receive funds from the federal government. This has not been a problem in most states, though the Florida Supreme Court ruled renewal and housing authorities unconstitutional in the 1950s. But local resistance to federal policies has manifested itself time and time again. By 1951, over thirty municipalities had voted against federally financed public housing. From 1949 to 1965, 40 percent of 250 referendum challenges to public housing were successful.[3]

To sum up, in this area of housing policy, the federal government took the initiative, implementing a vigorous program. But local governments quickly showed they could assert themselves, gaining a veto power over enactment of public housing within their boundaries.

2. Charles Abrams, *The City Is the Frontier* (New York: Harper & Row, 1965), pp. 211–254.
3. Leonard Freedman, *Public Housing* (New York: Holt, Rinehart and Winston, 1969), pp. 38–54.

The Scope of Housing Policy

Lest the reader assume that public housing constitutes the bulk of government effort in the housing area, a few facts are in order. Subsidized public housing is rented to about four million persons, less than 2 percent of the national population. Far greater in their impact on housing have been federal mortgage and income tax policies. Mortgage monies are provided by guarantees from agencies like the Federal Housing Administration (FHA) and the Veterans' Administration (VA) for those who wish to buy single-family homes. These programs, which began in earnest after the end of World War II, have contributed greatly to the growing suburbanization of the country. By enabling city dwellers to obtain mortgages on easier terms, through lower interest rates and less stringent eligibility criteria, the FHA and VA have enabled millions to attain their dream of a house "in the country."

Perhaps even more important than federal mortgage guarantees are the substantial subsidies indirectly provided to homeowners by the Internal Revenue Code. Since the Code allows homeowners to deduct the interest on their mortgages from their taxable income, it currently provides nearly fifteen *billion* dollars annually in tax credits to homeowners. Since few poor people can afford mortgages, this is a subsidy that goes almost entirely to the middle- and upper-income brackets.[4] Federal housing policy, then, is primarily directed toward the provision of middle- and upper-income families with owner-occupied single-family homes.

There are other government housing programs designed to rehabilitate housing that will then be owner-occupied. We will examine some of these later.

HOUSING NEEDS

All projections indicate that current policies do not meet the needs for housing. There is not enough new construction nor rehabilitation of existing stock to end substandard conditions. What are these substandard conditions like?

"Physically inadequate dwellings," in which seven million households lived in 1973, are those that are in dilapidated condition (needing, perhaps, a new roof, flooring, or the replacement of other crucial components), that lack complete indoor plumbing, or that do not have adequate heating. An excessive rent burden, paid by five-and-a-half million households, is defined as one in which the head of a family of two or more, earning under $10,000, pays 25 percent or more of his income in rent. The 700,000 overcrowded households

---

4. Henry J. Aaron, *Shelter and Subsidies* (Washington, D.C.: Brookings Institution, 1972).

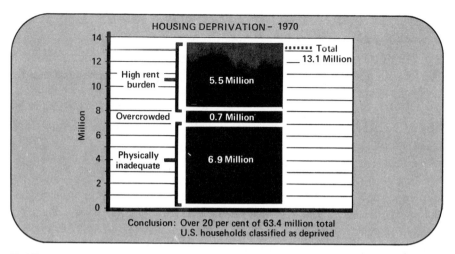

FIGURE 20.1 Housing Deprivation 1970. We have excluded households with incomes greater than $10,000 per year from all categories, on the assumption that such households have, in most cases, a reasonable opportunity by virtue of their income to acquire adequate housing. The categories are estimated in nonoverlapping terms—that is, a household experiencing more than one problem is counted only once.

SOURCE: Reprinted by permission of Joint Center for Urban Studies of MIT and Harvard University.

are those with under $10,000 income, consisting of at least 3 persons, with an average of 1.5 persons or more per room.[5] (See Figure 20.1).

The reader can gain better insight into what these conditions mean in human terms by examining some specific examples. In Washington County, Maine, there are log cabins with dirt floors, which lack electricity, plumbing, and central heating. Thousands of residents in the South Bronx in New York City live in crumbling tenements that have been abandoned by their owners. While residents live there rent free, they live under the same or worse conditions (except for the dirt floors) as the housing-deprived in Washington County. In Lowndes County, Alabama, families of six or more share one-room shacks. While most substandard housing is not this bad, millions of people in the U.S. live in these kinds of conditions, a fact many middle-class citizens do not realize.

The definitions given above overlook or ignore many relevant factors—such as adequate light and ventilation, and sanitary conditions. They also do not account for regional variations, for someone with an outside toilet in Mississippi is much better off than his counterpart in Maine. But the definitions do give us a sense of the overall shape and size of the problem. Now we can address the question of why—in spite of a 1968 act of Congress authorizing a national housing goal of 27.7 million new units by 1978—substandard housing is likely to

5. Fried, "Thirteen Million Families."

continue indefinitely as a major problem. At the same time, it should be noted that the housing stock has steadily improved in this century; things were much worse earlier in this century.

Local Government and Housing Construction

The housing industry is very different from the automobile industry. Four U.S. auto manufacturers produce over 80 percent of the cars sold in this country. These cars are manufactured by mass production assembly-line methods. The housing industry consists of thousands of small firms, none of which produces more than 2 percent of the total housing built annually. These small firms use a minimum of prefabricated materials, such as modular rooms, instead assembling the principal components of the house—roof, flooring, walls—themselves.

The reasons for the differences between these two industries lie in the fact that local government has been and remains the primary regulator of land use in this country. Local zoning and building code regulations are responsible for the absence of large, mass-production-oriented construction firms in this country. Over 14,000 local governments have land-use regulation powers, and all 14,000 seem to use them differently. One suburb may allow the construction of a house on a quarter-acre of land, while another insists on a minimum of five acres. Many localities prohibit preassembled wiring and plumbing systems. One town may require extremely stringent storm drainage facilities, while another may be lax in this area. One county may require roads in developments to have several layers of gravel and asphalt, as well as stone curbing, while another will allow the developer to leave the roads unpaved.

Under these conditions a mass-production industry is impossible, since many localities do not allow prefabricated units. The closest thing to mass production of housing is the mobile home or trailer industry, which now accounts for fully one-third of annual single family housing starts. Because they are mass produced, trailers are far cheaper than houses of the same size. Yet those who buy trailers are not allowed to place them on their own land in thousands of U.S. communities. In other localities, not even trailer parks, where trailer owners can rent a space and hook up to water, sewer, and electric lines, are allowed. If these restrictions were eased, trailer production would no doubt increase greatly and go a long way toward meeting existing housing needs.

As Massachusetts realtor Leslie J. Caulfield said in 1970, ". . . as fast as any federal or state agency comes up with the means of making low priced federal housing available, local governments will counter by making zoning changes and special municipal ordinances." Caulfield pointed out that zoning practices in greater Boston made it impossible not just for the poor, but for any

293

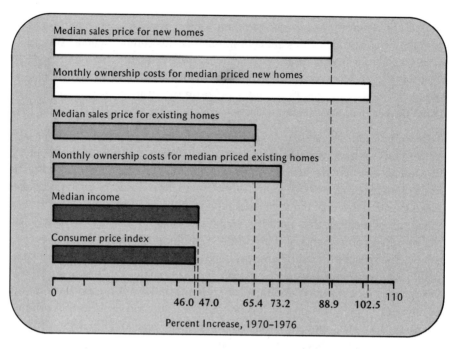

FIGURE 20.2   Homeowner Costs Strain the Average Budget, 1970–1976

SOURCE: Bernard J. Frieden, Arthur P. Solomon, et al., *The Nation's Housing: 1975-1985* (Cambridge, Mass.: Joint Center for Urban Studies), Figure 5.1, p. 119. Reprinted by permission.

family making under $20,000 in 1970 to live in suburbia.[6] Add the immense inflation which has occurred since 1970, and an understanding of why great numbers of the middle class are unable to buy a suburban house for themselves results.

ZONING AND THE ISOLATION OF THE CENTRAL CITY

Local zoning practices in suburbia have helped to destroy the central cities by making them the only place the poor can live. As poor people migrate to the cities from rural areas, middle-class city residents leave the city, in part to escape problems created by the poor. Our older central metropolises are well on their way to becoming *cities of the poor*. The scope of internal migration in the United States is tremendous: millions of people move every year. Many of those who move are the rural poor, who have watched their standard of living drop year after year as subsistence farming is replaced by large agricultural corporations. They come to the cities, in search of a better living.

6. Anthony J. Yudis, "Caulfield, the Maverick," *Boston Globe*, 1 November 1970, Section B, p. 59.

294

This migration illuminates the reasons behind the failure to do anything substantial about the most physically dilapidated housing in the nation. This housing is found in the poor *rural* areas from which the mass exodus to the cities comes. While there are housing programs available for rural areas, they are not of much use to the struggling poor, who have no means of support. Conditions like those in Washington and Lowndes counties are rarely matched in urban areas, except in abandoned buildings.

In 1950, over two-thirds of U.S. blacks, a majority of whom were poor, lived in the South. Today, less than 45 percent of blacks live in the South, and many of these have moved from the country to the larger southern cities, like Atlanta, New Orleans, Memphis, and Richmond. Over half the black population of the country now lives in fifty cities; one-third of the black population lives in fifteen cities. Blacks are concentrated this way largely because they cannot afford housing outside these cities.[7]

At the risk of repetition, we must note that the fact that the poor cannot afford housing outside the cities is caused not by economic but by political factors. Vacant land is plentiful within thirty miles of the center of every major city in the country. Without restrictive zoning, it would be possible to construct large numbers of housing units in the outer suburbs. In New York City, the 1971 cost per unit of public housing was well over $30,000, while apartments could have been built in the suburbs for well under $20,000 per unit if land costs and zoning restrictions were reasonable. They are not, because of government intervention through zoning laws that constitute "Ivy League Socialism." Restrictive zoning creates enclaves for the rich, which exclude low- and moderate-income families. This is *not* because of inevitable laws of economics, but because of government regulation, through zoning, of the market for land.[8]

One Response to Restrictive Zoning: Public Housing in the Central City

Attempts to improve city housing confront many problems. The history of public housing illustrates some of these.

Federally assisted public housing was created in 1933, conceived as a stopgap measure to help those hurt by the greatest depression in U.S. history. Planners in charge of public housing saw it as a refuge for widows and orphans, and as a temporary dwelling place for those hit hardest by the recession. Today there are families who have spent three generations in public housing.

7. Jack Rosenthal, "One-Third of Blacks Found in Fifteen Cities," *New York Times,* 19 May 1971, p. 20.
8. Linda Davidoff, Paul Davidoff, and Neil M. Gold, "The Suburbs Have to Open Their Gates," *New York Times Magazine*, 7 November 1971, pp. 40–60.

295

The population of low-income public housing has become increasingly made up of blacks (over 50 percent) and families on welfare (over 60 percent). The greater the influx of the poor on welfare, who tend to have far greater social problems, the more the working-class poor of all races left the projects. They could not stand the increased crime, vandalism, debris, and rowdiness. Public housing has thus become a dumping ground for the poorest families with the greatest problems. Because of this, it has lost much of the public support it enjoyed in the New Deal. Many middle- and working-class people regard welfare recipients as spongers who refuse to work, so they can be supported by tax-payers.

One ironic fact about public housing is that it has destroyed many more existing housing units than it has created. With only one or two exceptions, every city that has sponsored any public housing not exclusively for the elderly has ended up with fewer apartments than before. This means, of course, that the poor end up with fewer places in which to live.

In addition, even subsidized low-income housing usually costs more to rent than the units it replaces, so the poor have to pay more for the privilege of moving into public housing. As one critic remarked, the public housing program has spent several billion dollars to accomplish the feat of substantially reducing the nation's low-income-housing stock.

How could this happen? Primarily because public housing, after 1949, became less important than renewal programs that stressed the rebuilding of downtown central business districts. This change occurred as a wide array of interests, including city merchants, contractors, and real estate agents, discovered that much more money could be made from business renewal than from low-income housing. Often these businessmen united themselves with cultural and political leaders for mutual backpatting sessions extolling the wonderful work that was going on to rejuvenate the city. In New York City, for example, the vast Lincoln Center for the Performing Arts was created by evicting tens of thousands of low-income Puerto Ricans from their apartments.

Public housing, again because of greater profit for all concerned, began to involve middle- and upper-income housing instead of low-income housing. The following discussion between Senator Douglas of Illinois and Federal Urban Renewal Commissioner Follin, which took place in 1954, makes the point clear:[9]

> Senator Douglas: Have any of the slum clearance or urban redevelopment sites been made available for public housing?
> Mr. Follin: Yes . . . in three or four instances.

9. U.S. Senate Committee on Banking and Currency, *Hearings on Housing Act of 1954*, 83rd Cong. 2d sess., 1954, part I, pp. 91ff.

Senator Douglas: Out of how many?

Mr. Follin: There are fifty-two projects that are under contract.

Senator Douglas: Almost all the projects have been cleared and they have been used either for businesses or for residents for upper-income groups, but the people who were displaced from these areas are not rehoused in the areas themselves?

Mr. Follin: Only to some extent.

Senator Douglas: To a very slight extent.

Mr. Follin: Yes, sir.

Urban renewal proved a bonanza to many investors. The financing provisions of the act enabled speculators to enrich themselves at the public trough. Three Virginia businessmen, for instance, put up $6,000 for a $12.5 million project, and put themselves on the payroll for $20,000 each per year. When the building was completed, $2.25 million remained of the mortgage, which they pocketed. (To add insult to injury, they listed the mortgage as capital gains on their income tax, so they would not have to pay more than 25 percent of it back to the source from which it came).[10]

An additional disadvantage of much city low-income housing lies in its physical design. In many cases, towering ten- or twenty-story structures replaced two or three story houses, with unforeseen social consequences. Small children, unable to wait during the elevator ride or stair climb from playground to apartment, urinated on the stairs or elevator. The large buildings became muggers' delights. More fundamentally, in many cases neighborhoods whose residents felt a strong sense of attachment to the community were destroyed, with nothing to take their place. Boston's West End, an Italian community with shops and social clubs of all kinds, was wiped out in this manner. Those who could left the neighborhood for the suburbs or other similar ethnic city neighborhoods. Those who could not move were forced to remain in the new public housing. All concerned were bitter at the way government had intervened to destroy a vigorous and vital neighborhood.[11]

Another public housing disaster was the St. Louis high-rise project called Pruitt-Igoe. This vast complex of buildings proved to be such a social nightmare that many of its residents moved out rather than live in it. Finally, with an 80 percent vacancy rate for what had become a center of crime, drug addiction, and almost any type of social pathology one could name, much of the project was destroyed. The St. Louis Housing Authority dynamited several of the buildings in the complex in an attempt to make the remainder habitable—a vivid testimonial to the failure of this project. As Congressman John Monagan of Connecticut

10. Abrams, *The City Is the Frontier*, pp. 110–131.

11. Herbert Gans, "The Human Implications of Slum Clearance and Relocation," *Journal of the American Institute of Planners* (February 1959), pp. 15–25.

observed, "We are destroying it in order to save it. It sounds like something out of Jonathan Swift, or, better yet, Voltaire. It's a satire on the public housing program. . . ." [12]

The Growth and Deterioration of the Existing Central City Housing Stock

By the mid-1960s, it was clear that public housing had failed to solve either aspect of the housing problems—the shortage or the poor quality. But about the same time, researchers discovered that the exodus of the middle class had made the construction of new housing in the older central cities unnecessary. With the decline in population in the cities (St. Louis lost 17 percent of its population from 1960 to 1970; Detroit, 10 percent; Buffalo, 13 percent), more housing has become available. Unfortunately, current housing policies and social conditions combine to make it difficult to use this housing stock to alleviate the poor housing conditions of the central cities.

Thousands of city buildings have been abandoned by their owners, testimony to their disgust with the problem of coping with a changed urban environment. (The number of abandoned buildings in New York City exceeds the total housing stock of Boston.) A major study indicates that landlord abandonment is closely linked to social events like poverty, crime and vandalism, and overcrowded housing conditions. Landlord dissatisfaction with tenants, which expresses itself in complaints about vandalism and destruction, appears to be a crucial factor in the decision to abandon. Racial tensions are important here, since landlords, who are predominantly white, are much less likely to abandon structures inhabited by whites alone than they are to abandon buildings with black and Puerto Rican tenants. Black landlords are less likely to abandon than white landlords. [13]

The consequence of abandonment is the further deterioration of the housing stock until it is completely unfit for human habitation. Attempts to rehabilitate dilapidated structures in the city, whether these are abandoned or not, have met with little success. Most government effort has gone into destruction of existing units and construction of new ones, even though it would be much cheaper to rehabilitate existing housing. For such a policy to continue for over forty years, even in the face of frequent criticism, is evidence that those who stand to profit from construction dominate this area. Attempts under the 1968

12. William Lilley III and Timothy B. Clark, "Immense Costs, Scandals, Social Ills Plague Low-Income Housing Programs," *National Journal*, (1 July 1972,), p. 1079.

13. George Sternlieb et al., "Housing Abandonment in the Urban Core," *Journal of the American Institute of Planners* (September 1974), pp. 322–332.

Housing Act to rehabilitate housing suffered from the same defects as previous legislation, enabling unscrupulous operators to make a killing without much real improvement of the housing stock. One provision of the act enabled home-owners to have the FHA pick up most of the interest. This enabled speculators to buy houses, make cheap "cosmetic" repairs on them, and sell them for a huge profit. This was possible because the FHA assumed the mortgage over and above 20 percent of the owner's income, but did not inspect the house. In Paterson, New Jersey, for example, one entrepreneur bought a house for $1,800, made repairs of $450, and sold it for $20,000.[14]

One unforeseen result of federal attempts to spur home ownership by the poor has been the rise of the federal government as the nation's leading slumlord. Because of the high percentage of mortgage defaults by the poor, the federal government now owns more slum property than any other single owner in the country. It makes an unhappy landlord, disgruntled with its holdings, but unsure how to get rid of them.

Another attempt by the Federal Department of Housing and Urban Development (HUD) to rehabilitate city housing has been the urban homestead-ing program. This is a modern variant of the nineteenth-century policy that provided 160 acres of western land to anyone willing to settle on and improve it for five years. Urban homesteading offers abandoned or foreclosed housing free or at a nominal price to those agreeing to rehabilitate and occupy it over a given period.

In existence since May 1973, urban homesteading has been tried in some twenty-five localities, including Baltimore, Wilmington, and Philadelphia. These localities have not benefited from federal aid, and have only sponsored some several hundred homesteads. HUD started its own demonstration homestead project in twenty-three localities in late 1976.

Homesteading is not yet a program for the poor, but is designed to keep neighborhoods from deteriorating into slums. Since the homesteader must repay a rehabilitation loan that can amount to over $20,000, the poor are left out. But if the program can prevent housing deterioration, it may merit government support.

Baltimore homesteaders are dedicated to the program, reporting neighbors who throw garbage out the window to the health department and telling neighbors whose paint is peeling to paint their houses. The leading study of the subject concludes that while homesteading is not a panacea, it is one of the few positive initiatives taken to fight the snowballing abandonment problem.

14. Lilley and Clark, "Low-Income Housing Programs."

But substantial federal support will be necessary for the program to succeed in slowing city housing deterioration.[15]

This deterioration has been accelerated by two tactics. One is blockbusting, or sale by an unscrupulous real estate agent of one house in a previously all-white neighborhood to a minority family. Panic spreads among the residents, who fear that this change portends an invasion by low-income ghetto families and decline of the value of their property. The residents move out with great speed, selling their houses to speculators or others at prices below their real market value.

It is difficult to sum up blockbusting's impact. In some areas, middle-class whites have been replaced by middle-class blacks, with no real change in the character of the neighborhood. In other areas, where lower class minorities, unused to owning their own homes, have moved in, there has been a deterioration of the housing stock. In both cases, the effect of blockbusting has been to chase whites off to the suburbs, and leave the cities to grow increasingly nonwhite.

Hand in hand with blockbusting goes "redlining," a decision by banks not to lend mortgage money in areas where it seems likely poor minorities will move. Early stages of redlining are insidious: higher interest rates and mortgage down payments are required, and the loans must be paid back in a shorter period. In more advanced stages, loans are refused outright, or the lending institution claims it has no money to lend.

Homeowners are then forced to borrow from mortgage banking firms whose loans are usually insured 100 percent by the FHA or the VA. These lenders tend to be less concerned about the neighborhood, since they can't lose anything. At the same time, these credit sources involve more difficult terms for the homeowner, who now has no alternative.

As some housing begins to deteriorate, the rest of the neighborhood is likely to follow, since the absentee creditors are not concerned, and since it is difficult to obtain credit to improve one's property. Eventually the area becomes a slum—thanks to the self-fulfilling prophecy of redlining.[16] Consumer groups are presently trying to pass laws to force banks to end this discriminatory and destructive practice, but a strong federal law has not yet emerged.

In 1974 a new federal Housing and Community Development Act, which sought to place more initiative in the hands of local communities, was passed.

15. Bob Kuttner, "Ethnic Renewal," *New York Times Magazine*, 9 May 1976, pp. 18–30; and James W. Hughes and Kenneth Bleakly, Jr., *Urban Homesteading* (New Brunswick, N.J.: Center for Urban Policy Research, 1975).

16. James Vitarello, *The Redlining Route to Urban Decay* (Washington, D.C.: Joint Center for Political Studies, 1975). In November 1977, the Federal Home Loan Bank Board announced new regulations designed to stop savings and loan institutions from redlining.

Part of the Nixon-Ford "New Federalism" that had sponsored general revenue sharing, this act converted many specific federal grant programs into broader block grants that cities could use with a great deal more discretion. If one city wished to rehabilitate the existing housing stock, while another wanted to stress construction of new housing, each would have the freedom to follow its preferred option.

But because the new legislation did not subsidize mortgage rates, it is unlikely to help the housing problems of the central cities. Since private investors can get a higher return elsewhere, agencies like the Chicago Housing Authority report they have been unable to find any financing for rehabilitation and construction. Baltimore's Commissioner of Housing, Robert C. Embry, said, "I cannot understand this Administration's [Ford's] reluctance to admit the failure of the 1974 Housing Act."[17] There is no realistic prospect that the nation's housing problem is on its way to an early solution.

The Politics of Exclusionary Zoning—Why the Suburbs Remain Closed to the Poor

Mayor Henry Maier of Milwaukee has said, "The metropolitan establishment brags: 'There are no slums in suburbia.' Of course not: the slums of suburbia are in the central city."[18] While there *are* some suburban slums, the central thrust of Maier's statement is undeniable. Suburbs and cities make up one metropolitan area; their fates are inseparable; and the suburbs are placing an unfair burden on the cities by excluding the poor.

Why is this the case? As students of political science, we begin with the assumption that when change does not occur, it is because those who oppose it are more politically powerful than those who advocate it. Not only do a majority of metropolitan area residents live in suburbs, suburban residents have a lion's share of those resources that are correlated with political power: wealth, income, formal education, and higher-status occupations. The educated middle-income person is much more likely to be knowledgeable about government, to know where to go when he has a complaint or suggestion, and to know how to work with groups for or against certain government policies. Further, this knowledge and success in his own life give him self-confidence. The poor, on the other hand, are more likely both to be ignorant about and to lack confidence in their ability to influence government. They have been the passive objects of forces they cannot understand—unemployment, bureaucracies that dole out welfare

17. Ernest Holsendorph, "1974 Housing Act Helping Few of the Nation's Poor," *New York Times*, 2 November 1975, p. 1.

18. Address to the Midwest Ecumenical Symposium, Dubuque, Iowa, 29 October 1969.

benefits, and crime, to name a few. They lack both the motivation and political influence to get things done.

Such is hardly the case in the average middle-class suburb, where attempts to introduce low-income public housing will usually bring forth substantial numbers of opponents who will band together to fight the proposal. Using petitions, meetings, discussions with elected officials, demonstrations, referenda, and court cases, the opponents will do all they can to stop such projects. Such is understandable, if not commendable, because many suburbanites left the city precisely to escape from the poor minorities and the problems they now fear will follow them into their new dwelling place.

Because the white middle- and upper-class have a near monopoly of political power, change is unlikely to come out of either state legislatures or Congress. Attempts to end exclusionary zoning quickly run into the adamant opposition of suburbanites, who are not shy in letting their legislators know their feelings. And even when the courts act to end exclusionary zoning, opponents of such change can negate these rulings.

CHALLENGES TO LOCAL LAND USE DOMINATION

While local government still controls most uses of land, a number of harbingers of change have appeared. Because state governments have legal authority over their local governments, it has been possible for several states, including California, New York, and Connecticut, to enact statewide uniform building codes. Further, it has been argued that under the federal government's authority to regulate interstate commerce, it would be possible for it to enact *national* building code standards and zoning criteria to stop communities from zoning out the poor. Since a political coalition with enough clout to pass such laws does not exist, advocates of change have carried out a campaign similar to that followed earlier by groups opposing legally sanctioned racial segregation. That is, they have taken cases to court in which they have argued that current zoning practices are illegal and unconstitutional because they discriminate against one group of citizens.

In 1972, the New Jersey Supreme Court ruled that the township of Mount Laurel practiced economic discrimination through its zoning laws, and the court found these laws unconstitutional. In 1976, the State Superior Court ruled that eleven other New Jersey municipalities prevented low- and moderate-income families from purchasing housing. The presiding judge, David D. Furman, ordered the eleven towns to come up with plans—in ninety days—to allow for over 18,000 low- and moderate-income housing units by 1985.[19] Similar court challenges are being heard in a number of states across the country.

Recent federal court action relating to housing also merits attention. In September 1975, the city of Hartford went to court to try to stop seven of its suburbs from receiving four-and-a-half-million dollars in federal aid from HUD. Hartford argued that its suburbs had failed to offer adequate plans for low-income housing, thus leaving the city with the task of housing 90 percent of the region's poor. As Hartford City Councilman Richard Suisman said, "The question was: can one city supply all the services?" In January 1976, a federal district court ruled that the suburbs should *not* receive this money, since to do so would be inconsistent with the intent of the 1974 Housing and Community Development Act.[20] In 1977, the U.S. Court of Appeals reversed this decision.

Another major case is the April 1976 ruling of the U.S. Supreme Court that HUD can be ordered by courts to provide suburban low-income housing for city residents if federal housing programs have increased city housing segregation. The case, *Hills* v. *Gautreaux*, involving the city of Chicago, resulted in a federal lower court order to HUD to adopt a "comprehensive metropolitan area plan" for low- and moderate-income housing, instead of concentrating its efforts in Chicago.[21]

In addition, cases challenging the right of private corporations to move from cities to suburbs that practice exclusionary zoning are now in court. The Suburban Action Institute, a nonprofit corporation run by activist planners, has asked federal regulatory agencies to penalize or stop RCA, AT&T, and General Electric from moving from New York City to Connecticut and New Jersey suburbs with strict zoning laws.[22]

While predicting the exact impact of these court decisions is impossible, it is safe to say that such decisions alone will not end the housing problem in this country. They cannot, because the courts have not yet required legislatures to fund low-income housing. As town official Nicholas Glase of the Chicago suburb of Niles said about the *Hills* v. *Gautreaux* case, "The Court can decide what it wants, but as long as Congress does not appropriate any funds for public housing construction in the suburbs, there won't be any." Even more optimistic observers, such as Norman Threadgill, president of the Newark NAACP, feel "it

19. Walter H. Waggoner, "Eleven Jersey Areas Ordered to Zone for Less Affluent," *New York Times,* 6 May 1976, p. 1.

20. Lawrence Fellows, "Hartford Blocks Aid for Suburbs," *New York Times,* 29 January 1976, p. 1.

21. William E. Farrell, "Impact of Court's Ruling on Low-Income Housing Is Seen Far Off," *New York Times*, 26 April 1976, p. 42.

22. Davidoff, Davidoff, and Gold, "The Suburbs."

will take quite a few years before the decision has any measurable impact at all." [23]

The same holds true for the New Jersey decisions. While Judge Furman ordered the eleven affected towns to "pursue and cooperate in available federal and state subsidy programs for new housing and rehabilitation of substandard housing," it is still up to Congress and the state legislatures to fund these programs, and their current level of support makes it unlikely such goals will be met.

The experience of one state that passed a law restricting local zoning powers illustrates some of the difficulties state government faces in getting local governments to change their ways. In 1969, Massachusetts passed an "anti-snob zoning law," intended to overcome suburban large-lot zoning restrictions. Under the law, a locality can be ordered by the state to waive its zoning code to allow low- and moderate-income housing. [24]

Supporters of the law reacted to its passage with jubilation, feeling that the suburbs would now be open to the poor. Their opponents agreed that this would be the outcome, decrying what they thought would be a mass exodus of the poor to suburbia.

Both sides were wrong. By 1976, it was clear the law had had almost no effect on the suburban housing market. Every community that had decided to fight the law was successful. Some towns went to court, a tactic which bought time for several years. Others fought the plan before planning boards and city councils, stalling for time and exhausting the treasury of the groups backing anti-snob zoning.

In 1974, the Massachusetts Supreme Court upheld the law, but by then its proponents had other problems. Environmental restraints prevented construction of several projects, because they were to be located in part in swamps. These locations were not part of a scheme to sink the poor even deeper in the mire, but were the only land available at a reasonable price. When ecological groups argued that much animal life would be endangered and pollution would grow by building in the marshes, this meant that at least another couple of years of review would take place—with a good chance of defeat for the housing projects involved. In addition, federal funds available for this housing had dried up, and no other sources of money were visible on the horizon. As a result of

23. Farrell, "Court's Ruling."

24. Benjamin Taylor, "Court Test Over, But Progress Still Slow with Antisnob Zoning," *Boston Globe*, 24 February 1974, p. 1. In January 1977, the U.S. Supreme Court overturned a lower federal court ruling that would have required suburbs to rezone so that low- and moderate-income people could live there.

factors such as these, anti-snob zoning laws and court decisions probably will have little impact as long as they meet strong resistance from local communities.

There will probably be no substantial movement toward opening the suburbs until there is a revolutionary change in our housing policy, with the establishment of federal authority over land use. As former federal Secretary of Health, Education and Welfare, and now chairman of Common Cause, John W. Gardner has said: "I think one of the consequences of the great fragmentation of the housing industry is that a lot of these rigidities have only been tested at the local level, and not with very great force or public review. There's been no *national* debate on this subject." [25]

Yet even if there were now to be such a debate, it is unlikely that great change would result, as our examination of the political context of zoning has shown. We can expect for some time to come that the subnational level of government in this country will be the primary determiner of land use and housing patterns.

25. *Forbes*, 15 October 1969, p. 23.

PART SIX

THE SYSTEM IN ACTION:
CRIMINAL JUSTICE

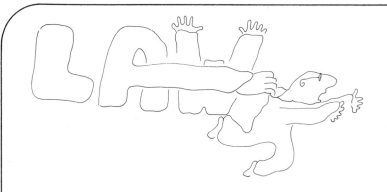

PROBLEMS IN CRIMINAL JUSTICE

CHAPTER TWENTY-ONE

Few governmental functions have become so heavily involved with, and so deeply embedded in, the subnational system as has criminal justice. State and local governments pay nearly 90 percent of all criminal justice costs and employ well over 90 percent of all criminal justice employees. In a very real sense, criminal justice in the United States has remained a largely subnational activity.

This state of affairs confers many benefits. It makes the criminal justice system more responsible and responsive to community values and causes it to yield to community concerns. In a vast and variegated country such as ours, communities display great differences in priorities and procedures. A decentralized system of criminal justice can more easily accommodate such distinctions. In so doing, it can engender more experimentation, and it can also elicit a

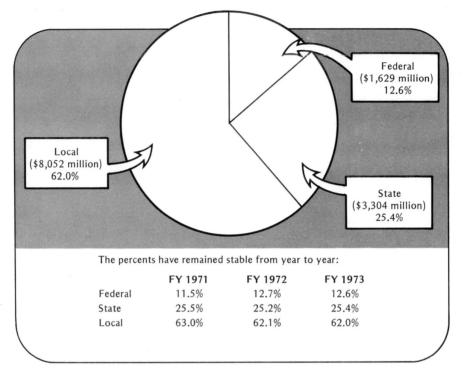

Federal
($1,629 million)
12.6%

Local
($8,052 million)
62.0%

State
($3,304 million)
25.4%

The percents have remained stable from year to year:

	FY 1971	FY 1972	FY 1973
Federal	11.5%	12.7%	12.6%
State	25.5%	25.2%	25.4%
Local	63.0%	62.1%	62.0%

FIGURE 21.1 Percent Distribution of Criminal Justice System Direct Expenditure by level of Government: FY 1973, $12,985 Million
SOURCE: U.S. Bureau of the Census and the Law Enforcement Assistance Administration.

much greater degree of public cooperation. Poll after poll has demonstrated that most citizens support the concept of decentralized justice.

But polls in recent years have indicated that citizens are becoming increasingly disturbed at the system's apparent shortcomings. Although they usually attach the blame elsewhere, many observers feel that the system's high degree of differentiation must bear some responsibility.

THE DILEMMAS OF DECENTRALIZED JUSTICE

To begin with, a fragmented criminal justice system makes a uniform application of the law or even uniform laws often impossible. If St. Louis in 1968 had 560 arrests for drunkenness while Atlanta during the same year had 40,000 such arrests, the discrepancy may derive more from differences in law enforcement than in occurrences of drunkenness.

310

Much more important from the standpoint of democratic values are the differentiations a community may make in applying the same law to different groups of people. For example, out-of-town traffic violators may be caught and punished more harshly than local violators. Some communities have earned considerable revenue by pouncing on "foreign motorists" and exacting from them heavy fines for speeding or for some other alleged infraction.

Small communities which have an expressway running through their borders have benefited the most from such practices. The three policemen of Monroesville, Ohio used to snare enough drivers along bustling Route 20 to produce, in traffic fines, over 40 percent of the town's total revenue. However, Fruithurst, Alabama did even better. This town of 300 people located on the Georgia line kept its four policemen working 72 hours a week and its City Hall open 24 hours a day. The result was that in 1974 it collected $200,000 in fines from motorists traveling the small strip of a U.S. highway that passes through the community.

The U.S. Supreme Court took action against Monroesville in 1972, ruling that since the town's mayor served as the traffic judge, and since the money he collected in fines enabled him to hold down the tax rate, he was unable to serve as a "neutral and detached judge."[1] Meanwhile, in Alabama the town of Fruithurst had to abandon its lucrative revenue-producing scheme when the state's ambitious attorney general secured an injunction against the community in 1975.[2] However, numerous other cities and towns continue to engage in these and similar discriminatory acts against those from beyond their borders.

In some instances, however, the system's decentralization works to the benefit of the nonlocal motorist. A 1965 study, for example, showed that one-fifth of all New York City's summonses for moving violations and a full half of its parking tickets went unheeded. The principal recipients of these violation notices were out-of-staters who knew that neither the city nor the state could punish them. Since then, the city has worked out an agreement with New Jersey authorities to gain some assistance in enforcing its traffic laws against violators from that state but it still remains quite helpless in dealing with violators from other jurisdictions.[3] Many other communities share the same problem. Out-of-state students with out-of-state license plates are the bane of many college communities.

The problems fragmentation produces also make themselves felt when it

1. *New York Times*, 15 November 1972.

2. *New York Times*, 6 July 1975.

3. However, in 1975 the city's Parking Violations Bureau disclosed that the single biggest defaulter on parking tickets was the U.S. Government. Cars owned by the seventy-seven federal agencies having offices in the city were accumulating five thousand unpaid parking tickets a month.

311

comes to coping with more serious offenses. Many cities have sought to regulate gun sales, but as long as other communities do not adopt such restrictions the would-be gun buyer need not worry. Even state governments experience difficulties in overcoming this dilemma. The mayor of Boston once pointed out that while his state had the nation's toughest restrictions on gun ownership in the nation, nearly half of his city's homicides were caused by firearms, a full 90 percent of which were purchased out of state.

Frequently, the system's many components not only fail to cooperate but actively compete with one another. On March 10, 1938 the then Manhattan District Attorney Thomas E. Dewey made a well-publicized arrest of a former New York Stock Exchange President, Richard Whitney, on a charge of embezzlement. The following day the state's attorney general arrested Whitney all over again, and blasted Dewey for "legal claim jumping."[4]

But if Dewey was subverting the actions of his attorney general, other prosecutors were doing the same to him. His crackdown on syndicated crime in New York had only sent the city's racketeers scurrying to New Jersey. From this sanctuary they continued to run their New York rackets. Some years later Dewey's successor, Frank Hogan, compiled evidence against a racketeer who was depositing nearly one million dollars a month in New York City banks. The money came from an illegal gambling casino in New Jersey. Hogan shipped his evidence to his counterpart in New Jersey, but there the matter ended. The New Jersey prosecutor claimed he could not find the casino, although newsmen had no trouble locating it since it was situated along a major highway and was lit up by a large neon sign.

Information sharing has spawned more numerous controversies. After the infamous kidnapping of the infant son of Charles Lindbergh, New York asked New Jersey for its evidence so that it could follow up some leads of its own in running down the culprit. The New Jersey authorities refused to comply although the man eventually arrested and convicted of the crime, Bruno Hauptmann, turned out to be a resident of New York. Some thirty years later the search for the "Boston Strangler" was hampered by the refusal of the many municipal police forces and prosecutorial offices involved to share their information with each other. The State's Attorney General, Elliot Richardson, finally set up a joint commission to oversee and coordinate the probe. (As it so happens, the man finally caught and convicted of the murders of the seven middle-aged women victims did not live in any of the communities where the crimes took place. Consequently, his local police department was not participating in the investigation.)[5]

4. John Brooks, *Once in Golconda* (New York: Harper & Row, 1969), pp. 271–272.
5. Gerold Frank, *The Boston Strangler* (New York: New American Library, 1966).

Such incidents as these have caused the Committee on Economic Development to bemoan the "patchwork structure" and "the organization and administrative chaos that characterizes the nation's uncoordinated system of criminal justice."[6]

EXILE AND EXTRADITION

The country's experience with the Articles of Confederation had convinced our founding fathers that their new constitution must contain appropriate constraints concerning relations between the states. The states must be prevented from sabotaging each other. To this end, the writers inserted the "full faith and credit" clause, which we examined briefly in Chapter 3. It states that each state must uphold the judicial proceedings of every other state and must render up any fugitive from justice from another state. Congress further strengthened these safeguards by passing the Fugitive Felon law, making it a federal offense for a person to cross state lines in order to avoid prosecution or to avoid giving testimony in trials.

Such constitutional provisions and congressional legislation would seem to resolve any problems that might arise from persons wishing to take advantage of the system's decentralization in order to evade complying with the law. In practice, however, problems have consistently arisen.

Prior to the Civil War, fugitive slaves created the most conflict. When a slave succeeded in escaping to the North, he would make a bid for freedom. The southern state from which he had fled would promptly seek to have him extradited. The northern state would often balk at doing so. In many cases, federal marshals would seek to bring back the fugitive but their efforts would often encounter serious obstruction. In 1856 antislavery Bostonians staged a near riot when federal officials sought to return a runaway slave to his southern master.

The Civil War may have ended this particular problem, but it did not put to rest all the turmoil that extradition can engender. Nor did it succeed in solving all the other kinds of criminal justice problems a system of divided sovereignty can produce.

To take one rather bizarre example, sometime around the turn of the century a North Carolina mountaineer named Hall shot and killed a Tennessee mountaineer named Bryson. Each was standing in his respective state at the time. North Carolina authorities arrested and tried Hall for murder but his lawyer took the case to the state's supreme court and won an aquittal. He successfully

6. *Reducing Crime and Assuring Justice* (New York: Committee for Economic Development, 1972), p. 14.

313

argued that the crime had occurred in the place where the bullet entered the victim's body and this had taken place in Tennessee. This prompted Tennessee to request rendition but once again Hall's lawyer managed to save him. Going again to the North Carolina court he argued that Hall could not be considered a fugitive from justice in Tennessee since he had never left North Carolina. The state's supreme court felt it had no choice but to agree.[7]

An even more bizarre but, in a sense, more typical case occurred in Kentucky a few years later. Two candidates, one named Taylor, the other named Goebel, were competing furiously for the governorship. The election was so close that the results were given to the state legislature for final determination. However, candidate Taylor, who was either fearful of what the verdict might be or was simply impatient, assassinated Goebel. Taylor was then inaugurated governor. However, his reign was short. A few days after taking office, he and his accomplices were indicted for Goebel's murder. Taylor and his band fled to Indiana, where a friendly governor refused Kentucky's request for rendition. Taylor stayed in Indiana until a governor from his own party was finally elected in Kentucky. The new governor pardoned Taylor and he returned home.[8]

Most extradition efforts run a smoother course but difficulties continually arise. Many of these have concerned Southerners fleeing north. One of the more famous of these was the case of the Scottsboro Boys, a group of young black men who were found guilty of dubious charges that they had raped two white women. They fled to New York and managed to defeat attempts to send them back.

White southerners have also made use of extradition proceedings to seek sanctuary in the North. For example, Arkansas petitioned Massachusetts in 1962 to send back an escapee from the state's prison. However, the escapee said that the prison administration had let him out after he had told them that he knew where a cache of stolen money was secreted. He was then supposed to return and divide up the loot with the warden and some other prison officials. But, said the fugitive, no such cache existed and he had merely used the story to flee the horrendous conditions at the Arkansas facility. The Massachusetts attorney general believed his story and refused Arkansas' request for extradition.

Domestic disputes give rise to many extradition entanglements. Husbands and fathers desert their families to seek a new life in another state. If they cause no trouble in their new home state, the state's authorities may prove reluctant to return them for prosecution for nonsupport. In another type of situation, many divorced or separated fathers in effect kidnap their own children

7. Robert S. Rankin, "Fugitives from Justice," in Rankin, ed., *Readings in American Government* (New York: D. Appleton-Century, 1939).
8. Ibid.

and take them out of state. Even if the mother can track them down, she often fails to get the sanctuary state's cooperation in returning the youngsters. And from time to time a couple with an adopted child whose natural mother decides she wants the child back will flee to another state to avoid surrendering the youngster.[9]

Not all extradition roadblocks are deliberate. Some simply result from technical difficulties. In 1967, the District Attorney's office of Queens County, New York secured an indictment against four members of the Mafia for the murder of a fifth. But the assistant district attorney who was to prosecute the case needed as a key witness another member who was then serving a sentence in a Florida state prison. The prosecutor went to Florida and there had to run a difficult obstacle course that required many phone calls back to the New York State governor's office for assistance. Although he obtained such aid, he was unable to get the convict extradited in time to testify. Partially as a result, the first Mafia killing to come to trial in Queens County in twenty years failed to produce a conviction.[10]

As this case further reveals, extradition is not only a sometimes controversial and complicated process, but also on occasion a costly one. Legal proceedings in other states plus transportation to and from them can run up big bills for the jurisdiction seeking extradition. But these are only part of the costs that a jurisdiction can incur as a consequence of the country's fragmented criminal justice system. Somerset County, Maryland, for instance, in 1972 found itself having to prosecute an out-of-state hitchhiker for the murder of an out-of-state motorist since the homicide took place within the county's borders. Because witnesses would have to be brought from Florida, New Jersey, and Indiana, the cost of the trial was expected to consume one-third of the county's law-enforcement budget. When the accused slayer escaped and fled to another state, many citizens asked the county prosecutor to let him go in order to save the county the expense of the trial as well as the expense of the extradition process. But the prosecutor said he had no choice but to demand extradition, hold the trial, and present the bill to the county.[11]

The desire to save money affects another aspect of decentralized criminal justice—exile. Exile has been a common punishment since ancient times, and a fragmented system of criminal justice has increased its practice. A jurisdiction

9. One example of this was the fight over "Baby Lenore," whose adoptive parents, residents of New York State, fled to Miami after a state court ordered them to return the child to its natural mother. The latter had given the child up for adoption at birth but then changed her mind. *New York Times*, 10 June 1971 and 5 July 1971.

10. The event is recounted in James Mills, *The Prosecutor* (New York: Farrar, Straus & Giroux, 1969).

11. *Time* (20 November 1972).

often finds it easier and cheaper simply to export its offenders and their problems and to let other jurisdictions worry about them. Use of this form of punishment has lengthy history in the United States. It was long a common practice for some communities to get rid of "undesirables" by having them run out of town. Today, although not so common as it once was, banishment still plays a role in U.S. justice. For example, a twenty-one-year-old college student accused of importing weapons and drugs into Central Islip, Long Island in 1970 was ordered into "exile" from the county as punishment. (He was originally from Alabama.)[12]

Dealing with an offender in this fashion obviously presents several drawbacks from the standpoint of furthering the ends of justice. It does not force him to come to grips with his problems and leaves him free to pursue his activities elsewhere. Crime is neither corrected nor curbed, but only displaced. In this way, banishment can result in greater crime at a later date.

Authorities in Oxnard, California once arrested nine girls and five young men for sleeping nude in a field. One of the girls, the mother of a newborn infant, was also charged with endangering the life of a child. However, the charges were dropped when the group agreed to leave the county. A year or so later one of the men, Charles Manson, assisted by four of the girls, committed one of the most grisly murders of the 1960s—the slaying of pregnant actress Sharon Tate and four dinner guests at the actress' Hollywood home.[13]

Exile and extradition constitute, along with many of the other problems discussed earlier, only some of the difficulties encountered in decentralized justice. We will see further ways in which this feature of our system conditions its operations as we examine its separate components.

12. *New York Times*, 25 August 1970.
13. *New York Times Magazine*, 4 January 1970, p. 30.

POLICE

CHAPTER TWENTY-TWO

Until fairly recently, no one really knew just how many different organizations fulfilled the function of law enforcement in the United States. In 1973 some students at Georgia State University undertook to make a thorough count. They came up with a figure of 20,114. Of this number only 37 were federal agencies.[1] The subnational system accounted for all the rest. As one can see, law enforcement in the United States is primarily a state and local activity.

1. John P. Granfield, "Publicly Funded Law Enforcement Agencies in the United States" *Police Chief* (July 1975).

STATE AGENCIES

Most crimes committed in the United States are violations of state laws. This stems from the fact that the federal government exercises only limited jurisdiction in most ordinary offenses, while local governments can only enact such laws, (called ordinances) as their state governments permit them to pass. (Customarily much local lawmaking is not related to the most common crimes, such as murder, robbery, burglary, etc.)

Despite the fact they have enacted most of the county's criminal laws, state governments long held back in enforcing these laws. Instead they allowed their local governments to do so. When the states finally began to move in this direction, they encountered opposition from the general public and from local police chiefs and county sherriffs. As a result, while Texas had established its famous Rangers for border control in 1835, it was not until 1905 that Pennsylvania set up the nation's first regular state police force. Labor unrest in its coal and iron mine areas persuaded Pennsylvania to take such a step. During the next few decades most of the other states followed suit. However, a much greater factor than labor violence in prompting them to do so was the emergence of the automobile and its use in intercity travel. A nonlocal police force was needed to patrol the highways and this function, it was felt, could only be fulfilled by a state agency.

Today, every state but Hawaii has a state police force. They range in size from less than 100 sworn officers in North Dakota to more than 7,000 in California. All told they number nearly 60,000 troopers.[2] But this figure constitutes only 12 percent of the more than half-a-million law enforcement officers in the nation. Furthermore, the majority of these state police forces remain confined to patrolling state highways. Only twenty-two state police forces possess any statewide investigative authority, and of these only seven can exercise a full range of police responsibility. And those that possess such general authority usually make use of it only in rural sections where they are often the only police force in the area.

Many state police forces do provide certain services to local police departments. In so doing they may operate crime laboratories, identification and data collecting units, polygraph (lie detector) units, and occasionally narcotics and other divisions. In recent years some have begun assuming additional responsibilities, such as running training academies for municipal police recruits. However, although they may, perhaps, play a greater role in law enforcement in

2. *Book of the States, 1974–1975* (Lexington, Ky.: Council of State Governments), pp. 419–423.

the future then they have in the past, they remain as of now a comparatively minor force in the criminal justice system.

Numerous other state agencies also discharge some law enforcement duties. These include the fire marshall's office, the department of conservation with its fish and game wardens, and the various regulatory boards and commissions that control the manufacture and sale of alcohol, drugs, and food or that license various professions and trades.

Many governors have on occasion employed their state militias for law enforcement purposes. Huey Long used National Guardsmen to conduct raids on illegal gambling casinos in the 1920s and Alabama sent in the guard to take over the administration of gambling-ridden Phoenix City in the mid-1950s. During the 1960s, some governors used the National Guard to quell riots by students and blacks. The governor of Massachusetts placed some of his Guard units on standby when demonstrations by whites protesting school desegregation in Boston in 1975 threatened to get out of hand.

COUNTY LAW ENFORCEMENT

County government figures prominently in American criminal justice. The counties carry out most of the system's prosecutions, run many of its court houses, and incarcerate a goodly number of its prisoners. They also do a good deal of law enforcement as well.

Unfortunately, county law enforcement shares many of the general problems of county government. The chief law enforcement officer is the sheriff. Like so many other county officials, he is usually elected. Only 11 of the county's 3,099 sheriffs hold their office through appointment. This means that the American sheriff is more often a professional politician than a professional policeman. In some southern states he often serves as the de facto county chief of his party. Furthermore, since most American counties lack merit systems, sheriffs often appoint their political henchmen as their deputies.

The size of sheriffs' offices varies considerably, ranging from 1 person serving on a part-time basis in a few rural counties to 7,000 in Los Angeles County. The duties of a sheriff's department may also vary considerably. In some counties, the sheriff carries out a full range of law enforcement functions and his office may include criminal investigation, juvenile, traffic and even vice divisions. In other counties, especially those in the Northeast, his law enforcement functions may be so limited that the position continues to exist only because it is authorized under the state constitution. Occasionally in one of these states a candidate will run for election as sheriff on the promise to abolish the post.

The political nature of so many sheriff's departments, coupled with their lack of visibility and accountability, has given county law enforcement a poor image. Many sheriff's departments are believed to suffer from too much corruption and too little competence. However, in some areas the office has undergone great changes in recent years. Some sheriffs, particularly those on the West Coast, have even moved to the forefront in spearheading progressive reform. Some, for example, require their recruits to possess college degrees. And one, the sheriff of Colorado's Jefferson County, actually advertised in 1976 for deputies possessing doctorates of philosophy. As a result of these and other changes, the reputation of county law enforcement may soon start to improve.

LOCAL LAW ENFORCEMENT

Police work in the United States began as a strictly grass roots function. Some of the first policemen, as a matter of fact, served only wards, not whole communities, and a suspect could sometimes elude their grasp by simply crossing the street. Gradually these neighborhood constabularies were replaced by community-wide forces, which today carry out most of the country's law enforcement.

Local police forces, like sheriff's departments, vary greatly in size from one part-time officer to the 28,000 men and women who police New York City. (They comprise a force that exceeds the Danish army in number.) Although most local police departments focus their major energies on enforcing the law, they frequently perform other duties as well. These may include licensing taxis and dogs, operating an ambulance service, and even taking the municipal census.

In many of the larger cities, the municipal police department is not the only police force. For example, New York City not only possesses the country's largest police force but also has the nation's tenth and thirtieth largest police forces. The former is the city's transit police force, which patrols its subways; the latter is the city's housing police force, which patrols its housing projects. In addition, the Port of New York Authority, a joint New York–New Jersey special district, has its own police force to guard the city's airports, bus stations, and other facilities under its jurisdiction.

Some cities maintain special police forces to patrol their parks. Others have separate systems for maintaining law and order in their schools. Over 400 colleges and universities support police forces whose members, duly deputized by their local municipal departments, exercise full police powers on their campuses. Finally, although not included among the 20,114 official police organizations, there are the thousands of private security agencies whose employees also are involved in law enforcement. California alone has nearly four hundred firms engaged in the industry. Nationally, these firms in all employ some 800,000 people. This adds up to a law enforcement establishment of nearly one-and-a-quarter-million people working for nearly 25,000 official and nonofficial agencies.

POLICE PROBLEMS

The Limits of Decentralization

In 1972 a group of plainclothesmen from the Detroit Police Department raided a gambling game and sought to arrest the participants. Some of the gamblers, however, pulled out their guns. Shooting broke out, killing one man and wounding three others. The Detroit policemen did not know that the card players were deputy sheriffs, while the deputies had pulled their guns not knowing that the armed men who had barged into their playing room were police officers.[3]

The incident illustrates the problems a vast array of law enforcement agencies can produce. Although the disorganization and divisiveness within our fragmented law enforcement system does not usually lead to such grim consequences as the Detroit shoot-out, it causes numerous conflicts. When police forces do not actually clash, they often compete, and even when they do not compete, they often fail to cooperate. As a result, the ends of justice suffer.

One group that has benefited substantially from this situation is organized crime. As far back as 1951, the U.S. Senate Crime Committee found that local policing "lends itself to buck-passing and evasion of responsibility which can only insure the advantage of gansters and racketeers. And it makes it possible for hoodlums to find those cities and towns where law enforcement is low and to concentrate their operations there."[4]

Even the handling of minor matters often becomes snarled. A tourist in Florida who heard a prowler at her motel door had to telephone three different police departments before she could obtain some assistance. A speeding motorist in Louisiana was pursued by police cars from seven municipalities before finally being flagged down. Another motorist reporting a stolen car to the Buffalo police found, after the police had come and carefully studied the location, that his car had actually been stolen in West Seneca. By the time the proper jurisdiction had been established, the thief and the car were long gone (neither was ever found). When a woman drowned in somewhat mysterious

3. *New York Times*, 31 August 1971.
4. Estes Kefauver, *Crime in America* (Garden City, N.Y.: Doubleday and Company, 1951), p. 16.

321

circumstances in Lake Michigan, the wrangling between two shorefront communities as to who had jurisdiction reached such a point that the U.S. Coast Guard had to intervene.[5]

The system is not only confusing but also costly. In the 1960s Los Angeles County created its Lakewood plan, under which communities could pay the county to provide them with services they did not wish to provide for themselves. Studies done at the time showed that most communities would save substantial sums of money through abolishing their own police forces and affiliating with the county system. West Covina, for example, would be able to cut its police costs by 15 percent and Signal Hill could reduce its expenditures by around 40 percent by adopting the scheme. Furthermore, both communities would obtain for these reduced expenditures more rather than less police service. These studies illustrate the savings obtainable through even small-scale consolidation.[6]

Efforts to bring about consolidations, however, have floundered. Neither West Covina nor Signal Hill, for example, voted to accept the county policing plan despite the advantages it offered. And many other communities have also rejected proposals that would cause them to lose direct community control over their local constabularies. However, more and more positive sentiment for such steps is being voiced. The National Advisory Commission on Criminal Justice Standards and Goals, for example, has urged the merger of all police departments with fewer than ten sworn officers; the Committee on Economic Development suggests twenty as a more effective cut-off point. The Committee also advocates a greater role by the state police in the overall law enforcement system.

Some movement in these directions has been achieved. Some seventy-five counties in the United States now have county-wide police forces. And state police departments, as we have seen, have begun to operate training academies as well as to furnish other services to local forces. However, our citizens continue to show a deep-seated and understandable attachment to the system as it now exists. Thus, further advancement along these lines will undoubtedly come only at a gradual pace.

Corruption, Coercion, and Competence

In 1844 , New York City established the nation's first full-fledged police department. Within a few years it became evident that the city's policemen were

5. Henry S. Reuss, *Revenue-Sharing* (New York: Praeger Publishers, 1970), pp. 48–49.
6. Gordon E. Misner, "The Police Service Contract in California," *Journal of Criminal Law, Criminology and Police Science* (November/December 1961).

322

collecting "rewards" for the recovery of stolen property. Some were even refusing to deal with complaints of theft unless promised such a reward. Police corruption has continued to plague New York and the rest of the country ever since. In 1974, for example, complaints of widespread police corruption were under investigation in Chicago, Philadelphia, Cleveland, Indianapolis, Houston, and Denver, as well as in New York City.[7]

Police corruption takes many forms. At the lowest level it may consist of an officer accepting a free lunch at a local diner in return for giving the eatery a little extra protection. At a somewhat higher level it may take the form of police accepting gratuities in reciprocation for overlooking petty offenses such as traffic violations. However, it sometimes assumes more advanced molds. Police officers may shake down prostitutes, homosexuals, tavern owners operating after hours, and drug dealers, for money. In dealing with drug traffickers, some officers have confiscated the dealer's contraband material only to turn around and sell it themselves. And some police officers have formed burglary rings and systematically looted stores and other businesses on their beats.

Perhaps the most intensive investigation of police corruption ever undertaken in the United States was carried out by the Knapp Commission in New York City in the early 1970s. The Commission, which was set up by Governor Nelson Rockefeller in response to revelations supplied to the local press by two outraged policemen, Francis Serpico and David Durk, found a pervasive pattern of corruption. It was not simply a case of a few "rotten apples," said the Commission. Rather, large numbers of the city police force were engaging in such practices.

The Commission did differentiate degrees of corruption. It classified corrupt police officers into two groups, "meat eaters" and "grass eaters." The "meat eaters" were the truly aggressive officers who sought to squeeze every possible financial advantage from their positions. The "grass eaters" took a much milder approach, confining themselves largely to accepting gratuities, discounts, and other favors in return for furnishing some extra service, or for overlooking some extralegal activity. Most of the city's corrupt police officers, said the Commission, fell into the grass-eater category. However, the grass eaters were the real problems, for their minor depredations created a tolerance that allowed the worse activities of the meat eaters to flourish.[8]

Like corruption, police coercion also has a long history in the United States. The police have frequently trampled on individual rights and have often used physical brutality in their attempts to solve crimes and impose law and

7. "Making Police Crime Unfashionable," *Time* (6 May 1974).
8. *New York Times*, 7 August 1972.

323

order. Unlike corruption, however, police coercion only became a major issue in our country in the 1960s. Since then it has stimulated a steady stream of controversy. Many of these issues have been, at least in theory, settled by the Supreme Court. As a result of the Court's rulings, for example, police are forbidden to search a person or his residence without a warrant, or to compel a suspect, through either physical or psychological coercion, to confess to a crime. However, many other issues have been left for local and state authorities to decide.

Several of these involve the use of force. Should police be allowed to carry and use high-powered revolvers rather than the standard .38 caliber special?[9] Should they be furnished, or be allowed to furnish themselves, with dum-dum bullets? High-powered revolvers, their supporters contend, help police officers bring down a fleeing felon who, if allowed to escape, would probably go on to commit other crimes. But opponents claim that such weapons do more damage to a suspect than a policeman has a right to inflict, and also increase the danger to bystanders. Proponents of dum-dum bullets claim not only that such ammunition is more effective in bringing down a suspect but also that it is safer for bystanders since the bullet expands on contact and does not ricochet. Opponents contend that such bullets, which have been outlawed for military use, are far too cruel since they tend to tear up the insides of any person they strike.

A more serious and sustained source of contention concerns restrictions on the police officer's right to use his weapons, whatever they may be. When should he shoot and when should he not? Traditionally, the police have been granted the right to use their weapons fairly freely when it comes to subduing a resisting suspect or stopping an escaping one. However, such policies have encountered increasing resistance in recent years.

Finally, there is the question of police effectiveness. Only slightly more than one-fifth of all reported major crimes in the United States result in an arrest. And since unreported crimes are believed to be two or three times as numerous as reported ones, the crime clearance rate is actually much lower. Minority groups in particular have become greatly concerned over the issue of police competence. Though they formerly were in the forefront in protesting police brutality, they have begun to concentrate more of their fire on police negligence.

---

9. An Associated Press survey in 1974 showed that twelve states—Washington, Arkansas, Texas, Colorado, Wisconsin, Montana, Utah, New Mexico, Nevada, South Dakota, New York, and Connecticut—issue high-powered magnum revolvers to their state troopers while two more states, Oklahoma and California, permit their troopers to buy them on their own. No comprehensive survey has yet been done on the practices of local police departments in regard to this issue.

Some measure of progress on all of these fronts is being made. The fact that police corruption and coercion have become such serious and such sensitive issues testifies to this trend. What was formerly accepted resignedly is now being protested vigorously. Police departments are coming under increasing pressure to clean house and to crack down on their errant members. They have also begun to draw up and promulgate regulations regarding the use of firearms. Grand juries have begun to indict law enforcement officers who fatally shoot suspects without seemingly good reasons for doing so.

Police effectiveness, as judged by the ever-increasing crime rate, might seem to be decreasing. Yet, many of the factors contributing to this increase lie beyond police control. Furthermore, numerous experiments now underway hold out hope for improved police responses to the crime problem. Palo Alto, California has begun to tie police pay raises to decreases in the crime rate. New York City has launched a family-dispute squad. Syracuse, Dayton, and other cities have instituted a new patrol concept called team policing. Other communities are pioneering in other ways. Although the fragmentation of the police continues to pose problems, it has encouraged a good deal of innovation, some of which seems likely to produce beneficial results.

Underlying much of whatever progress has been achieved is a change in the caliber of those entering the police field and of those rising to leadership positions within it. These new officers are, first of all, much better educated, on the average, than their predecessors. Some thirty-two states have now set minimum training standards and a few offer extra pay or other inducements to those possessing or pursuing college degrees. Second, they are much more representative of our population, for police departments, often in response to court and community pressures, have begun recruiting and promoting more minority-group members. Women, too, are becoming increasingly visible in police work.

In short, the police may have changed as much in the past twenty years as they changed in the entire previous century. But they will probably come under increasing pressure to change still more in the decades ahead.

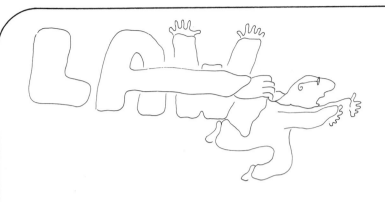

PROSECUTION AND DEFENSE

CHAPTER TWENTY-THREE

American justice is adversary justice. It thrusts the state into an arena with the defense, there to fight it out in the expectation that justice will emerge. The police furnish the government with many of its weapons in the form of evidence; the judge acts as the referee; the jury customarily decides who has won. But the fighting itself falls on the shoulders of the prosecutor. More than anyone else on the side of the system, he determines the outcome of the battle.

One scholar has summed up the situation in these words:

> The prosecutor rather than the judge or the defense attorney plays the key role in administering criminal justice. In most cities the prosecutor must make or contribute to each of the key decisions: whether to charge an offense, which offense to charge, whether to accept a plea of guilty, which charges to drop, whether to

prosecute concurrently or separately if several charges are pending and what sentence to recommend to the judge. Most of the decisions are made in the privacy of the prosecutor's office; neither newspapers nor television intrude to report the results. [1]

The fact that so much of what the prosecutor does is done privately, away from the public view, increases his discretion. For example, if he wishes, for one reason or another, to "throw a case," he can, in the secrecy of the grand jury room, present such a weak argument that the jurors will refuse to indict. And if the jury does indict, he can "plea bargain" away most of the government's case to the point where the defendant escapes with almost no punishment. If, on the other hand, he wishes to go after someone, he can usually succeed in at least subjecting his prey to the ordeal of pretrial and trial proceedings, thereby inflicting great damage on the suspect's financial resources as well as on his reputation.

A U.S. Supreme Court decision in 1976 sheds considerable light on the ramifications of prosecutorial power in the United States. A deputy district attorney in Los Angeles had knowingly used perjured testimony to try to convict a suspect. Subsequently the use of perjury was discovered and the convicted man won his freedom. However, when he sued the prosecutor for damages, the court ruled the prosecutor to be immune from such penalties. The justices admitted that "this immunity does leave the genuinely wronged defendent without civil redress." But allowing prosecutors to be sued for damages, said the court, would "prevent the vigorous and fearless performance of the prosecutor's duty that is essential to the proper functioning of the criminal justice system." [2]

Who are these people who wield such power? At the municipal level prosecutors are the city or town attorneys who represent their communities in all legal matters. However, these attorneys do very little criminal prosecution. Most of the cases they try only involve alleged violations of municipal ordinances such as building and housing codes. Typically they result in punishments carrying no more than a small fine.

At the state level, there is the attorney general. However, although his office usually ranks next to the governor in power and prestige, the attorney general does not customarily play a major role in criminal justice. To be sure, he is often referred to as the state's chief law enforcement official. But only thirteen states give him unrestricted power to initiate local prosecutions, while thirty states give him authority to do so under certain conditions (for example, if the governor

1. Herbert Jacob, *Justice in America* (Boston: Little, Brown and Co., 1975), p. 180.

2. Howard Zinn, "A True-False Test about Law and the Supreme Court," *Boston Globe*, 5 March 1976.

requests him to do so). Furthermore, only thirteen states allow him to supersede a local prosecutor and only two states empower him to remove a local prosecutor from office.[3]

Most state attorneys general have been reluctant to use even the abbreviated legal authority they possess. In those states where the attorney general can take over the prosecution of a case from the district attorney, he rarely does so. More often than not, attorneys general have been content to confine themselves to their other important functions, such as serving as legal advisor to the governor and/or legislature or representing the state in civil matters, while leaving most criminal prosecutions to district or county attorneys.

It is the latter group, then, who prosecute most of the country's criminal cases. The key decisions prosecutors must make in our adversary system fall primarily on their shoulders. As former U.S. Attorney General Ramsey Clark observed, "The power of a district attorney is immense—the public has entrusted many of its most cherished rights to his discretion."[4]

DISTRICT ATTORNEYS

The district attorney is usually a county official and in some jurisdictions is actually called the county attorney. Most often he is elected. Of course, exceptions do exist. In five states district or county attorneys are appointed. In a few states several rural counties have been banded together to form a prosecutorial district with one prosecutor in charge of all prosecutions within the district. However, the typical district attorney is an elected official serving one county.

The appeal of the position varies greatly. In rural areas most seasoned lawyers shun the post, for it usually confers little in the way of pay or prestige. Oftentimes only a young lawyer fresh out of law school will seek the office. But in more populous areas, the situation is quite different. In these areas it is usually a political prize of the first importance. In all areas, however, the position can serve as a springboard to higher office. Many of our governors, senators, and congressmen started their public service careers as district attorneys, and nearly one-half of all federal judges served at one time in a prosecutorial capacity. As Robert Traver, a former district attorney from upper Michigan has noted, "No class is politically more on the make than ex-D.A.'s."[5]

The fact that district attorneys exercise considerable power, that they

3. For an informative view of the relations of state attorneys general with local prosecutors see: President's Commission on Law Enforcement and Administration of Justice, *Task Force Report: The Courts* (Washington, D.C.: U.S. Government Printing Office, 1968), p. 4.

4. Ramsey Clark, *Crime in America* (New York: Simon & Schuster, 1970), p. 190.

5. Robert Traver, *Small Town D.A.* (New York: E. P. Dutton, 1958), p. 42.

usually hold their office through election, and that they often seek to use the office to advance their careers opens up possibilities for numerous abuses. Unfortunately, few systematic studies of district attorney offices have ever been done. But such evidence as has become available indicates that such abuses have, at least sometimes, occurred. To wit:

A district attorney in Pittsburgh killed himself in 1974 as a federal grand jury was getting ready to indict him. The jury claimed that he had collected substantial "protection" payments from racketeers that he had failed to include on his income tax form.[6]

An investigator for a special crime commission in Massachusetts reported witnessing "a well-known gaming operator, who served time in state prison on a murder charge, paying workers $20.00 apiece in a barroom for services rendered in behalf of one seeking the nomination for district attorney."[7]

Some years after the assassination of President Kennedy, a New Orleans prosecutor claimed to have uncovered evidence that the killing was plotted by a group in his own city. He named a respected and retired business leader, Clay Shaw, as the ringleader. Although he was never able to convict Shaw, the district attorney subjected him to extensive prosecutorial proceedings that brought Shaw to the brink of financial and physical ruin.[8]

A Florida district attorney felt compelled to seek an indictment of a woman reporter after she had published material dealing with a supposedly secret grand jury proceeding. However, it was later learned that the material had been furnished to her by the district attorney himself.[9]

The problem of district attorneys using their offices to advance their public careers or their private fortunes is compounded by the fact that most of the more than twenty-five hundred district attorneys in the United States work only part-time. Even the prosecutors in counties encompassing such large cities as Houston, Little Rock, Cleveland, and Baltimore are allowed to carry on their private practices simultaneously. And the same holds true for the numerous assistant district attorneys as well.

Of course no part-time prosecutor can defend a person on a criminal charge in his own jurisdiction, but he can usually defend someone facing charges

6. *Boston Globe*, 6 March 1974.

7. Massachusetts Special Crime Commission, *Final Report, 1957*, p. 18.

8. Shaw, after a trial jury found him innocent, went on the lecture circuit in an effort to rebuild his depleted fortunes. However, the strain of the prosecutor's proceedings had apparently taken its toll on his health for he died soon after of a heart attack. His prosecutor, District Attorney Jim Garrison, was subsequently indicted by a federal grand jury for accepting bribes to protect illegal gambling but a trial jury later found him innocent. See "Garrison vs. Everybody," *Time* (8 October 1973).

9. Whitney North Seymour, a former prosecutor himself (he was a U.S. attorney for southern New York) says, "Publicity seeking is one of the chronic potential abuses in prosecutors' offices." Seymour, *Why Justice Fails* (New York: William Morrow & Co., 1973), p. 97.

in a neighboring jurisdiction. And he can almost always represent a client on a civil matter within his own county. Both situations can cause problems. When defending someone on a criminal charge in a neighboring jurisdiction the district attorney can usually expect favored treatment. After all, he is also part of the prosecutorial system and enjoys a vocational kinship with those who are trying to convict his client. Someday they may be defending a suspect in his own jurisdiction and will want special treatment from him.

Being part of the system also helps the district attorney in civil trials within his own bailiwick. Though the trial is a civil proceeding, he still comes into court on a firmer footing and enjoys a more developed relationship with the judges, court officers, and other court personnel. His clients thus enjoy advantages. If he is truly corrupt, he may on occasion "go easy" on a suspect in return for some private legal business the suspect or his friends may throw his way. The situation is fraught with the potential for abuse.

Efforts at correcting these conditions have, on the whole, made little headway. In 1952, the National Conference of Commissioners on State Laws, working with a special committee of the American Bar Association, promulgated a Model Department of Justice Act. The proposal would have greatly strengthened the power of attorneys general to oversee county prosecutors. However, in 1969, the National Association of Attorneys General noted that in the seventeen years since the Act was drawn up, not one state legislature had enacted it, even in modified form. The situation remains essentially the same today. Aside from undertaking further consolidations to provide larger prosecutorial districts, most states have refused to tamper with the district attorney's duties and discretion. He remains the system's primary prosecutor.

Attorneys general, meanwhile, have found fruitful fields for endeavor in other areas. As the consumer movement began to gain ground in the 1960s, many attorneys general set up special divisions to handle consumer protection. The rise of the conservation movement caused many of them to start prosecuting polluters as well.[10] But these were matters local prosecutors had shown little interest in pursuing. When it comes to prosecuting more traditional types of crimes, the district attorney in most states still reigns supreme.

CORONERS

Another county official who aids in the prosecutory process is the coroner. It is his responsibility to investigate any death in which there is reasonable suspicion of foul play. Usually no prosecution of a suspect can take place unless the coroner has first studied the case and ruled it to be a homicide.

10. *Wall Street Journal*, 7 January 1972.

In fulfilling this function, the coroner may conduct autopsies. He may also conduct hearings, call inquests, and assemble a jury of six persons to hear the evidence and make a report. He may even issue arrest warrants if he or the jury finds that the victim's death resulted from the commission of another crime.

The coroner is frequently an elected official. Very often he is not required to have any medical training. These two features have understandably bothered most of those who have studied the office. Congressman Henry Reuss, for example, says that "of all the thousands of elective officials in the United States, the county coroner is unquestionably the most archaic and absurd." [11] He points out that the American Medical Association, the American Bar Association, and the National Civil Service League once issued a joint statement calling the coroner system "a national scandal."

One common consequence of electing coroners with minimal qualifications is that many deaths are ruled accidents when they should be ascribed to other causes. Reuss quotes one pathologist as estimating that 3,000 to 10,000 murders a year go undetected thanks to the erroneous judgements of county coroners.

An eighty-one-year-old Pennsylvania woman was found dead at the foot of the basement stairs in her nephew's home. The nephew said the woman had caught her heel on a broken step and fallen. The coroner accepted his explanation and ruled the death an accident. But neighbors later told the police of hearing frequent quarrels between the pair. The police investigated and found a month-old will leaving the nephew $20,000. Then they turned up a blood-stained stick. Finally they exhumed the body and found it had sustained more extensive injuries than would be compatible with a simple fall. The nephew was tried and convicted of first-degree murder.[12]

In another case, the body of an eleven-year-old boy was found hanging from a tree. Despite the fact that the boy's hands were tied, his back was heavily scratched, and his clothing was soiled, the coroner ruled the death to have been accidental. Complaints of local citizens eventually resulted in the arrest of a sex deviate who confessed to the crime.[13]

In some cases, coroners rule wrongly not out of ignorance but out of compassion. They do this when they judge an obvious suicide to be an accident, thereby allowing the victim's family to collect life insurance. For example, a Kansas man once leaped from a twenty-four-story window; the coroner determined the cause of death to have been a heart attack.

11. Henry S. Reuss, *Revenue-Sharing* (New York: Praeger, 1970), p. 50.
12. Ibid., p. 51.
13. Ibid., pp. 52–53.

Fortunately some progress is being made in correcting these conditions. By 1970 some fifteen states had abolished the office of coroner outright, replacing it with statewide systems of appointed medical examiners. Nine other states had retained their coroners but made them appointed rather than elected. Some states had set up medical examiners to work in association with coroners. Louisiana and Ohio now require coroners to be licensed physicians, and this practice is becoming widespread. Slowly, the position of coroner in the criminal justice system is succumbing to the forces of change.[14]

DEFENSE

Until the 1960s, state and local governments gave little thought to the defense. Defending suspects was not considered to be a government function. The sole exception was the provision of counsel for those charged with a capital crime who had no resources to engage counsel on their own. Other impoverished defendants had to make do as best they could.

This situation changed sharply in 1963 when the U.S. Supreme Court received a pencil-scrawled petition from an indigent prisoner named Clarence Gideon. The letter bore the postmark of a Florida state prison. Gideon claimed that the state of Florida, in convicting and jailing him for a felony without furnishing him counsel, had deprived him of his rights. The Supreme Court eventually agreed and so the criminal justice system began to assume a new and necessary responsibility.

State and local governments presently rely on two basic alternatives to discharge their obligations to impecunious defendants. One is to assign them a lawyer from the regular bar association; the other is to establish a public defender system that employs lawyers on a full-time basis for this purpose.

When the assigned counsel procedure is used, the judge usually chooses the attorney who will represent the defendant. He may make the election from among the junior members of the bar who have not yet established full-time practices. He may appoint one of the "courthouse regulars," that is, one of the marginal lawyers who hang around courthouses hoping to pick up a case. He may give the case to a lawyer whom he likes and who needs to make a little extra money. (Fees are not high for such work but, then, the work is often not arduous since most such cases never come to trial, but are settled through plea bargaining ahead of time.) Many judges, to be sure, do their best to secure the best possible counsel for the defendants, and some jurisdictions have instituted procedures to

14. Advisory Commission on Intergovernmental Relations, *Making the Safe Streets Act Work: An Intergovernmental Challenge* (Washington, D.C.: U.S. Government Printing Office, 1971), p. 29.

further this end. In Houston the entire active membership of the bar association takes turns defending indigent persons accused of crimes. In Detroit, judges have made it an established practice to assign seasoned attorneys to this task. Other jurisdictions have adopted these or similar measures. Still, by and large, the system of assigned counsel often leaves much to be desired.

The increasing awareness of the inadequacy of many assigned counsel systems has awakened interest in public defender programs. The first office of public defender originated in Los Angeles in 1913. By 1970, eleven states had instituted public defender offices throughout the state while another twenty-three states had established such offices in their principal cities. The remaining sixteen states that continued to rely exclusively on assigned counsel were mainly rural states with relatively low crime rates.

Though many yet remain unsatisfied with the protection public defenders provide, most observers believe that they do, on the whole, a better job for the poor than do court-assigned counsel. One study showed that professional public defenders were more capable than the "courthouse regulars" and more experienced than appointed attorneys from the civil bar.[15] Not only does the public defender acquire increasing competence through devoting full-time effort to this function, but he also benefits by being an official of criminal justice and having contact with, and access to, its other functions and functionaries. Some of the more outstanding public defenders have become judges.

Financing the defense of the indigent accused varies greatly. Some states shoulder the entire cost, some pay part of it, and some cover none of it. Wisconsin, for example, pays the entire bill while Oregon pays only for public defenders and lets local governments pay for assigned counsel. As might be expected, counties and municipalities have displayed little desire to put up money for such purposes, leading the states to assume an ever-larger role.

15. Herbert Jacob and Kenneth Vines, eds., *Politics in the American States* (Boston: Little, Brown and Co., 1965), p. 68.

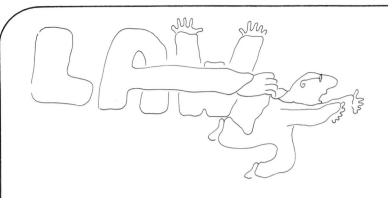

ADJUDICATION

CHAPTER TWENTY-FOUR

Every state operates a fairly elaborate court system and no state's system duplicates that of another state. For example, some states allow justices of the peace with no legal training at all to impose sentences of up to a year in jail on those they find guilty. Other states restrict their justices of the peace largely to performing marriages. Other states have abolished the office completely. Some states have specialized courts for, say, traffic or domestic disputes. Other do not. In some states, the counties run most of the courts. Other states do so themselves.

Even the nomenclature varies greatly from state to state. What is called a magistrate court in one state will be termed a district court in another. When a New Jersey resident mentions his state's supreme court, he is referring to his state's ultimate bench, which, like the U.S. Supreme Court, hears only appeals. When a New Yorker talks about *his* state supreme court he is referring to a middle-level court that tries cases, for in New York the trial court is called the supreme court. And what constitutes a surrogate court in New York is a probate court in Connecticut, and so on. Sorting out the various state court systems is a complicated process.

All state court arrangements do, however, break down into three basic levels or types. At the lowest level are the courts of limited jurisdiction. They may hear all kinds of cases and may make preliminary findings or final judgements. If the crime in question is a misdemeanor, these courts can often make a final judgement and prescribe the penalty, with the accused being given the right to appeal to a higher court if he wishes. If the crime is more serious, these courts may be limited to deciding whether or not the accused shall be held for trial. The next level is the one at which most trials take place and from which most sentences for felonious crimes are handed down. Above these trial courts there is always a court of last resort where, upon appeal, the state's final judgement is pronounced. However, over half the states have set up intermediate appeals courts between their trial courts and their supreme court. These courts decide some appeals on their own, passing up only the more complex or the more sensitive for determination by the justices who sit on the court of last resort.

State courts now process over three million cases a year, compared to about 150,000 by the federal courts. They are consequently important institutions. They are also busy institutions, and they are becoming busier all the time. This has put them under increasing pressure and made their problems more pronounced. Examining some of these problems will provide some insight into their proceedings.

SELECTING JUDGES

Clad in his black robe and sitting on his elevated bench, the U.S. judge presides over the legal system with some degree of majesty. His role may be more that of referee than participant, but in justice, as in baseball, the umpire has the ultimate word. Furthermore, he is usually quite an active umpire, one who can schedule the event, decide who can play and how, and even at times decide who has won and who has lost. And he hands down all the penalties. He can also discipline anyone involved in the event, including those who are only spectators. He commands more prestige and exercises more visible power than any other actor in the judicial arena.

Selecting judges, therefore, becomes of primary importance. In our system this selection has involved either election or appointment or a combination

336

of both. Election has been the most popular process by far. Although not as prevalent as it once was, it is still the dominant method for judicial selection in about thirty states. Half of these states, most of them in the Far West and northern Mid-West, elect their judges on nonpartisan ballots. The other fifteen states, located principally in the South, chose their judges on partisan ballots. However, in all these states judicial candidates must win voter approval and, if elected, must present themselves periodically before the electorate for renewal of their mandates. Election is never for a life term.[1]

The rationale for electing judges is deeply rooted in our political tradition. Originally all magistrates were appointed by the King of England and quite naturally, leaned in his favor in deciding disputes between the colonists and their royal overseers. This fact, plus the rising spirit of democracy, caused many colonies to opt for electing judges once they became independent. The frontier spirit nourished this tradition. If the law comes from the people, so should those who administer it.

Supporters of the elective method today argue that it keeps judges from becoming isolated from modern society. The law is closely bound up with the realities of life, and the elected judge is much more likely to realize this fact. He can never completely turn his back on the people and their everyday problems.

Electing judges, it is further contended, is also a way of controlling them. They know they must at regular intervals answer to the people for their deeds and misdeeds. Awareness of this fact will temper any corrupt tendencies. Furthermore, awareness by party officials that a poor judicial candidate will weaken the party's whole ticket should guide them in the nomination process. They will tend to winnow out the weaker candidates and nominate only the stronger ones.

Finally, electing judges, it is said, leads to a more representative judiciary. It should offer more opportunity for those from all classes and groups to serve on the bench. Appointment processes frequently tap only the upper levels and the dominant groups of society for judicial manpower.

Opponents of the system, and their numbers seem to be increasing, contest these claims. To them the election system has resulted in more corruption than would otherwise be the case. Party leaders often hand out judicial nominations as rewards for faithful service. Sometimes such nominations are actually put up for sale to the highest bidder.[2] Even when these abuses do not occur, the elected judge must frequently campaign and this may force him to solicit support from the attorneys who will appear before him. How can he

1. Donald Dale Jackson, *Judges* (New York: Atheneum, 1974), p. 16.

2. For a look at how such a system operates in one state, New York, see: Martin Tolchin and Susan Tolchin, *To the Victor . . .* (New York: Random House, 1971), Chapter 4. See also the *New York Times*, 23 June 1970 for an anonymous interview with one judge on this and related issues.

remain completely impartial, for example, when presiding over a trial in which the attorney for one side backed his election while the attorney for the other supported his opponent? Campaigning for election may also detract from the dignity of the office.

Opponents of the system also feel that pressures from the electorate may catalyze rather than curtail abusive behavior. Some traffic court judges, for example, persistently allow parking violators to go unpunished. They fear that the violators will punish *them* at the next election by voting for their opponents. On the other hand, a judge may deal overly harshly with an unpopular malefactor, such as a notorious child molester, lest an aroused populace turn him out of office at the next election. The barometer of public opinion may serve as a poor guide to the goals of justice.

These problems are further aggravated by the fact that the average citizen only becomes conscious of a judge's behavior when he comes into contact with the judge directly or when the judge is presiding over a headline-making trial. Otherwise most citizens know little and care less about what the judge is doing. In a 1952 special election in Florida to chose a judge for the state's highest court, fewer than 13,000 voters out of well over a million eligibles cast ballots. During the same year in a judicial election in Evanston, Illinois, a city with 45,000 eligible voters, only 88 showed up at the polls[3]

Even when a voter wants to exercise his franchise in picking his judges he finds it difficult to do so on an intelligent basis. Voters in a 1973 election in Philadelphia, for instance, faced the task of selecting 47 judges from a list of 263 candidates. [4]

When it comes to choosing candidates for lower-level judgeships almost anything can happen. In Lawrence, Kansas, a twenty-three-year-old college dropout, who admitted to being a dope pusher, once won election as justice of the peace. His constituents came largely from a hippie colony near the University of Kansas. But many of the 6,000 votes he received came from people who simply did not know who he was. Said the newly elected justice, "Secrecy was the secret of my success." (He said he would continue peddling dope because "you can't earn much as a J.P. around here.")[5]

Even when it comes to electing judges at the highest level, voters frequently vote blindly. A chief justice of the Texas Supreme Court has told of meeting, while on the campaign trail, a voter who told him, "I'm glad I have finally met a candidate for the supreme court. This time I can vote for a man I've

3. Jackson, *Judges,* p. 382.
4. *New York Times,* 2 May 1973.
5. United Press International dispatch in the *Boston Globe,* 14 November 1973.

met. You know, most people just vote for the man whose name is first on the ballot; and so I have made it a practice to vote for the man whose name is last on the ballot just to neutralize the vote of the uninformed."[6]

The ten states in which the governor or the legislature appoints most of the judges manage to avoid some of these problems. Those who obtain such appointments have usually been screened by the local bar association. Governors especially dislike naming a judge that the bar has found to be unqualified. Once appointed, a judge usually holds his appointment for life. He never needs to solicit campaign funds or votes.

But appointment also presents problems. Although it may result in generally better-qualified judges, political considerations do often play a role. For a long time Massachusetts was the only state in the nation that did not elect any judges. As a result many judges named to the bench met only the bar association's minimum qualifications, and some were appointed over the bar association's objections. One governor in the mid-1960s gave a valued probate judgeship to an attorney who had flunked the state bar examination sixteen times before finally winning the right to practice law. (He had been practicing for less than four years when the judgeship was conferred on him.)[7]

Judges appointed for life also can become too pompous and preemptory. Secure in their seats, they sometimes tend to dispense justice as if they were dispensing favors. They may also dispense rude insults, capricious commands, and erroneous judgements. Elected judges may and do frequently behave the same way, but the possibility that at least some of those to whom such behavior is directed will seek revenge at the polls may curtail somewhat their tendency to do so. The appointed judge is subject to no such check.

The desire to do away with some of these deficiencies has led to the creation of a new method of judicial selection. Called the Missouri Plan after the state which first adopted it, it has become the dominant device of selecting judges in at least nine states. Essentially the plan allows the governor to appoint judges but limits him to choosing from a list of nominees (usually three) presented by a special commission. The commission is composed of judges, lawyers, and laymen. The chief justice of the state's highest court usually heads the commission. A judge appointed in this fashion does not hold his position for life. Periodically, usually every ten years, his name goes before the voters, who decide whether or not they wish to retain him. If they vote no, then the commission submits a new list of nominees and the governor makes a new appointment.

6. Fred Gant, Jr., Irving O. Dawson, and Luther B. Hagard, Jr., eds., *Governing Texas* (New York: Thomas Y. Crowell Co., 1966), p. 207.

7. *Boston Globe,* 17 April 1965.

The Missouri Plan has won the endorsement of many reform groups. Since the governor can only appoint a nominee who has won the approval of the special commission, he is prevented from naming incompetents to the bench. And the fact that the judge so appointed must come up for voter approval every so often may help keep him from misbehaving while in office. Although studies indicate that governors often manage to manipulate the commission in order to obtain nominees they like, nevertheless the plan has usually prevented incompetent people from becoming judges.[8] Furthermore, once on the bench, most Missouri Plan judges have conducted themselves reasonably well. Though far from a perfect solution to the selection problem, this scheme, or versions of it, seems likely to become increasingly widespread in the future.

THE CONGESTED COURTS

The 1960s saw an upsurge in crime accompanied by an upsurge in demands for defendant's rights. These two trends have swelled the number of cases coming into court and have multiplied the number of steps needed to process them, making it more and more difficult for courts to keep abreast of their case calendars. By the early seventies criminal cases in some jurisdictions took a year or more to come to trial. Civil cases sometimes took as long as three years before adjudication.

Such a situation poses grave problems for the administration of justice. The longer a trial is delayed, the more the prosecution's case tends to weaken. Witnesses may die, move away, or become less certain in their testimony as their recollections fade. Evidence may be destroyed or lost. Victims may also die or disappear, or may simply lose interest. On the other hand, the defendant may also suffer, for if he is unable to make bail, he may have to serve many months behind bars awaiting trial. Nearly half of all incarcerated men and women in the early 1970s had never been convicted of anything. They were simply waiting for their cases to be called.

One outgrowth of this situation has been a dramatic increase in what is called plea bargaining. Under this system the defendant waives, in effect, his right to trial, in return for being allowed to plead guilty to a lesser charge. It is believed that over ninety percent of all criminal cases are now disposed of through this means. In New York City, for example, the number of arrests made for felonies rose from a little over 35,000 to nearly 95,000 during the 1960s.[9] Yet

8. Richard W. Watson and Rondal G. Downing, *The Politics of the Bench and Bar* (New York: John Wiley & Sons, 1969).

9. Whitney North Seymour, *Why Justice Fails* (New York: William Morrow & Co., 1973), p. 79.

only 552 of these cases actually came to trial. One city policeman said he had served on the force eight years and had averaged about 200 arrests a year. Yet he had never had one arrest that went to trial.

The practice of plea bargaining has aroused much animosity. The Committee for Economic Development, for example, claims that "plea bargaining undertaken merely to mitigate intolerable congestion of court dockets is a travesty of justice. . . . The guilty ought not to take advantage of congestion and the innocent should be assured of a fair trial." [10] Others have pointed out that plea bargaining makes the prosecutor the real judge, since it is he who makes the decision on the guilt or innocence of the defendant.

But plea bargaining has its supporters, too. They claim that without it the system would collapse. Among the defenders of plea bargaining is the chief justice of the U.S. Supreme Court. "Properly administered," says Warren E. Burger, "it is to be encouraged. If every criminal charge were subjected to a full-scale trial, the states and the federal government would need to multiply by many times the number of judges and court facilities." [11]

As is obvious from Justice Burger's statement, the defense of plea bargaining rests not so much on its alleged advantages as on the dire consequences that would ensue if it were eliminated. In an attempt to crack down on congestion more effectively, state and local governments have begun to seek out other remedies.

One step they are taking is easing up on the prosecution of what are called victimless crimes. These are crimes involving drunkenness, drug use (but not trafficking), prostitution, and the like in which there is no real victim except, perhaps, the perpetrator himself. Nearly one-half of all cases that flow into U.S. courtrooms involve such crimes and nearly one-half of all prisoners are serving time for behavior that injured no one except themselves. In the move to clean their court dockets, some six states by 1975 had erased public drunkenness from their statute books. Some states had moved to "decriminalize" possession of small amounts of marijuana. Many other states, along with many local police departments, had become less eager to enforce many of the marijuana laws that remained on their statute books. The expansion of legalized gambling, it is hoped, may further reduce the number of victimless crimes.

Another area of increasing activity is court administration. Practitioners and observers are gradually coming to the realization that courts may be among the worst-run institutions in our society. Forty-two states have established court administrator offices, and programs to train people in court administration are

10. *Reducing Crime and Assuring Justice* (New York: Committee for Economic Development, 1972), p. 24.
11. Quoted in Jackson, *Judges,* p. 74.

springing up in colleges and universities throughout the country. Some new administrative measures being adopted by courts to cope with their congestion woes include "omnibus" hearings, at which both prosecution and defense are required to state all their intentions at the beginning; master calendars to sort out scheduling conflicts; and the establishment of a maximum time allowed between arrest and trial. The very knowledge that a suspect must be brought to trial within a given period of time, or else be released, has jogged many court systems into moving more expeditiously.

The key factor in all this is, of course, the judge. If he allows the attorney for either side too many continuances (postponements), he contributes to congestion. (Defense lawyers often seek as many continuances as they can get.) If he takes long vacations or puts in short days, the cases pile up. (A New York City Study in 1973 showed that the average judge spent only three hours and twenty-one minutes a day on the bench.) And if he makes errors, either intentional or unintentional, in his conduct of the case, he lays the way open for lengthy appeals. Thus, improving the selection of, as well as the supervision over, judges holds the key to clearing up much of the congestion in the courts.

PASSING SENTENCE

The average convicted murderer in the United States serves ten years—but this is only an average figure. If convicted in Florida he could expect a sentence of only five years. In California he would probably draw a sentence of fourteen years. And in Pennsylvania he would have to anticipate serving seventeen to eighteen years behind bars.

These figures point up the vast discrepancies among sentencing procedures in the United States. These differences also exist within states. A man found guilty of a $7 armed robbery in northern Wyoming receives a ten-to twelve-year sentence; another man found guilty of a $124 armed robbery in southern Wyoming draws a sentence of two to three years. [12] Persons convicted of crimes in New York City receive, on the whole, substantially lighter sentences than those found guilty of similar offenses in upstate New York. And within New York City itself, a person picked up for failing to pay his subway fare can expect to pay a fine of $10.49 if he comes before a judge in the city's Queens section; if he comes before a Bronx judge his fine will average ninety-nine cents. [13]

Vast disparities in sentences occur not only between sections but between judges and even between various phases or days of an individual judge's term

12. Ibid., p. 367.
13. *New York Times,* 3 March 1976.

on the bench. This lack of uniformity tends to make a mockery of the supposed impartiality of the laws and it tends to undermine the whole concept of equal justice. Many agree with former U.S. Attorney General Elliot Richardson that the sentencing practices of American courts have reached scandalous proportions.

These divergences in sentencing are not the result of mere whims. Certain patterns reveal themselves. Studies suggest that a suspect is likely to receive more lenient treatment if he is white, if he is not poor, and if he pleads guilty and has his own lawyer. Of course, it is difficult to make hard-and-fast statements about such distinctions. If blacks are treated more harshly than whites for the same offense, this *may* be related to their often being poorer than whites. Some studies show that in some situations, blacks are actually given lesser sentences than whites. However, even in this latter case, discriminatory practices may be at work. Most black crime is directed against other blacks, so that in treating such crime more indulgently, the courts may be showing that they do not consider crimes against blacks to be very important. (Only about 2 percent of all judges, it should be noted, are black.) Generally speaking, a black person committing a crime against a white person is punished more severely than if he had committed the same crime against a member of his own race.

Women have also received discriminatory treatment in our courtrooms. However, here the "chivalry factor" has weighted the balance in their favor. Research indicates that "women are less likely to be arrested by male police officers for the same offenses, less likely to be convicted if brought to trial and only half as likely to be sent to prison if convicted" as men are. Furthermore, their prison sentences are likely to be much shorter than those that would be given to men for the same offenses.[14]

Some sentencing practices follow party lines. One researcher found that Democratic judges tend to side with the defense more often than do Republican judges. Democratic judges, his statistics show, also more often find for the tenant in a landlord-tenant case, for the consumer in a sale-of-goods case, and for the government in a business regulation case.[15] Even religious persuasion can correlate with sentencing practice. Protestant judges are likely to deal more harshly with the defense than are their Catholic colleagues.[16]

More often than not, however, variability in sentences reflects the differences among individual judges and their own individual ideas and idiosyn-

14. *New York Times,* 14 March 1976. The statement quoted is by Tom Buckley in a news story headlined "Critics Assail Linking Feminism with Women in Crime."

15. Stuart Nagel, "Political Party Affiliation and Judges' Decisions," *American Political Science Association* 55 (1961): 843–851.

16. Stuart Nagel, "Ethnic Affiliation and Judicial Propensities," *Journal of Politics* 24 (1962). For an interesting, related study see: Kenneth N. Vines, "Southern State Supreme Courts and Race Relations," *Western Political Quarterly* 15 (1965).

crasies. As a judge told one researcher, "Justice is what my gut says it is." [17] Furthermore, any individual judge may vary his sentences depending on his mood of the moment. As another judge told the same researcher, "You know, some days I feel lousy and I'll give a guy six months. Other days I feel good and I might fine somebody fifty dollars for the same thing. I figure it all evens out." [18]

The problems of sentencing have aroused a good deal of concern in recent years, and several states have moved to correct them. Some states have adopted mandatory sentencing for certain crimes. Indiana forbids suspended terms for rapists, New York requires a jail term for a second felony, and Massachusetts imposes a one-year prison term on anyone illegally carrying a gun. But mandatory sentencing strikes many as being a far from perfect solution. No two crimes are exactly alike and no two criminals are ever the same. The mandatory sentence, in its inflexibility, makes no allowances for this. Furthermore, it makes defendents less likely to plead guilty or to cooperate in other ways.

Another possible way of correcting the variability of the sentencing system is the use of more than one judge. New York City in late 1972 began using three-judge panels to prescribe sentences. And the chief judge of New York has recommended that a correction authority or some other agency take the sentencing task entirely out of the hands of the judiciary. [19]

In the meantime, one encouraging trend has already emerged. This is the growing tendency to hand out sentences that help both the community and the criminal. Thus, an Arizona physician found guilty of selling "speed" (amphetamines) was sentenced to devote one-third of his professional services to charity for seven years. A Michigan youth convicted of shooting a protected swan was ordered to work for two weeks at a state game preserve. And a Miami man who shot a gun into the home of an interracial couple was told to attend Saturday breakfasts at a church in the city's black community for six years. This trend may help curb, though not correct, the problems that characterize the sentencing practices of state and local judicial systems.

CONTROLLING JUDGES

Many of the sentencing scandals at state and local levels arise out of the awesome authority judges seem to possess. Lawyers and litigants curry their favor, while the press customarily withholds its criticism. The problem probably affects appointed judges more than elected ones, but the latter also customarily

17. Jackson, *Judges*, p. 100.
18. Ibid., p. 35.
19. *New York Times*, 28 September 1972 and 3 October 1972.

344

command a remarkable degree of deference. It would be surprising, then, if even the best judges did not eventually succumb to such treatment and start to preside in an autocratic manner. As a Texas judge reportedly remarked. "It's hard not to get the feeling that your ass is the divinity if it's been gettin' kissed for twenty years."

Controlling judges has long been a major problem in U.S. criminal justice. Although a higher judge may overturn his verdict, and although the voters may repudiate him at the polls, the individual judge is left with a vast amount of discretion. Removal of a judge in most states requires a formal impeachment proceeding, and such proceedings rarely occur. A study done some years ago indicated that the majority of states had never even instituted such a proceeding.

In recent years, however, many states have taken steps to exercise more direct control over their judges. One such step is to set up a special commission to hear complaints against judges, investigate them, and take disciplinary measures when the evidence so warrants. California first set up such a commission in the early 1960s. By 1974, some thirty states had followed suit. Though the powers of these commissions vary, they all provide some constraint over judicial capriciousness.

Other steps include setting up hierarchical structures, so that at each level a judge must answer to a superior who wields some supervisory authority over him, and requiring all judges to retire at age seventy. Only a relatively few states have yet moved forcibly to adopt these and other corrective controls, but we can expect more action along these lines in the future. Both the press and the public are slowly becoming more conscious and more critical of judicial practices. This trend, coupled with somewhat improved selection procedures, is gradually making some inroads into judicial misbehavior.

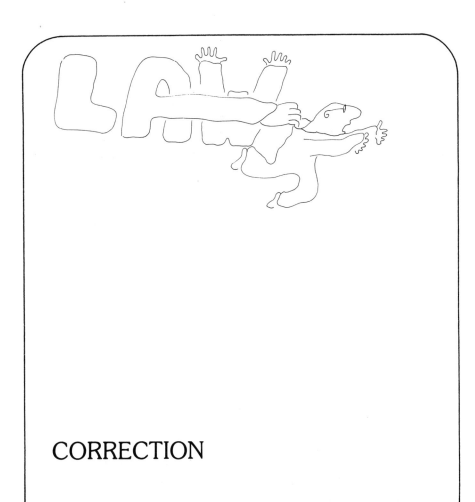

CORRECTION

C H A P T E R T W E N T Y - F I V E

Nearly one-and-a-half-million of our citizens live under correctional authority of one kind or another, and all but 5 percent of them come under the jurisdiction of state and local governments. These governments employ nearly 150,000 people and spend well over one billion dollars a year in carrying out this function. But almost no one feels that they are doing so in a satisfactory fashion.

The first problem we encounter when we survey the subnational correction scene is the familar one of fragmentation. The fifty states, most of their counties, and a majority of their larger cities each have one or more facilities for detention. This adds up to nearly 4.5 thousand jails and prisons. State governments handle most parole services but only one-quarter of all probation cases. County and, in some cases, municipal governments take care of the rest. Only a handful of states have organized their correction activities into a single department. In most of these, probation works independently of detention, and detention at one governmental level has little to do with that at another level.

"Correction today is characterized by an overlapping of jurisdictions, a diversity of philosophies, and a hodge-podge of organizational structures which have little contact with one another," notes a federal government report.[1] Another study claims that "structurally, correction is the most fragmented component of the Criminal Justice System."[2] This situation is believed to be responsible for many of the system's other shortcomings. As Ramsey Clark has observed, "Jails across the street from each other—one run by the county, the other by the city—are still commonplace. The time spent moving prisoners from one facility to the other and the risk involved each time are reasons enough to abolish one." And, he adds, "The waste in manpower and resources . . . is outrageous."[3]

This waste of resources and lack of central responsibility, coupled with the limited interest that the public and its political leaders have usually shown toward correction, have produced many of its more visible problems. These include overcrowding, filth, brutality, and inadequate rehabilitative services. County jails are probably the worst offenders but many state prisons have been seriously remiss.

Correction personnel frequently aggravate rather than ameliorate the situation. Most correction officers are white and middle-aged. Most prisoners are young and a large percentage of them are black. Correction officers are often undereducated—nearly half did not have a high school diploma in 1971—and poorly paid. (In 1970, nearly four-fifths were earning less than $8,000 a year.)[4]

These personnel practices contribute to the corruption that is found in so many county and local jails and in not a few state prisons. Some guards smuggle in drugs, liquor, and even, on occasion, weapons for sale to the prisoners. And some will give favorable treatment to those who can afford to pay for it.

Guard brutality against prisoners does take place, but guard indifference to the brutality that goes on among the prisoners themselves overshadows it. Often the guards themselves fear the most violent prisoners, and in any case frequently find it too difficult to control them. As a result, the strong may prey on

1. Joint Commission on Correctional Manpower and Training, *The Public Looks at Crime and Corrections* (Washington, D.C.: U.S. Government Printing Office, 1968), p. 2

2. Advisory Commission on Intergovernmental Relations, *Making The Safe Streets Act Work: An Intergovernmental Challenge* (Washington, D.C.: U.S. Government Printing Office, 1971) pp. 137-138

3. Ramsey Clark, *Crime in America* (New York: Simon & Schuster, 1970), p. 234.

4. *New York Times*, 26 September 1971.

348

the weak while those in official command try to look the other way. One study of Philadelphia's jails showed that some two thousand sexual assaults had taken place in a twenty-six-month period.[5] During a three-year period in West Virginia's State Penitentiary, fifteen inmates met death at the hands of fellow inmates.[6]

CORRECTING CORRECTION

Correction has been the last component of the criminal justice system to feel the currents of change. But by the mid-seventies it too had begun to experience some rather dramatic efforts at improvement. In four states, Arkansas, Maryland, Mississippi, and Massachusetts, federal judges ruled that prison conditions were so bad that they deprived inmates of their constitutional rights. The states were ordered to correct them. Growing prison unrest, culminating in the bloody uprising at New York's Attica prison, had also focused more attention on the problem. And the growing realization that too many prisons were developing rather than deterring criminality was also assisting the forces of change.

Many correction departments have launched work-release and prison furlough programs. Many jails have instituted work therapy and psychotherapy programs. A few systems have set up college degree programs. Conjugal visits, which permit prisoners to spend time privately with their wives, are becoming more common. And several correction systems now permit male and female inmates to spend a certain amount of supervised time together.

One of the more noteworthy examples of this metamorphosis is the county jail in New Orleans. In 1971 it was considered one of the worst (if not the worst) detention facilities in the county. Even the sheriff who ran it called it a "filthy pigsty." However, as a result of a federal court ruling to improve it, its budget rose nearly 300 percent in five years. The structure itself was rehabilitated and numerous new services were added. One interesting and welcome consequence was that attempted escapes and assaults on guards dropped markedly.[7]

Much remains to be done in cleaning up correction, and progress will not be smooth. One of the biggest obstacles is the growing realization by reformers that most rehabilitation programs, even when wholeheartedly embraced and

5. Whitney North Seymour, *Why Justice Fails* (New York: William Morrow & Co., 1973), p. 119.

6. In November, 1976, the Massachusetts Commissioner of Correction disclosed the discovery of a "Death Squad" operation among the inmates at the state maximum security institution at Walpole. The squad was believed responsible for numerous inmate deaths.

7. United Press International dispatch in the Boston *Herald-American*, 20 March 1976.

carried out, have rarely achieved much success.[8] Other difficulties involve funding improvements, and finding employers and other members of the community to assist such rehabilitation efforts that hold out hope of succeeding.[9] However correction does seem to have turned a corner during the past decades. It is no longer the neglected stepchild of state and local justice.

8. For two rather startling but heavily researched articles on this point, see: Robert Martinson, "What Works? Questions and Answers about Prison Reform," *Public Interest* (Spring 1974); and Gordon Tullock, "Does Punishment Deter Crime?" *Public Interest* (Summer 1974).

9. A poll by Louis Harris in November 1967 showed that 59 percent of our population did not want taxes raised to pay for better correctional programs.

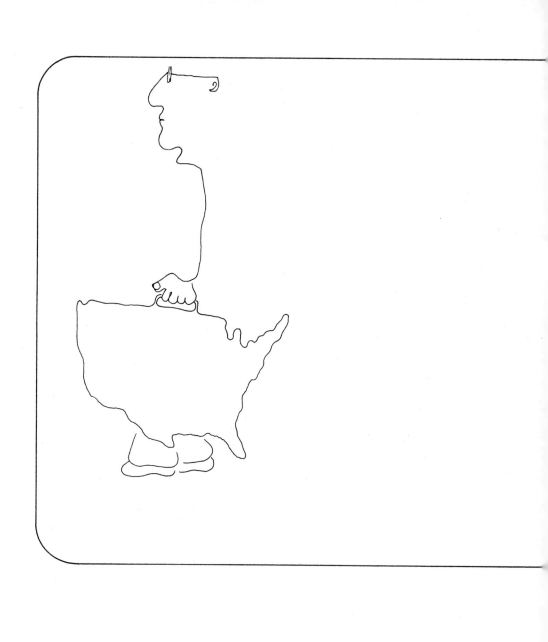

PART SEVEN

CONCLUSION

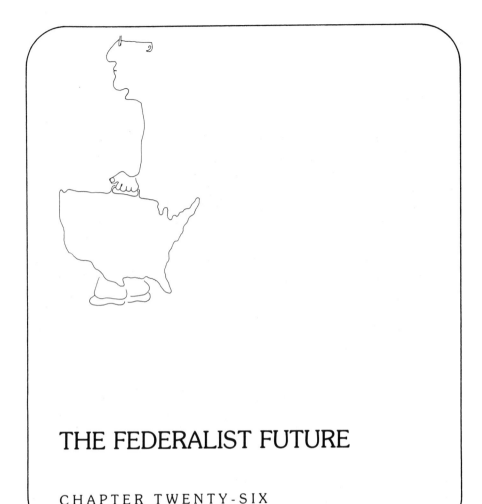

THE FEDERALIST FUTURE

CHAPTER TWENTY-SIX

One overriding trend has characterized the federal system during the past quarter-century. This has been the persistent shifting of more and more responsibilities to higher levels of governments. The federal government has become increasingly involved with matters that formerly lay within the exclusive or near-exclusive jurisdiction of the states. The states, meanwhile, have begun to play a larger role in what were once considered to be purely local affairs.

Dollar signs document this upward shift. In 1954, federal aid to the states amounted to only 21.5 percent of what the states were spending from their own revenue sources. During the next twenty-two years, state spending rose rapidly, but federal funding of state activities rose even more. Thus, by 1976, federal financial aid to the states had surged to over 40 percent of the revenues the states were collecting from their own sources.

The situation in local government shows the same trend. In 1954, the amount of aid local governments were receiving from both their state and federal governments came to 43.5 percent of all the revenue they were raising on their own. By 1976, this figure had shot up to 75.5 percent.[1]

Of course increased aid doesn't necessarily require its recipients to surrender responsibility to those who are supplying the aid, but in practice it usually entails some subordination. Those who bestow generally assume some power over those who benefit. And today we see the federal government and the state governments exercising increased influence in areas where they formerly maintained a hands-off attitude.

For examples of this trend the student need only review our chapters on the environment, transportation, welfare, etc. These include numerous illustrations of how the federal government is becoming an ever-greater actor in what were once strictly state and local activities.

That the trend goes beyond the statehouse is borne out by a 1976 study by the Advisory Commission on Intergovernmental Relations. The Commission found that nearly one-third of all the communities it surveyed had, during the previous decade, transferred, either voluntarily or involuntarily, one or more of its functions to another unit of government. And the larger the community, the more functions it had managed to cast off.[2]

What governments took on these new functions? The survey showed that counties and special districts were the most common recipients. But states also shouldered some of these duties. Thus, Rhode Island abolished all city and town health departments and transferred their responsibilities to the state. Vermont, Massachusetts, and Delaware assumed all responsibility for public welfare. Florida phased out all its municipal courts, transferring their duties to state courts. Maryland made property tax assessment a state function.

Not all this upward shift takes the form of a complete switch of functions from one level of government to another. U.S. federalism, being the marble cake that it is, apportions most areas of government activity among the various levels. Many activities have remained divided up among two or more levels of governments but here too we find some upward movement.[3] In 1957–1958, for

1. *Intergovernmental Perspectives* (Fall 1976), p. 2.

2. The ACIR report was entitled *Pragmatic Federalism: The Reassignment of Functional Responsibilities.* For a summary of its findings see: Wayne F. Anderson, "State and Local Governments Shift Functional Responsibilities—Mainly Upward," *News and Views* (November 1976). (*News and Views* is a monthly publication of the American Society for Public Administration.)

3. Advisory Commission on Intergovernmental Relations, *Improving Urban America: A Challenge to Federalism* (Washington, D.C.: U.S. Government Printing Office, September 1976), p. 45.

example, local governments paid for 56.6 percent of all public school expenditures. The states supplied 39.4 percent and the federal government contributed the remaining 4 percent. By 1974–1975, the local contribution had dropped to 48.6 percent while the state share had increased to 43.6 percent and the federal government's portion had risen to 7.8 percent.

Criminal justice expenditures show a similar, though more moderate, trend. In 1965, the states were responsible for 27 percent of all criminal justice expenditures. By 1975, this had increased to 30 percent. Similarly, the counties were bearing 32 percent of the local criminal justice expense burden in 1965, and in 1975 they were shouldering 35 percent. Meanwhile, the federal government's portion had nearly doubled, reaching 13.1 percent in 1975.

In general, then, it can be said that the overall tendency within the federal sphere over the past two decades has been for the larger and broader levels to play an ever-greater role in the overall governmental arena.

WILL THIS TREND CONTINUE?

Certainly no one can predict the future with any degree of certainty but such indications as exist point to a continuation of this trend. We may well find the lower levels of the federal system yielding more and more of their rights and responsibilities to those above them.

At the national level, we may see Washington assume an increasing share of the responsibility for welfare. In 1974, the federal government nationalized aid to the aged, blind, and disabled. In 1976, the Advisory Commission on Intergovernmental Relations called for full federal financing of all federal welfare programs, including general assistance and Medicaid. As the Commission put it, "The programs are so inter-state in nature and already so largely dominated by federal policy that only complete federal financing makes sense." [4]

Of course, the Commission is only an advisory body. It can recommend but not command. However, the Family Assistance Plan President Nixon proposed in 1970 would have effectively transferred welfare to the national level. And President Carter has proposed a rather sweeping program that would, as we have seen, have the federal government assume a larger share of the financial load.

Meanwhile, grass roots pressures for placing the welfare burden in Washington's hands are growing. The Northeast and North Central states, along with California, have particularly felt welfare to be an expensive encumbrance. Their comparatively liberal payment policies, coupled with their growing unemploy-

4. Ibid., p. 16.

ment problem, have made their welfare roles rise relentlessly. In 1975, the chairman of the Michigan Manpower Council, Dr. Daniel H. Kuger, voiced a desire to pay welfare recipients $5,000 apiece just to leave the state. Though he doubted the legality of such a move, he said it would save "ample amounts of money for taxpayers."[5]

These Northeast and North Central states that are pressuring for a federal assumption of welfare costs are the states that already feel shortchanged in terms of federal aid. A study published in 1976 showed that the federal government during the previous year had collected nearly $11 billion more from the area than it spent there.[6] The Northeast governors, at a post-election conference in mid-November 1976, called on the incoming Carter administration to rectify this imbalance. One way of doing so would be to nationalize welfare costs.[7]

We may also expect to see the federal government step up its involvement in other areas, such as education and health. President Carter expressed the desire to initiate greater federal activity in both these areas during his campaign.

The federal presence may loom larger not just in the spending of money but also in its collection. The Tax Reform Act of 1976 eased the restrictions on the use by the states of the Internal Revenue Service to collect state income taxes. Thus, more states may make use of the federal government's offer to "piggyback" their income tax onto the federal income tax, letting the federal government collect the state income taxes while it collects its own.

The federal government may also move to take over many state "severance taxes." These are taxes that those states blessed with abundant mineral or other natural resources have placed on the sale of those resources. The energy crisis has enabled some states to impose stiff taxes on coal. Montana now taxes coal from its mines at 20 to 30 percent of its wholesale price, while North Dakota imposes a 15 to 20 percent coal tax. Such taxes greatly enrich the coffers of these states at the expense of consumers in other states. A report prepared for the National Science Foundation has suggested that the federal government intervene in order to see that the benefits of the nation's huge supply of coal do not become overly weighted in favor of those relatively few states that possess most of this vital fuel.[8]

Meanwhile, the states seem likely to play a greater part in the performance of hitherto local functions. They are being pressed from a variety of sources

5. *Moneysworth* (13 October 1975), p. 3.
6. "Where the Funds Flow," *National Journal* (26 June 1976).
7. *Boston Globe,* 14 November 1976.
8. Associated Press dispatch in *The State,* 28 November 1976.

to assume more and more of the financial costs for elementary and public schools. Some of this pressure is coming from their own courts, where by 1976 at least fifty separate suits had been filed to equalize educational expenditures. Some of this pressure is coming from teacher associations, which generally favor greater state, as well as federal, aid to education. And some of this pressure is coming from various good government groups that view the present system of local financing as a distortion of democratic principles. By the mid-1970s thirty-five states had taken, or were preparing to take, some action in this matter.

Land use also seems destined to receive more statehouse scrutiny. Hawaii established statewide zoning in 1961. No other state has gone so far, but Vermont, Maine, Florida, Delaware, Oregon, and California have all launched moves to regulate the use of land. Given the fact that there is only a fixed supply of land to accommodate a still growing population, such initiatives no doubt will increase and intensify.[9]

Criminal justice offers still another field for greater state action. The states have already begun to set recruitment and training standards for local police departments and two states have taken over most of the recruitment and training task for these local police forces. We can probably expect to see more of them do the same. Some states now offer extra pay to police officers for college credits. States may also take over more and more of the financing of courthouse and county jails, although the power of many local sheriffs may delay the day when such facilities are commonly part of the state government. Attempts to increase state intervention in the prosecutorial process may prove even harder given the power of local prosecutors. The ACIR has suggested that the state governments should pay one-half of all local prosecutorial costs and that the attorney general should possess stronger powers to oversee their work.[10] However, few states have dared to move very far in this direction.

The states of necessity have already started, and doubtlessly will continue, to exercise more oversight over their local governments. The financial disaster that almost overtook New York City, and the perilous financial position in which Boston, Philadelphia, and many other communities, large and small, have found themselves, has served notice on the states that they must keep better tabs on how and what their local governments are doing. Home rule once served as a local government battle cry as many communities sought greater freedom from state control. In the future, however, we may hear this demand uttered less and less as more communities turn to their statehouses for support.

9. Shirley K. Werthamer, "The State Role in Land Use: New York in the Seventies" *National Civic Review* (October 1976).

10. Advisory Commission, *Improving Urban America,* p. 16.

IS GRASS ROOTS DEMOCRACY DOOMED?

The flow of functions to higher levels would seem to presage the decline of what we call grass roots democracy. Yet this need not, and quite possibly will not, be the case. Much remains to be done at the grass roots level and local government will doubtlessly continue to play a significant part on the governmental stage.

Local government itself, however, may undergo some change. For one thing, it seems likely that counties will in many instances assume greater importance. In some cases, counties will serve as the basic structure for metropolitan government, consolidating their own functions and those of their localities into one governmental apparatus. As we saw in Chapter 13, this occurred in seven counties from 1969 to 1973. In Nevada, Clark County and Las Vegas came close to merging in 1976—a State Supreme Court decision blocked the move temporarily—and were expected to do so in 1977.

But even where such consolidations fail to take place, we can expect the county to become an increasingly important factor in the governmental system. County revenues and expenditures are already growing at a faster rate than municipal revenues and expenditures and seem likely to go on doing so. As political scientists John DeGrove and Carolyn B. Lawrence reported in 1976, "The major development in local government in the next several decades will be the continued strengthening of county government as the critical link between multi-county, state and federal levels on the one hand, and sub-county levels on the other." [11]

But the survival and possibly even the strengthening of grass roots democracy may come from another trend, the trend toward *administrative* decentralization. Under administrative decentralization, basic policy may be made at higher levels but the decisions to implement that policy are made closer to the scene. Such administrative decentralization permits and even promotes a good deal of local participation.

The federal government has taken several steps in recent years to decentralize its administrative apparatus. It has consolidated many of its field services into ten regional headquarters and given its field officials more leeway in responding to local demands. Washington has also begun to make increased use of block grants in its community development and health programs. (However, it has established goals and guidelines for such grants and set up monitoring systems so as to escape the problems that have beset the Law Enforcement

11. *National Civic Review* (October 1976), p. 472.

Assistance Administration in its use of such grants. We examined some of these problems in Chapter 9.)

Many states have also started to decentralize some of their activities. For example, the Massachusetts Department of Mental Health has broken the state down into districts and established a field office and a citizens' advisory council for each district. Other states have divided themselves into planning districts complete with field offices and citizens' committees in each district.

Many municipalities have also succumbed to this trend. They have set up neighborhood city halls, neighborhood citizens' councils, and/or other mechanisms to develop responsiveness to their residents. When Dayton, Ohio decided to raise the city's income tax in 1975, it organized one-hundred neighborhood meetings to enable the city's citizens to tell the city's officials how they wanted the increased revenues to be spent.[12] Thus, through a variety of devices, grass roots democracy continues to survive and even thrive in the federal United States.

PROSPECTS AND PROBLEMS

The signs of progress within the federal system scarcely signal the end to all the problems that beset it. Much remains to be done. Furthermore, a new and major problem has reared its head. While it may hasten the resolution of some of the system's difficulties, it may also hamper other needed action. This problem is money.

As we saw at the outset of this book, the subnational system has grown remarkably in recent decades. This upward surge has imposed increasing costs on our citizens, and the citizens are beginning to react. The 1976 elections saw several states voting on referenda designed to place absolute limits on state spending. While none of these referenda passed, the fact that they were initiated, plus the fact that most of them received substantial support from the voters, should serve as a warning to many state officials.

The same negative reaction to government spending has also surfaced at local levels. Voters have become increasingly reluctant to approve any new spending proposals. School districts in Oregon, Connecticut, and other states had to suspend classes in 1976 when voters refused to approve their budgets.

This taxpayer revolt has prompted an increasing number of our 80,000 governments to launch efforts designed to streamline their operations. Many

12. James H. Winchester, "Dayton's Unique Do-It-Yourself Government," *Reader's Digest* (June 1976).

states and local governments have called on private business for help in making their operations more effective and less costly. Wisconsin, for example, used such outside aid to improve the functioning of its Division of Motor Vehicles, while New York City did the same to improve the operation of its courts. [13] Some states, led by Colorado, have passed sunset laws. And nearly all state and local governments have become more resistant to demands from government employee trade unions. The voters of San Francisco, once considered a very pro-labor city, overwhelmingly approved a charter change in 1976 that will give them the right to decide, in case of a management-labor deadlock, whether or not a city employee union's final offer is to be accepted.

The mounting antagonism to increasing state and local expenditures will undoubtedly spur on some efforts at reorganization and reform. To the extent that they can be shown to save money, such efforts may elicit considerable public support. But to the extent they may require additional funding, they may only succeed in arousing further animosity. The public's new mood should encourage those who wish to cut down on the confusion that now characterizes so much of the subnational system, but only if they can demonstrate that their efforts will also tend to cut costs as well.

The new concern on costs will also affect employment possibilities. The major growth in payrolls seems, at least for the foreseeable future, to have come to an end. At the same time, however, we may see some more job opportunities for the better-educated and the better-trained since their talents will be increasingly needed. For those with the skill and the desire, the system should provide more than its share of challenges and satisfactions in the years ahead.

13. Trevor Armbuster, "They're Trimming the Fat from State Government," *Reader's Digest* (May 1976).

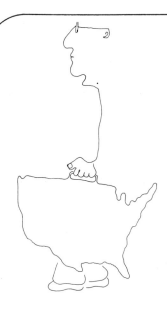

A COMPARATIVE
LOOK AT SUBNATIONAL
GOVERNMENT

CHAPTER TWENTY-SEVEN

Governing regions and localities is not a concern common to the United States alone. Virtually all countries, except for tiny principalities such as Luxembourg or Monaco, need a subnational system of one kind or another. Although all countries are unique, with factors and forces peculiar to themselves, the goal of effective subnational governance still poses problems of general applicability. We can therefore deepen our understanding of our own system by examining how other modern industrialized democracies approach this task.

GREAT BRITAIN[1]

The United States started out as a British colony equipped with basically British institutions and animated by essentially Anglo-Saxon attitudes. To some extent this continues to be the case today. We still make use of such British institutions as the sheriff and the coroner, and such ancient Anglo-Saxon procedures as *habeas corpus* and trial by jury. Yet, remarkable divergences now exist between the political systems of the mother country and its former colony. And nowhere, perhaps, do they more fully reveal themselves than in the area of subnational government.

The most striking difference lies in their contrasting approaches to centralization. While the United States has nearly 80,000 governments, Britain has fewer than 500. To put it another way, while Great Britain's population equals 25 percent of our own, its number of subnational governments amounts to less than 1 percent of ours.

To begin with, Britain is a unitary, not a federal, nation. Consequently, all sovereign power rests in the hands of its national government in London. It has no sovereign states or any other entities that can challenge the national government or carve out for themselves areas of authority where the national government cannot intrude. All regional and local governments in Britain are, legally at least, a reflection of the will of the national one.

Britain's subnational system consists essentially of two tiers. The larger and more encompassing tier is the county. The smaller tier is called the district. There are about 435 districts and they are grouped into some sixty counties. The districts vary greatly in population, from less than 75,000 population to over a million. The counties range in size from a quarter of a million to over three million. It is interesting to note that Manchester, Britain's second largest city, is a mere district and is one of nine such districts housed within its county.

Districts are supposed to be in charge of education, personal social services, fire and police, consumer protection, recreation, libraries, rubbish collection, food safety and hygiene, communicable disease protection, regulation of building construction, care of cemeteries, and other similar matters. They do make some input into parks and recreation affairs and they do fill in the details of the county's overall plan as it affects themselves. In addition, the larger

---

1. This section is based upon research conducted by one of the authors (Berkley) in England in 1972 and by his research assistant, Mrs. Donna Galen, in 1976. For further information on this topic see: George E. Berkley, "Community Control in Britain: Going, Going . . . ," *National Civic Review* (May 1973); and Berkley "Britain's New Town Blues," *National Civic Review* (October 1973).

districts are given some say in education and social services. Nevertheless, the counties clearly enjoy the dominant role.

But even the counties' role is not as strong as it seems. If we were to examine the system more closely, we would find the hand of the national government nearly everywhere, shaping and moulding local governance to its own desires.

Planning, for example, is a vital activity in Britain. Planning determines how many people are to dwell in a locality, what kinds of jobs they are to have, where they are to live, etc. The counties draw up the basic plans and allow their districts to fill in some of the details. However, all such county and district plans must be approved by the national government, and the latter is not at all adverse to altering these plans to suit its own needs. For example, it is not unusual for the Ministry of the Environment to require the plan to include a shopping center even if the county and the districts where it is to be located do not want one. If the shopping center will serve those from other districts who need one, these local objections will not necessarily prevent its construction.

Policing is also ostensibly a local matter in Britain, but in reality it is not. The Home Office of the national government can consolidate police forces basically at will and, as a matter of fact, has done so frequently since World War II. As a result, there are now only forty-seven police forces in Britain, which means that some encompass more than one county. Furthermore, the Home Office sets all the recruitment, pay, and promotion standards and does all the police training. And the Home Secretary must approve the hiring of any police chief and he can dismiss any police chief at any time.

The situation with the fire service is much the same. Indeed, even the size of hose couplings is nationally determined.

Education was long considered sacrosanct, relatively free from the influence of London. However, that is true no longer. The national government sets minimum performance standards. It also sets a maximum on expenditures. Consequently, there is far less variability in educational performance within Great Gritain than in the United States. Although the national government does encourage local initiatives, it formulates basic educational policy and local governments can do little without national approval.

The same holds true in housing as well. Local initiative is encouraged, but the national government continues to hold the trump cards. It sets all basic and often less general policies and enforces them rigorously. When a local housing authority refused to raise its rents in 1972, the Ministry of Housing stepped in and did so.

Underlying this control by London are the financial arrangements be-

365

tween the capital and the local governments. The local governments must rely almost exclusively on the property tax for their tax revenues. Yet, property taxes remain, by U.S. standards, quite low. The owner of a London townhouse worth $100,000 may pay only about $500 a year in property tax. The reason for this is that local governments derive most of their funds from the national government. Grants from the latter paid nearly two-thirds of all local expenditures in 1975.

Bearing these facts in mind, it should come as no surprise then to find that local political leaders really do not have much to do. The county and district councils that govern subnational Britain almost never meet more frequently than once every two weeks and often hold sessions only once every six weeks. Furthermore, those elected to serve on these councils do not receive a salary, although they are eligible for reimbursement for expenses.

Local government elections are partisan affairs and thus are highly contested, for each party uses them to demonstrate its national popularity. For example, when the local elections go against the party that is in power in Parliament, it is taken as a sign that the people are dissatisfied with the national government. But aside from their use as a bellwether of public opinion on national concerns, local elections have little impact on policymaking. Only about one-third of all eligible Britons bother to vote in their local elections although over three-quarters of them cast their ballots in national contests.

Governing London

Approximately one person out of every eight in Britain lives in London. This gives the capital city a position in British life far greater than that held by any city in the United States. This has given rise to some special arrangements for governing the metropolis.

The overall governing authority for London and its suburbs is the Greater London Council. It is comprised of one hundred elected councilors, and sixteen aldermen whom the councilors themselves have selected to join them. There is also a lord mayor, but his duties are almost wholly ceremonial.

The councilors are elected on a partisan basis, as in all British local elections. The members of each party sit together as a group and generally vote as a bloc. The party having the majority appoints the council chairman, as well as the chairmen of the various standing committees. The council meets every other week.

Within the county of London there are, in addition, some thirty-two boroughs and the city's financial district, which, though not called a borough, to all intents and purposes functions as one. Each of these boroughs has a council

366

of its own with up to twenty-four councilors, with the number depending somewhat on population. As has been seen, London's governing apparatus to a great extent parallels that of the rest of the county with an overall county government made up of several districts.

The Greater London Council, or GLC as it is customarily called, exercises full responsibility for fire and water service, refuse disposal, principal roads, main sewers, the licensing of public entertainment and horse tracks, research, and all scientific and supply services. It prepares the overall development plan, including all large-scale projects—especially those that straddle borough lines. It also handles education in the twelve inner-city London boroughs. Finally, it sets and collects the property tax. (Property assessment throughout Great Britain, however, is done by the national government.)

The boroughs, each of which is comparable to a fair-sized city in population, are in charge of libraries, refuse collection, street cleaning, parks and open space, lesser roads, off-street parking, and inspection services related to health. The boroughs also have primary responsibility for housing, and the twenty outer boroughs have responsibility for education as well.

But again we find that these responsibilities are not as extensive as they seem. The national government keeps, if anything, a closer eye on what happens in London than on what happens in the countryside. When Prime Minister Edward Heath got caught in a bad traffic jam in the late 1960s, the national government served notice to the GLC to take action on its traffic problems. When it comes to law enforcement, the GLC does not even exercise nominal control, for the Home Office directly administers the London police and appoints its commissioner.

Summary

The approximately 500 local authorities that govern subnational Britain today are a comparatively new invention. They were created in 1974 as part of a sweeping reorganization put into effect by the national government. Previously, the country's political system operated through 1,900 units of government. Thus the reorganization consolidated the system considerably, creating fewer and larger units to replace smaller and more numerous ones.

Many hoped that the larger units would restore some vigor to the non-national political system. The new local authorities, it was believed, would be more viable and therefore more capable of contributing to the governing process. But such has not proven to be the case. Although local authority employment has grown faster than national government employment, local authority enterprise has withered. The need for more national control over Britain's increasingly troubled economy, plus the failure of the local governments to act in a responsible and resourceful manner, has diminished their role. As one prominent British magazine, *The Economist,* observed in 1976, "As a whole local government now has less power than before reorganization. . . ."

More interesting for an observer from the United States, perhaps, is the response of the British themselves to this trend. In general, they have remained quite unconcerned. Comments *The Economist,* "As far as public opinion goes, if centralizing refuse collection from Westminster [London] would be shown to save money that is what the rate payers [taxpayers] would want."

At the heart of this calmness in the face of growing centralization lies a fundamental difference in defining democracy. To many Americans, decentralization and democracy go hand in hand. The British, however, feel that centralization and democracy are quite compatible. In some cases, centralization may, in their view, enhance democratic values. As one British government document puts it, " . . . there are many areas of local authority activity— education, police, fire and so on—where the citizen will expect to receive a certain standard of service regardless of where he may live. It is the central government's responsibility to see that this happens."

FRANCE[2]

At first glance, the French subnational system strikes the observer as much more decentralized than the British one. France has an elaborate network of regional and local governments totaling over 41,000 in all. This network is not only greater than Britain's, but, on a population basis, is even more extensive than our own set-up. Added to this is the fact that the French turn out for regional and local elections much more avidly than either the British or we do. It is not unusual to find over three-quarters of all eligible voters showing up at the polls for a municipal election.

But things are not always what they seem. Appearances of decentralization can prove deceptive. France, despite the fact that it has so many nonnational governments, and despite the fact that its citizens take their local elections so seriously, is a highly centralized state. In many respects it even surpasses Great Britain in the degree to which the national government rules the roost.

2. Material for this section was drawn from a variety of sources, the most important being *L'Administration Regionale et Locale De La France,* by Hewé Detton (Paris: Presses Universitaire De France, 1972). For an English-language summary of some of the issues now confronting subnational government in France see Flora Lewis' dispatch headlined "Regional Autonomy Gains Dramatically in Lorraine while Lagging Elsewhere in Centralized France," *New York Times,* 18 April 1976.

Governing Provincial France: Forms and Functions

The main unit in the French regional-local checkerboard of government is the *department*. Although it is spelled the same way as the English word department, it has a somewhat different meaning. The French *department* is actually an administrative district, somewhat larger, perhaps, than the typical U.S. county but a good deal smaller than the typical U.S. state. France consists of ninety-five departments, which form the cornerstones of the country's subnational system.

Each department is presided over by an official called the *prefect*. He (and it is always "he" for no woman has, as yet, ever been given a prefectoral post) is appointed by the national government. The inhabitants of the department have virtually no say in his selection. He is a career employee of the Ministry of the Interior, and it is the Ministry that determines where each prefect will serve.

Prefects are usually outstandingly capable men. They are often selected from among the top-scoring graduates of France's prestigious and rigorous National Academy of Administration (*Ecole Nationale d'Administration*). They customarily begin their careers as subprefects and then move up. The Ministry of Interior regularly rotates them in order to sharpen their skills and to keep them from becoming too attached to any one department. For the prefect serves, first to all, the nation, and only secondly his district.

The prefect, then, is an administrative agent of the national government. He receives his orders primarily from Paris. Assisted by two to four subprefects and other staff aides he governs the department. As such, he not only implements policy but creates it as well.

A mechanism does exist, however, for the citizens of the department to make their wishes known. This is the General Council, whose members are elected for three years. The Council consults regularly with the prefect and oversees his activity. It also enjoys some limited discretion in developing new programs and eliminating others. But for the most part its activities are advisory. It is primarily a talk shop.

Actually, department councils in France do not even have much chance to talk. They meet only twice a year, for fifteen days in the spring and for one month in the Fall. What's more, the prefect can send the councilors home if he finds them too rambunctious or too recalcitrant. In practice, however, prefects try to work as amicably as possible with their councils and will frequently defer to their desires when it comes to minor matters. Nevertheless, the prefect at almost all times is in control.

The departments vary considerably in size. The smallest has fewer than 100,000 inhabitants. The largest, the Department of the Seine, which embraces

Paris, approaches nearly ten million. As a result, the councils themselves also vary somewhat in size. Furthermore, the seats are unequally apportioned, with rural areas being given more than their due and with cities often being shortchanged. For example, Nice, contains nearly half the population of its department, but elects only four members to its thirty-one-man departmental council. Thus, the prefect's awareness that he is not dealing with a fully representative body may temper still more his willingness to accommodate its demands.

Each department includes three types of jurisdictions, *arrondissements*, *cantons*, and *communes*. The first two primarily serve as election districts and play little real role in local governance. The communes, however, warrant careful consideration.

A commune is essentially a municipality, any municipality. Small villages with less than a hundred inhabitants qualify as communes. So does Paris, with a population of over six million. In other words, little organizational distinction exists among municipalities in France. With a few exceptions, all have fundamentally the same form of government.

The communes, like the departments, elect councils for six years. However, unlike those of the departments, the communal councils do exercise some real powers. They may make certain policy decisions and may appropiate or withhold funds in keeping with those decisions. One of their most important tasks, however, is to elect the mayor.

The French mayor, unlike his British counterpart, is not merely a ceremonial figure. He is entrusted with the enforcement of law and order. He is in charge of the registration of births and deaths. He performs marriages. (All marriages in France must be solemnized in a civil wedding ceremony, in addition to whatever religious ceremony the participants may have selected.) He also can promulgate some laws and appoint some officials on his own.

Strengthening the mayor's hand is the fact that once appointed by the council, he cannot be removed, at least not by the councilors themselves. Thus, they are, in effect, stuck with him for six years. Communal councils tend to be quite large, numbering over sixty members in the larger cities. This makes it difficult for the councils to act decisively, leaving a vacuum that an energetic mayor can fill. Indeed, a strong mayor can dominate the life of his commune.

However, before we start considering the mayor as the champion of his commune against the forces of centralized power, we should take note of one important fact: French law makes the mayor not only the leader of his municipality but also an agent of the national government. In other words, anyone elected mayor becomes an employee of the French government and therefore subject to its direction. Many of the functions he performs result from requirements imposed upon him from above.

370

This brings us back to the prefect. He sees to it that the mayor and his communal council do what they are supposed to do and behave as they are supposed to behave. The prefect may suspend any mayor from office for a month without a hearing; his superiors at the Ministry of Interior may, upon his request, extend this suspension period for another three months. And they may bring charges in court to remove the mayor from office completely. The prefect may also suspend or even dissolve the communal council.

In reality, such suspensions, dissolutions, and removals are rare. And under the watchful eye of their prefects, communes and their mayors often exhibit a good deal of enterprise. Local governments in France have exclusive right to the property tax and can impose other taxes as well. Their main source of tax revenue comes from a broad-based sales tax that, though only 1 or 2 percent in most cases, covers all commercial transactions within the municipality. Many also tax luxuries, including pets and pianos. (That is, they tax not just the purchase but the ownership, on an annual basis.) Many communes also operate profit-making enterprises. For example, nearly all pawnshops in France are owned and operated by local governments.

But although the municipalities of France enjoy certain freedoms and exercise certain responsibilities, they never escape the presence of Paris and its prefect. Though the communes set the tax rates, the central government collects the taxes for them. The communes maintain the school buildings and hire the custodial staff, but Paris hires the teachers and determines the curricula. The commune can initiate new programs, but the prefect or one of his deputies must approve them. At the same time, the prefect will require them to allocate certain minimum sums for education, fire service, and the like, and to keep their budgets balanced.

One indication of the limited role of subnational government in France is the fact that though the mayor is by far the most important local official, his job is almost never full-time. Even mayors of the country's largest cities usually continue to hold other positions. Some have served in the national legislature while holding down the mayoralty of their municipality. And a mayor of Bordeaux, France's third largest city, managed to serve simultaneously as the country's prime minister. The nation's capital, Paris, is where the power is. As Napoleon once expressed it, he who rules Paris, rules France.

Recent Trends

A good deal of discord over this centralized system has surfaced in recent years, and the national government has taken some small steps to assuage it. One of these has been to give the prefect more power. This might seem like a strange way to decentralize but actually it does signal a step in that direction. Although the prefect has wielded great power in relation to local officials, he has not fared so well in controlling other officials of the national government within his department. Most police chiefs, school superintendents, highway engineers, and others, we should remember, work for the national government, and in the past they have preferred to take their orders directly from their own ministries in Paris. But the prefect is the only field officer who deals on a day-by-day basis with local leaders. By strengthening his hand, the government has, at least to some degree, put itself in a position where it can respond more effectively to local demands.

The national regime has also started to make increasing use of grants-in-aid. These grants are never given without numerous restrictions, but in many cases they are earmarked for projects that have been initiated by the communes themselves. In general, Paris is listening more to its provinces. Indeed, it is also easing up somewhat on the very tight control it has exercised over the capital city itself. A reform that went into effect in 1977 gave Paris a locally selected mayor for the first time. (Up to now, the prefect of the Seine has performed the functions of both mayor and prefect.)

A development related to the drive for decentralization has been increased regionalism. France originally consisted of a series of regions that were, in themselves, virtual nations. But heretofore the growth of centralized power has given little recognition to this fact. Most of these regions have been divided into several departments. They have lacked a governmental apparatus of their own. This is now starting to change. The movement to do so is coming from both the top and the bottom. At the grass roots level, local ethnic and subethnic groups are starting to assert their identity. Bretons (from Brittany), Corsicans, and others are demanding more recognition; some of the more extreme elements are seeking to secede from France itself and set up a new nation. In the summer of 1976 two policemen lost their lives in an effort to quell a small-scale nationalist uprising in Corsica.

The French government, meanwhile, has become increasingly aware that the country's departments are too small to serve as effective units for economic planning. Large-scale economic development requires larger areas to work with. New roads, railroad lines, power facilities, universities, factories, etc., nearly always have an impact on several departments. Consequently, the government has grouped the country into twenty-one regions, each guided by a coordinating- or super-prefect. Whether or not these regions develop into viable mechanisms for decentralizing power and invigorating nonnational government, however, remains to be seen.

372

WEST GERMANY[3]

After World War II, West Germany, struggling to get back on its feet, adopted a new constitution. The constitution was designed to give the defeated nation something it had never had, namely a strong and stable democratic form of government. One of the most important ingredients this new constitution contained was federalism.

The West Germans had good reasons for adopting a federal form of government. The shaky and short-lived democracy the Germans had set up after the first World War had also been a federal state. Thus, the country had had some experience with such a system. Then, both the United States and France wanted a federal West Germany. (The United States felt that federalism would be more democratic; France hoped that federalism would help keep West Germany from becoming too aggressively powerful.) Finally, the nation's leading political party, the Christian Democrats, believed in federalism.

As a result, West Germany today has a governmental system that in some ways is similar to our own. There is a national government that shares its sovereignty within ten state governments. As in the United States, the states differ considerably in size, with two of them (Hamburg and Bremen) being simply single cities while others contain numerous cities, towns, and rural areas. Furthermore, as in this country, the federal system has permitted a good deal of diversity but has also produced a fair degree of discord.

The Role of the States

The West German states, unlike their American counterparts, play a direct role in national policymaking. The membership of the upper house of the West German Parliament consists of delegations from the various state governments. These delegations range from three to five members, depending on the state's size. This differs considerably from the composition of our own upper house, which consists of independently elected senators. To be sure, our senators are elected on a state basis but they are not emissaries of their state governments. (Indeed, there is no *formal* connection at all between the U.S. senator and the government of the state from which he has been elected.)

Another distinction between the U.S. Senate and West Germany's upper house (*Bundesrat*) is the allowance made for the differences in size. In the United

3. Information for the following section was drawn largely from materials made available by the German Information Service in New York City. For an earlier summary of some of these points see: George E. Berkley, "Crisis and Change in German Federalism," *National Civic Review* (April 1970).

States, Rhode Island has as many seats as California. In West Germany, as we have seen, the number of votes from each state varies (within, to be sure a rather small range). Another distinction is that in West Germany, each state's votes must be cast as a unit. In our country, each senator votes independently and often the two senators of a state vote differently on many issues.

The direct role given to the state governments in the passage of national legislation is modified somewhat by another feature of the West German Constitution. In our country, each house of Congress possesses an absolute veto over all legislation. If a bill becomes blocked in either house, it fails to become law. In West Germany the upper house can stop a bill only if it casts as many votes against the measure as the lower house cast for it. Consequently, if a bill passes the lower chamber with a ten-vote majority, the state delegations in the upper house would have to muster a ten-vote majority against it in order to keep it from becoming law.

Despite this slight limitation on the power of the state-controlled upper house, there is no denying the fact that the West German state governments enjoy more *direct* influence over the national government than our own state governments. Their direct control of one of the two branches of the national legislatures insures the states of a strong say in both the initiation and implementation of national policy.

Yet despite this seemingly secure foothold in national affairs, the West German states still suffer from diminished status when compared to their U.S. counterparts. A look at the country's constitution will show why. West Germany's constitution gives the federal government *exclusive* jurisdiction in eleven fields. Generally, they are the same fields in which our own national government exercises total control. They include defense, foreign trade, citizenship, monetary policy, and the like. However, the constitution also gives the national government *concurrent* jurisdiction in twenty-three other fields. To all intents and purposes, these cover most areas of governmental activity. Moreover, if any conflict arises between the West German federal government and one of its states, the federal government always has the final word. Its power is essentially supreme. "To a very considerable extent it is a system of centralized legislative power tempered by local administration."

For the most part, the states have been given discretionary power in only two areas: education and the police. But even here the federal government makes its presence felt. In education it contributes to the cost and oversees the general financial arrangements set up by the states. In law enforcement, the federal government pays for all the costs of police training and oversees the operation of the training academies. Since police training in West Germany lasts

374

from three to four years, during which period the recruits spend considerable time out on the beat as well as in the classroom, this practice gives the national administration considerable control over police operations generally. (The national government also operates some police forces of its own, including a national detective agency. Furthermore, it promulgates a criminal code that serves the entire country.)

This does not mean that the West German states have nothing to do in other areas of governmental concern. Actually, they do a good deal. In 1974 there were 1,367,000 people working for the state government compared to only 296,000 employed by the central government. But most of the state government employees were engaged in implementing nationally determined policies and programs. It is no exaggeration to say that the West German states serve primarily as the administrative apparatus for the country's national regime.

On the local level, West Germany in the 1960s had nearly 25,000 governments. Due to consolidations, it has only 11,000 today. Furthermore, most of them, except for those few that are city-states, play little role in the policymaking process. They do operate fire departments and some recreation programs, including, in the larger municipalities, municipal theatres and opera companies. They also maintain parks, construct and clean streets, and carry out some other functions as well. A few communities in the south of Germany still support local police forces. Nevertheless, most government employees in the typical West German community are working for their state government and, more often than not, they are carrying out federal legislation.

Trendlines

As the foregoing discussion indicates, federalism in West Germany does not go so far or extend so deeply as it does in this country. But the fact that it has remained limited has not prevented the West Germans from voicing a desire to see it eliminated entirely. One poll in 1969 showed 70 percent of the people as "against federalism." The country's most prestigious newspaper, *Die Zeit (Time),* has blamed the nation's federal system for imposing increased costs and hampering the country's efforts to deal with its present-day problems.

For a long time the inequalities in the country's decentralized taxation system produced a great deal of rancor. Under the old system the states collected all personal and corporate income taxes, gave 35 percent of the receipts to the federal government, and kept the rest for themselves. Though they spent much of the money they retained for nationally decreed and therefore uniform programs, some states ended up with much more revenue than

375

others. Since 1970, however, the states have had to turn over all their revenues from these sources to the national government, which reallocates them on a roughly proportionate basis in terms of population.

The central government has also begun to intervene more directly in other arenas as well. It has stepped up its financial aid for education, and thereby increased its influence in this hitherto largely state function. And it has begun to administer directly any public program for which it pays 50 percent or more of the cost.

Some West German political figures have even started to think about what for American politicians would be the unthinkable: namely, the *possibility* of reducing the number of states through consolidation. Plans have been put forth for amalgamating the ten West German states into five. However, both the smaller states and the richer states oppose such a move, since both feel they would lose in the process.

To sum up, federal West Germany appears to be moving toward increased centralization, and this trend seems likely to continue. However, it also seems unlikely that the country will eliminate its federal system altogether. If for no other reason, the country's major political parties rely on the state governments to provide both elective and appointive positions for their leading members. And the system, as we noted at the outset, does have a fairly long tradition in the country. Consequently, while we may see German federalism shrink somewhat, we will probably not see it wither away altogether.

SWITZERLAND[4]

Generally, large countries find federalism most appealing and attractive. Their very size and diversity make them more amenable to the decentralized approach and apparatus federalism implies. Switzerland, however, offers a striking exception to this rule. This small republic has developed a governmental system that in its degree of decentralization rivals and may even surpass that of the United States.

Switzerland's adherence to decentralization stems from the fact that while it lacks size, it does not lack diversity. On the contrary, it is one of the most heterogeneous nations in the Western world. Its population consists of three different language groups—German, French, and Italian—each of which shows a cultural affinity to another European country. (The German-speaking Swiss

4. Material for the following section was drawn largely from "The Federal Government of Switzerland," by George Arthur Codding, Jr. (Boston: Houghton Mifflin Co., 1961). Supplemented and updated by some interviews and first-hand observation by one of the authors in Switzerland in 1973.

376

relate to Germany, the French-speaking Swiss feel some closeness to France, and the Italian-speaking Swiss demonstrate a kinship with Italy). These cultural differences have been reinforced by the mountainous character of Switzerland, which in the past has made communication among the separate sections of the country somewhat difficult. The result has been the development of a governmental system that has no parallel in the modern world.

Cantons and Communes

The sovereign subunits of Swiss federalism are called *cantons*. They are the rough equivalent of our states except they are more like our counties in size. Switzerland has twenty-two cantons in all, each of which elects representatives to the upper house of parliament.

These Swiss cantons enjoy powers and privileges that are denied to our states. They can sign, on their own, certain agreements with foreign powers, though few of them in recent years have sought to do so. They may also set their own standards for citizenship within the limits prescribed by the federal government. This can be quite important, for a foreigner wishing to acquire Swiss nationality must win the approval of his cantonal government. A Chinese who lived in Berne for twenty-five years, for example, was refused citizenship by cantonal authorities on the grounds that he had not sufficiently become part of the community.

The cantons may also add their own rules and requirements to the national standards governing the right to vote. Some cantons deny voting rights to those guilty of habitual drunkenness, or to those who are on welfare through their own fault. Some cantons allow women to vote only on certain matters, while others *do not permit women* to vote at all. Some cantons require all their eligible voters to vote in every election; others make voting completely voluntary.

Most of the traditional domestic functions of government are lodged with the cantonal governments. They possess the basic powers in such fields as health, education, welfare, criminal justice, etc. They also possess the basic powers to levy and collect taxes. The national government was only gradually given the right to impose income and sales taxes. (It took the depression of the 1930s along with World War II for the central government to acquire such taxing powers.) Finally, Switzerland has no supreme court to declare a law or an action of the cantonal government unconstitutional.

However, the distribution of power is not quite as one-sided as these observations might seem to suggest. The federal government controls foreign affairs, the army (there is, of course, no Swiss Navy), customs, the coinage of

377

money, the issuing of banknotes, extradition, and the movement of foreigners within Switzerland.

The central government also exercises an exclusive monopoly over the manufacture and sale of gunpowder, as well as the manufacture and sale of alcohol and the emission of radio and television programs. It owns and operates the railroads, the telephone and telegraph company, and the postal service. It has general authority over navigation, major highways, automobiles, food and drugs, conservation, infectious diseases, and related matters. Constitutional amendments give it the right to take steps to eliminate unemployment, protect the family, and provide a minimum of social security. As one authority on Swiss politics has observed, the county's present-day constitution "gives the Swiss federal government at least a supervisory function in all aspects of political life."

Proceeding further we find that, though no court exists that can declare a cantonal law null and void, still all cantons must submit their constitutions, and any amendments they may wish to make to them, to the federal government for approval. Any conflict between the cantons and the federal government is settled in the latter's favor. Furthermore, the country has only one criminal code, which is promulgated by the central government.

When it comes to education, the cantons, while they retain primary responsibility, must meet certain federally imposed regulations. These require them to operate school systems that are adequte, obligatory, nonsectarian, and free. (In the United States, it will be recalled, no state can be required to make school compulsory and one state, Mississippi, still does not do so.) In higher education, the federal government operates a polytechnical school and subsidizes the country's seven cantonal-run universities. The federal government can intervene more directly if any of the cantonal universities let their standards slip or experience other trouble.

This policy of using subsidies to exert influence runs through most of the country's domestic programs. The federal government helps fund old age and survivor insurance, unemployment services, and other supposedly canton-controlled activities. And with such funds comes federal oversight. The profits from its enterprises and monopolies frequently supply the money the federal government uses to extend such help.

As for the municipal governments, called *communes*, their powers and functions remain quite limited. For example, Zurich, Switzerland's largest city, does have a police force of its own. But it is made up exclusively of traffic patrolmen who carry no weapons and catch no criminals. Most other Swiss cities don't have any local constabulary. Subnational government in Switzerland is essentially, though not exclusively, a cantonal enterprise.

The small role of the municipalities and the growing role of the federal government make Switzerland a more centralized country than would at first appear to be the case. In some respects it carries decentralization further than does the United States. In other respects, however, it does not go as far as we do. On balance, it presents an interesting example of dispersed authority within a cohesive, and essentially harmonious, system.

CANADA[5]

Canada, like the United States, started out a British colony. Like the United States, her large size and diversified population induced her to adopt a federal system. Indeed, the Canadians had more reason to choose federalism than we had since their country not only covers a greater geographic area than our own, but also comprises two different and contrasting cultures, British and French. Between one-quarter and one-third of all Canadians speak French as their native tongue and share a heritage that differs quite sharply from that of the Anglo-Saxon majority. A federal framework thus seemed to be the best way to accommodate this diversity and to allow each group the maximum degree of discretion.

Self-government for the Canadians, however, came much later than it came for us. They were consequently in a position to benefit from our experience. Their constitution, called the British North American Act, was drafted during the time of our Civil War. The Canadians wanted to make sure that they would never have to face such a calamity. As a result they made sure that their central government would always have the upper hand in dealing with its sovereign subunits.

The Federal-Provincial Relationship

As the reader will remember, the U.S. Constitution describes only those powers specifically conferred on the federal government. All other powers, says Article Ten of the Bill of Rights, are reserved for the states. The Canadians, in framing their constitution, took the opposite approach. The British North American Act (BNA) itemizes the powers to be enjoyed by the ten sovereign subunits, which are called provinces. All other powers and prerogatives rest in the hands of the

5. Much of the information for the following comes from "The Shifting Balance in Canadian Federalism," by Donna Galen (Unpublished paper, Northeastern University, 1976), and from "Ontario Maps the Way to Metro Reform," *Business Week* (21 November 1970). Some interviewing one of the authors undertook in Nova Scotia in the fall of 1970 was also helpful, as was an interview with Professor Robert J. McLaren, a former faculty member at the University of Regina in Regina, Saskatchewan. A dispatch in *New York Times,* 21 December 1975 on Montreal and its problems was also useful.

federal government. Thus, in Canada the so-called residual power is national, while in our country it belongs to the states.

What are the powers given to the provinces? They are reasonably broad. The provinces control education, health, welfare, their own municipalities, and to some degree, the administration of justice within the province. They share power with the federal government in the areas of agriculture and immigration. The latter is a power our states do not have since they are forbidden to enact any legislation affecting immigration matters. (The Canadians probably felt obliged to give the provinces some authority in this area out of the need to accommodate Quebec. This province, being French-speaking, would obviously wish to exercise some control over the kinds and numbers of immigrants that would settle within its borders.)

The provinces received somewhat limited taxing power. They could impose sales, property, and many other types of taxes, but were and are forbidden from enacting and enforcing income tax laws on their own. The personal income tax remains an exclusive prerogative of the federal government in Ottawa. (The federal government can, however, give a province the right to impose an income tax of its own and Quebec, with national approval, now does so.)

Ottawa handles all foreign affairs and defense matters and regulates all commercial affairs that it chooses to regulate. Unlike our own national government, it does not have to limit itself to those economic activities having an interstate character. It enacts the country's one criminal code and appoints most of the country's judges. Finally, it possesses, as the ultimate weapon, the right to disallow any law passed by a province so long as it does so within one year of the law's enactment.

As one can see, the balance of federal-state power is skewed much more to the center in Canada than it is in the United States. The national government seems firmly ensconced in the driver's seat when it comes to determining what government shall do and what it shall not.

However, the provinces possess more authority than may at first seem to be the case. They do exercise basic authority and initiate general policy in many important domestic matters. And although Ottawa has the right to keep them from doing anything it does not want them to do, in practice it uses this weapon somewhat sparingly. Furthermore, many court decisions in recent decades have tended, in contrast to court decisions in this country, to expand provincial power.

Actually, the Candian federal government has found a better device for getting the provinces to do what it would like them to do in many instances. This is the same device our own constitutionally weaker federal government uses for the same purposes: money. Grants-in-aid and revenue sharing have been a

380

feature of Canadian federalism since its inception, and over the years the use of such devices has been greatly enlarged.

The degree of aid distributed by the central government varies greatly. Newfoundland, the least developed of the Canadian provinces, receives nearly 80 percent of all its revenues from Ottawa. However, Ontario, one of the richer provinces, can count on the national government for no more than 40 percent of its budgeted outlays. As do our states, the Canadian provinces frequently complain about the restrictions that govern these grants. But, in general, such rules have been more flexible in Canada. The grant formulas for any province are frequently worked out through discussions with the provincial officials, and to some degree are tailored to meet the provinces' desires. Furthermore, the province can opt out of some programs and receive the money, or some portion of it, in comparatively unrestricted lump sum payments. Quebec frequently chooses this route.

In summary, then, the Canadian provinces are by no means vassals of their Ottawa overlords. They initiate policies as well as carry out programs. But, to a greater extent than our states, they have remained the junior partner in the federal relationship.

The Provincial-Local Relationship

If the province finds itself in a comparatively weaker position than the U.S. state in its relationship with the federal government, it enjoys a comparatively stronger position in its dealings with its localities. Local government in the United States, though it lacks sovereign power, does possess, as we have seen, a good deal of political clout. This is far less true of its Canadian counterpart. When it comes to subnational politics in Canada, the provinces dominate the scene.

Each Canadian province is, in effect, a miniature parliamentary republic. Each has a parliamentary assembly that selects a provincial prime minister and cabinet. In practice, the prime minister is nearly always the head of the majority party and has a good deal of say in who is to serve in his cabinet. All of these provincial assemblies are unicameral, with the possible exception of Quebec, which has a weak second chamber of sorts consisting of members appointed for life.

These provincial parliaments and their cabinets handle most of the important governmental business that takes place within the province. For example, they customarily shoulder much more of the educational burden than do most of the American states. They sometimes appoint the members of the local school boards and usually furnish much of the funds they spend. As with federal-provincial grants-in-aid, provincial aid to local education varies a good deal depending not only on provincial policies but also on the degree of local need. It is not unusual for a provincial government to pay 90 percent of the school costs for its poorer localities.

The provinces also handle nearly all matters concerning public health and also take major responsibility for law enforcement. And although local government may impose and collect property taxes, provincial officials assess the properties and make the valuations.

One factor that impels the provincial government to take on many of the duties discharged by local governments in our own country is that much of Canada is not municipally organized. Although Canada has forty-six hundred municipalities, which, on a population basis, is somewhat more than we have, most of them are miniscule. In addition, they are often clustered in the more populous sections of the country. Only the southern sections of the western provinces and less than half of Quebec are municipally organized. Indeed, less than 1 percent of the land area of Newfoundland is governed by municipalities.

Of course, Canada does have many large cities where one can find a broad range of functions being performed at the local level. Many of these cities have adopted metropolian forms of government. The Montreal Urban Community, for example, is in charge of police, sanitation, transportation, sewage, planning and economic development, and promotion for Montreal and its suburbs. An even more noteworthy example of metropolitanism is Toronto. This city has joined with twelve of its suburbs in constructing a two-tiered government in which the upper metropolitan tier handles or supervises most important governmental functions. (See Chapter 13).

But the metropolitan movement itself only serves to illustrate the vigorous role the provinces play in local affairs. Impressed by metropolitan Toronto's achievements, the provincial authorities in Ontario launched a drive at the beginning of the 1970s to consolidate the province's 908 municipalities into 30 two-tiered municipal units. (In a two-tiered set-up, the upper tier forms the government for the entire jurisdiction; the lower tier consists of the separate local entities that carry out some functions on their own.) On the Niagara Peninsula, to take one example, the provincial authorities eliminated two counties and seven villages and consolidated twenty-six towns into twelve governmental units. These local governments were then brought together to form the Regional Municipality of Niagara which handles most of the same services that the metropolitan governments of Toronto and Montreal provide.

Although any U.S. state could legally undertake a similar program with respect to its municipalities, it would be difficult to conceive of any of them doing so. Local government here is too firmly entrenched in our political system and

382

too enshrined by our political culture. But Canada is different. It has no deeply rooted tradition of home rule. Indeed, some municipal mayors and councilors have welcomed provincial-imposed consolidations, even though such mergers have eliminated their positions. Perhaps they felt that, given the limited powers and resources of their offices, they were not surrendering very much.

Canadian Federalism at Work: Law Enforcement

A brief look at how the police function is exercised in Canada should furnish us with a fuller idea of how the Canadian system operates.

The federal government has one major police force, the Royal Canadian Mounted Police, or RCMP. The "mounties," however, no longer ride horseback or dress in red tunics except under special circumstances and on ceremonial occasions. They drive cars or go on foot; they also wear more conventional police uniforms and sometimes plainclothes. They form the largest single constabulary in the country.

The mounties carry out most of the federal government's law enforcement activities. In addition, they provide police services to those provinces that want them. Of Canada's ten provinces all but two, Ontario and Quebec, have contracted with the RCMP. In return for a stipulated sum from the province, the mounties serve as the province's state police.

In serving as the provincial police, the RCMP take on many more duties than are customarily fulfilled by the state police in our country, for, most of Canada's municipalities have no local police of their own. Consequently this national police force actually serves as the local police force as well. To be sure, the larger and medium-sized cities do have their own police forces. But since there are comparatively few such cities, as so little of Canada is municipally organized, the RCMP is the only police force in most areas of the country.

In Ontario and Quebec, the policing pattern more closely approximates our own. These provinces have their own provincial (state) police, while their cities are patrolled by local police forces. But here too there are some differences. First of all, their provincial police possess full police responsibility and exercise such responsibility more widely than do state troopers in this country since so much of the territory of these provinces is without local law enforcement. Secondly, most of their local policemen work not for a municipal government, but for a metropolitan or regional authority.

Thus, while it is possible to find police in Canada at all levels of government, the overall policing pattern is much more centralized than it is in the United States. Both the national and the provincial governments play a greater

383

role in law enforcement, while the municipalities play a much smaller one. And much of the role that local government does play takes place at the metropolitan or regional level.

To sum up, Canadian federalism exhibits, like our own, a varied pattern of power and performance. One can find examples of vital activity at all levels of government. But with the federal government enjoying the residual power, with the provinces taking responsibility for many matters that would be local concerns in this country, and with consolidations of local governments occurring frequently, the Canadian system does not nearly equal the decentralization that characterizes the United States. [6]

6. It was becoming evident at the start of 1977, however, that the forces of fragmentation had begun to threaten the Canadian union as never before. The victory of the separatist party in Quebec had only stimulated separatist sentiment throughout the country. Furthermore, the growing importance and value of the country's natural resources was making many provinces unwilling to share the proceeds of such resources with the federal government. Even impoverished Newfoundland, which had hitherto virtually lived off Ottowa's largesse, was now contemplating the delights of going it alone, thereby keeping for itself all the prospective income from its potential offshore oil and gas reserves. Although it appeared unlikely that the Canadian union would break apart under these pressures, it did seem certain that Canadian federalism's greatest challenge lay just ahead.

384

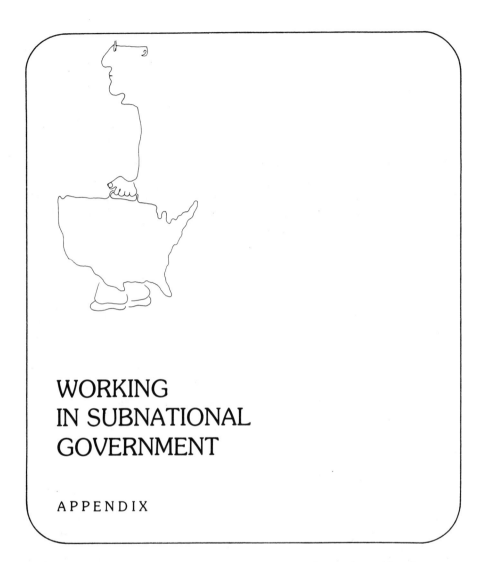

WORKING
IN SUBNATIONAL
GOVERNMENT

APPENDIX

The previous chapters have conveyed the concept that state and local government is where the domestic problem-solving action is. Subnational government
continues to expand in budget and employees at a rate three times faster than
that of the federal government or the private sector. Grass roots government is
the level where all the problems of those policy areas examined in this book and
many others are actually confronted. The federal government provides funds to
help face these problems, but the implementation of programs is up to state and
local government employees. Careers in subnational government pay much
more than they used to—though not as much as the federal government—and
offer a meaningful and challenging career.

WHERE ARE THE JOBS?

While 80 percent of civilian government jobs are found at the subnational level, not all of these jobs are accessible or attractive to every job seeker. Fully *one-half* of state and local jobs are in public education. The bulk of professional jobs in this area are classroom teaching jobs. For elementary and secondary education, teaching certification is needed; for college teaching, the Ph.D. has become a union card without which it is increasingly harder to remain in the classroom for long, even at the two-year community college level. A decline in the birthrate means that far fewer elementary and secondary school teachers will be needed in the future; those contemplating a career in education are well-advised to concentrate on allied fields such as counselling, or areas like special education, as a backup to conventional teaching or administrative careers. At the college level, enrollments in the liberal arts and humanities are declining, while the demand for practical vocational courses, such as computer programing, law enforcement, and business and public administration increases as middle-aged students enter college in mid-career.

Job prospects are decidedly different in fields like public health, mass transportation, environmental protection, criminal justice, recreation and leisure, and general administration. All of these fields are expanding, and all can use qualified, well-trained personnel. While they are by no means the only expanding programs, they illustrate the rapidly changing nature of government.

Health care, which has increased its share of the gross national product from 3.6 percent in 1929 to 5.9 percent in 1965 and 8.2 percent in 1975, is on the verge of a major expansion. Some kind of a national health insurance program, at least for catastrophically expensive illness, is a likelihood in the near future. Since the government share of health spending increased from 13.3 percent in 1929 to 42.2 percent in 1975, and continues to rise, it makes sense to think of health care as a government function. The need for health and hospital administrators and staff personnel in functions like budgeting, management, and personnel is great. One need not be a nurse or doctor for a career in health care.

States, fueled by federal funds, are devoting more resources to mass transit by rail and bus at a time when the relative share of the budget spent on highways is contracting. From West Virginia's People Mover to San Francisco's new subway system to Camden's (New Jersey) Dial-a-Mini-Bus program, innovations in mass transport are proceeding apace. The mass transit divisions of state transportation departments have grown, as have the bus and subway departments of some central cities. The demand for transportation planners and those qualified to run surveys of transport needs and use patterns should continue for some time.

Much the same is true in environmental protection, which has expanded rapidly. Environmental planners and monitors will be in demand for some time. Energy and consumer protection agencies are also proliferating in many states.

The soaring crime rate and supplies of federal funds to the field of criminal justice mean that it will remain for the foreseeable future an area where well-trained personnel in court administration,, corrections, probation, and police work will be valued. As a result of growing professionalism in law enforcement, it is now easier for criminal justice personnel to transfer to departments and levels of government other than their own than it was in the past.

The growth of leisure time can be measured by increasing government attention to recreation, parks, forests and other programs designed to fill leisure and retirement hours. The need for recreation personnel has expanded greatly, and the field should continue to burgeon. In addition, all the states and many big cities have agencies dealing with aid to cultural and arts organizations, and the prospects for sustained long-term growth here are excellent.

Not all areas of state and local government are expanding. While some social welfare programs are increasing in size and scope, others, like AFDC and public housing, have reached an equilibrium level. And some areas are being cut back, in the face of taxpayer revolts. But even in declining areas, certain types of jobs are in demand, and it makes sense to train for them.

TRAINING FOR THE JOB HUNT

The key to subnational government job seeking is the applicant's training and experience. Students with the proper background will be eligible for opportunities not only in the executive branch, but also in the fast-growing professional staffs of the state legislature and judiciary. Students without the necessary skills will get clerical or unskilled jobs, if they get anything at all.

There are two specific strategies between which the student thinking of a career in government can choose. The first is to acquire a thorough grounding in a particular skill such as accounting, nursing, engineering, or the like. Students with these qualifications will be able to compete for jobs in business and in nonprofit corporations, as well as in government. The second strategy is to concentrate on acquiring general administrative skills as well as some specialized skills generally in demand in government today. The student following this second strategy would take courses in public administration and in more specific areas, like police, educational, health, or recreational administration. Courses in business administration should also be carefully investigated. In addition, the student may want to take related courses in the social sciences, especially political science, economics, and sociology.

387

Specialized skills strongly in demand today include those in accounting, computer science, and statistics. The demand for these skills reflects the enormous increase in information and the necessity of being able to manage and analyze these data. Any government office contains information on thousands of individuals and/or things, and those who run the offices must be increasingly interested in better ways to use this knowledge.

While most students would probably not be scared off by an introductory semester of accounting, many shy away from statistics and computer courses. They shudder at the thought of entering these "math-oriented" courses. But they are needlessly nervous, for introductory courses in both subjects taught outside mathematics departments do not require any knowledge of higher mathematics. A student can get a thorough grounding in both computer science and statistics without recourse to algebra, geometry, trigonometry, or calculus.

Some students may wonder why they should simply get a grasp of these skills through introductory courses rather than get a more intense education in them. Students who become interested in any of these subjects may want to continue in them, but a good introductory course is enough to enable the student to speak and understand much if not most of the language used in these areas. The job seeker can thus establish his credentials in these areas. In addition, as a responsible government official, he can understand and detect faulty accounting, computer printouts, and statistical analyses.

The combination of general administrative skill courses and accounting, computer, and statistics courses will produce what we call a policy analyst—a generalist able to devise an action plan for an agency, to check on its implementation, and to evaluate its success. Persons with this background will be eligible not only for positions in line agencies, like agriculture and transportation, but also for jobs in staff agencies, such as bureaus of budget, management, audit and personnel. In addition, this combination, together with a master's degree, is well-suited to a career in city management. (Remember, the city manager form of government is the most prevalent form for all cities over 10,000.) Finally, the desire to achieve economy and efficiency leads to the employment of additional policy analysts even when agencies are shrinking. In New Jersey, for example, the state college system laid off scores of teachers in 1976 while adding policy analysts to its central staff.

Another ingredient essential to this package of skills is an internship experience, a program that places the student in a government agency, enabling him simultaneously to gain invaluable practical experience and academic credit. In some schools, government internships are run by the department of political science or public administration; in others, by a central office of cooperative education. In schools where there is no such program, students should see if they can devise an internship of their own and earn independent study credit for it. A good internship experience will be well worth the time put into arranging and carrying it out.

Those students who either specialize in one vocational area or train themselves in general administrative skills will be in a strong competitive position when the time to begin the job hunt comes. This assertion applies not only to jobs in state and local government, our concern here, but also to federal government, nonprofit corporations (foundations, cultural organizations, hospitals, colleges, and political, social cause, religious, service, and professional organizations), as well as some business positions.

At the same time, we must point out that the job applicant with a graduate degree in administration, usually the Master's in Public Administration (M.P.A.), will have the advantage over other job seekers. This is often true even when others have substantial practical experience. Many jobs listed today stipulate the M.P.A. as a condition for consideration. Whether this makes sense or not (and the authors share some misgivings about it), it is a reality we have to confront. One strategy followed by many students who have just received their bachelor's degrees and who have to earn some money is to get a job and study for the M.P.A. at night. The M.P.A. is now offered at most good-sized universities, so it should not be a problem to locate a program.

JOB HUNTING

Michael A. Murray has made what may be the most multifarious analysis of the job market in government, and we will draw on it in this section.[1] Murray notes that while there are both many government jobs and academic programs training people for these jobs, students have difficulty landing positions. Why is this so?

One reason is that graduates of public administration (P.A.) programs don't know where to get their first job, because P.A. lacks the clearly defined career path of professions like law or medicine, or of the private business sector. Another problem is that P.A. graduates generally lack access to public decision makers. Few government agencies do on-campus recruiting, and job seekers usually have contact only with the personnel officer, rather than the line

---

1. Michael A. Murray, "Strategies for Placing Public Administration Graduates," *Public Administration Review* (November/December 1975), pp. 629–635.

agency official with the authority to hire. A final problem is the lack of an informal network of contacts between the schools and government. P.A. programs, most of which are relatively new, compare unfavorably in this aspect to more established programs like business, law, medicine, and education.

What can the job hunter do to break down these barriers? The key is to shift from inertia to action. First, students should decide what they want to do and where they want to do it. This is the most important decision, forcing a student to catalog his skills and interests. The student should next do research and focus on jobs that match his skills and interests. The final crucial step is to communicate with those who actually have the authority to hire.

A superb guide to this active job hunt is Richard Bolles' *What Color Is Your Parachute?*[2] The author argues that conventional approaches to the job search are too passive and thus unlikely to succeed. For example, students should shun personnel offices and the mailing of resumés. The job search is too important to be left to others, and employers are inundated with hundreds of resumes for most jobs. These, however, are general recommendations. What can the student do more specifically to search for government employment?

First, he can develop a list of contacts in key agencies, by asking his academic advisors, fellow students, and any other likely sources for names of those in a position to hire or who are knowledgeable about hiring. When the student talks to the contact, he should try to get the names of several additional contacts as well.

Another approach is to wait on the doorstep of those with the authority to hire until they agree to talk. The student should not fear making a nuisance of himself, because he has almost nothing to lose anyway. It is more likely that the official will react to this persistence with admiration than with irritation.

A further step is to do political campaign work, an excellent place to develop the managerial skills of judgment, motivation, good guessing, and dealing with political reality. Campaign work pays little, if anything, but it lasts only a few months, and the contacts made and experience gained may net one a good job. The same applies to volunteer work for "public interest" groups like the League of Women Voters, Common Cause, or Ralph Nader's state consumer advocacy groups.

Another way to generate contacts is at conferences of groups like the American Society for Public Administration, the Municipal Finance Officers Association, City Management Associations, and the Personnel Management

2. (Berkeley, Calif.: Ten Speed Press, 1976). The 1976 edition sells for $5.95, plus $.50 for mailing. Write the publisher at Box 4310, Berkeley, California 94704.

Association.[3] Faculty can help by reducing entrance fees and providing an initial contact; after that, the assertive student can meet a host of possible employers.

An additional way to switch from the passive to the active mode concerns the results of one's performances on written civil service entrance exams. In large governments, such as those of a populous state, county, or city, these scores are circulated to government agencies, who then contact the applicant if they wish. What many students do not realize is that it is also entirely legitimate for *them* to call the agency of their choice once they get their test scores and ask for an interview. Again, the best possible person to interview with is the one actually authorized to hire.

WORKING IN THE BUREAUCRACY

While the concerns of government cover the complete and complex range of human behavior, it is possible to make a few general comments about the bureaucratic environment that will keep those working in it attuned to reality. These remarks apply even to those who would like to see a great deal of change take place, because the best way to begin work on those changes in a stable society like the United States is within the system. Bureaucratic "guerrillas" can "infiltrate" the government and work into positions of influence.

As this book has argued again and again, our fragmented government flourishes in delay, confusion, overlap, and failure to deliver services with efficiency and effectiveness. Decision making takes place in a political context, so that the best-laid plans are often vetoed by the politicos. A beginning bureaucrat

---

3. Following are the addresses of some of these groups:

American Society for Public Administration
1225 Connecticut Avenue, N.W.
Washington, D.C. 20036

Common Cause
2030 M St., N.W.
Washington, D.C. 20037

International City Management Association
1140 Connecticut Ave., N.W.
Washington, D.C. 20036

International Personnel Management Association
1313 E. 60th Street
Chicago, Illinois 60637

Municipal Finance Officers Association
1313 E. 60th Street
Chicago, Illinois 60637

National League of Cities
1612 K St., N.W.
Washington, D.C. 20006

391

who does not grasp these facts will be doomed to disappointment, and sink into ineffectiveness. One who does understand them can work around them to a considerable extent by persuasion and persistence. He will have to take the long-range view, for his favorite reorganization or policy reform scheme will not take place tomorrow. Change will be the result of tireless talking to legislators, the chief executive, department heads, and interest groups. If the career official is able to convince these powers that his proposal is in their own best interest, because it embellishes their esteem, power, or popularity, he will get much of what he wants. If he cannot do this, he can usually write off his proposal.

Government employees must be capable of compromise, because no one in the system gets everything he wants. If someone does not want to bargain, government is not the place for him. U.S. politics is usually a politics of gradual change, but cumulative changes can result in substantial shifts over time. In 1965, for example, few states had departments of environmental protection and consumer protection—but many do today. Numerous states and localities have now passed "sunshine" laws, making agency meetings and records hitherto unavailable open to the public. In spite of all its handicaps, government accomplishes great tasks daily, whether these involve moving millions of people by rail, removing sewage and solid wastes, teaching, or ministering to those in need. Professional work in subnational government is often frustrating, but it is not boring for those who are able to apply their energies to problem solving.

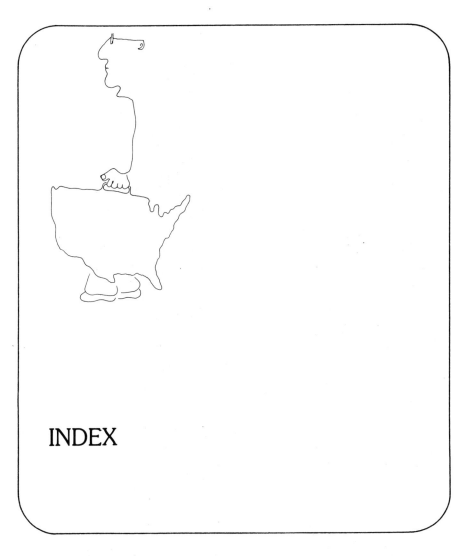

INDEX